# General Eoin O'Du

## *The Political Life of an Irish Firebrand*

JACK TRAYNOR

McFarland & Company, Inc., Publishers
*Jefferson, North Carolina*

**ISBN (print) 978-1-4766-9326-2**
**ISBN (ebook) 978-1-4766-5133-0**

Library of Congress and British Library
cataloguing data are available

Library of Congress Control Number 2023054483



Front cover image: President of Fine Gael (United Ireland Party) Eoin O'Duffy, portrait photograph, circa December 1933 (courtesy of the National Library of Ireland).

Printed in the United States of America

*McFarland & Company, Inc., Publishers*
*Box 611, Jefferson, North Carolina 28640*
*www.mcfarlandpub.com*

# Table of Contents

# Preface

This book examines the life and career of General Eoin O'Duffy. It is essentially a political history which utilizes a biographical lens to examine what O'Duffy's life tells us about the momentous developments of the revolutionary period (1916–23) and the political culture of early independent Ireland. Unlike those who entered a red martyrdom during the revolutionary period which ensured their posthumous veneration, O'Duffy remained a prominent figure in Irish public life at every step of the journey from the immediate post–Easter Rising period until the final stages of the Second World War.

Chapters 1–3 trace O'Duffy's early life and involvement in the revolutionary period as a commandant of the Irish Republican Army in County Monaghan and Ulster. Like many young men of his generation, he became immersed in the cultural and sporting nationalism of the fin-de-siècle, which enabled his elevation through the ranks of the republican movement. Chapters 4–6 examine his support for the Anglo-Irish Treaty and his subsequent service to the Irish Free State as a Civil War general and as commissioner of the Garda Síochána. His involvement in the sporting world is also analyzed, particularly his role in Irish athletics and involvement in the 1932 Summer Olympics. Chapters 7–9 detail his entry into the political fray of the 1930s, as director-general of the Blueshirts, as leader of Fine Gael and the opposition, and finally as leader of the National Corporate Party. Chapter 10 examines his ill-fated involvement in the Spanish Civil War fighting for Franco's forces. Whilst support for the Spanish Nationalists was widespread across Ireland, O'Duffy's conduct in Spain profoundly damaged his domestic reputation and effectively ended his political career. Chapter 11 analyzes the final years of his life during the period of the Emergency, including his association with Ireland's pro-Axis underground, his curious rapprochement with the IRA, and his final involvement in athletics.

Although during his lifetime O'Duffy frequently exploited his revolutionary record, it has been overshadowed by his political activities during the 1930s. The launch of the Decade of Centenaries (2012–23) program helped to blow away many of the cobwebs of the revolutionary period. Its focus on "remembering" historical events "with sensitivity" rather than singularly commemorating and celebrating heroic narratives has helped to reappraise the role of several key personalities of the period. In particular, a more objective recognition of the important role played by O'Duffy in the War of Independence has emerged in recent works. Particularly in

Monaghan his seminal role in the independence struggle locally has been acknowledged, as distinct from his tarnished political legacy.

This book hopes to shed light on O'Duffy's role as a conduit who influenced many northern IRA men to support the Anglo-Irish Treaty in 1921 and subsequently aided their enlistment in the Free State army. This speaks to a wider theme of O'Duffy as a proponent of a dynamic strand of pro–Treaty nationalism which was particularly militant on the question of partition. Although he served the conservative Cumann na nGaedheal government loyally during the early Free State period, his instincts were often radical. Time and again, he was called upon to rescue the pro–Treaty regime, as seen by his appointment as commander of the army during an internal army mutiny in 1924 and his appointment as leader of the political opposition to Fianna Fáil in the early 1930s. Pro-Treaty nationalism was not a homogenous bloc but rather a loose collection of various ideologies and instincts. Although it was initially held together under the charismatic sway of Michael Collins, his death stymied this diversity. Hereafter, pro–Treaty nationalists served the cautious and conservative regime of the 1920s.

O'Duffy's ignominious reputation may cause eyebrows to raise at the suggestion that he even "deserves" a new biography. Fearghal McGarry's 2005 study of O'Duffy helped to demythologize many aspects of his life. McGarry examined O'Duffy not simply as an interesting yet unrepresentative historical character, but as a mirror to the values of Irish society. In addition to charting his career, McGarry argued that O'Duffy's self-constructed heroic image was profoundly at odds with his mounting personal failings and inherent contradictions. However, the impression of O'Duffy as essentially the odd one out within pro–Treaty nationalism remains largely uncontested. Viewing the political career of O'Duffy with presentist values may immediately condemn him in the eyes of a modern reader, but to allow O'Duffy to act as the lightning rod for anti-democratic views during the 1930s is to allow a litany of historical figures to emerge unscathed from scrutiny. Particularly within the pro–Treaty nationalism of the 1930s, a sneaking regard if not an outright identification with fascistic ideology was commonplace. The Cumann na nGaedheal party newspaper printed articles which extolled Italian fascism for restricting the franchise to those who "can use it properly" at a time when O'Duffy served as garda commissioner under the first Fianna Fáil government. This complexity requires considerable examination. By reintegrating O'Duffy within the amorphous camp of pro–Treaty nationalism, it challenges the residual historiographical narrative of a Civil War divide between pro–Treaty democratic state-builders and anti–Treaty dictators, which still holds some popular currency.

Finally, this work hopes to contribute to the recent growth of international and comparative studies of fascism. It seeks to contextualize and expand on O'Duffy's international fascist links whilst correcting some dubious claims which have cropped up in Irish historiography about O'Duffy's involvement in international far-right networks. It is hoped this examination of the political views and activities of O'Duffy, when contextualized, can contribute to our understanding of the ideological underpinnings of the early independent Irish state and the widespread pro–Treaty anxieties of the 1930s.

# 1

# Beginnings

Owen Duffy Jnr, later known as Eoin O'Duffy, was born on 28 January 1890 in the townland of Cargaghdoo, near Castleblayney in County Monaghan.[1] Cargaghdoo, also known as Carrickaduff, is an Anglicization of An Charraigeach Dhubh, which translates as "the black rocks."[2] In the 1911 census, there were just 78 people living in this townland in Monaghan.[3] Rural life necessitated a close-knit relationship between neighbors, particularly at harvest time. The youngest son of a small farmer, his father farmed 15 acres of land. During important agricultural seasons, the neighbors worked together in a cooperative model for the common good of the community, without the relationship of employee and employer.[4] This tradition, *Meitheal*, is deeply rooted in Ireland's Gaelic heritage. Its earliest reference can be found in the ancient law tracts. It was also mentioned in the early Christian period in the lives of St Brigid, St Ciarán of Clonmacnoise, St Colmcille, and St Mochuda.[5] An awareness of Ireland's intertwined Gaelic and Christian heritage informed O'Duffy's worldview.

The Duffy surname, one of the most common in Monaghan, is Anglicized from Ó Dubhthaigh, a Gaelic clan notable for "the extraordinary number of parish clergy of the name."[6] The surname means "black." Although his family were undistinguished and apolitical, O'Duffy believed he was related to James Connolly, the prominent socialist-republican born in Edinburgh to Monaghan parents.[7] Whilst his family experienced hardship, O'Duffy's humble origins have been overstated in some accounts, including his own. In addition to his farm earnings, Owen Duffy Snr worked on the roads to supplement his income. O'Duffy later described road workers as "well-to-do people" which included both Catholics and Protestants.[8] This surplus income left the family financially better off than many of their neighbors.[9] Born eight years after his second youngest sibling, O'Duffy was spared much of the laborious agricultural work expected of his four brothers. The family experienced emigration. His brother Peter left for the United States while his brothers Frank and Jim "stole away to Glasgow."[10] Another brother, Patrick, worked as a stonemason and continued to live at home with his sister Mary and their father, who died in 1915. Neither Patrick nor Mary married.[11]

As a boy, O'Duffy was doted over by his mother, Brigid (née Fealy), from the nearby parish of Donaghmoyne. For his first four years she dressed him in traditional boy's petticoats. She sold eggs, butter, and chickens at the market in Castleblayney. O'Duffy recalled accompanying her to the town via a donkey and cart.

After stabling the donkey, he would venture off "to listen to everything and peer at everything in the town."[12] Despite having a majority Catholic population, most local businesses in Castleblayney were Protestant-owned. From a young age, O'Duffy was aware of the religious demographics which distinguished Monaghan from other counties. By 1911, a quarter of Monaghan's population of 71,455 was Protestant: 8,725 Anglicans, 8,512 Presbyterians and 860 other denominations (mostly Methodists).[13] Historically, the county experienced an influx of Protestant settlers in the 17th century who benefited from statutory discrimination against Catholics and their forced displacement. This generated significant local tensions, particularly around the question of land ownership.

A landlocked county, Monaghan is one of the nine counties which make up Ireland's northern province, Ulster, then the only region in Ireland with an overall Protestant majority. At the time of his birth, Monaghan was in the grip of the nationwide Plan of Campaign, a period of agrarian agitation spearheaded by the Land League. Irish tenant farmers demanded better conditions and the ability to purchase the land they farmed from large landlords, many of whom were Protestant. A profile of O'Duffy's career in July 1934 claimed: "to the vast majority of people the name Monaghan conveys no meaning save of a townland near the border. It is just an ordinary Irish town, but yet it has a deeper meaning for loyal Irishmen. For it was Monaghan that gave us General O'Duffy. It was that county that sheltered the boy who was afterwards to hold the destiny of Ireland in his hands."[14]

Although his family were monolingual English speakers, the young O'Duffy was swept up by the patriotic fervor of the Gaelic revival at the turn of the century. He soon adopted a Gaelicized form of his name: Eoin Ua Dubhthaigh or Eoin O'Duffy. Nationalist contemporaries elsewhere underwent a similar identity transformation; Kevin Higgins, a future colleague, became Kevin O'Higgins. At age 14, O'Duffy became a "regular competitor" at feiseanna festivals which promoted native poetry, dance, language, and culture. He also joined the Gaelic League, established in 1893 by Dr Douglas Hyde to de-Anglicize Ireland. For O'Duffy and his compatriots, Irish language classes were not simply about learning Ireland's historic language, but a way to express their nationalism. "We all vowed to encourage Irish industries, and nobody would risk the scorn of his classmates by turning up in clothes made outside Ireland instead of in good Irish tweeds.... Few of us smoked, but those who did only used Irish made cigarettes," he wrote.[15]

The dominant political force in Ireland was the Irish Parliamentary Party (IPP), a constitutional nationalist party which espoused the creation of a home rule parliament in Dublin. Although the party stopped short of endorsing the separation of Ireland from the United Kingdom, it clamored for a significant measure of Irish legislative autonomy. The party was supported by most Irish Catholics. Fr Hugh MacMahon, a godson of O'Duffy, wrote that although there was "general enthusiasm for the Irish language and culture" in O'Duffy's native area, this did not translate into support for separatist nationalism.[16] Home rule was the major force of Monaghan politics until 1916.

He remembered his early life in Monaghan as a rural idyll. He wrote,

> God did give joy to my youth. I had enough of eating, enough of laughing and dancing and singing. If I had a sorrow here and there, a head sore from a cuff, muscles sore almost beyond bearing with farm work that seemed too great, well, I have been none the worse of it since.

This reflected his nostalgia for what was already a bygone age when he started writing his memoir in the early 1940s. O'Duffy felt a deep affection for his mother. By contrast, his father was somewhat distant and preoccupied with farm work. O'Duffy recalled "he appeared to take little interest in my existence." While still a child, his mother's health declined as she developed cancer. He assisted her by performing duties like keeping the fire ablaze in her room and bringing her what little food she would eat. But, as he recollected, "slowly the smile she had for me as I strutted about my sickroom duties grew fainter, her eyes more tired."[17] Her illness hung like a dark cloud over the family for five years until she died in 1902, when O'Duffy was 12 years old. The death had a profound impact on him. He wore her wedding ring for the rest of his life in her memory.[18] She was buried in her native parish, four miles from the family homestead. Tragedy struck again when his brother Peter died in the United States the year after his mother's death. O'Duffy credited his family's religious devotion as a major source of strength. Together they prayed the Rosary every evening and attended Sunday Mass.

◆ ◆ ◆

Following these tragedies, the Paterfamilias took a "rough but kindly" interest in his youngest son. His father insisted O'Duffy continue his education, hoping he would become a teacher. Owen Snr did not learn to read or write until he was in his fifties but ensured his children were educated to a sufficiently high standard.[19] As "the scholar of the family," he was spared the grueling farm work which his brothers endured. An ambitious student, O'Duffy regularly studied until past midnight with the dim flicker of an oil lamp as his sole companion. He performed well academically. At Laggan national school, he came under the influence of a teacher, Mrs. Jane Lambe. He was "devoted" to her. He developed a well-rounded knowledge of subjects like mathematics but admitted he was not a "serene-faced cherub with a snow-white copy book" and "shared fully … the scholar's interest in the welfare of the school clock."[20] After completing his primary education, he progressed to a school in Laragh, outside his home parish. Laragh, near Broomfield in County Monaghan, prospered in the early 19th century and hosted three thriving flax mills which provided local employment for upwards of 300 people.[21] By the time O'Duffy commenced his studies in Laragh, the village had passed its peak.

At Laragh, O'Duffy was strongly influenced by his maternal uncle, a teacher, who provided the pupil with a rich education. Among his classmates was Peadar MacMahon, who later became chief-of-staff of the defense forces. O'Duffy felt "the atmosphere at Laragh was different somehow" from Laggan. After a bout of measles, he developed a stammer and became more withdrawn. Described as "shy and lonely," he "worked hard to fulfill his determination to excel in everything he undertook" and was aided by an excellent memory.[22] He soon abandoned his shyness and regularly attended traditional Irish *céilí* dances and enjoyed playing cards with his peers.[23] He became indispensable to his illiterate elderly neighbors. They gathered around the hearth in his father's rambling house to listen as the young pupil read aloud from the newspaper, including reports from the local court of assizes and international news from the Boer War. O'Duffy recalled that his neighbors strongly supported the Boers. He fondly remembered the folkish charm of the aroma of turf burning on the stove and tobacco smoke as he read aloud. As a teenager, he read works by the young nationalist poet Brian O'Higgins and studied John Locke, the Enlightenment philosopher.[24]

After finishing his studies, O'Duffy intended to become a teacher and fulfill the career plan charted by his father. He successfully sat an examination for a scholarship to enter St Patrick's teacher training college in Drumcondra, Dublin. But O'Duffy abandoned ambitions to become a teacher at the eleventh hour. He believed there was a scarcity of teaching vacancies and feared he would struggle to find employment. Instead, he opted to apply for a civil service position as a clerk to the county surveyor in Monaghan in 1910. Ten days after sitting the clerk's examination, he received a notice informing him that he had placed first in a field of 20 candidates. He benefited from his fluency in Irish.[25] The nationalist-controlled council in Monaghan introduced one of the first language requirements for hiring new civil servants, which led to an uptick of interest in learning the language.[26] The decentralization of power to local government was a small concession introduced by the British government in 1898 to mollify Irish demands for home rule.

Aged 19, O'Duffy became a junior surveyor with Monaghan County Council. He gained an extensive knowledge of local geography, which became important when organizing activities during the War of Independence. Over the next two years, his tasks in Monaghan included the completion of pay-sheets and the preparation of drawings, specifications, draught estimates, and calculations for County Works. He was responsible for making arrangements for extensive steam-rolling and machine-breaking of stone. His work was highly praised by the county surveyor.[27]

On 15 April 1912, O'Duffy was informed that he had successfully qualified as an assistant surveyor in the recent civil service examination, "taking fifth place in Ireland."[28] His promotion brought him to the town of Clones. The county surveyor, James Hannigan, wrote that O'Duffy was "energetic and zealous in the discharge of his duties" as junior surveyor.[29] He also secured the personal recommendation of Bishop Patrick McKenna of Clogher, who was "personally acquainted" with O'Duffy. He praised the young man's "splendid ability" and "highest character."[30] Receiving the bishop's recommendation indicated his family's social status was not as lowly as he later implied. He undertook a brief apprenticeship in County Wexford in 1913 before returning to Clones where he became well respected.[31]

In Clones, he stayed for a time in the Provincial Hotel, which was owned by friends of his family. He was commended locally for rejecting attempted bribes of money and alcohol to secure favorable planning decisions. He proudly described himself as "strictly sober" and "a Prefect of the Pioneer Total Abstinence Association."[32] By the time of his father's death in 1915, O'Duffy was already achieving success in life. He was self-confident enough to request a salary raise from his employers in February 1916, shrewdly alluding to a lucrative vacant assistant surveyorship in nearby Fermanagh. Recognizing it could ill afford to lose him, the Monaghan County Council granted O'Duffy a salary increase from £100 per annum to £110, to be raised by £20 every three years to a maximum of £150.[33] He took pride in the fruits of his labor and regularly referred to the roads across Monaghan as "my roads," a habit he found difficult to break even years after leaving the job.[34] Upwardly mobile and highly ambitious, he soon threw himself into cultural nationalist activism with gusto. Many of his contemporaries came from similar backgrounds and soon distinguished themselves as part of what has been dubbed the revolutionary generation.

◆ ◆ ◆

As an assistant county surveyor in Clones, O'Duffy lived in the village of Newbliss. Here he joined the Sarsfield's Gaelic football club.[35] The sporting body known as the Gaelic Athletic Association (GAA) was founded in 1884 to promote the reemergence of native Irish sports like Gaelic football and hurling. From the outset, its ethos was firmly nationalist. It opposed the creeping dominance of "foreign" sports like soccer and rugby, pejoratively known as garrison games. Michael Cusack, the GAA's founder, featured in James Joyce's novel *Ulysses* as the Citizen character. Joyce's roman-à-clef portrayed Cusack as an "anti-Semitic, chauvinistic figure" who espoused an insular nationalism.[36] Enthusiasm for Gaelic sports and nationalist politics frequently overlapped. "At the time the GAA was founded," O'Duffy wrote, "games here were in the grip of men hostile to the aspirations of the Irish people, men who were either English or *shoneen*—which is to say, little Johneys, or Irish sycophants of the Crown."[37] The GAA banned its members from playing "foreign" games until 1971 under Rule 27. O'Duffy supported the ban, arguing in the aftermath of Ireland's partition that "until Ireland is free and we need not trouble about the imperialist propaganda which at present is supporting the unnatural division of our land and people, it will be time enough for the ban to go."[38]

The GAA was first constituted in Monaghan on 27 December 1887 at a meeting in a small Carrickmacross hotel.[39] O'Duffy was a member since 1910 but his involvement with the GAA began in earnest in September 1912. Aged 22, he was appointed honorary secretary of the Monaghan County Board. Two months later, a vacancy arose for the secretaryship of the GAA Ulster Council, which O'Duffy was chosen to fill. He claimed the appointment came without his knowledge and in somewhat desperate circumstances owing to the resignations of five previous secretaries in a single year. O'Duffy enjoyed the patronage of Patrick Whelan, president of the GAA in Ulster and a fellow Monaghan native. He was impressed by the young man's energy and fluency in the Irish language. Whelan, chairman of the Newbliss Gaelic League, first encountered O'Duffy through the language movement.[40] The Ulster Council resolved to conduct its business entirely through Irish. Once again, O'Duffy's knowledge of the language stood in his favor.

The GAA in Ulster faced hostility from northern Protestants, something which was not a factor for GAA clubs elsewhere. Attacks by Protestant loyalists against players, supporters and property were not uncommon.[41] Tensions rose following the monumental passage of home rule legislation in 1912 by the Liberal government, which depended on the votes of Irish nationalist members of parliament for its survival. Although the House of Lords vetoed the bill, the recent Parliament Act 1911 diluted the upper house's power and ensured the peers could only postpone the commencement of legislation for two years. The prospect of impending home rule for Ireland rallied unionist opposition and prompted the establishment in 1913 of the Ulster Volunteers, a paramilitary force pledged to defy the introduction of home rule.

As a GAA administrator, O'Duffy channeled his natural ability as an organizer and helped to put the Ulster Council on a stable footing. Ulster GAA benefited from a rise in membership and the accompanying increase in subs helped place the organization in the black. Locally, O'Duffy's intervention helped the Monaghan team win the Ulster Senior Football Championship in 1914 for the first time in seven years. His administrative ability was praised highly in the local *Anglo-Celt* newspaper: "Mr O'Duffy came on the scene at a time when the GAA was at a very low ebb in Monaghan, but the martial instinct of the indomitable and unconquerable Gael was strong in his soul, and by his relentless energy he had taken a noteworthy part in placing Monaghan in the vanguard of Ulster Gaeldom."[42]

The period in which O'Duffy served as secretary of the Ulster Council was a turbulent time in modern Irish history. In response to the formation of the Ulster Volunteers, the Gaelic scholar Eoin MacNeill published an influential article "The North Began" in November 1913 which advocated the formation of a rival armed force to uphold the British government's commitment to enact Irish home rule. Nationalist opinion concurred. The Irish Volunteers (IV) was duly founded at a public meeting in Dublin's Rotunda Rink. MacNeill was elected president of the new force. From the outset, the Royal Irish Constabulary (RIC) was concerned that the GAA "could supply an abundance of first class recruits" for the IV.[43] Enthusiastic Irish nationalists flocked to join the Volunteers, which soon swelled to reach 180,000 men. Civil war in the United Kingdom seemed probable when a section of the British army in Ireland mutinied in the Curragh camp and refused to contemplate implementing home rule. Meanwhile, the Conservative leader of the opposition, Andrew Bonar Law, tacitly endorsed violence and mutiny to block home rule.[44]

The IV attracted the attention of the constitutionalist IPP led by John Redmond, who demanded the force be placed under his party's control. He was particularly concerned by the presence of members of the secret oathbound Irish Republican Brotherhood (IRB). Its members were committed separatists and successfully infiltrated the central committee of the IV. In January 1914, O'Duffy attended the first meeting of the Volunteers in Monaghan which elected Patrick Whelan as president of the local unit. O'Duffy initially remained outside the IV and continued to focus on sports administration. Praised as "a tireless worker" and a "great organizer," he was "instrumental in getting GAA clubs established throughout his own county and the entire province."[45] His involvement in the GAA was the perfect apprenticeship for his later involvement in revolutionary advanced nationalism.

The outbreak of World War I in late July 1914 soon produced a split in the IV. In September, Redmond addressed a meeting in Woodenbridge, County Wicklow, where he urged nationalist Ireland to support the British war effort. Whilst most of the Volunteers sided with Redmond and formed the National Volunteers, a recalcitrant 12,000 men rejected his call and reconstituted themselves under MacNeill's leadership. Many from Redmond's majority faction subsequently enlisted in the British army. The rump of the IV was dominated by the clandestine IRB, which began to plot a rebellion in Ireland while British military power was concentrated on fighting the Central Powers on the continent. The IV split also led to inactivity in the GAA. O'Duffy stated in his spring 1915 report that "the Volunteer movement had knocked it out" in Antrim and Tyrone. He continued to focus on the GAA, proposing the name Breffni Park for a new stadium in Cavan. He was later presented with a gold watch by the Ulster Council in recognition of his service to the GAA.[46]

◆ ◆ ◆

On 23 April 1916, O'Duffy attended the annual congress of the GAA in Dublin. Like most Irish people, he was oblivious about the secret plans for an insurrection in Dublin to be launched the next day, the Easter Rising. Most of the republican combatants with links to the GAA came from outside Ulster. A single northern GAA man, Patrick Rankin from Newry, cycled to Dublin to join the rebellion.[47] The Easter Rising was the culmination of a scheme spearheaded by the military council of the IRB. Fifteen hundred men, mostly from the IV and James Connolly's Irish Citizen Army, turned out on Easter Monday for the Dublin-based insurrection. They successfully captured key buildings across the capital city to the surprise of British authorities. From the rebel headquarters in the General Post Office, a republic was proclaimed under a provisional government made up of several youthful leaders of the Gaelic revival as well as veteran IRB plotters. Although connections were forged between the IRB and Germany, the failure of German rifles to successfully reach southwestern Ireland shortly before the planned insurrection damaged its chances of success. Republicans held their outposts for a week under heavy fire from a hastily assembled British force commanded by General John Maxwell. On 29 April, the rebel leader Patrick Pearse issued an unconditional surrender in the interest of avoiding further loss of life.

The Easter Rising "seemed to catch the entire North by surprise" but its aftermath was to have "a deep and lasting effect on the life of the GAA and its members."[48] For young men like O'Duffy who had not participated in the rising, they were consumed by the groundswell of support for republicanism which came in its aftermath. The ill-fated decision of the British government to introduce martial law in Ireland and to execute the key leaders of the rebellion has often been credited with turning the tide of public opinion on the rising from one of hostility to one of sympathy. Prominent republican leaders involved in the rising were executed in the months after the surrender including Pearse, an educator and nationalist writer; Connolly, a trade unionist and ardent champion of the working class; Tom Clarke, a veteran IRB organizer; and Seán Mac Diarmada, a young poet and journalist. Roger Casement, although captured prior to the rising when trying to import German rifles off the coast of Kerry, was executed in August. Casement was a former diplomat who was knighted by the British crown for his services to human rights in the Congo and Peru. He became a staunch republican after 1913. The executed leaders soon became martyrs. Many survivors of the uprising were transported to prison camps in England and Wales, where they planned their next campaign. As Dorothy Macardle wrote, "Irishmen learned by the costly experience of Easter Week" and devised that a new revolution should follow tactics of guerrilla warfare to challenge the might of the British Empire.[49]

Public support for Redmond's party suffered as support for republicanism grew. The British press erroneously dubbed the insurrection the "Sinn Féin Rising," mistakenly blaming the political party led by Arthur Griffith for organizing the rebellion. "As Ireland became pro-insurrection she became Sinn Féin, without knowing what Sinn Féin was, except that it stood generally for Irish independence," wrote P.S. O'Hegarty. Sinn Féin (SF), he continued, benefited from "a great public emotional wave towards the insurrection" and led to an influx of republicans into the party.[50]

Although O'Duffy was sympathetic to the ideals of the rising beforehand, he quickly became involved in rebuilding the republican movement in the rising's aftermath. On 22 June, he wrote to the newly established Irish National Aid and Volunteers' Dependents' Fund about starting a local collection in Clones.[51] The Fund was headed by Kathleen Clarke, the widow of Tom Clarke. She later employed Michael Collins as secretary to manage the Fund, which allowed him to contact members of the IRB and reorganize the secret society under his direction. Collins fought in the Easter Rising and was interned in Frongoch prison camp in Wales until its internees were released in a general amnesty in December 1916. He came to play a major role in the War of Independence.

O'Duffy seems to have joined the IV in May 1917. In September he was elected as the captain of his local IV company in Clones, then the only company in Monaghan. O'Duffy took advantage of his administrative role in the Ulster GAA to make the sporting association a recruiting ground for the reconstructed IV. It soon attracted patriotically minded athletes prepared to fight for Irish independence. Under O'Duffy's direction, the politics of the GAA in Ulster transformed from "a stance of relative moderation before 1917 to central involvement in the republican (para)military movement over the next five years."[52] He claimed to have recruited "virtually every able-bodied member or supporter of the GAA into Volunteer activities."[53]

Shortly after his election as an IV captain, he received instructions from General Headquarters (GHQ) to oversee the formation of new companies elsewhere. He soon succeeded in forming companies in Newbliss and Scotstown, which were then merged into battalions of which he was appointed commandant. He was also involved in republican politics, hosting meetings of SF at the newly acquired premises of the GAA club in Clones as early as January 1917.[54] He attributed the source of his enthusiasm to his first meeting with Collins in November 1917 at Croke Park. He was introduced to Collins by Luke O'Toole, secretary-general of the GAA. Due to O'Duffy's patriotic instincts, Collins had "no difficulty in kindling his feelings into a flame."[55] Henceforth, he became a devoted acolyte of Collins. He was also inducted into the IRB by Collins. IRB links were exploited to accelerate O'Duffy's advancement within the Ulster GAA.[56]

The poet W.B. Yeats wrote in the aftermath of the Easter Rising, "All changed, changed utterly; a terrible beauty is born." Although these lines are often quoted, they accurately describe the transformed landscape of Irish society following the rising's failure. SF, reconstructed as the political wing of the revolutionary movement, emerged as the major force in Irish nationalism and successfully displaced the IPP during the period between the Easter Rising's defeat and the December 1918 general election. The telos of Irish history departed from an incremental development to home rule towards a sudden outburst of revolutionary enthusiasm. O'Duffy and others of his generation emerged from humble origins to assume the towering heights of leadership and responsibility for steering the destiny of their country.

# 2

# Eoin O'Duffy's War

Nineteen seventeen saw the political and military reorganization of the republican movement. Although principally a militarist, O'Duffy spoke at the establishment of a SF club in Ballybay in October. Hecklers from the IPP and associated organizations like the Ancient Order of Hibernians (AOH) tried to interrupt the proceedings but were forcibly ejected.[1] The establishment of SF clubs came on foot of a series of successful by-elections, beginning with the victory of George Noble Plunkett, the father of an executed Easter Rising leader, in the Roscommon North by-election in February. Plunkett adhered to the SF policy of abstentionism, whereby elected members of parliament refused to recognize or attend the British parliament. The trend of SF successes continued when Joseph McGuinness, a republican prisoner in Lewes, was elected in a narrow victory over his IPP opponent in South Longford in May. The next by-election was held in July in East Clare. SF's candidate was Éamon de Valera, an Easter Rising commandant at Boland's Mill. Imprisoned in England post-Rising, he was released on 10 July 1917. Winning over 70 percent of the vote, de Valera's electoral victory added further wind to the sails of SF. The death of Thomas Ashe on hunger strike in September left de Valera as the most senior surviving commandant from the Easter Rising, a status which soon propelled him to the leadership of the republican movement.

Concomitant to the development of SF as a political force, the IV was reorganized in March 1917. Richard Mulcahy became chief-of-staff and Collins director of organization (DO). Mulcahy, second-in-command to Ashe during the rising, helped to achieve one of the IV's few successful engagements in the form of a pincer movement which captured several policemen in Ashbourne, County Meath.[2] GHQ initiated a root-and-branch reform of the IV across Ireland, beginning with the adoption of orthodox military structures such as companies, battalions, and brigades. A company corresponded to a local village or parish, whilst a brigade generally constituted a county. A company captain was often elected based on his prowess on the football pitch or due to his fluency of the Irish language.[3] O'Duffy described the intertwine of Gaelic sport and preparations for warfare, writing that "from the national games the Volunteers turned to the national struggle for independence. Their Irish-Ireland ideals illuminated them in battle as in play, but they shouldered rifle instead of *caman*, wore bandolier instead of jersey."[4]

The symbolic unification of the military and political wings of Irish republicanism came in October 1917. On 26 October, Griffith abdicated SF's presidency to de

Valera. Henceforth, SF adopted a more firmly republican program, scrapping Griffith's previous policy of a "dual monarchy" in which Ireland would retain the British monarch as king of Ireland. The party platform spoke the parlance of contemporary international diplomacy, positioning Ireland's claim to independence as a fulfillment of President Woodrow Wilson's promise of a post-war right to self-determination for small nations. The day after the SF congress, a secret IV convention was held which elected de Valera president of the body. Cathal Brugha became chairman of the resident committee. Directors were appointed to strengthen the force in key areas. It is disputed whether Brugha effectively became chief-of-staff at this point or whether Mulcahy retained the post. In Mulcahy's recollection, the IV national executive accepted a GHQ staff with himself as chief-of-staff, Collins as DO, Seán MacMahon as quartermaster general, Richard McKee as director of training, and Rory O'Connor as director of engineering.[5] The overlap in leadership roles between SF and IV personnel was deliberate. Mulcahy described this unification as having "fashioned and planted the two great tap-roots around which the new national movement was to grow."[6]

P.S. O'Hegarty claimed previous Irish revolutions had failed because they "had no public policy … to fall back on when the revolutionary policy failed them." Post-Easter Rising, he claimed republicanism benefited from "the clear intellectuality of Sinn Féin."[7] But the historian Michael Laffan argued that "people joined Sinn Féin in their tens of thousands because they were attracted by its image, not because they believed in its ideology." He characterized SF ideology as vague and populist, appealing to the sentiment that "freedom from Britain would be a panacea."[8] Seán Lemass remembered there was "a lot of nonsense associated with the old Sinn Féin organization.… It had collected all the cranks in the country and there were people making speeches in favor of vegetarianism and the single tax, all sorts of queer cranks."[9]

Writing in March 1938, O'Duffy identified 11 core principles of revolutionary SF. In his view, it stood for the reform of the Irish education system along nationalist lines; the creation of a consular state that prioritized the Irish diaspora abroad as a counterbalance to the "interests of the English Commercial houses"; the establishment of a national civil service; the creation of a national bank and stock exchange that could "bring pressure to bear on Irish banks to adopt a policy more in sympathy with Irish trade and industry"; the creation of a "national council of transit" to "develop Irish waterways under [the] control of popularly elected bodies—the County Councils"; the reform of the poor law system to direct money spent on workhouses towards "Irish goods and productive works"; the establishment of a mercantile marine based on a Norwegian model that would pursue foreign markets for Irish goods without "English interference"; the creation of an economic policy of protectionism and tariffs to encourage the state-led growth of native Irish industry; the conduct of a survey of Irish mineral resources with an eye towards quarrying native marble; the creation of national courts of arbitration that would supersede "the ordinary courts of law in civil cases, and thus deprive the corrupt Bar of Ireland of much of its incentive to corruption"; and finally, the promotion of the policy of abstentionism whereby Irish parliamentarians would refuse to take their seats in Westminster and instead establish a national assembly, the Council of Three Hundred, which would "form a de facto Irish Parliament."[10] This was O'Duffy's understanding of what SF meant, but the party's ambiguous platform allowed it to act as all things to all men.

◆ ◆ ◆

In Monaghan, O'Duffy formed a close association with Dan Hogan, a railway worker originally from County Tipperary heavily involved in the IV and GAA. Both men served on the committee of the SF James Connolly club in Clones.[11] Hogan and O'Duffy formed a powerful alliance and acted as the driving force behind the development of the IV in Monaghan. They also established a successful auctioneering business in Clones, which within its first few months netted over £2,000 in profit. The venture provided local Catholics with the opportunity to do business with a Catholic-owned firm. Although O'Duffy foresaw "a big practice in the three counties of Monaghan, Fermanagh, and Cavan," his focus on the IV hampered the growth of the business.[12] O'Duffy traversed the county by bicycle, organizing local companies. One local volunteer recalled that he and a group of friends contacted O'Duffy in June 1918 with a request to form an IV company. O'Duffy arrived in Wattlebridge by bicycle on a Sunday afternoon and delivered a 20-minute speech to the local GAA team. He outlined the IV's structure, history and succinctly summed up their ultimate objective, "the overthrow of British rule in Ireland." The 20 men were told by O'Duffy that if they were not prepared to use force, they should not join the IV. At least six of the men never joined, but the rest eventually joined.[13] By the end of 1917, O'Duffy, as secretary of SF in North Monaghan, reported that there were 22 clubs embracing a membership of almost 2,000. He explained that "with a little more organization and perseverance they would have enrolled in Sinn Féin practically the entire Catholic population of North Monaghan."[14]

The onward march of SF faced a setback in early 1918 when it lost two successive by-elections in Ulster. In South Armagh in February and East Tyrone in April, the SF candidates failed to replicate earlier victories and overturn the IPP majority. Ulster remained a regional stronghold for residual IPP support, particularly due to the organized presence of the AOH, a fraternal Catholic nationalist association. It provided the backbone of the IPP's political machine in the northeast under the domination of Belfast's Joseph Devlin. There was a strong mutual hostility between the AOH and republicans. One republican from Tyrone characterized the Hibernians as being "worse than the unionists."[15] A by-election in East Cavan in June saw SF's candidate, Arthur Griffith, defeat his IPP opponent. In addition to its central plank of establishing an Irish republic, SF attracted mass support due to its staunch opposition to the prospect of the introduction of conscription in Ireland. Moreover, the spurious "German plot" alleged by the British administration in Ireland, which led to the arrest of prominent republicans in May 1918, quickly unraveled and generated a further surge of support for the interned SF leaders. In each of the three Ulster by-elections O'Duffy mobilized the IV under his command for impressive election day parades. Even before the commencement of the War of Independence, O'Duffy was demonstrating his competency as an organizer.

As 1918 progressed, the increased frequency of IV marches, drills, and formations training was noted with concern by the RIC. Suspicious that IV activities were being organized under the auspices of the GAA, Dublin Castle issued a proclamation in July which required GAA clubs to obtain permits to hold hurling or Gaelic football games. In response, the GAA organized a nationwide day of defiance on 4 August which arranged hurling and Gaelic football matches across the country without a single permit being granted. The event, known as Gaelic Sunday, marked "the GAA's most public demonstration of identification with the rising tide of public disaffection in Ireland," according to Tim Pat Coogan. Realizing that repression would be counter-productive, the British authorities backed down and allowed the matches to go ahead unimpeded.[16] On 14 September, at the half-way point of the Gaelic football championship between Cavan and Armagh held in Cootehill, a squadron of RIC men arrived "in full battle dress" to proclaim the event an "illegal assembly." O'Duffy, the match referee, was singled out by one policeman who placed his hand on O'Duffy's shoulder and informed him he was under arrest. He was handcuffed as he rose from his seat and was marched off with a police officer on either side of him. Dan Hogan was also arrested. O'Duffy smiled defiantly at his supporters as he was led away to the police barracks.[17] He had reason to smile as the RIC's decision to break up a peaceful football match sparked an immediate popular backlash.

Supporters followed O'Duffy and Hogan to the police barracks, cheering along the way. Some were later charged with using seditious language. There was a considerable build-up of a military and police presence in the town. O'Duffy was struck in the face by a British soldier at Clones train station. It was reported that "no provocation was given whatsoever by Mr O'Duffy," who bled from the blow.[18] From Clones, O'Duffy and Hogan were transported to Belfast jail to await trial. They were held in a republican wing, which allowed SF prisoners from across the country to mix freely. His day was highly regimented. Each morning, he rose at 7.30 and said his morning prayers before breakfast at 8.15. The days consisted mostly of parades and meals. However, he wrote letters and received mail during the day. Additionally, he taught a daily Irish class in the afternoon. The Rosary was prayed at 6 p.m., with lights out at 9.45 p.m. On Sundays, Mass began at 7.30, although O'Duffy disliked the celebrant and his sermons, suspecting he was hostile to the republican prisoners. The men received parcels of food from the Belfast Cumann na mBán, the women's auxiliary to the republican movement.[19]

Hogan and O'Duffy were transported from Belfast jail to Clones for their trial on 21 September where they received "a hero's welcome." Their train was "mobbed by supporters at every train station in the county" as they returned to Monaghan.[20] The arrest "sent thrills of indignation through every Gael in Ireland," reported one regional newspaper.[21] At the trial, a farcical charge was laid against O'Duffy of using a whistle while in the role of referee during a football match. This was roundly mocked in the press. In court, O'Duffy refused to answer questions in English. When questioned by the head constable, Mr. Johnstone, O'Duffy replied in Irish: "Don't pay any heed to the English courts.... I haven't a thing to say to you" and sarcastically asked if the constable did not understand "the Hottentot language."[22] This elicited a burst of applause in the courtroom. The public were warned that if there were any further "futile interruptions" the courtroom would be cleared. The judge then sentenced O'Duffy and Hogan to two months of imprisonment in Belfast jail. The convicts were given an enthusiastic send-off as a crowd assembled to show their support for the felons.[23]

Collins despaired that the jailing of O'Duffy was "another hellish loss." He regarded O'Duffy as "the best man by far in Ulster."[24] Collins respected his administrative abilities in the GAA and IV and his enthusiasm for advancing the republican movement. O'Duffy wrote that "Collins knew well the merits of the GAA from the national viewpoint. He came from an old Gaelic clan in Cork, and when he went to a job in London as a boy he joined the Gaelic Athletic Association, becoming secretary of the Geraldines Football and Hurling Club."[25] In addition to a shared appreciation for the utility of the GAA to advance militant nationalism, they were of one mind on core political issues.

◆ ◆ ◆

Eoin O'Duffy, convict number 1089, served 67 days in Belfast jail from 14 September to 19 November 1918.[26] Shortly before his release, World War I ended on 11 November with the victory of the Allies over Germany and the Central Powers. The British coalition government led by David Lloyd George soon called a UK-wide general election for 14 December. The results returned the wartime-era national government to power. Although a member of the Liberal Party, Lloyd George headed a coalition mostly supported by Conservative members of parliament. In Ireland, the results demonstrated the clear shift of allegiance towards SF, which won a majority of 73 parliamentary seats from a total of 105 Irish constituencies. Unionists, mostly in the northeast, won 22 seats. Meanwhile, the IPP trailed behind with just six seats mostly elected from its residual pockets of support in Ulster.

Adhering to the republican doctrine of abstentionism, elected SF members of parliament met on 21 January 1919 in the Mansion House, the official residence of Dublin's Lord Mayor. As many of the SF members of parliament were still in prison following the German Plot arrests, just 27 SF delegates attended the meeting which constituted the inaugural assembly of the First Dáil. This revolutionary parliament passed a declaration of independence, agreed a democratic program, and proclaimed a message to the free nations of the world seeking international recognition for the newly ratified Irish Republic. It was a highly choreographed but symbolically important meeting. On the same day, an IV column in Tipperary commanded by Seán Treacy and Dan Breen ambushed and killed two RIC men near Soloheadbeg. The volunteers captured a consignment of gelignite, the material used to make explosives. Although Treacy and Breen were acting on their own initiative and without the approval of GHQ, the attack signaled the beginning of the Irish War of Independence.

The establishment of the Irish Republic remolded the IV as the republic's military. It was soon styled the Irish Republican Army (IRA). Volunteers swore an oath of allegiance to the republic and its revolutionary parliament. In Monaghan, one local IRA captain queried if their oath superseded all other oaths. O'Duffy answered in the affirmative. The captain hoped the new oath would render allegiance to the oathbound IRB secondary in importance.[27] The War of Independence was characterized by regional and irregular patterns of sporadic violence. In Monaghan, violence was initially limited. O'Duffy concentrated on building the strength of the IRA locally, assuming command over all IRA units in the county. Driven and energetic, O'Duffy was at one stage honorary secretary of "no fewer than ten voluntary organizations." He recalled, "not only did I need to work sixteen hours a day, but I had to suffer irregular meals and widely varying hours of sleep. But, thank God, I was always physically fit, and had the ability to sleep through earthquakes."[28] There was a clash of personalities between O'Duffy and Dr Conn Ward within the Monaghan IRA. Ward and O'Duffy became lifelong rivals. "Both of these men were ambitious, and each wanted to be boss," recalled IRA volunteer John Shields.[29]

O'Duffy gained a reputation as a stern disciplinarian. His authority in Monaghan was strengthened by his ability to exploit the IRB's network to build an intelligence organization for the IRA.[30] Collins took O'Duffy under his wing in the IRB and he rapidly ascended the ranks of the secret society. The same local captain who queried O'Duffy on the oath to the republic was dismayed to discover an IRB organizer attempting to recruit two of his lieutenants. When questioned, the IRB organizer revealed he had been given their names by O'Duffy. The captain ascribed the disproportionate presence of IRB men among IRA officers in Monaghan to "the influence which Eoin O'Duffy exercised in that area."[31] However, O'Duffy prioritized competence over IRB membership. He was "disappointed with the work of the 5th (Carrick) Battalion and had no confidence in the Commandant P.J. Daly," an IRB member who tried to ensure the secret organization dominated his unit. O'Duffy asked Brian MacMahon (non–IRB) to take over from Daly. Despite being advised not to become entangled in the complicated situation, MacMahon accepted the appointment. He recalled that O'Duffy was "sticking out his neck" in replacing an IRB member with a non-member. Nonetheless, he frequently invited MacMahon to join the IRB and asked his brother, Peadar MacMahon, to "put pressure on me to join." He recalled,

> I knew O'Duffy all my life, as we were born and reared a stone's throw from each other and were close friends until the IRB question intervened somewhat. We had had several heated arguments as to the validity of the Brotherhood or its necessity and I should have known then that if I should ever come up against the IRB I could not rely on his support.[32]

British authorities described the IRA leader in Monaghan as "clean-shaven, but now may have a small reddish mustache; smart-looking; speaks well, brown eyes [sic], long thin nose, pale complexion, thin face, slight make, 5 feet 9 inches high, about 30 years of age: walks with long strides and swings his arms."[33] O'Duffy could unnerve people by the "piercing blueness" of his eyes which "undoubtedly had a disturbing effect on the individual on whom they concentrated their gaze."[34] Captain Liam Walsh, O'Duffy's future secretary, recalled that O'Duffy's eyes gave one "the uncomfortable feeling he was cognizant of your every thought."[35] Although strict, O'Duffy seemed to have earned the respect of his men. He regularly dipped into his own savings to provide transport for the IRA men under his command to and from rallies.[36]

Although violence was rare in Monaghan throughout 1919, the IRA tried to assert republican authority by intimidating local enemies and launching boycotts of the British administration including its courts and police force. Public protest meetings in Monaghan regularly appealed to the Peace Conference in Paris to apply the principle of self-determination to Ireland while condemning the actions of the British administration. At a public meeting in Clones in mid–March 1919, O'Duffy seconded a motion which called for Irish self-determination and demanded the release of SF political prisoners from Belfast jail.[37] Appealing to the Paris Peace Conference was a central aim of the republic's foreign policy. An Irish delegation led by Seán T. O'Kelly failed to gain entry to the Paris Peace Conference. Representatives of other small nations, like the Egyptian Wafd party, faced a similar response. However, roving Irish diplomatic envoys on the continent produced copious amounts of pro-republican propaganda which they disseminated to drum up international sympathy for the Irish cause.

To complement the republic's international strategy, the SF leader, New York-born Éamon de Valera, embarked on a nationwide tour of the United States from June 1919. The objectives of the mission were threefold: to acquire recognition for the Irish Republic from the American government; to energize the Irish diaspora and Irish American organizations in support of the republic; and to raise a loan of $5 million from public subscription.[38] The legality of raising such a loan was disputed. As the Irish Republic was an unrecognized state, its hopes of accessing international money markets were dashed by the existence of American blue sky laws.[39] In America, de Valera clashed with Irish-American leaders Daniel Cohalan and John Devoy. This produced a rupture among supporters of the Irish republican cause in the United States. As de Valera toured North America from June 1919 until November 1920, the administration of the revolutionary republic at home and the prosecution of the IRA's war effort fell to subordinates. In particular, Collins accumulated significant powers in the republican government and IRA during de Valera's absence. As minister for finance, Collins established a Dáil loan to fund the revolution. From late 1919, bonds were sold across Ireland. Of Ulster's nine counties, Monaghan was the most successful county for uptake in subscriptions to the Dáil loan.[40] O'Duffy personally purchased £25 worth of shares in the republican loan.[41]

◆ ◆ ◆

During the period of de Valera's sojourn in the United States, the Irish War of Independence intensified. In January 1920, the infamous "Black and Tans" arrived in Ireland to restore British law and order in the "troubled" island. These men were officially recruited to replenish the ranks of the RIC, which saw an exodus of policemen since the beginning of hostilities. Recruits from Britain tended to be veterans of World War I who struggled to find post-war employment. They earned their nickname due to donning a combination of standard British army uniforms and RIC uniforms. The Black and Tans gained a notorious reputation due to their poor discipline and a tendency to regard all Irish as the enemy. Responding to this intensification in Monaghan, O'Duffy oversaw preparations for the first major engagement of the county's IRA in February 1920. Conferring with IRA staff, O'Duffy and Hogan produced a detailed plan for a raid on the police barracks in Ballytrain, a village eight miles outside Castleblayney. It included a scheme to block roads across the county to prevent reinforcements from arriving at the RIC garrison. Ernie O'Malley, a young IRA officer attached to GHQ, traveled to Monaghan in advance of the raid to inspect the quality of the Monaghan IRA. "The work had all been done before O'Malley was informed of our plans," one local IRA man recalled.[42]

The attack went ahead on the night of 14 February. O'Duffy took command of the raid. A detachment of five or six IRA volunteers broke the windows of a house directly opposite the RIC barracks in Ballytrain, swiftly occupying the building. Once inside, they opened fire on the barracks across the street. At the same time, a party of IRA raiders entered the barracks' lock-up store, where they planted an explosive mine at the building's gable end. O'Malley had trained the Monaghan men in the use of grenades. A volunteer recalled O'Malley was "very successful in every effort." Less than an hour after the commencement of the attack, O'Duffy ordered all men to move down the road, where 25 of them assembled and trained their rifles on the barracks. O'Duffy demanded that the occupants of the barracks surrender, giving them three chances to comply. Each call was answered with the fire of a rifle from the RIC. Having received his answer, O'Duffy ordered his men to explode the mine. One witness recalled that O'Duffy spoke through a megaphone "in a loud distinctive voice" and shouted the order "let off the mine!" A loud explosion followed. The building's slates could be heard falling. The IRA were ordered to charge the barracks via the gaping hole in its gable wall, which was left "in a heap of rubble." The upstairs floor was "sloped down resting on the rubble." The IRA raiders scrambled up the destroyed stairs and reached the room where the RIC had taken shelter.[43] It was only after the explosion of the mine that the police surrendered and came out with their hands up.

Magnanimous in victory, O'Duffy shook hands with the surrendering Constable Gallagher, telling him: "we did not come here to do injury, but only for arms."[44] When another policeman drew attention to £60 stored in a safe, O'Duffy informed him, "we don't want your money." His conduct resembled good-natured sportsmanship on the football field rather than what might be expected from the guerrilla leader of a night time raid. As the IRA seized a supply of rifles, revolvers, and ammunition from the captured barracks, Dan Hogan used a first-aid kit to treat an abrasion Gallagher had suffered from the explosion.[45] O'Duffy even apologized for the lack of a doctor available to treat the injured policemen and complimented them "on the fight they had made."[46] The battle was distinguished by its apparent chivalry. It lasted for four hours and resulted in damage to property of over £10,000.[47]

The Ballytrain raid was a major success for O'Duffy and enhanced his reputation with GHQ. It was described by Terence Dooley as marking "the beginning of the War of Independence in earnest in Monaghan."[48] Historian Michael Hopkinson explained that the "charismatic leadership" of O'Duffy was a major factor in pulling off "one of the first successful police barracks attacks" in north-eastern Ireland.[49] His "military acumen and precision" during the Ballytrain raid was reported to GHQ by a highly impressed O'Malley. The raid "brought the name Eoin O'Duffy to prominence."[50] O'Duffy basked in this achievement throughout his career, later caustically drawing attention to the absence of Dr Ward who "failed to turn up on the night of the attack." It was a rather unfair remark, as Ward was not living in Monaghan at the time but in Dundalk, County Louth.[51]

The aftermath of the well-reported raid caused the RIC considerable embarrassment. In late April, O'Duffy was present at an Armagh meeting of the GAA Ulster Council in his role as secretary when it was noticed by attendees that the meeting place was being surrounded by the police. Suddenly, the room was raided and O'Duffy was placed under arrest. Supporters booed as the police escorted him away.[52] Dan Hogan was also arrested. Both were arrested without charge. O'Duffy's latest French leave caused activity in the Monaghan GAA to reach "a complete standstill."[53] The arrest prompted a series of reprisals by the Monaghan IRA, who burned police barracks in Clontibret and Smithborough and nearby Middletown, County Armagh in April.[54]

Following their arrest, Hogan and O'Duffy were transported to Crumlin Road jail in Belfast. Over the course of its lengthy history, Crumlin Road jail has been "dotted with hunger strikes, escapes, floggings, and riots."[55] IRA men were frequently sent to prisons in Belfast where it was hoped the mainly Protestant anti-republican population of the city would make escapes less feasible. Paul Mulcahy, a County Tipperary IRA prisoner, recalled being transported to the Quays area of Belfast, where "we were charged by an Orange mob and a party of Carson's boy scouts in uniform, who flung stones, bolts and nuts at us."[56] Soon after arriving, O'Duffy, who was a well-known and respected commander in the northern IRA, was co-opted onto the political prisoners' military council. The council intended to organize a hunger strike, demanding the release of political prisoners. An ultimatum signed by O'Duffy and three others from the prisoners' council was presented to the governor "on behalf of 145 uncharged and untried men in Belfast." It demanded their "immediate and unconditional release ... failing this we go on hunger-strike to-night, Monday, 26th April 1920."[57] The hunger strike went ahead. By Wednesday, one of the hunger strikers fainted during the evening as the men prayed the Rosary. Eleven IRA men were exempted from partaking in the hunger strike for health or age reasons.[58] O'Duffy soon became leader of the hunger strikers. He threatened the prison doctor that he "would be held personally responsible" if any of the strikers died. The threat was effective, as the doctor began discharging prisoners on medical grounds.[59] After just a week, the hunger strike had eroded the confidence of the prison authorities. They were soon released.

During the hunger strike, the IRA in Monaghan staged its own "protest against the treatment meted out ... by the British authorities." The IRA "closed down local British institutions and institutions friendly to the occupation for a short period," which often meant forcibly shutting down pro–British businesses in Monaghan.[60] This was coupled with the enforcement of the Belfast boycott, a campaign launched by the IRA in 1920 in response to a drastic increase in anti–Catholic "pogroms" in Belfast. The boycott forbade Irish businesses from doing trade with northern Protestant businessmen deemed complicit in the violence. A total of 498 people were killed in Belfast during the violent period 1920–22.[61] O'Duffy was a strong supporter of the boycott against firms seen as anti-national. O'Duffy characterized the Bank of Ireland as "without doubt the most *shoneen* & anti–Irish bank in the country" and described an occasion when he tried to lodge a check signed in Irish which was refused.[62]

Upon their return to Monaghan, the freed prisoners received a hearty welcome. A motion of congratulations for O'Duffy was passed by Monaghan County Council on his resumption of duties as assistant surveyor. The chairman praised him as "one of the most intelligent and competent men" employed by the council and expressed his support for O'Duffy's recent "great victory" in Crumlin Road jail.[63] One of the first meetings O'Duffy attended following his release was the Ulster Association of Municipal Engineers and Assistant County Surveyors in Portadown as the delegate from Monaghan. He claimed that despite the religious differences with most other delegates and his status as a "convicted nationalist felon and jailbird," he received cheers from the other delegates.[64]

His position as an assistant surveyor employed by Monaghan County Council was disputed in March 1921. Recognizing that his status as a wanted man made him unable to fully discharge his duties, O'Duffy asked to step back from his position in March 1921.[65] At a council meeting, Colonel Madden, who served as a unionist councilor on the local government body, asked questions about how O'Duffy received his wages given he was "on the run." O'Duffy was defended by Dr Conn Ward, who queried why Colonel Madden was "so anxious about this man" and whether he was simply "looking for information." The council subsequently voted that O'Duffy should continue to receive his full salary and that the county surveyor would appoint a substitute until O'Duffy could return to full-time work. The three unionist councilors dissented.[66]

◆ ◆ ◆

By May 1920, the IRA were organized in virtually every parish in Monaghan. There were 1,000 volunteers in the county. The success of the Monaghan IRA prompted GHQ to transfer the IRA's Clogher company in neighboring County Tyrone to O'Duffy's brigade.[67] For a time, O'Duffy stayed "in a very comfortable farmhouse in the hills" behind Clogher with the McConnell family.[68] P.V. Hoey, a company captain, defended O'Duffy's reputation: "in view of the fantastical stories one hears occasionally concerning compulsion on the IRA to undertake certain activities, it is well to state that Commandant O'Duffy pointed to the dangerous work that lay ahead and gave each man the option to leave the IRA if he so wished. Not a single man in the Battalion area availed of this offer."[69]

By the end of 1920 the "national resistance" in County Monaghan had reached a high, wrote Hoey. He claimed the forces of the republic were firmly entrenched across the county: "The enemy had withdrawn from their rural posts to their last stronghold in the Battalion area, their fortified barracks in Carrickmacross."[70] Although he exaggerated the scale of the IRA's dominance, the republican movement had successfully made its presence felt. In Clones, the IRA paraded the streets at night while the RIC was confined to its barracks.[71] The Dáil introduced a republican court system across Ireland which meted out justice and tried to settle local disputes. In June, a meeting at St Macartan's Hall in Monaghan was "crowded with delegates" from local government, poor law guardians, representatives from SF clubs, representatives from each company of the Monaghan IRA, delegates from trade unions and clergymen from the Catholic Church. The meeting established Dáil courts in Monaghan and appointed several judges, including O'Duffy.[72] Sittings of the Dáil courts were generally held in town courthouses. Hoey claimed "the enemy did not interfere, except in Carrickmacross, where Sergeant McGolderick and some other RIC men held a 'watching brief' for the Crown."[73]

The IRA in Monaghan was frequently involved in raids against illegal distilleries producing *poitín*, an illicit form of home-made alcohol analogous to moonshine. Fiercely intolerant of drunkenness, O'Duffy took a leading role in the crusade against *poitín*. On one occasion after a traditional *céilí* dance in Clones, O'Duffy learned that "a certain gentleman" had offered to sell another man *poitín*. The seller was arrested by the IRA, who used him as a guide to find the origin of the stock. The IRA discovered the distillery was owned by a Protestant who was likely to resist them by force. Twelve IRA men led by O'Duffy traveled by bicycle to the owner's home, where they used a battering ram to smash his front door and take him by surprise. The owner was interrogated and his property searched. The IRA found a four-gallon crockery jar containing the illicit substance. "With due ceremony, O'Duffy smashed this jar on the laneway leading to the house," one volunteer recalled.[74] A shotgun was also seized during the raid but O'Duffy returned it to its owner. He explained, "it is a *poitín* raid I am conducting, not an arms one."[75]

But O'Duffy was still not satisfied and made further enquiries which led him to the house of the salesman from the dance. In the garden, buried in potato drills, the men discovered the "worm" of the still. A *poitín* still is an apparatus used to distill or separate alcohol from a mixture known as "the mash." Because alcohol has a lower boiling point than water, when heated the alcohol turns into vapor and rises to the top of the still. It then is caught in the connecting tube and directed into the worm. The worm is a copper pipe coiled into a spiral shape and submerged in cold water, so when the hot vapor inside the worm reaches the section submerged in the cold water it condenses back into liquid form. This distillate is then caught in containers at the end of the worm which protrudes from the condensing barrel.[76] The Clones IRA men sawed the worm into short lengths to stop it ever being used again.

On another occasion, the Monaghan IRA captured a lead pipe that weighed 70 pounds, used in the production of *poitín*, and converted it into buckshot for use against British forces. P.V. Hoey claimed the IRA's raids were so successful that in a short space of time illegal *poitín* traffic in Monaghan was "practically eliminated."[77] Excessive alcohol consumption was viewed with extreme disapproval by idealistic nationalists like O'Duffy. SF advocated sobriety, arguing that Ireland's annual contribution to imperial taxation would be cut by £4 million if alcohol consumption were halved.[78] Patrick Pearse had similarly bemoaned "the two great evils in country places at present … stagnation and drink."[79]

◆ ◆ ◆

Under O'Duffy's command, the Monaghan IRA was involved in several controversial executions of people alleged to be spies or informers. The issue of executions carried out by the IRA remains a contentious historiographical topic. In Peter Hart's view, the "loose, localized nature" of the IRA coupled with the "radicalizing pressures of a guerilla war" bred an environment whereby a "low-level but widespread, and occasionally intense, persecution" festered.[80] Hart claimed Protestants were the main group persecuted by the IRA, followed by individuals regarded as social misfits, members of the Traveler community, or those who were seen as too pro–British or hostile to republicans. Hart's methodology has been criticized by, among others, the historian John Regan.

On 9 March 1921, the bodies of two young Catholics, Patrick Larmer and Francis McPhillips, were discovered in the village of Aghabog. Notes attached to the bodies suggested they were convicted informers who had been executed by the IRA. Twenty-three-year-old Larmer was a republican sympathizer who carried messages for the IRA. But following his capture by British forces, Larmer broke under interrogation. John McGahey, an IRA volunteer in Rockcorry, pleaded for O'Duffy not to order Larmer's execution. McGahey felt he was nearly successful in convincing O'Duffy to spare the young man's life when Dan Hogan arrived and "intervened in a manner most aggressive towards myself."[81] Larmer was soon after executed, although McGahey primarily blamed the untimely intervention of Hogan.

McPhillips was 21 years old and the only son of a widow who farmed 30 acres in the village of Aghabog. He was a member of the AOH. The IRA suspected McPhillips of providing information to the police and engaging in indiscreet conversations with Protestant neighbors about the activities of local republicans. A month before his death he was abducted and tied to the railings of the local church as a warning. The execution was controversial as many believed the murder was carried out purely because of his AOH membership. The parish priest of Aghabog thought the young man "should not have been put before the [firing] squad" as "he was generally acknowledged as not up to the normal mental standard."[82] Another AOH man, Arthur Treanor, was killed in June 1921 for allegedly providing information to the police. He was a prominent member of the community and a vocal opponent of SF. Even subsequent IRA testimonies acknowledged that the case against him was more ambiguous than others, as "Treanor was intelligent and shrewd and more difficult to involve."[83] It was reported that the IRA extorted £10 from Treanor on 24 June, but that he was still shot the next morning.[84] In 1925, a Celtic cross memorial was erected to Treanor by the AOH. In a speech marking the occasion, Treanor was called "a stumbling block" to SF due to his local popularity who was murdered by "blood thirsty rogues and robbers."[85] Ill-feeling between the AOH and IRA remained potent throughout the War of Independence and beyond.

O'Duffy's ruthless streak was displayed in his claim to have executed a volunteer for making disparaging remarks that Terence MacSwiney, the Lord Mayor of Cork who died on hunger strike, had committed suicide. Frank Aiken, another northern IRA commander, doubted the veracity of the anecdote. The actual reason for the execution, according to Aiken, was that this Monaghan volunteer was a "traitor" who was shot "for giving away about twenty men of his own Company to the Peelers." The man allegedly confessed what he had done and begged O'Duffy to shoot him.[86]

The IRA execution of civilians alleged to be informers has understandably remained a controversial subject. An *Irish Times* "missing list" of 22 August 1921 included the names of James Gaffney and Francis Boyle from Monaghan as two civilians missing since 9 July, likely shot by the IRA.[87] However, the death of Kate Carroll on 17 April 1921 was particularly controversial due to her gender and a reputed sectarian dimension. It was mistakenly reported that Carroll was Protestant. Historian Terence Dooley recently corrected the prevailing error about Carroll's religion. She was, in fact, an unmarried Catholic farmer.[88] It was highly unusual for a woman to be executed by the IRA. Her body bore a note from the IRA which suggested she was a spy or an informer. McGarry suggested her involvement in *poitín* distilling and refusal to pay fines to the IRA could have been the motivating factor which led to her death. He quoted a report by the county inspector which attributed her death to a letter to the RIC intercepted by republicans in which she informed on rival distillers.[89] However, the same report indicated that Carroll had ceased distilling before her death. Rumors abounded locally that Carroll had "communicated information to Crown Forces."[90] One IRA man claimed that Carroll was "giving information to the British" and that the IRA intercepted letters containing a check intended for Carroll "for services rendered."[91] In another IRA testimony it was stated that the evidence against her was "very strong." He continued, "she was scarcely normal and was not sufficiently intelligent to cloak her activities."[92] The motive behind Carroll's execution remains uncertain, but it would be disingenuous to discount the IRA's professed reason of executing a known informer.

◆ ◆ ◆

After Ballytrain, O'Duffy launched a general raid for arms directed against the unionist population in Monaghan. He suspected local Protestants of hoarding arms and reasoned that IRA raids would equip his force with weaponry whilst defanging a hostile "fifth column." Brian MacMahon estimated local loyalties in the southern barony of Farney as follows: 20 percent "ardent Sinn Féiners and out and out supporters of the IRA"; 35 percent "mild supporters" of SF and the IRA; 15 percent "mild adherents" of the IPP, but not connected to the AOH; 20 percent "rabid supporters" of the IPP and members of the AOH; 10 percent unionists.[93]

Philip Marron recalled leading raids against ten houses in Milltown, a unionist area hostile to the IRA: "It was known to us that many of the inhabitants were in possession of firearms including rifles."[94] A house owned by the Millar family was described by John McGahey as resembling "a military fortress in size and strength." 18 IRA men from the Rockcorry company participated in the raid. They knocked on the front door to gain admittance but were immediately met with gunshots from six men inside the house. "We were forced to take cover and we then replied to the fire" before retreating to some sheds behind the house. The IRA realized they "could not force an entrance to the house" and the attack was abandoned.[95] Three IRA men were killed, and another later died from his wounds. Although other raids were more successful, O'Duffy had underestimated "the ferocity of loyalist resistance to their raids." Whilst loyalists in Monaghan remained a potent force, they eventually succumbed to defeat at the hands of the IRA.[96] Unlike their counterparts in

Northern Ireland, Monaghan loyalists failed to maintain their domination over the Catholic nationalist population in the long-term.

Raids on the Crawford, Fleming, Hawthorne, and Lester families by the IRA in August and September left two IRA men dead and more injured.[97] Pat McDonnell later doubted the wisdom of the raids, arguing the campaign "did more harm than good as it made the Unionists and Hibernians more antagonistic than ever."[98] Local Protestants formed militias and defense committees in response to the raids. Dooley wrote that an "escalating cycle of violence was to be one of the clear impacts of the general raid for arms." Aside from IRA deaths during the raids, loyalists also targeted those associated with SF such as Fr James McPhillips who was killed in November 1920.[99]

In August 1920, the British government upped the ante by introducing coercive legislation which "virtually abolished the principle of trial by jury and established military law."[100] On 21 November, Collins' "squad" of IRA men eliminated the Cairo Gang, killing 15 British intelligence operatives in a carefully planned operation in Dublin. The Black and Tans retaliated the same day. In an act of terrorism, they fired on civilians attending a GAA match in Dublin's Croke Park. Fourteen civilians were killed in what became known as Bloody Sunday. Dan Hogan's brother, a player in the football match, was killed during the attack.[101] O'Duffy was in Draperstown, County Derry with Dan Hogan when he learned of Bloody Sunday. Reading the newspaper accounts, he asked Dan Hogan if he knew Mick Hogan of Grangemockler. "Yes," answered Dan. "He's my brother. What about him?" O'Duffy hesitated before handing him the newspaper. Hogan said nothing for a while before asking O'Duffy for permission to attend the funeral. "No, Dan," he answered. "One tragedy is enough for your mother to bear." The decision was accepted. The men then knelt together to pray a Rosary for the repose of Michael Hogan's soul.[102]

A week after the events of 21 November, the IRA's 3rd Cork Brigade led by Tom Barry ambushed 18 Auxiliaries in Kilmichael and killed 16 of them. The incident alarmed the British cabinet and impressed upon them that a full-fledged military campaign was required to subdue Ireland. The events of November 1920 "made nonsense of the assumptions that the end was in sight," according to historian Ronan Fanning.[103] As 1920 ended, O'Duffy prepared the men under his command for a tough period of brutal fighting which would eventually produce a breakthrough. He told his men in December to prepare for "a war to the death in Monaghan against the enemy who has threatened to wipe out the Young Republic." He stated that any officers who displayed ill-discipline in the coming year would be demoted without hesitation, "no matter of what rank or how useful otherwise."[104]

◆ ◆ ◆

The revolution intensified in 1921. The passage of the Government of Ireland Act 1920 by the British parliament had partitioned Ireland into a 26-county entity termed Southern Ireland and the north-eastern six counties which were incorporated as Northern Ireland. Three of Ulster's nine counties (Monaghan, Cavan and Donegal) fell within the territory of Southern Ireland, which was intended to serve as a home rule parliament within the United Kingdom. However, republicans strongly rejected the imposition of partition. The new border became a flashpoint for violent incidents. In January 1921, George Lester, a Protestant and member of the Orange Order, assaulted two Catholic boys whom he accused of running IRA messages in Roslea, County Fermanagh. Upon learning of the incident, O'Duffy ordered Monaghan IRA volunteer James McKenna to shoot Lester. John T. Connolly, Patrick Prunty, and McKenna went to Roslea armed with two shotguns and a revolver. They waited opposite Lester's house until he opened his shop and shot him. Lester was wounded but survived. The IRA men had only five cartridges for their two shotguns and one of the guns misfired, so only one shot hit Lester.[105]

The Lester shooting led to an immediate explosion of recriminations against Catholic civilians in Roslea by loyalists. Many Protestants joined the Ulster Special Constabulary (USC) in November 1920, the new northern police force's volunteer auxiliary wing, (the B Specials). O'Duffy believed that 620 Monaghan men were part-time members of the USC.[106] Many were ex-members of the Ulster Volunteers and British army. In the end, two Catholic men were badly wounded, and eight houses were razed during the attacks. A Catholic curate's house was also targeted by the loyalists. The attack prompted the IRA to plan reprisals against B Specials and prominent Orangemen in Roslea, Smithboro and Scotstown, villages which straddle the border between Fermanagh and Monaghan.[107] O'Duffy dispatched Dan Hogan to Dublin to seek permission from Collins for the campaign of reprisals. James McKenna recalled that O'Duffy "got a free hand in the reprisals. All arrangements had been made prior to Commandant Hogan's return. We had agreed that four Sergeants of the B Specials should be shot, and sixteen houses burnt."[108]

John Connolly was asked by O'Duffy if the local nationalist population in Roslea "would stand behind the IRA when the reprisals were carried out." The young volunteer assured him they would.[109] With the reprisals, the War of Independence in the north acquired a strongly ethno-religious dimension as northern Protestants became more involved in the conflict. Tim Pat Coogan described the killings of Protestant loyalists along the border as a direct response by the IRA to the overt anti-Catholic persecutions carried out by the loyalist Protestant leadership. "It is certainly the case that O'Duffy's reprisals and the counter-reprisals which heavily followed, were grisly in the extreme," wrote Coogan.[110]

The war's intensification was matched by the Black and Tans, who burnt Cork city in December 1920. A contemporary memorandum penned by Art O'Brien, a republican envoy in London, is revealing. He observed how the Black and Tans' marauding was negatively impacting the prestige and discipline of the regular British army.

> I am told on what I would say is at all events fairly reliable authority, that even Sir Henry Wilson, who of course, with Churchill is chiefly responsible for the whole reign of terror, is getting nervous of these results. I am also told from another source that Churchill himself is peevish and annoyed and doubtful. That seems quite understandable from a Military point of view. Of course, they promised that six weeks of Black and Tan terrorism would kill the demand for an independent Irish Republic. Six week's bloody spree might be curable with a few months strict discipline, but if continued very long the disease might be incurable.[111]

Immense international pressure from prominent officials in the United States was brought to bear on the British government to resolve the Irish crisis. Secret talks were held between SF representatives and British government envoys in December 1920, mediated by Archbishop Clune of Perth. The tentative negotiations failed due to British demands that the IRA decommission its arms. However, the Clune talks indicated Britain's willingness to find a compromise. Nevil Macready wrote, with the benefit of hindsight, that the "cup-and-ball game between repression and conciliation" would soon come to an end.[112] In fact, War of Independence casualties doubled in the first half of 1921.

◆ ◆ ◆

In early 1921, steps were taken by GHQ to reorganize and professionalize the IRA through the process of divisionalization. The IRA was strongest in the extreme south of Ireland in counties like Cork and Kerry. Cork IRA officer Florence O'Donoghue wrote it was logical that the first IRA divisions would be formed from the southern brigades "which had attained the highest organization and fighting efficiency."[113] In the north, divisionalization was initiated to breathe life into the moribund Ulster brigades. GHQ had dispatched Kerry's Charlie Daly to Tyrone to take the lead locally. Daly was disappointed by the "slave mind and lack of enthusiasm and military spirit in the population in this part of Ireland."[114] In March 1921 a conference of Ulster IRA officers convened, including Daly from Tyrone, Joseph McKelvey from Belfast, Dan Hogan and O'Duffy from Monaghan. The northern leaders plotted an intense campaign of IRA activities north of the border. They were concerned the creation of Northern Ireland would act as a bridgehead which British forces could use as a base to launch a reconquest of the south.[115] To preempt this, the northern IRA planned a campaign along the border. A greater role for the northern IRA required that it would be included in GHQ's scheme for divisionalization. In spring 1921, GHQ set about creating Northern Divisions which united several brigade areas under one divisional commandant. Monaghan fell within the remit of the 5th Northern Division.

In April, GHQ asked O'Duffy to take over the new post of Officer Commanding (O/C) of the 2nd Northern Division, which included Tyrone and Derry. Anxious not to lose his base in Monaghan, O'Duffy wrote to GHQ on 28 April:

> I would like to know my position as regards my own area, Monaghan. After years of hard work building up the organization in that county alone and unaided, I naturally do not like to sever my connection with it or lose my grip with it. In my letter to the Chief of Staff [Richard Mulcahy] I made this clear; in his letter to me of 26th Jan he told me that if I accepted this position in Tyrone I would retain nominally and to a certain extent actually my control over Monaghan.[116]

GHQ understood O'Duffy's concerns and allowed him to keep a foot in Monaghan and Tyrone/Derry. By appointing Dan Hogan as O/C of the 5th Northern Division, O'Duffy retained considerable influence in the military affairs of his home county. Under Hogan, the war in Monaghan continued in much the same vein as under O'Duffy's leadership. Hogan led attacks and ambushes against the RIC and Black and Tans, while he continued the policy of raiding for arms against unionists and members of the B Specials. During the period, the Monaghan IRA also continued to enforce the boycott, raided for enemy mail, guarded IRA headquarters, blocked roads, enforced decrees of the republican courts, and tried to prevent the operation of British rule in the county.[117]

As O/C of the 2nd Northern Division, O'Duffy found lodgings with a Catholic curate, Fr Edward McNamee. He lived in the presbytery of Feeny, County Derry.[118] The local IRA was in a state of disarray. Immediately, O'Duffy overhauled the existing command staff. Charlie Daly became Vice O/C in the divisional staff. William J. Kelly, a Tyrone IRA officer, recalled the new O/C's arrival: "O'Duffy's first job was to get the Division organized, Brigade areas defined, and officers appointed on the staffs of the Division, the Brigades, and where necessary, in the Battalions. In some areas O'Duffy made small adjustments in the Battalion areas."[119] His remedy for ill-discipline was to dismiss problematic officers and initiate a policy of "drastic punishment."[120] In Derry, he ordered each unit to carry out some operation every week, "it didn't matter how simple it was, cutting of wires, trenching roads, etc."[121]

During his time with the 2nd Northern Division, O'Duffy oversaw a series of ambushes and skirmishes against the RIC, B Specials, and militant loyalists. Attacks against the RIC were planned in ten villages across Tyrone. On the night of the attacks, a patrol of B Specials was ambushed by five IRA men as they reached a police barracks in Dromore. One participant recalled, "We threw a hand grenade into the party and then opened fire with revolvers. Two of the Specials were seriously wounded, and the Barrack window was damaged." The next day the B Specials initiated a reprisal in Dromore. "The town was completely cut off from the surrounding districts and no person was allowed by the Orangemen to leave their houses. The invaders indulged in terrorizing tactics, shooting up the town the whole night."[122] By the end of the day, three Catholic civilians were killed. He ordered "that reprisals be carried out against the B men in Dromore."[123]

Counter-reprisals materialized on the night of 14 May. The IRA singled out the head constable, Matthew Henderson, for assassination. An ambush of nine policemen by seven IRA volunteers resulted in the wounding of four RIC men while one IRA volunteer was killed, 19-year-old Edward McCusker. Another clash with the police in Tyrone broke out in Five-Mile-Town on 11 June. O'Duffy arranged for a detachment of Monaghan IRA men to bolster the ranks of the Tyrone IRA in advance of future ambushes. An ambush was soon launched in the rural townland of Ardfad as B Specials passed along the crossroads, searching passers-by. As they stopped to smoke, an IRA party of nine men opened fire, killing three. That night the B Specials carried out a reprisal by burning six Catholic houses in the town.[124] The trend of reprisal and counter-reprisal characterized O'Duffy's time as O/C. The men did not always obey O'Duffy and feared offensive actions could lead to loyalist attacks against the innocent Catholic population. Militarists like O'Duffy and Frank Aiken often failed to understand this reality.[125] As O/C of the 2nd Northern Division, O'Duffy cultivated contacts with his counterparts elsewhere in Ulster, such as Joseph McKelvey and Séamus Woods in Belfast. These personal relationships soon became critically important.

During the War of Independence in Monaghan, O'Duffy was wounded in several ambushes and even lost his left index finger in battle.[126] His reputation as an able IRA commander brought him to the attention of GHQ and enabled his promotion. His role in the IRB and the patronage of Collins further helped him to climb the greasy pole. The role he played during the "four glorious years" of Ireland's War of Independence propelled his career forward and thrust him into the spotlight of national leadership, a status he came to relish. He was seen principally as a patriotic soldier rather than a political figure, an image he tried to maintain throughout his career.

# 3

# From Truce to Treaty

O'Duffy became part of the beating heart of the revolutionary movement in 1921. On 24 May, a general election was held to elect deputies to the newly formed Southern Irish and Northern Irish home rule parliaments. SF used the elections to return a new slate of Teachtaí Dála (TDs) to the parliament of the Irish Republic, forming the Second Dáil. In Monaghan, O'Duffy was selected as a candidate for the new three seat constituency. His candidacy was proposed by a Catholic priest, Fr Eugene Coyle, and seconded by his brother Patrick. He was joined on the ticket by two northern republicans, Seán MacEntee from Belfast, and Ernest Blythe, then resident in Lisburn, County Down. Both MacEntee and Blythe were incumbent TDs, having been elected in 1918. No candidates were present at the handing in of their nomination papers in 1921 for fear of arrest, instead they were represented by their respective proposers and seconders.[1] O'Duffy's local rival, Dr Conn Ward, was interested in securing a SF nomination to stand and even visited O'Duffy in Derry in March 1921 to request that he be added to the ticket.[2] But there was simply no room for another candidate. O'Duffy was not prepared to stand aside in Ward's favor. The men had a longstanding rivalry. In 1918, O'Duffy asked Blythe to contest the North Monaghan constituency as a compromise candidate due to a "quarrel between Dr Ward and Seán MacEntee." A northern Protestant who by his own admission "had never been in Monaghan except for [one] week," Blythe was regarded as a suitable candidate who would raise "no local objection."[3]

In the 1921 election in Southern Ireland, a SF nomination was tantamount to election due to the absence of any challengers from the IPP or Labor Party. John Dillon, leader of the IPP, "advised [his] friends not to take any part in the Southern elections" to avoid discord and bitterness.[4] Meanwhile, the Labor Party, which was successful in the 1920 local elections, stood aside in favor of SF. One hundred twenty-four SF candidates were elected unopposed. In Northern Ireland, SF won six seats, the Devlin-led nationalists also won six seats, and the remaining 40 were won by unionists. Whilst SF elected representatives naturally continued their policy of abstentionism and continued to sit in the Dáil, the Devlinites refused to enter the Northern Ireland parliament until 1925 due to a strong rejection of partition.[5] In Monaghan, the three SF candidates were returned unopposed. As a TD, O'Duffy made few contributions in the Dáil. He was described as lacking the patience of a politician, but "he spoke openly and without fear."[6] He was one of 50 new SF members elected to the Second Dáil.

O'Duffy's election was partly enabled by the IRB's role in the selection of SF candidates. Collins became president of the secret society during the War of Independence and "picked Volunteer officers and IRB men to go forward" for election.[7] Non-IRB republicans disliked the secret society. Brugha, the minister for defense in the republican government, left the IRB in the aftermath of the Easter Rising, believing it had fulfilled its purpose. He later accused the IRB of being involved in a corrupt arms deal in Scotland.[8] Brugha intensely disliked Collins. In time, O'Duffy and Brugha came to loggerheads over the former's elevation within the IRA. The significance of Collins' IRB activities was twofold. Apart from allowing him to cultivate a coterie of supporters whose loyalty to the Dáil was questionable, the IRB constitution considered its president to be, ipso facto, president of the republic. De Valera had assumed the title president of the republic during his tour in the United States, a status which was accepted by the Dáil. Although Collins never publicly claimed the presidency of the republic, he and de Valera frequently clashed as the War of Independence progressed. The men strongly differed in temperament and style: Collins was a "bombastic and chain-smoking young man."[9] In contrast, de Valera was more strait-laced.

◆ ◆ ◆

O'Duffy was asked by Collins in June 1921 to become DO, a position previously held by Collins. O'Duffy accepted and left Derry for Dublin to become part of GHQ staff. The IRA's central leadership in Dublin prized bureaucratic talent and administrative ability over one's prowess during ambushes. As historian John Regan noted, "Collins and Mulcahy represented the new revolution, based on administrative efficiency, intelligence, results and above all else tangible success."[10] O'Duffy was another military-bureaucrat, unlike the rough and ready regional IRA commanders like Dan Breen in Tipperary or Tom Barry in Kerry. As commandant in Monaghan, he was a consistent record keeper and produced "long reports" for GHQ, "very well typed in red" rather than hastily hand-written.[11] The Dublin IRA O/C, Oscar Traynor, resented Mulcahy's invocations that he should emulate O'Duffy, whose reports Mulcahy was "always terribly impressed by." Traynor recalled that Mulcahy "once showed me reports by O'Duffy... 'Isn't it a magnificent report,' he asked? It was all 1. 2. 3. 4. a. b. c. d. 'Now what strikes me about the man,' I said, 'is that he must have plenty of time on [his] hands.'"[12]

O'Duffy's predecessor as DO, Bob Price, was pushed out of the position in the aftermath of the Battle of the Custom House, which occurred under his watch. The IRA's attack on Dublin's Custom House on 25 May was a major operation which involved 120 men from the Dublin Brigade. Although they successfully captured the building, it was besieged by British forces. It was then set aflame. The capture of the Custom House was a symbolic action which struck at the center of British rule in Ireland. However, IRA losses were considerable: five men were killed, three wounded, and up to 80 were captured by British forces. Three civilians were also killed in the crossfire, while a further seven were wounded.[13] Price was scapegoated and accused of poorly planning the operation.

On his first day as DO, O'Duffy was introduced by Price to Frank Henderson, an officer attached to GHQ. Henderson had expected to be named DO and was taken aback to discover he was not being offered the post. After a few days, Henderson believed he "could be of no further use" to O'Duffy and asked to be transferred back to the Dublin Brigade.[14] Henderson likely lost out due to O'Duffy's seniority in the IRB. Initially, O'Duffy operated from an office at Barry's Hotel in Gardiner Row. He was not long in his position before the War of Independence drew to a close. In early July, a Belfast IRA man, Joseph Murray, was brought to meet O'Duffy at his office. Murray was a wanted man in Belfast and was to be transferred elsewhere in the country. He was attached to the new DO for just a few days before O'Duffy told him he would not be sending him down the country "as negotiations were going on which would probably end up in a truce." Murray was surprised to learn the end of the Anglo-Irish conflict was in sight.[15]

By June 1921, it was understood that the war could not continue indefinitely. Prosecuting the war in Ireland placed a significant financial burden on the British exchequer, whilst the marauding Black and Tans generated considerable embarrassment for the British government. Meanwhile, GHQ was eager to end the war, recognizing that the imprisonment and death of several of the IRA's leading members was hamstringing the force. The beginning of the end is often dated with the opening of the Northern Ireland parliament on 22 June 1921. Here, the British monarch appealed to "all Irishmen ... to forgive and forget" and seemingly extended an olive branch to republicans.[16] The speech was designed to produce settlement negotiations. Two days after the king's speech, David Lloyd George invited de Valera to London to commence peace talks. A military truce was soon brokered between the IRA and the British army. The truce talks were mediated by the Irish unionist peer Lord Middleton and its terms were agreed at the Mansion House on 8 July. The truce came into force at noon on 11 July.[17]

◆ ◆ ◆

The coming of the truce on 11 July 1921 led to an explosion of Irish nationalistic fervor. It was believed that after 700 years of British occupation, Irish freedom was now on the horizon. The truce generated a remarkable spike of interest in cultural nationalism. The sale of Irish language grammar books, dictionaries, and textbooks soared during the period.[18] Bonfires were lit in towns and villages across Ireland. In Derry, the suspension of curfew "was hailed with such delight that many people remained out until after midnight and around bonfires which blazed in some thoroughfares" and national airs were "lustily sung."[19] In the IRA, many volunteers saw the truce as a temporary period of ceasefire and anticipated a resumption of hostilities. Ernie O'Malley and his men, then stationed in Tipperary, thought the Truce would last for just two or three weeks. The truce also brought a phalanx of fresh recruits to the IRA. These late recruits have pejoratively been dubbed "trucileers." Between July and December 1921 the on paper membership of the IRA rose from 30,000 to 75,000.[20]

Early in the truce period, the IRB began to strengthen its hold over the Irish nationalist movement. Séumas Robinson, a northerner active in the Tipperary IRA, met Collins in early July who brought him to meet Seán Ó Muirthile, secretary of the supreme council of the IRB. Ó Muirthile tried to persuade Robinson to rejoin the IRB, but he refused on similar grounds as Cathal Brugha, "that a secret society within the IRA was undesirable." Ó Muirthile flew into a fit of rage, shouting "Brugha and yourself should be shot, and maybe some day ye will." Collins intervened and ordered Ó Muirthile out of the room.[21] The incident illustrated a growing divide within Irish nationalism between the Collins loyalists within the IRB and "others" (including some IRB men) who held a mismatch of views. As treasurer of the secret society, O'Duffy was a member of its supreme council with Ó Muirthile and Collins.[22] To prevent a fissure in the IRA, it was necessary that the fighting men were brought along with a potential compromise settlement. Collins was seen as key to a potential compromise, as the IRB effectively controlled GHQ whilst Collins' agency "may have controlled much else," according to Regan.[23] The British believed that "90% of the gunmen will follow Collins."[24]

The truce ended O'Duffy's active period as DO. He was soon appointed as the IRA's Ulster liaison officer, stationed in Belfast. He was responsible for upholding the truce and ceasefire across Ulster's nine counties plus County Louth in Leinster. Liaison officers were required to troubleshoot problems directly with British and police counterparts. Northern unionists were distressed to learn the truce would apply across the island of Ireland, irrespective of partition. The USC, the northern militarized police force, was demobilized in July. However, USC men retained their arms and continued to underhandedly operate in Northern Ireland.[25] In addition to his role as Ulster liaison officer, O'Duffy became IRA deputy chief-of-staff on 1 August. The appointment was apparently made by Mulcahy without the approval or knowledge of Brugha, who continued to believe Austin Stack was the deputy chief-of-staff. Stack was seemingly not aware of his demotion either as he seldom attended GHQ meetings. The irregular appointment later became a major bone of contention between GHQ and the civilian government.

Whilst the truce brought a degree of stability and peace to most of Ireland, it was short-lived north of the border. The truce coincided with the Orange marching season which commemorated the victory of the Protestant king William of Orange over the Catholic king James II in 1690. Orange marches regularly produced inter-communal violence in the north. Belfast's Roger McCorley remembered that "the pogrom lasted 2 years, but the truce itself lasted six hours only."[26] Belfast became the scene of widespread sectarian violence. Nine thousand Catholics were expelled from their jobs in shipyards.[27] When O'Duffy arrived in Belfast in early August, he found the city in "a veritable state of war." He witnessed "the peal of rifles, frenzied mobs at street corners, terror-stricken people rushing for their lives, and ambulances carrying the dead and dying to hospitals." He was astonished at the bedlam unleashed in Ireland's second largest city.

In Ulster, O'Duffy tried to ensure the influx of new IRA recruits received adequate training. IRA-controlled "factories" began to manufacture and stockpile explosive devices and munitions. In Armagh, the Ballymacnab Company established an engineering section and began to construct concrete landmine casings.[28] These were not the activities of an army which anticipated peace. There was an increase in southern IRA officers who traveled north to provide the local men with training during the truce period. This was partly a recognition that if hostilities resumed, the Ulster IRA was likely to be at the coalface of a renewed military campaign. Tipperary's Dan Breen arrived to assist the northern men. He later wrote that GHQ "was devoting special attention to the northern areas in an effort to equip local units in order that, if the fight were to be renewed, they would play a more active part and thereby lessen the burden of the southern counties." Breen spent five weeks in the north with Charlie Daly, "a Kerryman and a true patriot." They spent their time "instructing the northern boys in the use of the gun and the bomb." He remembered "it was hard work but I enjoyed it. We saw a great part of Ulster in our long walks and infrequent pleasure-drives. To make it more exciting, we paid an occasional visit to Belfast" which was in a state of chaotic violence at this time.[29]

O'Duffy set up headquarters at St Mary's Hall in Belfast's Bank Street, the former headquarters of the 3rd Northern Division. The three-storey building could contain up to 500 people. O'Duffy ensured that IRA raids and military engagements were carefully recorded and verified.[30] As liaison officer, he undertook a tour of Ulster. Outside Belfast, most places were judged to be in a comparatively quieter state and with "little to complain of."[31] In Newry and south Armagh the cycle of reprisal and counter-reprisal (which O'Duffy had participated in as divisional commandant in west Ulster) largely ended with the imposition of the truce.[32] Even the local RIC in Armagh observed that "since the advent of the truce there has been a total absence of political crime and as a consequence a genuine feeling of relief prevails amongst the people."[33] In Armagh, O'Duffy consulted with Aiken of the 4th Northern Division. In Belfast, O'Duffy initiated contact with his British counterparts in an effort to deescalate the city's violence.

From July, several IRA men in the city were shot by loyalists "to make an impossible atmosphere for the Truce." O'Duffy praised the local IRA for exercising "wonderful restraint," who "refused to be drawn into acts of retaliation" and displayed a discipline which "staggered our enemies." He condemned incitement by loyalist politicians in "blood-curdling platform orations" and consequent acts of violence.[34] Despite making up just a quarter of the city's population, Roman Catholics were half of the fatalities during the period in 1920–22.[35] O'Duffy told the press of various crimes allegedly committed by members of the USC. He claimed a 50-year-old man was ordered down from a ladder, struck with an iron bar, asked his religion, and then shot dead. In another case, a bomb was thrown towards a group of women and children by B Specials. Loyalist snipers near Belfast's Mater Hospital took pot-shots to prevent wounded patients from being admitted. Such atrocities tested his restraint. He considered these incidents "callous in the extreme." He despaired that "vain appeals were made by my assistant at St. Mary's Hall" to the police to act; the next day they appealed to the military to enforce the rule of law.

The situation worsened as the B Specials continued to cause havoc. On one occasion, a group of B Specials acquired an armored car which they drove into a Catholic quarter of the city before randomly unloading 20 bullets into the street. A 13-year-old boy was killed as he ran across the street. On 31 August, there was heavy firing at Henry Street from a sniper located on top of a telegraph pole. When a contingent of USC arrived on scene, an IRA man attached to O'Duffy's headquarters told the police sergeant of the sniper's presence. He replied "Go to Hell and mind your own business," refusing to defuse the situation. In all likelihood the sniper was one of their own.

There were several attempts on O'Duffy's life during the truce period in Belfast. On one occasion, two armed men took up position outside a house where he was staying and prepared to ambush him as he left. A man walked cautiously towards the house and was immediately pounced upon by would-be assassins. The man was quick to draw a revolver, leaving the attackers wounded on the ground. The attackers had ironically mistaken "the fastest-shooting detective in Belfast for O'Duffy."[36] He was determined that no threats or attempts to end his life would intimidate or prevent him from "standing by or falling with my fellow Catholic men and women in Ulster in the crisis through which we are now passing."[37]

By early September, O'Duffy's restraint broke down. He found it impossible to continue to uphold his end of the truce whilst such fragrant breaches occurred. He ordered the IRA to "take action to protect our people." Volunteers were placed at vantage points all over the city, and within a few hours they "made their presence felt." Almost immediately, the news that the IRA were "in action" resulted in a mobilization from the British military. O'Duffy considered this to be a sign of British bad faith, as the British army had failed to react to weeks of loyalist violence. An emergency meeting of the Northern Irish cabinet was held to discuss the situation. O'Duffy reacted by stating: "no such conferences were held, or requisitions made when the streets were red with Catholic blood, but until things were getting hot for the loyalists." On 10 September, O'Duffy ordered an end to the mobilization. He stated that his men would not go into action "until it is absolutely necessary for the protection of our people." But, he warned, if "the Orange mob are allowed to continue murdering our people, and the police appear to act in connivance and the military refuse to turn out, then there is no other course open to us but to strike." He predicted that this strike would not be confined to Belfast but to "any other area [in Ulster] where the lives of our people are endangered."[38] General Macready recalled that the orders had been given by O'Duffy, whom he considered a pugnacious IRA leader.[39] Ordering the IRA into action was part of O'Duffy's flare for the theatrical and the dramatic.[40]

He told the press that southern IRA volunteers were not being funneled into the north, commenting that if called upon the southern IRA would undoubtedly come to their aid, but that "the IRA in Belfast is in itself sufficiently strong to cope with any situation which may arise if the forces of the Crown act impartially or withdraw altogether." The IRA continued to "rigidly adhere" to the truce and was actively engaged in intelligence work, gathering information on snipers and rogue B Specials who committed atrocities. This information was passed to the police, but it was never acted upon.[41] O'Duffy's press interview elevated his status among republicans in Ulster. His duty was described as a "herculean task" but one he handled with "courage and tenacity."[42]

◆ ◆ ◆

Whilst O'Duffy endeavored to uphold the truce in Ulster, negotiations were ongoing between Irish republicans and the British government. An initial round of talks in London between de Valera and Lloyd George broke down on 20 July. The British offered dominion status for Southern Ireland, the statelet they had created in 1920 and which was unrecognized and unwanted by Irish republicans. Rejected by de Valera as falling far short of meaningful independence, the negotiations collapsed. In a moment of high drama, Lloyd George tested de Valera by delivering an in-person ultimatum: "But you realize this means war? Do you realize that the responsibility for it will rest on your shoulders and yours alone?" De Valera answered, "No, Mr Lloyd George. If you insist on attacking us, it is you, not I, who will be responsible."[43] Instead of war, 15 letters and telegrams between the two men aimed at restoring negotiations ensued. The correspondence was long and meandering, but eventually produced a second attempt at negotiations.

On 30 September, de Valera announced that a new delegation would participate in renewed talks with the British government in London. He planned to remain in Dublin during this period. The agenda of the negotiations was to explore "how the association of Ireland with the community of nations known as the British empire might best be reconciled with Irish national aspirations."[44] An Irish delegation of plenipotentiaries was headed by Arthur Griffith, the republican minister for foreign affairs. He was joined in London by Collins, the supposedly militant counterbalance to the "moderate" Griffith. There is a widespread impression that de Valera felt threatened by Collins' accumulation of power. As Frank Pakenham acknowledged, in Collins' determination to see that the war was won, "he never hesitated to overstep the theoretical jurisdiction of his office, or usurp the legitimate functions of others."[45] The Irish delegation also included Eamonn Duggan, Robert Barton, and George Gavan Duffy. Pakenham observed that the delegation was hobbled by the absence of de Valera's leadership. But Griffith and Collins, the two principal Irish negotiators, were "splendid representatives, far out of the common run of men." They were united by their "love of Ireland" and shared a mutual "enormous physical strength and vitality, they were both extremely quick and shrewd in a deal."[46] As the negotiations progressed in London, O'Duffy remained in close touch with Collins. O'Duffy played a minor role in the negotiations, traveling to London to assist the Irish delegation in "military conferences."[47] He was "one of the Irish advisors" who attended meetings of the Naval and Air Committee during plenary sessions held on 17–18 October.[48]

Many republicans believed the IRA could not emerge victorious from the war against Britain. GHQ compiled figures which showed the army had on average only 43 rounds per rifle, 34 per automatic, 14 per revolver, and a mere six cartridges per shotgun. As far as GHQ was aware, the IRA had only 3,295 rifles in total.[49] However, on the eve of the truce there was a significant windfall of arms which arrived in Waterford via the ship *The Dortmund*, following a successful mission undertaken by IRA volunteers Robert Briscoe and Charles McGuinness in Germany. It was "the largest single arms shipment ever to reach the Irish Republican Army."[50] An exact picture of the IRA's strength is unclear. GHQ officers who favored a compromise exaggerated the IRA's paucity of arms. The argument that the IRA could not withstand a resumption of hostilities persuaded many SF deputies to support the eventual settlement.

**Eoin O'Duffy as General Officer Commanding in the southwest, 27 July 1922 (courtesy the National Library of Ireland).**

◆ ◆ ◆

O'Duffy constructed a public image of himself as a militarist, a defender of northern Catholics, and a humble patriot who spoke with a soldier's honesty. On 22 August, O'Duffy and another TD, J.J. Walsh, strongly rejected de Valera's proclaimed stance that an independent republic would permit "each county power to vote itself out ... if it so wished."[51] O'Duffy told the Dáil that "as far as they in Ulster were concerned, they thought force should be used against [the northern government]." He claimed that without the military and political support of the British government, Northern Ireland would be unable to withstand the force of the IRA as "the [loyalist] Ulster people had very little power themselves" and there were "sufficient Volunteers in Belfast to hold [Ulster] for Ireland." O'Duffy struck a militant tone when he told the Dáil that he "had dealt with them by force in Monaghan, Fermanagh and Tyrone, and those people were now silent." He explained that northern Protestants "realized they could not exist without the rest of Ireland."[52]

The most obvious display of O'Duffy's identification with militarism was seen in comments made at a rally in Armagh city on 4 September. O'Duffy accompanied Collins on his "first official visit to the city."[53] Collins was an elected member of the Northern Ireland parliament for Armagh city. A rally was held outside the Charlemont Arms Hotel with a reputed turnout of 10,000 people. Collins spoke in Irish before switching to English and paid tribute to the sacrifices of the IRA:

> With matchless bravery our badly equipped Volunteers stood up against troops who had seen service in many lands, who enjoyed the most perfect modern equipment, every contrivance, every facility for making terrible and destructive war. Our inexperienced, ill-trained men stood up to the enemy, and proved themselves always a match for him no matter how great the disadvantages against our side.

He disputed unionist claims that an independent Ireland would lead to the ruination of Ulster. He cited the decaying economic situation of the supposedly "prosperous" province, pointing to its falling population and rising emigration rate. Collins told northern nationalists that "no matter what the future may bring," they "shall not desert them." Mary MacSwiney, the sister of Terence MacSwiney, felt Collins' speech in Armagh was much too "safe."[54]

O'Duffy's speech was belligerent. It was a remarkable performance. He removed his hat and began to speak, recounting his work in Belfast and relaying how he had recently ordered IRA sentries to make their presence felt. Although he ordered a ceasefire on that occasion, he warned that "Ulstermen would now have to decide whether they were for Ireland or for the British Empire. If they decided against Ireland we will have to put on the screw of the boycott, and we will turn that screw, and if necessary we will have to use lead against them!"[55] It was a display of sheer militarism. The threat of "the lead" made O'Duffy a bête noire for northern unionists. O'Duffy believed his speech was misinterpreted. He claimed to oppose "the coercion of Ulster by force," but stated he would, if his pleas were ignored, "advocate taking the necessary steps to protect the Catholic and Nationalist population from the bigoted rabble."[56] He later tried to clarify that "if the Orangemen were to murder our people in cold blood as they had done in the past, then they should get the lead. If they continue to do this my prescription remains the same."[57]

Ó Murthuile, who also spoke in Armagh, believed O'Duffy's comments were an attempt to challenge de Valera, whose tolerance of county secession raised many republican eyebrows. Ó Murthuile claimed the speech "caused indignation," but, he continued, "when one comes to think of it, it was the speech of an Ulster Catholic, who had grown up among the scenes of the bigoted fury of anti-Catholicism, and again one ought not to be too mercilessly criticized for maintaining that majorities have a right to use force against rebellious minorities."[58] Loyalists nicknamed him "Give 'em the lead" O'Duffy, a moniker he was evidently proud of. In an entry for the *Biographical Encyclopedia of the World* in the 1940s, O'Duffy noted he delivered a "famous speech at Armagh" as part of his political history.[59] Aiken, another witness, recalled that it "did a lot to infuriate the Orange mob" but reflected that O'Duffy's attitude was "merely representative of that of the whole army. We were great believers then in the power of the gun alone to cure all evils."[60]

◆ ◆ ◆

A significant backdrop to the negotiations in London was the boiling over of tensions between personalities and different factions within the republican movement. Brugha, the minister for defense, resented the power of Collins. He disliked Collins' associates, particularly his "squad" and his "brothers" in the IRB. Brugha and de Valera were concerned that the IRB exercised far too much control over IRA

GHQ, which undermined the principle of civilian government. Aware of the need to prepare the IRA for a compromise settlement based on his own formula, de Valera tried to reassert the Dáil cabinet's authority over GHQ by initiating reforms in the IRA.

In September, Brugha was furious to learn that O'Duffy had been appointed deputy chief-of-staff by Mulcahy without his approval or knowledge. In a venomous letter of 6 September, Brugha wrote to Mulcahy: "before you are very much older, my friend, I shall show you I have as little intention of taking dictation from you as to how I should reprove inefficiency or negligence on part of yourself or the Director of Intelligence [Collins] as I have of allowing you to appoint a Deputy Chief of Staff of your own choosing."[61] This secret appointment was the final straw for Brugha. He considered it a challenge to his authority. T. Ryle Dwyer noted that Brugha felt Mulcahy had failed to "control" Collins on GHQ staff and hoped to install Stack "in order to control the Big Fellow."[62]

As deputy chief-of-staff, O'Duffy inspected several IRA training camps across the country. In Tipperary, Ernie O'Malley recalled that O'Duffy "inspected the camp and was pleased with the progress. He questioned each officer about the detailed organization of his area, and put them through what we called the third degree.... After a long discussion on administration, organization and intelligence, the special services were examined one by one." He was later described by Mulcahy as a "tireless, effective, distinguished" deputy chief-of-staff.[63] During the inspection of Tipperary, O'Duffy implied that GHQ was planning for a resumption of war due to a "deadlock" at the negotiations in London. He remarkably suggested to O'Malley that "we ourselves should break the truce ... by attacking the British posts without giving the agreed seventy-two hours' warning."[64]

Brugha and de Valera's scheme to reform the IRA and bring it under civilian control involved re-issuing commissions to all IRA officers. In effect, this would shift the source of the officers' authority from GHQ to the minister for defense. In November, letters were issued to serving IRA officers with commissions for the "new" army. The content of one letter (sent to Charlie Daly) is reproduced below:

> In view of the possibilities of further fighting and in order to put the army in an unequivocal position as the legal defense forces of the nation, under the control of the civil government, the cabinet had decided to issue fresh commissions to all officers, and to offer re-enlistment to all ranks. The new army will date from the 25 November, the anniversary of the foundation of the Irish Volunteers in 1913.
>
> On the authority of the president and the cabinet, acting as the duly appointed executive of Dáil Éireann, I hereby offer you a commission as O/C 2nd ND with the rank of commandant general in the new army.
>
> Signed,
> Cathal Brugha
> Minister for Defence.[65]

Considerable confusion was generated among the rank-and-file of the IRA by the new commissions. Most IRA men were unaware of the power struggle within the republican movement between elements of the government and GHQ. A commission as director of organization was offered to O'Duffy, but he replied in a lengthy letter to Brugha on 24 November rejecting the offer. He considered the offer an unwarranted demotion: "I feel I have the confidence of all the Officers in the army, and they will not understand why I should be reduced in rank now." He continued, "I am reluctantly compelled to interpret the reduction in rank as a personal slight and a grave dishonor which I submit I do not deserve."[66]

A conference was held on 25 November at the Mansion House in an effort to resolve the burgeoning crisis between the republic's civil-military leadership. An initial meeting was held between Mulcahy and the Dáil cabinet. De Valera tried to broker a compromise, proposing that O'Duffy could continue as deputy chief-of-staff but that Stack would return to GHQ as a joint deputy chief-of-staff. Stack was to hold a watching brief and would act as "Cathal's ghost on the Staff."[67] Mulcahy flatly refused the proposal. At this point, the rest of GHQ staff and several officers attached to GHQ were ushered into the drawing room. De Valera sat at a small table at one end with his Ministers alongside him. Collins was absent in London. The uniformed IRA officers faced de Valera and his cabinet ministers. De Valera tried to explain his position to the officers and described how he wanted to reform the staff and asked for their opinions. One leading officer J.J. "Ginger" O'Connell captured the mood of the room by replying, "the General Headquarters Staff had been a band of brothers" and he did not support seeing it broken up. This objection was echoed across the room by various officers, until it reached O'Duffy, who was second last on the right. O'Duffy's intervention worsened the situation in an already tense meeting. He forcefully told de Valera how he considered the recent proposals to be "an insult and a criticism" of himself, given the furore centered on his appointment as deputy chief-of-staff. An officer present recalled that O'Duffy's voice became somewhat shrill with emotion and even had "a slight touch of hysteria" to it. The mounting emotions burst when de Valera leapt excitedly from his chair, pushed out the small table in front of him and declared "in a half-scream, half-shout": "You all may mutiny if you like, but Ireland will give me another Army!" He then dismissed all the IRA officers from his sight.[68]

In the aftermath of the tempestuous meeting between the cabinet and GHQ, it appeared that a temporary resolution had been arrived at. Unwilling to risk a split, GHQ acceded to allow the men to accept the new commissions. However, schemes for a new army were dropped. Deputizing for Mulcahy, O'Duffy wrote on 30 November 1921:

> To all Divisional Commandants,
>
> Some time ago, you have, I presume, received a communication from the Minister for Defense offering you a commission with rank of commandant general. It might be inferred from this document that a new army was being formed, but this is not really so—the idea being to offer fresh commissions to certain officers. The whole situation has been examined at a joint meeting of the cabinet and GHQ Staff and an understanding arrived at. You should write to the Minister for Defense accepting the commission.
>
> Beir beannacht, [Take Victory]<br>
> Eoin O'Duffy<br>
> For Chief of Staff.[69]

The controversy "represented the most important and potentially dangerous division within the revolutionary movement," wrote Regan.[70] De Valera's choice to grasp the nettle and try to assert his authority over the IRA was a curious one which came at "a time when a breakdown of the talks in London was entirely possible." It has been seen as an attempt to put his man at the center of the military apparatus. In anticipation of a split within the ranks over a compromise treaty, de Valera sought to hold as much civilian control over the IRA as possible. Another view is that de Valera was trying to maintain Brugha's support and brittle loyalty at a crucial time as cracks within the republican movement's stony edifice were beginning to show.[71]

◆ ◆ ◆

On 6 December, the Anglo-Irish Treaty was signed in London under controversial circumstances. The British prime minister threatened a return to war if it was not signed, leading many to view the agreement as having been signed under duress. Lloyd George's threat was not simply a return to the small-scale Black and Tan guerrilla war, but an "immediate and terrible war." Collins later claimed the threat was "probably a bluff" and "the immediate tactics would surely have been to put the offer of July 20, which the British considered a very good offer, before the country, and, if rejected, they would have very little difficulty in carrying their own people into a war against Ireland."[72]

The deliberations had been a long, protracted process. During the talks, a rift emerged within the Irish cabinet. De Valera obdurately insisted that the plenipotentiaries should demand "external association," a concept he invented. It was partly inspired by the United States' relationship with Cuba and South America. "The externally associated state would, for matters of common concern such as defense and external relations, be voluntarily associated with the dominion of the Empire." The British monarch would be recognized by Ireland as the head of the associated collection of states but not of the Irish state itself. Ireland would voluntarily leave the Empire and then rejoin the Empire on its own initiative, a precedent which if enacted would have "far-flung implications" abroad.[73] A memorandum by de Valera of 27 October argued that only external association could give meaning to the precedent set by leading British political leaders when speaking of other dominions, such as "the terms 'complete control of their own destinies' (Bonar Law) and 'controls its own destiny in the fullest sense' (Lloyd George on South Africa at Paris June 1919)."[74] De Valera leaned on Wilsonian self-determination but within the structure of the British Commonwealth.

However, external association was not included in the articles of agreement signed on 6 December. It created a British dominion, the Irish Free State, which would be subordinate to the British Crown, including the requirement that public officials swear an oath of allegiance. The oath became a major item of contention, as it contradicted the oath sworn to the Irish Republic. It was alleged that at a meeting of the Dublin Brigade in January 1922, O'Duffy and Mulcahy each struck the table and emphatically announced that, despite their support for the Treaty, they would never swear an oath of allegiance to the crown.[75] The Treaty also required a mutual defense policy with Britain (including control over three Irish harbors), provisions in relation to Ireland's contribution to the overall British debt, and the continued payment of pensions to ex–British public servants and members of the RIC.

The Treaty essentially accepted the partition of Ireland by allowing the Northern Ireland parliament to secede from the Free State. The agreement contained a provision for the establishment of a "Boundary Commission" which planned to review and redraw the border of the new Irish Free State and Northern Ireland. There appeared to have been much credence placed on the outcome of the boundary commission, particularly the suggestion that it would cede significant portions of Northern territory to the Irish Free State. Nationalists believed this would render the northern rump state economically unviable. The majority–Catholic counties of Fermanagh and Tyrone were obvious starting points, but also the majority Catholic town of Newry and Derry city. There were significant pockets of County Derry and south Armagh which were mostly Catholic. Meanwhile, a significant amount of Belfast's population were Catholics. Many supporters, and arguably even opponents, of the Anglo-Irish Treaty interpreted the boundary commission as an instrument to erode and undo partition. Eventually, the boundary commission met in 1924–5 but its leaked report resulted in a fiasco. Its findings advocated only moderate adjustments to the Irish border, including the annexation of some Free State territory into Northern Ireland. O'Duffy was deeply perturbed by the "deception" and "betrayal" of northern nationalists who had supported the Anglo-Irish Treaty: "So much was expected, so little was got."[76]

The fact Collins signed the Treaty was seen by many within the British establishment as a surprise, who considered him an extremist gunman. Famously, Collins viewed the Treaty as an opportunity to attain certain limited freedoms and from that foundation build further upwards towards eventually achieving an independent republic. Notably, Collins was not a doctrinaire republican and claimed that the particular form of government was meaningless, arguing "if we had still a descendent of our Irish Kings left" then an Irish monarchy would be acceptable.[77] His incrementalistic approach was visible in his speech urging the Treaty's ratification on 19 January 1922. He argued that whilst the Treaty "does not give us freedom, not the ultimate freedom that all nations desire and develop to," it provided "the freedom to achieve it."[78] This "stepping stone" theory influenced many militarists to adopt a pro–Treaty stance, perhaps contrary to their radical instincts. His personal appeal and charisma were significant in attracting support for the agreement.

Inside the IRA, the Treaty came as a bolt from the blue. As seen during O'Duffy's inspection of the Tipperary IRA, he gave the impression that the negotiations would probably break down. On another occasion, he told Frank Aiken that "GHQ had asked the President to keep the negotiations going until the winter," the optimum seasonal conditions for waging a guerrilla war.[79] Although the Treaty brought a measure of freedom to 26 of Ireland's counties, with the possibility of further territorial concessions being made via the boundary commission, for many in the IRA it fell short of the republic for which their comrades had fought and died.

# 4

# The Treaty

Like many militarists, O'Duffy was initially skeptical of the Treaty. He was in Dublin when it was first published. SF deputy Dr James Ryan recalled that O'Duffy was "dead against" it. He told Mulcahy, in Ryan's presence, "the army won't stand for this, Dick." Mulcahy urged "wait until you see Collins" and advised that the Treaty allowed the Irish to "build up your army ... and then knock the hell out of England."[1] This was a compelling argument, and one which O'Duffy soon repeated. On 7 December 1921, he attended a *céilí* dance in Clones which included several IRA divisional commanders including Aiken; Seán MacEoin, O/C of the 1st Midlands Division; and Joseph McKelvey from the 3rd Northern Division. Aiken remembered that "O'Duffy assured us, with great vehemence, that the signing of the Treaty was only a trick; that he would never take that oath and that no one would [be] asked to take it. He told us that it had been signed with the approval of GHQ in order to get arms to continue the fight."[2] The northern IRA's positive opinion of O'Duffy helped encourage many in its ranks to support the Treaty.

On 7 December, de Valera gave the plenipotentiaries a tongue lashing for signing the articles of agreement without his approval. In turn, they argued their status enabled them to sign an agreement without referring it to cabinet and drew attention to de Valera's own absence from the negotiations. At the time the Treaty was signed, de Valera was in the southwestern city of Limerick, which frustrated reputed attempts to contact him.[3] A vote of the cabinet was taken on whether to refer the settlement to the Dáil for a final vote or not. It passed by four votes to three. Collins, Griffith, Robert Barton and W.T. Cosgrave voted in favor; while Brugha, Stack and de Valera opposed the motion. Two days after the vote, de Valera met GHQ staff in the Mansion House's Oak Room. The agenda was to discuss whether the IRA was ready to resume hostilities if necessary. Mulcahy believed the meeting was an attempt by de Valera to ascertain whether GHQ would support him if he successfully persuaded the Dáil to reject the Treaty. De Valera assured Mulcahy and O'Duffy that if the Dáil ratified the Treaty he "would not stand for a moment for mutiny in the Army."[4]

Many of the areas which saw the heaviest fighting during the War of Independence were commanded by local IRA leaders who resented GHQ's influence and disliked Dublin's interference in their affairs. They were instinctively hostile to the Treaty and believed the IRA was winning the war. Most were equally suspicious of external association. A number of "hot-headed patriots" in the IRA had even urged de Valera to arrest the Treaty's signatories for "high treason" when they returned to Ireland. De Valera refused, arguing that a "very definite constitutional way" could be found to resolve the growing issues.[5] Collins, Mulcahy and O'Duffy mobilized the IRB network to sell the Treaty to the IRA's fighting men. In particular, Collins "set out to win over dubious comrades using his considerable influence within the IRA, and his position as president of the supreme council of the IRB."[6] There was an intense devotion to Collins among ordinary volunteers. Robert Briscoe, who opposed the Treaty, felt particularly aggrieved by Collins' support for it: "Collins, our man of steel and granite, our fearless fighting leader, trusted and beloved; what strange malaise had weakened Michael Collins? … His most effective weapon was the trust our people had in Michael Collins. Man after man would say, 'What's good enough for Mick is good enough for me.'"[7]

Joe Sweeney, O/C of the 1st Northern Division and TD for Donegal West, thought "to hell with this, this is not what we were fighting for" when he learned of the Treaty. Sweeney, an IRB member, traveled to Dublin where he met O'Duffy and Collins. He asked O'Duffy "what's the position with regard to the IRB and the Treaty?" O'Duffy replied, "you're free to do as your conscience dictates." Sweeney then deliberated with his allies in Donegal before arriving at a pro-Treaty conclusion.[8] Ernie O'Malley, who strongly opposed the Treaty, remembered that "personalities rather than principles seemed to have swayed many" and that Collins was largely seen as having a genius for intrigue. O'Malley wrote: "Many men had followed him, thinking that he would beat the British, the masters of duplicity, by his own duplicity and probably he wanted to give weight to his promises by aggressive action." He also put considerable credence in the theory that Collins' use of the IRB became "the strongest element to support the Treaty" and that although "it did not work openly … its effects could be felt."[9]

◆ ◆ ◆

O'Duffy participated in the Dáil debates held from 14 December 1921 until 7 January 1922 in the University College Dublin senate chamber of what is now the National Concert Hall, Earlsfort Terrace (the Mansion House was unavailable due to a booking from the annual Christmas fair). The room was long and narrow, with a low ceiling which negatively impacted its acoustics. A young IRA volunteer, Seán MacBride, helped to guard the building during the debates. He remembered "a series of long speeches, predictable on both sides."[10] Historian Mel Farrell argued that the emergent pro-Treaty party utilized a disciplined parliamentary strategy to appeal to moderates and hardliners alike. This underlined how the Treaty could mean different things to different people.[11]

O'Duffy delivered his first pro-Treaty speech, and second ever parliamentary contribution, on 17 December. O'Duffy leaned on his status as a fighting man and a defender of northern nationalists during his speech. Although even supporters recognized his speech was "not great … judged by oratorical standards" it was felt he gave "an honest speech delivered at a time when passions were running high."[12] O'Duffy began by admitting he had "not studied the document in great depth," he nonetheless identified "two points in it" which "commended themselves to me." The first was that the Treaty removed "the British soldier and British Peeler" from Ireland. The British military had been billeted in Ireland since the 18th century and its permanent removal represented a tangible result of the settlement. The second selling point was the creation of a native Irish military, "fully armed and equipped."[13]

Whilst de Valera opposed the Treaty, he produced his own alternative to the settlement which was quickly dubbed Document No 2. It was similar to the Treaty but incorporated de Valera's nostrum of external association. The document was notable for its absence of an oath of allegiance to the British monarch, a feature of the Treaty which became a sticking point for many republicans. However, Document No 2 failed to address the partition issue. De Valera's alternative was not popular even among republican deputies instinctively hostile to the Treaty. Pro-Treaty speeches frequently hammered Document No 2 as bearing little substantive difference to the articles of agreement signed in London. O'Duffy was, according to a sympathizer, unprepared "to risk another life or the destruction of further property for the difference between one document and another, between Tweedledum and Tweedledee."[14]

O'Duffy defended the honor of the plenipotentiaries against criticism that they failed to "bring back a republic" and therefore "let us down." "We have given our trust to those men, and we should not revile them when they have shown themselves worthy of our trust." He rejected the suggestion that supporters of the Treaty were war weary. "For me war has no horrors. I am not a bit afraid of war and the men as I know them have no fear of it.... The only pleasure in freedom is fighting for it." He claimed the Dáil had a duty to protect the lives of the young men of the IRA but argued he would be "in the forefront" if war was resumed. He heavily endorsed Collins' stepping stone theory and claimed it was the best means to achieve a republic. "I hold that the action I am taking in this case is towards the Republic. I feel that to act otherwise would be to deny the men that would secure the Republic arms. I recognize it as a stepping stone only, I regard it as not being final, otherwise I would be false to my oath and my country."[15] Throughout his life, O'Duffy remained performatively committed to the ideal of a republic as the symbol of ultimate freedom, although he occasionally flirted with monarchism. In 1935 he stated, "we should be honest with the North ... and tell them straight that our aim is a Republic for all Ireland. A Free State for all Ireland will not satisfy the aspirations of the people."[16]

A neurotic and deeply emotional side of O'Duffy's character emerged during the period of the Treaty debates. Mary MacSwiney, initially impressed by the passionate young GHQ officer, urged him not to vote for the agreement which "constituted a real betrayal of the Republic." Tears swelled in O'Duffy's eyes and emotion was present in his voice as he told MacSwiney, "I wish to God I had died half an hour ago before being told that I would have betrayed the Republic." Several people later told MacSwiney that her suggestion that he would betray the republic left him "heartbroken."[17] He was deeply sensitive to accusations of treason. He told the Dáil, "if there is one man or woman who feels I have turned down the Republic I will not seek their suffrages."[18]

A vote on the Treaty was long fingered as the Dáil broke for Christmas. During this recess, the influential powerbrokers of the Catholic hierarchy and national press heavily supported the settlement. Christmas-Day homilies urged faithful Catholics to back the Treaty.[19] The historian Patrick Murray wrote that during the crucial period of the Dáil debate, "bishops and many of their clergy exerted considerable influence on public opinion generally and on the Dáil deputies in particular to secure the passage of the agreement."[20] The intervention of the hierarchy was notable. During the War of Independence O'Duffy acknowledged "the Catholic Church in Ireland was not very friendly disposed towards Sinn Féin" but affirmed "at no time was there any trace of anti-clericalism."[21]

A few instinctively anti–Treaty deputies changed their minds during the recess, shifting to a pro–Treaty stance by the time the Dáil returned on 3 January. For instance, P.J. Ward from Donegal went home opposed to the Treaty, but he found "the voice of the best elements in the constituency" favored the settlement.[22] Newspapers mostly backed the Treaty and influenced public opinion. From the outset, the Treaty was presented in the media as being popularly backed by the people. A deluge of pro–Treaty resolutions were carried nationally in SF clubs, local associations of businessmen and farmers, and other influential societies. O'Duffy returned to Monaghan during the recess, already an advocate of the Treaty. Clones district council passed a motion which urged the three Monaghan TDs (Blythe, O'Duffy, and MacEntee) to support the Treaty. The resolution claimed an exaggerated 99 percent of the electors in Monaghan supported it.[23] Whilst Blythe and O'Duffy favored the Treaty, MacEntee opposed it. Clones district councilors urged MacEntee to "see the folly of taking up the attitude he did when he spoke against the ratification."[24] However, the fault lines were drawn. MacEntee later voted against ratifying the Treaty and remained a lifelong follower of de Valera.

The Dáil returned on 3 January 1922. The debates were characterized by deep acrimony. On 4 January, O'Duffy spoke. He announced that too much time had been "wasted in idle recrimination" and blaming others. He called for the cabinet, president and Dáil deputies to pull together in the interest of achieving "the freedom of our country" irrespective of whether "we only differ in ways and means." O'Duffy urged the acceptance of the Treaty on the basis it was supported by the people and claimed only "one or two" of his 35,000 constituents were anti–Treaty. He appealed to deputies not to disobey the "unanimous voice of the sovereign people of Ireland" by rejecting the Treaty and warned that "the people's will is mightier than the sword." According to John Regan, O'Duffy was a "tactical democrat," who supported majority votes when they went his way.[25] O'Duffy also compared the Treaty to the contemporary constitutional status of South Africa, arguing it was not dishonorable for the Afrikaners to agitate politically for the reestablishment of their republic and neither would it be for Irish republicans to accept the Anglo-Irish Treaty. Anti-Treaty deputy Erskine Childers, who had considerable first-hand experience of South Africa, rubbished the idea of South African sovereignty.

O'Duffy was one of the few deputies to speak on the issue of partition. The historian F.S.L. Lyons estimated that of the official 338 pages of the debate printed in the Dáil report, just nine are devoted to the question of partition; of these nine pages, two-thirds were contributed by deputies from Monaghan.[26] The apparent absence of partition from the Dáil debates has led to a somewhat misleading assumption that the status of Northern Ireland was irrelevant to nearly all SF deputies. O'Duffy was a highly respected voice on northern matters, being regarded as the "unofficial leader" of the IRA in Ulster.[27] He claimed to know Ulster "better than any man or woman in this Dáil" and somewhat belabored his reputation as an advocate of using "lead" against hostile loyalists: "I have faced Ulster's lead on more than one occasion with lead, and in those places where I was able to do it. I silenced them with lead. I would have silenced them in every case with lead if I had as much lead as they had." Evoking gruesome imagery of loyalist violence, he claimed in Cookstown "they took out our people's eyes" and "put sticks down their throats." He urged the Dáil to provide active support to northern Catholics. This portion of his speech appealed to onlooking northern nationalists that the pro-Treaty regime would defend them.[28] A supporter claimed it was known among northerners that O'Duffy "loved and served the North" and that "he understood its particular problems."[29]

◆ ◆ ◆

Seen as an honest broker interested in preserving unity, O'Duffy was invited to participate in a subcommittee aimed at finding a compromise before a vote was held. This "peace committee" included representatives from both camps. On the pro-Treaty side, it included Patrick Hogan, Joseph McGuinness, Michael Hayes and O'Duffy; meanwhile, its anti-Treaty members included Seán T. O'Kelly, Liam Mellows, Patrick Ruttledge, Art O'Connor and Seán Moylan. It met in O'Kelly's home. The subcommittee proposed that, if the Treaty was passed, de Valera's "active services" as president would be "preserved for the nation" and that the emergent pro-Treaty provisional government would be responsible to the Dáil. The IRA was to be responsible to the provisional government. The proposed compromise sought to prevent "a dissipation of our whole movement" at a "crucial point where all can be lost or gained."[30]

O'Duffy was enthusiastic about the work of the peace committee. On the morning of 6 January, he asked the Dáil to postpone further debates until after that evening's anticipated publication of the "substantial agreement" reached by the nine Dáil deputies "to avoid a split in the country."[31] Richard Mulcahy and Countess Markievicz supported the request. The sitting of parliament was adjourned until the following morning in a show of support for an eagerly awaited national unity.[32] On 7 January, the Dáil met behind closed doors to hear the report of the peace committee. However, the media learned that the committee "had failed to agree" and the Dáil resumed public session that afternoon.[33] But why did the peace committee's proposal fail? The compromise agreement rested on utilizing de Valera as the figurehead of the revolution to stave off a split in the event of the Treaty being ratified and a provisional government proclaimed. However, de Valera vetoed the idea. He clung stubbornly to his external association concept and advocated Document No 2 as a counterproposal.[34] Without de Valera's endorsement, the peace committee's scheme ran aground.

A division was taken on the Treaty on 7 January Although O'Duffy did not speak on the day, he voted for the Treaty alongside 63 other deputies. Meanwhile, 57 TDs voted to reject the Treaty. It was a close-run thing, but the Treaty was narrowly passed by the Dáil. The emergent pro–Treaty regime leaned heavily on this democratic legitimacy, including O'Duffy.

A tense atmosphere enveloped the Dáil in the aftermath of the vote. As de Valera rose to speak, he appealed for the discipline of the past four years to endure before his voice broke with emotion. "Burying his face in his arms to hide his tears, he sank back onto his little chair," recalled Briscoe.[35] De Valera resigned as president, to be replaced by Arthur Griffith on 10 January. O'Duffy welcomed the election of Griffith but regretted that de Valera "thought it well to place his resignation in our hands." He urged the Dáil "now that the Treaty is approved of, we should get on with the work."[36] He then signaled his hope that a compromise could still be reached to avoid a split. He asked anti–Treaty republicans to allow a provisional government to be formed "without opposition, for the sake of the people of Ireland, and for the sake of giving Ireland a chance."[37] However, over the next six months Ireland sleepwalked towards civil war as the gap between former comrades became unbridgeable.

◆ ◆ ◆

Anti-Treaty deputies rejected the legitimacy of the provisional government formed on 14 January in the aftermath of the Treaty vote. Collins became its chairman. This transitional administration was to last a year until the formal creation of the Irish Free State in December 1922. Hostility to the Treaty was widespread in the IRA. Some estimates suggested 75 percent of the fighting men took an anti–Treaty stance in the wake of the Dáil's vote.[38] A delegation of senior IRA officers hostile to the Treaty asked Mulcahy to schedule an IRA convention to decide their position on it. Mulcahy tried to mollify tensions in the IRA, agreeing in principle to hold a convention. However, pro–Treaty GHQ staff immediately spearheaded a "quiet process of reorganization" in the force and turned GHQ into "the nucleus of the professional army for which the Treaty provided." On 15 January, Mulcahy became minister for defense in the provisional government. O'Duffy replaced Mulcahy as chief-of-staff.

Republican historian Dorothy Macardle wrote that "these men of the IRA, although they were supporting the Treaty, no doubt believed that they were not deserting the Republic."[39] A core of pro–Treaty militarists which surrounded Collins genuinely believed the Treaty could pragmatically be used to forge an independent Irish state and professional army which would establish a republic at a later date. However, efforts by pro–Treaty officers to wrest control of the IRA were internally resisted. Rory O'Connor, director of engineering, led a faction of IRA officers known as the "Acting Military Council" which informed Mulcahy and O'Duffy that the IRA would not obey orders from the new leadership which were not also countersigned by himself on behalf of his ginger group.[40] This derailed the efforts of the emergent pro–Treaty leadership to consolidate its control over the IRA.

A triumvirate of Collins, Mulcahy, and O'Duffy emerged to steer the early months of the fledgling pro–Treaty regime. "Young and untrained," they now "found themselves with many complex problems."[41] Although a minority in the IRA, the pro–Treaty position had considerable advantages in early 1922. Most experienced GHQ officers sided with the Treaty and tried to shore up support nationally. The IRB network was heavily utilized by Collins to appoint key men to positions of authority in the fledgling regime. By contrast, aside from a shared antipathy towards the Treaty, there was not much unity among anti–Treaty republicans. Some hawkish republicans favored a preemptive strike against the provisional government, whilst others were involved in negotiations to find a compromise.

In January, Collins called a meeting to establish a clandestine entity known as the Ulster Council or Northern Military Command. This body was headed by Frank Aiken, who initially adopted a neutral stance on the Treaty. His deputy was the pro–Treaty IRA leader from Longford, Seán MacEoin. The Northern Command was meant to be ecumenical on the Treaty question and to oversee IRA activities north of the border. Of particular importance were efforts to combat the widespread persecution of northern Catholics. Collins tried to project an image of the provisional government as the foremost defenders of the northern nationalist minority. O'Duffy was key to winning support for the provisional government north of the border. He initially persuaded Joseph McKelvey to support the Treaty. McKelvey was misled on the meaning of the boundary commission and mistakenly believed "even the Falls Road can vote itself out" of Northern Ireland. A Belfast IRA volunteer recalled McKelvey "told us that all our areas could vote themselves out so there would be little left of the northern government, and as a result they would have had to come in with the rest of Ireland."[42] In Ballybay, O'Duffy told northern officers the Treaty was a ploy to build up a national army which could import arms and "blow the shit out of" the remaining British forces in northeastern Ireland.[43]

A new army was created from the rump of the pro–Treaty IRA in February. O'Duffy also became chief-of-staff of this force. Henceforth, he was often known as General O'Duffy. However, among Collins' "squad," O'Duffy's appointment was resented as he was seen as a threat to their authority and prestige. The provisional government oversaw the establishment of the National Army as most of the IRA nationally had effectively gone rogue and either supported local independent commanders, adopted neutrality, or otherwise disobeyed GHQ's orders by supporting O'Connor's group. To demonstrate his commitment to ignoring partition, O'Duffy appointed Séamus Woods from Belfast as deputy chief-of-staff. Although pro–Treaty, he was a dyed in the wool militarist and adopted a pugnacious attitude towards the Northern Ireland government. He considered the Treaty's ambiguity on partition to be its major weakness.[44] Anti-Treaty elements of the IRA rejected the legitimacy of the new force headquartered at Beggar's Bush barracks in Dublin. Many pro–Treaty IRA officers held simultaneous ranks in the new National Army which blurred the lines between the two entities.

O'Duffy signaled his intention to actively disregard partition following a northern crisis in late January. As chairman of the provisional government, Collins tried to negotiate a bilateral settlement with the northern premier, James Craig. The "Craig-Collins pact" was agreed and aimed to end loyalist violence against northern nationalists in exchange for Collins' agreement to lift the Belfast boycott. However, the agreement unraveled due to mutual mistrust and the failure of both leaders to implement their respective ends of the deal. A final break in the pact came when Dan Hogan, O'Duffy's close associate, was arrested by the police in Northern Ireland. Hogan was set to captain the Monaghan GAA team in the Ulster Final with

Derry. As most of the players were also members of the IRA, they "traveled armed with their usual revolvers." At a checkpoint in Dromore, County Tyrone, six cars containing the Monaghan footballers were stopped and searched by the police. The men were arrested and transported to Derry jail, where they were scheduled to be hanged. O'Duffy was incensed by these events but his complaints to the British authorities fell on deaf ears.[45] Collins initially planned to dispatch his "squad" to assassinate the hangman in England. O'Duffy formulated an equally radical plan to prevent the death sentences being carried out. O'Duffy informed Collins,

> I have arranged for the kidnapping of one hundred prominent Orangemen in Counties Fermanagh and Tyrone. This was to take place last Tuesday, the 24th inst., but on account of the agreement arrived at between Sir James Craig and yourself I postponed action until tomorrow, Tuesday, 31st inst. And failing to hear from you to the contrary the kidnapping will commence at 7 o'clock tomorrow evening.[46]

Although postponed for a week, on the night of 8 February the plan was implemented. The 2nd Northern Division launched the raids. At Wattlebridge, County Fermanagh, the IRA ambushed a group of B Specials in a Crossley Tender armored car. The B Specials abandoned the vehicle and retreated, leaving it in the hands of the IRA.[47] 42 prominent loyalists and B Specials were taken hostage by the IRA and transported south. The operation stunned Craig. He schemed an extreme counterattack. Plans were drafted to mobilize 5,000 USC men for an attack on the south to forcefully liberate the loyalist hostages. Lloyd George realized the disastrous consequences of Craig's planned attack. If enacted, it could provoke a north-south civil war. Pressure was brought to bear on Craig to call off the operation. A settlement, mediated by the British government, released the jailed IRA men in exchange for freeing the loyalist hostages.[48] The incident demonstrated O'Duffy's propensity for risk taking. It further pointed to his belligerent attitude towards Northern Ireland despite his acceptance of the Treaty.

The northern crisis occasionally spilled across the frontier into Irish Free State territory. On 11 February in Clones, the regional headquarters of the IRA's 5th Northern Division, a trainload of 19 uniformed and armed members of the USC arrived in the town outside their jurisdiction. Local IRA commandant Matt Fitzpatrick and three others leapt into a car upon hearing the news and arrived at the train station. As Fitzpatrick approached, he ordered the USC men to surrender. He was immediately shot dead. Pandemonium erupted in the town. A party of 20 IRA volunteers engaged in a shootout with the USC. A witness recalled,

> After we had been seated for about two minutes, shots suddenly rang out, about six being fired into our carriage in quick succession, one of the bullets flashing across my face and grazing my hat. I could hear shots being discharged all over the train mingled with the yells and screams of the men in the other carriages. I heard one man appeal for mercy, and another call for his mother.[49]

Four USC men died, while the IRA suffered the single loss of its commander. The "Clones affray" incident profoundly impacted O'Duffy. Fitzpatrick was an "outstanding Volunteer leader" who demonstrated continuous service from 1917 until his death, O'Duffy recalled. The incident illustrated that "activities against the common enemy did not come to an end in Ulster at the Truce or at the Treaty" but in fact the war "only intensified." O'Duffy offered an insight into the psychology of the northern IRA at the time: "the Volunteers did not concern themselves about the pros and cons of the Treaty. The murder pogrom in Ulster had only then reached its peak, and the most reprisals on our part were essential if our nationals in the North were not to be brutally wiped out."[50] This unique situation allowed the northern IRA to remain largely under pro–Treaty GHQ's orbit as the IRA nationally began to fracture over the contentious issue of the Treaty.

◆ ◆ ◆

Perhaps one of the strongest points of the Treaty from a republican perspective was that the British garrison in Ireland was to be removed. As the British army began to vacate barracks across the country, Mulcahy promised in January, as chief-of-staff, that local IRA units would be allowed to occupy the vacant barracks without distinction to their views on the Treaty. This neutral policy was mostly honored until 10 March. In Limerick, the 2nd Southern Division commanded by Ernie O'Malley was set to occupy the vacated barracks. However, his anti–Treaty views were well known. The provisional government considered Limerick too important a city to fall into the hands of a belligerently republican IRA commander. As such, the Clare-based 1st Western Division led by the reliably pro–Treaty Michael Brennan was ordered by GHQ to occupy the barracks before O'Malley's men arrived. O'Malley reacted by bringing his anti–Treaty unit into Limerick.[51]

The crisis which brewed in Limerick threatened to unleash civil war. Mulcahy and O'Duffy arrived in the city to broker peace. However, the anti–Treaty forces refused to meet the GHQ leadership at their headquarters, whilst Mulcahy and O'Duffy refused to meet O'Malley and his associates on neutral ground. A row between O'Duffy and the local anti–Treaty leader in Limerick over the phone was described as "not as polite as it might have been." Mulcahy and O'Duffy returned to Dublin "highly incensed," having failed to even meet O'Malley or the anti–Treaty IRA in Limerick.[52] On 10 March, Cork officer Liam Lynch and the Dublin Brigade's Oscar Traynor were summoned to meet Collins, Mulcahy and O'Duffy in Dublin. The GHQ triumvirate asked Lynch and Traynor to confer with O'Malley in Limerick and find a reasonable compromise. Meanwhile, the civilian provisional government bayed for Brennan to take immediate action, even if it resulted in civil war. Arthur Griffith was particularly vehement on this point. However, an agreement mediated by Lynch was reached whereby his 2nd Southern Division would vacate the city, but the pro–Lynch mid–Limerick Brigade would take control of the barracks. Brennan's division was also to leave Limerick. It was an uneasy compromise and one which caused controversy among some Free State army officers like J.J. "Ginger" O'Connell who believed Mulcahy had capitulated to Lynch. O'Duffy supported the compromise agreement in the hope it would avert civil war.[53]

A fortnight after the Limerick incident, the anti–Treaty officers Rory O'Connor and Liam Mellows proceeded to hold an IRA convention. Mulcahy, as minister for defense, proscribed the convention and forbade IRA attendance. However, most of the IRA had already defected from obedience to GHQ and the provisional government. Most IRA divisions were represented at the convention. Resolutions were passed which rejected the Treaty. The convention further repudiated the authority of the provisional government and of the Second Dáil, which had voted to ratify the hated agreement in January. The headquarters staff led by O'Duffy was ruled null and void. A new IRA executive was elected with Lynch chosen as chief-of-staff. He was joined on the governing body by McKelvey, who reversed his initial support for the Treaty. McKelvey also brought a contingent of men from the 3rd Northern Division along. The convention essentially marked the end of the unified IRA. It was within the context of the convention that O'Connor gave an infamous press interview. When asked by a journalist if "we are going to have a military dictatorship then?" O'Connor replied, "you can take it that way if you like."[54] Meanwhile, de Valera's career reached its nadir during this time as he was overtaken by republican militarists. His alternative to the Treaty, Document No 2, was cast aside as the anti–Treaty forces pledged their commitment to an independent republic. De Valera was humbled enough to enlist in the IRA with the rank of a private.

Upon learning of the presence of the 3rd Northern Division at the banned convention, O'Duffy sought out Roger McCorley, a Belfast IRA officer. McCorley said the Belfast men had been offered arms and ammunition by the anti–Treaty force and advised O'Duffy that he intended to recommend his comrades to shift their allegiance to the new executive. O'Duffy replied that GHQ would be far better placed to provide the arms they needed. He explained that the provisional government could access world markets and legally import large quantities of arms. Whilst he recognized this advantage, McCorley remonstrated that GHQ had "not been very generous with supplies" so far. He explained he was "in the market for the first time" and his "support would go to the people who would help us to honor our obligations to the nationalists in Belfast." It was a typically northern attitude to the emerging split. Northern republicans were less concerned with abstract debates about the oath of allegiance and instead favored the faction which could provide beleaguered northern Catholics with materiel aid.

O'Duffy made McCorley and the northern IRA "a definite promise" that GHQ "would provide all the supplies necessary within a very short space of time." McCorley was satisfied and duly advised the Belfast men to support GHQ, "with whom my personal sympathies lay." Like O'Duffy, the Belfast officer believed the article of the Treaty "which would allow the Irish people to maintain armed forces" was its strongest point.[55] The northern IRA fell in line with GHQ for several practical reasons but the impact of personal interventions by pro–Treaty leaders like O'Duffy and Collins should not be underestimated. After O'Duffy's promise to McCorley, 600 rifles were earmarked for delivery to the Belfast IRA. The rifles had been supplied to the Free State army by the British government. An operation successfully organized by the Northern Command saw arms shipped "in a little twelve-ton motor boat" to Gunns' Island, just outside Ballyhornan beach, County Down. The operation successfully landed 200 rifles and between 30–40,000 rounds of ammunition. In addition, there were two Thompson submachine guns.[56]

From February, O'Duffy held the interchangeable roles of chief-of-staff of the Free State army and chief-of-staff of the (pro–Treaty) IRA. The Free State army, based in Beggar's Bush, recruited men outside the IRA's ranks. Before the IRA convention in March, O'Duffy's claim to be chief-of-staff of the entire IRA was largely theoretical. Most units defected from GHQ. O'Duffy tried unsuccessfully to assert control over the entire force by dismissing errant anti-Treaty officers. For example, he sacked Charlie Daly, O/C of the 2nd Northern Division, on 4 March.[57] The pretext for Daly's dismissal was inefficiency, but his known anti-Treaty stance was the obvious reason.

O'Duffy principally focused on establishing the new provisional government-controlled Free State army on a steady footing. Existing IRA officers were enticed by the allure of a commission in the Free State army and a steady paycheck. A regular salary was particularly important in influencing the northern IRA, many of whom were unemployed and faced discrimination by Protestant employers. Under the auspices of the Northern Command, the provisional government paid the salaries of northern IRA officers.[58] Patrick Diamond, a Derry IRA officer and later a commandant in the Free State army, recalled: "Officer personnel who had seen active service in pre–Truce days would be given officer rank and put into some serving battalion. Those who had not pre–Truce service would be sent to officer training corps school and be given a rank higher than they possessed in pre–Truce times." He claimed Dan McKenna and John Haughey took advantage of this offer and joined the Free State army as officers.[59]

◆ ◆ ◆

On 14 April, an anti–Treaty force of 200 occupied the Four Courts in the heart of Dublin city, the principal palace of justice. This became the anti–Treaty IRA headquarters under the command of Mellows and O'Connor. The occupation threw down the gauntlet to the provisional government. However, Collins refused to order the Free State army to recapture the building. The occupation of the Four Courts escalated tensions in Ireland. P.S. O'Hegarty said the country was "a huge armed camp with, in most towns, armed men glaring at each other from opposite sides of the street."[60] Collins hoped to negotiate a compromise with Lynch. Whilst Lynch served as chief-of-staff of the anti–Treaty IRA, the Four Courts garrison was led by more radical elements inside the republican camp. Lynch hoped that a deal could be reached with the provisional government and was prepared to concede much to avoid civil war. He was assured by Collins that the constitution of the Irish Free State would be "definitely republican" and would omit references to the British crown. Lynch was urged to wait for its publication.[61] A committee headed by the independent nationalist Darrell Figgis was responsible for drafting the constitution in the first half of 1922.

In conjunction with awaiting the publication of a republican constitution, Lynch was cajoled into agreeing to a scheme for the reunification of the IRA in May. It proposed to form a coalition army council which would include pro– and anti–Treaty officers. O'Duffy was to retain his portfolio as chief-of-staff, while Lynch would become deputy chief-of-staff. His fellow Cork anti–Treaty officer Liam Deasy would be joint deputy chief-of-staff. Florence O'Donoghue, a neutral Cork officer, would become adjutant general. Meanwhile, the pro–Treaty officers Seán

MacMahon and Gearóid O'Sullivan would become quartermaster and director of intelligence respectively.[62] It was apparently intended that O'Duffy would soon relinquish the post of chief-of-staff to Lynch to head up the Free State's police force. Deasy would then become the sole deputy chief-of-staff to Lynch. Ernie O'Malley doubted the sincerity of the provisional government in the negotiations, believing they "were playing for time until they felt strengthened and secure."[63] Lynch's openness to compromise in the first half of 1922 contrasted with his posthumous image as an ultra-republican militarist. IRA officer Seán Dowling observed that Lynch was "close to neutral in the weeks prior to June 28th; indeed for a while he was proposed as deputy to Eoin O'Duffy" but after the outbreak of civil war, Lynch was "reincarnated as the leader of an army that would not give in."[64]

The negotiations initially seemed successful. A secret arms "swap" scheme was arranged between the two sides. The Free State army would trade British manufactured arms for an equivalent number of weapons held by the Four Courts' arsenal. The latter guns, now in the possession of the Free State forces, were to be smuggled north for use by the northern IRA. This was done to cover the tracks of the provisional government in funneling weapons north of the border. Additionally, the provisional government and Lynch agreed a truce to forbid skirmishes which occasionally arose over the occupation of barracks. Further recruitment into the Free State army and IRA was also to be ceased. On 8 May, Lynch and O'Duffy issued a joint statement that ordered an indefinite continuation of the truce to "allow the army and Dáil committees to bring their work to completion."[65]

The working relationship between Lynch and O'Duffy was strained. The negotiations came close to collapsing when O'Duffy accused Lynch of hording arms in Cork which were destined for the northern IRA. O'Duffy's statement was published in the *Irish Independent* on 26 April. Lynch refuted the accusation the next day.[66] It was incredible that this dispute was aired publicly. Tensions also arose between the two men over the truce. On 10 May, O'Duffy accused the anti–Treaty forces of breaking the truce and told the Dáil he could identify "sixty breaches of the truce on the other side, but I do not wish to do that." He also falsely claimed the National Army was not recruiting during the period of the truce.[67] Both the anti–Treaty IRA and the National Army continued to clandestinely recruit during the period of the shaky truce.

◆ ◆ ◆

A remarkable scheme to reconcile republicans and the provisional government was concocted in May. Although O'Duffy told the press on 13 April that there was "no expectation of renewed trouble on the border," a military campaign in Northern Ireland was widely seen as a potential means to reunify the fissured republican movement.[68] Brugha told the Dáil on 17 May that he was "sick of politics" and urged all sides to come together to end "the ruffianism going on in the north," "we have some fighting to do." He continued,

> If this proposal be not accepted and there are no further efforts at peace, it is quite obvious that we will have fighting here in what are called the twenty-six counties. I for one would prefer to die by an English bullet or an Orange bullet rather than by a bullet fired by one of the

> men with whom we have been fighting together during the last six years, on and off. I am never going to fire a bullet at any of these men and I hope that I am not going to die by a bullet from any of them. Now we have a means of unity.[69]

A secret plan for an ambitious military campaign north of the border was devised which involved Mulcahy, O'Duffy, Mellows, Lynch and O'Connor. It was agreed that a joint invasion of Northern Ireland would be launched in May. At one meeting of the coalition army council which included the above-named leaders, Mulcahy laughed at the suggestion that the Four Courts should be evacuated. He explained that for as long as the Four Courts remained under IRA occupation, the intended attacks in Northern Ireland would be attributed to them. O'Connor commented, "we, of course, had no objection."[70] The plan proposed that the joint force dubbed the "Army of the North" would be led by Frank Aiken. This force would stage a "Rising" in Ulster and would be reinforced by joint IRA divisions from the south. Details have remained murky, but a strong hint of naivety surrounded the grand plan. Aiken declined to lead the operation and was reluctant to participate in the planned northern "Rising" at all.

The operation was launched on 19 May with a series of botched raids and minor skirmishes. It immediately unraveled when the northern government interned IRA leaders. O'Duffy received a desperate plea from Séamus Woods which begged for reinforcements. O'Duffy tried to oblige by issuing an order to Aiken to mobilize his 4th Northern Division, but he refused the order.[71] Blame for the operation's failure has been laid on all sides by subsequent observers. Historian Donal Hall blamed O'Duffy "who allowed the operation to go off piecemeal, instead of at the agreed time in a coordinated manner," although he acknowledged it was bound to fail anyway.[72] Thomas Kelly, a northern IRA man, expressed gratitude to leaders like O'Duffy and Collins for taking "a staggering risk in supplying weapons and ammo."[73] However, the failure of the "Rising" effectively marked the end of the northern IRA. It was possible that the British got wind of the provisional government's involvement in covert activities north of the border. An ominous letter from Churchill to Collins in May warned him that British weapons should not fall into "bad hands" as "you never know whom a bomb will kill; very likely a woman, probably a widow."[74]

The failure of the joint northern offensive contributed to a further breakdown in the brittle unity between the rival military factions in Ireland. Rhetoric hardened on both sides in June. On 8 June, O'Duffy addressed an anniversary commemoration of the Cratloe ambush near Meelick, County Clare. He suggested that the volunteers who died at Cratloe would have taken the pro–Treaty position and claimed they would "blush in shame" at the "shameful things done at present in the name of freedom" by the anti–Treaty IRA.[75] His charged speech illustrated the extent to which army reunification had failed.

◆ ◆ ◆

Following many months of political wrangling, a general election was scheduled for 16 June 1922. Although regarded largely as a popular referendum on the Anglo-Irish Treaty, several small parties and independent candidates participated in the election. In line with other negotiations to avoid civil war, an electoral pact was agreed between Collins and de Valera on 20 May. The pact presented a panel of united SF candidates in line with the breakdown of the original Treaty vote. The elected representatives would then form a coalition government to include pro- and anti-Treaty cabinet ministers. The pact was not simply a delaying tactic or a pointless compromise, but an effort to offset the impact of the continued British threat of immediate and terrible war which hung over the Irish electorate in 1922. This threat of reinvasion if an anti-Treaty majority was returned undoubtedly impacted the vote and cast doubt on the election's democratic legitimacy.

The pact fell apart on the day of the election when a draft of the Free State constitution was publicized. Due to pressure from the British government, it failed to omit references to the British crown and retained the detested oath of allegiance. In a well-publicized speech in Cork delivered on the eve of the poll, Collins urged electors to vote for the best candidate irrespective of the pact. This has been regarded as a repudiation by Collins of the pact. Pro-Treaty posters told electors: "You can get the Republic for all Ireland through the safe and sane method of the Treaty." Briscoe called such promises "bloody lies."[76]

In Monaghan, O'Duffy and Blythe were selected as SF candidates from the pro-Treaty faction. The presence of an independent candidate, Thomas McHugh, ensured there would be a contest for the three seats. Seán MacEntee, who voted against the Treaty, was not selected by the anti-Treaty side to contest the seat in breach of the pact's terms which stipulated that each incumbent would be re-selected. Anti-Treaty SF replaced MacEntee with Dr Patrick MacCarvill, a decision which was rejected by the pro-Treaty party. MacEntee may have stood down due to the perception that he had broken a promise to resign his Dáil seat rather than vote against the will of his constituents during the Treaty debate. In the event, he voted against the Treaty but did not resign. McHugh was fielded as a third implicitly pro-Treaty candidate "in reserve." Blythe and O'Duffy campaigned in Monaghan on the merits of the Treaty and encouraged electors to lend McHugh their third preference vote. McHugh largely focused on agricultural issues during the election. Although the pact broke down across the country, the nature in which it broke down in Monaghan was unique.[77]

Blythe and O'Duffy spoke at a campaign husting on 14 June. O'Duffy was "greeted with loud cheers" as he rose to speak. He repeated many of the themes of his contributions during the Dáil debate. When asked about his labor policy by a trade unionist, he asked that he be judged "by what he had done in the past for the poor rather than by eloquent promises of what he would do in the future."[78] On the question of Northern Ireland, he revealed a tolerance for northern Protestants whom he regarded as Irish citizens and expressed his appreciation for the contributions of Anglicans and Presbyterians to Irish society. He welcomed any unionists present at the meeting and asked that they play a role in building the Irish nation. He tried to clarify his notorious belligerent speech at Armagh, "if [loyalists] should attempt to shoot me down, or shoot my comrades, I would defend myself, but apart from that I do not desire that any man should suffer for his religious beliefs." In the aftermath of the hustings, a northern unionist newspaper carried the sarcastic headline: "O'Duffy the Lead in a new vein: His heartfelt love for Protestants."[79]

On polling day in Monaghan, pro–Treaty candidates received three quarters of all votes cast. 15,473 first preference votes were cast for pro–Treaty candidates. Dr MacCarvill received 5,046 first preference votes. O'Duffy came first in the election, winning 7,298 first preference votes or 35.6 percent of the total first preference vote. In the second count, MacCarvill won the second seat. Finally, Blythe won the final Monaghan seat. Nationally, pro–Treaty SF candidates won 58 seats compared with the 36 won by anti–Treaty SF. The election was notable for the strong performance of the Labor party led by Thomas Johnson which won 17 seats. Nine independents and seven Farmers' Party deputies were also elected to the new parliament. These small parties and independents were implicitly pro–Treaty in outlook. Anti-Treaty SF continued to adhere to its abstentionist doctrine and rejected the legitimacy of the Free State parliament.

# 5

# The Civil War

Although Ireland remained divided between two armed camps, life in the country continued in a state of quasi-normality. On 21 June, O'Duffy acted as best man in the wedding of his friend General Seán MacEoin in St Mel's Cathedral, Longford. The press reported that Collins seemed "in high spirits" and "delighted to be with his old friend" MacEoin. The same report described O'Duffy as "a slim, boyish figure and must be under thirty years."[1] MacEoin and O'Duffy were close allies. As chief-of-staff, O'Duffy delivered "a pompous little homily" to soldiers under MacEoin's command in Athlone.[2] On 23 June, MacEoin was congratulated on his marriage and invited by an anti-Treaty IRA officer in Donegal to visit their headquarters, "we can at least respect one another in peace."[3] The invitation showed that whilst relations between republicans and the provisional government remained tense, personal friendships and civility continued to cross political allegiances. However, on 22 June a major incident set off a chain reaction which led to an irreparable breakdown between republicans and the provisional government, setting them on a collision course of civil war.

The 22 June assassination of Field Marshal Henry Wilson, former chief-of-staff of the British Imperial forces, at his home in London was immediately blamed by the British government on the anti-Treaty IRA in the Four Courts. Wilson was an Irish loyalist and acted as a military advisor to the Northern Ireland government. He was regarded as particularly sectarian and a proponent of a British reconquest of Ireland. Whilst there has been considerable historiographical debate on the motives of the two London-based IRA men who shot Wilson, it is unlikely they were affiliated to the anti-Treaty IRA. Some historians have detected the hand of Collins or the IRB in ordering the assassination.[4] Rory O'Connor issued a statement which denied culpability for the shooting of Wilson. Nonetheless, the British government blamed his anti-Treaty faction. Domestic pressure compelled Lloyd George to act on this "violence in their own sacred capital."[5] The British government ordered General Macready and his outpost of British soldiers in Dublin to prepare an attack on the Four Courts. However, Macready wisely delayed the attack, suspecting it would become a catalyst to reunite the divided republican movement with a common enemy. Instead, he asked that pressure be brought to bear on the provisional government to move against the Four Courts. Lloyd George acceded. He cabled an ultimatum to Collins on 22 June:

> The assassins of Henry Wilson had documents clearly identifying them as individuals with the Irish Republican Army and they further reveal the existence of a deeper conspiracy against law and order in this country. We have information that the Irregular elements of the IRA are to resume attacks upon lives and property of British subjects both in England and in Ulster....
>
> The ambiguous position of the Irish Republican Army can no longer be tolerated by the British government. Still less can Rory O'Connor be permitted to remain with his followers and his arsenal in the heart of Dublin in possession of the Courts of Justice organizing and sending out from this center enterprises of murder in your jurisdiction, the six counties and Great Britain.
>
> The British government feels entitled to formally ask you to bring it to an end forthwith. We are prepared to place at your disposal the necessary pieces of artillery ... or otherwise to assist you as may be arranged. Continued toleration of this rebellious defiance of the principles of the Treaty [is] incompatible with its faithful execution.... Now that you are supported by the declared will of the Irish people in favor of the Treaty, they have a right to the necessary action to be taken by our government without delay.[6]

The provisional government agonized over their next steps. Collins mistakenly believed a rupture within anti–Treaty republicanism between moderates like Lynch and extreme elements like O'Malley and Mellows in the Four Courts could be exploited. The latter faction had ousted Lynch as chief-of-staff shortly after the general election. He was replaced by McKelvey. Collins planned to rout the hardliners from the Four Courts and anticipated that he could then negotiate a settlement with Lynch, without a full-scale civil war erupting. Using the 27 June arrest of General J.J. O'Connell by the anti–Treaty IRA as a pretext, an ultimatum was delivered to the Four Courts garrison the same night by General Tom Ennis. It ordered that the Four Courts be evacuated, and General O'Connell released by 4 o'clock on the morning of 28 June. However, the republicans refused to obey the ultimatum which prompted the Free State army to begin an artillery shelling of the building, igniting the Irish Civil War. O'Duffy later reflected that the conflict was a "fratricide" and regretted that it happened at all.[7]

Heavy fighting in Dublin strongly evoked memories of the Easter Rising. A contemporary anti–Treaty poster stated: "Easter Week repeats itself. The IRA still defends the republic." O'Duffy's involvement in the battle for Dublin was mostly limited to administration from his headquarters. General Tom Ennis and General Paddy O'Daly were the chief commanders of the Free State army during the battle. In his memoirs, Macready wrote that he received "frantic telephone messages" on the evening of 28 June from O'Duffy and British civil servant AW Cope requesting to borrow the British army's explosive artillery shells. When Macready informed O'Duffy he "would have to wait till next day for more high-explosive shells," O'Duffy and Cope "metaphorically turned their faces to the wall and gave up the enterprise as lost." Macready continued, "O'Duffy did not fail to tell me it was my fault, and that he would telegraph Mr Churchill to say so, an Irishism for which I was quite prepared."[8] O'Duffy emphatically denied Macready's claim: "I never met General Macready in my life; I never wrote him; never communicated with him by phone or otherwise; I don't know anything about the man, and the only thing I am proud of is that he doesn't pay a tribute to me in his memoirs.... He insults me as far as he possibly can."[9] There are some misnomers and factual errors in Macready's memoir. For example, he erroneously described O'Duffy as the general "who apparently had replaced the kidnapped O'Connell as Commander-in-Chief."[10] In fact, O'Duffy had been chief-of-staff since February whilst O'Connell was deputy chief-of-staff, the successor to Woods. Macready dismissed all Irish officers as incompetent except Emmet Dalton because he fought with the British army in Belgium. IRA experience notwithstanding, J.J. O'Connell served in the U.S. army, which Macready appeared unaware of.

Liam Lynch tried to leave Dublin in the early stages of the fighting to take command of the IRA in the 1st Southern Division. Oscar Traynor was left to command the republican forces in Dublin. As Lynch left his headquarters in the Clarence Hotel for Kingsbridge railway station with Deasy and Seán Culhane they were arrested by Free State soldiers commanded by Liam Tobin. The men were then taken to Wellington barracks to be questioned by O'Duffy. However, O'Duffy made the surprising decision to free the captives, telling them, "you'd better be on your way south." He expressed ambivalence about the conflict and told Deasy, "this war is too bad, Liam."[11] Afterwards, Lynch told Seán Moylan that O'Duffy had asked his views on the situation to which he replied, "I think ye're all mad." This may have led to a misunderstanding on O'Duffy's part, that he understood Lynch to have meant the people in the Four Courts were mad.[12] O'Duffy claimed to have received Lynch's "word of honor" that he disapproved of the Four Courts IRA's policy and would not assist them. Meda Ryan speculated "perhaps it was through goodwill that O'Duffy had allowed Liam to go free believing he might have helped to limit the Civil War in the south."[13] O'Duffy believed Lynch to be a moderate. He potentially judged it would be preferable for the agreeable Lynch to assume command over the anti–Treaty forces instead of a more belligerent IRA leader like Tom Barry. O'Duffy was "anxious not to antagonize" Lynch and "probably inferred more than Lynch intended by his casual remark."[14]

By 7 July, it was apparent that the anti–Treaty IRA was on the backfoot in Dublin. In the Hammam Hotel on Sackville Street (O'Connell Street), Cathal Brugha ordered the men under his command to evacuate the building. The men were arrested by the Free State army outside the hotel. As they awaited his surrender, Brugha emerged from the doorway engulfed by flames. He ignored demands to surrender and produced revolvers in both hands, shooting as he charged the line of soldiers. Brugha was shot and fell onto the ground. "With his enemies howling around him and their bayonets raised ready to plunge them into his body, Cathal Brugha said, 'No, I will not!'"[15] He survived long enough to be brought to the Mater Hospital where he died that night from his wounds. Unaware of the severity of Brugha's injuries, de Valera wrote to him the same day: "You were scarcely justified ... in taking the risk you ran, and we were all more than vexed with you, but all's well that ends well."[16] The opening stage of the Civil War in Dublin ended with the capture of Mellows, O'Connor, McKelvey and other prominent anti–Treaty leaders who were confined to Mountjoy jail.

◆ ◆ ◆

Shortly after the conclusion of the battle, the Free State army's most senior officers were "routed from their beds" at Portobello barracks for a hastily arranged conference to draw up a war plan. At this "disheveled breakfast" it was decided that O'Duffy would take command in the southwest against the anti–Treaty IRA. On 12 July, the provisional government announced the formation of the "War Council of Three" to oversee the period of the Civil War. It included the familiar triumvirate of Collins, Mulcahy and O'Duffy. Collins became commander in chief of the 6,000-strong Free State army, lending considerable personal prestige to the force. By the end of the Civil War, there were 60,000 men serving in the army. Mulcahy took over the duties of chief-of-staff of the army from O'Duffy, who was appointed general in command of the southwestern division.[17] Notably, all three were senior members of the IRB. Republicans pointed out that "the Free State higher command and the civil offices of the Provisional Government" were manned with "members of the same camarilla."[18] The three-man council was decried as a military dictatorship and the war described "not as a war for the security of the people" but as "a war for the supremacy of the IRB."[19] Historian John Regan proposed that Collins' assumption of political and military power at the outset of the Civil War amounted to the creation of a military dictatorship. This dictatorship was buttressed by the internal constitution of the IRB, which considered Collins the de jure president of the republic. Significantly, Collins prorogued the meeting of the parliament elected in June and applied martial law. These actions "describe the structure and agency of a military dictatorship," wrote Regan.[20] A future associate of O'Duffy's, Liam Walsh, wrote that the IRB was then "in fact as well as by right, the sole Government of the Irish Republic." Tellingly, he crossed out the words "the sole" and substituted "an important actor in the Government of the Irish Republic."[21]

In July, Dominick Doherty, the O/C of the Newry battalion attached to Frank Aiken's neutral 4th Northern Division stationed in Dundalk, decided to "rebel against the rule of Aiken & co ... without fee or reward." He reported to O'Duffy and Mulcahy, who ordered Doherty to return to Dundalk and prepare the way for an attack on Dundalk barracks by Dan Hogan.[22] O'Duffy had advocated a seizure of Aiken's headquarters in Dundalk since the spring.[23] Under O'Duffy's orders, Hogan attacked Dundalk in late July, ending the Free State army's toleration of Aiken's neutrality. Dundalk was a strategically important barracks along the border. Henceforth, it was used as a recruitment station for enlistees in the Free State army from Northern Ireland. Tom Fitzpatrick, former O/C of the 3rd Northern Division and later a colonel in the Free State army, arranged the transport of Belfast IRA men to Dundalk "for service with the National Army." Notably, all fares were paid for out of Belfast Brigade funds.[24]

Colonel Séamus Woods was irate when he learned of the attack and complained to Hogan and O'Duffy. Woods then wrote to Mulcahy to request the release of Aiken from jail. Woods believed Hogan was jealous of him due to his closeness to O'Duffy. At a meeting in Portobello barracks, Woods rebuked Hogan: "that was a marvelous military operation of yours the other night." Hogan replied, "I wish you had been there," suggesting he would have liked to take Woods prisoner too. He then placed his hand on his revolver. Woods drew his own revolver. However, O'Duffy managed to defuse tensions. Whilst O'Duffy was on business in Dublin in mid–August, he tried to reconcile Hogan and Woods by inviting them for tea in County Wicklow with the chairman of the County Down GAA. On the way home, Hogan insisted that Woods and he stopover in Dundalk barracks. Woods was reluctant and wanted to continue back to Belfast. In the early hours of the morning, Aiken's 4th Northern Division launched an attack on Dundalk barracks. Hogan then suspected Woods of conniving with the anti–Treaty IRA to ensure Hogan was absent from Dundalk at the time of the raid. His eagerness to hasten back to Belfast appeared to further endorse this suspicion. Hogan and Gearóid O'Sullivan considered Woods a secret "Irregular" (anti–Treaty).[25]

O'Duffy's appointment as general officer commanding (GOC) in the southwest placed him at the coalface of the Civil War. He established his field headquarters outside Limerick. The image of General O'Duffy as a national military figurehead dated from his command in summer 1922. He was described as a "sparely built, keen faced young man" and a "quiet man." He regularly poured over maps and planned strategic engagements until late into the night. A journalist painted a glowing picture of O'Duffy in command. Described as youthful, quiet but intense, efficient, and bureaucratic, he was the opposite of the "flamboyant red faced, white mustached generals of fiction." He was flatteringly compared to a new generation of brilliant generals who distinguished themselves during World War I and "brought brains rather than seniority." The journalist continued:

> [O'Duffy was] full of brains and determination which mask a shy and unassuming manner. You forget when you are talking to this kindly man, he is very little over thirty, that you are in the presence of one who is practically the military dictator and has power over life and death in a very wide area of Ireland. As a matter of fact, you are apt to forget everything except wonder at the extraordinary brightness of his eyes; and the quiet humor with which he makes a jest or parries a question he does not want to answer.

As GOC in southwestern Ireland during a time of martial law, O'Duffy oversaw civil administration in the region. He ensured that the provisional government's writ ran smoothly in the areas under his occupation. He avoided the impression of being aloof and tried to "show the troops that he is not one who sends them to face bullets, while he remains comfortably secure behind brick walls."[26]

Liam Lynch recognized the strategic importance of capturing Limerick. He wrote on 15 July, "if Limerick is won it will take us a long way to upholding the Republic."[27] A unit loyal to Lynch was in occupation of the city's principal barracks since March. Anti-Treaty forces were mostly concentrated in the southern province of Munster. According to Meda Ryan, O'Duffy's appointment "canceled any hope which Liam had of maintaining stability in the south and the west."[28] The truce which dated from the Limerick crisis was still in effect by the time of O'Duffy's arrival. Lynch appeared to harbor hope that it could remain in force and was reluctant to reenforce his position in the city. Reticence characterized Lynch's leadership of the early period of the Civil War. By contrast, the belligerent O'Duffy was quoted as saying, "the army of a nation will sacrifice its last soldier to carry out the nation's will."[29] From his field headquarters outside Limerick, O'Duffy issued a statement to the people of Limerick heralding their arrival "to help the people who are being trampled upon by men, some of whom, at least, believe they are patriots, but the majority of whom are out for loot and appropriation of property of the people."[30] It displayed a hardening of his attitude towards the IRA, who were engaged in a sabotage campaign of cutting railway lines, barricading roads, and exploding canals.

On 19 July, O'Duffy launched a surprise operation to seize Limerick city from the small pro–Lynch unit. Commandant-General Dermot MacManus recalled that "O'Duffy, as he was inclined to do, had jumped to conclusions" based on reports of Lynch's weak position.[31] In launching the attack, he violated the uneasy truce Lynch helped to negotiate in March. Utilizing artillery, the National Army successfully captured Limerick for the provisional government on 20 July. O'Duffy described it as "the finest operation in the present war."[32] The campaign was hardly the work of strategic genius. MacManus believed O'Duffy "had far more information than he did."[33] In fact, the operation was an impulsive gamble, but it successfully took the cautious Lynch by surprise. The latter's indecision and failure to occupy Limerick left the city open to O'Duffy. The anti–Treaty IRA retreated southwards with little fighting. During the summer campaign in southern Ireland, the Free State benefited from the support of the British Royal Navy, which acted as "the eyes and ears of isolated National Army units" due to the IRA's sabotage campaign which had crippled Irish infrastructure.[34] Traditional methods of communication were interrupted by the sabotage campaign which prevented news from Dublin from reaching Limerick in a timely manner.

O'Duffy basked in his victory at Limerick. He received the praise of the press, which was unanimously pro–Treaty in outlook. The city was "beginning to assume a normal condition" and had been "quiet for the last few days, but some sporadic sniping with revolvers goes on at night."[35] General Michael Brennan recalled that "the whole Civil War really turned on Limerick" as control of the River Shannon was considered the key to holding the south and west of Ireland.[36] If republican forces had captured Limerick it would have isolated MacEoin's command in Athlone from Brennan's command in Clare and Galway. "Republican success in Limerick and the south-east could have become a springboard for a move on Dublin," wrote historian Michael Hopkinson.[37]

In early August, O'Duffy conferred with his second in command, W.R.E. Murphy, a Free State general with British army experience from World War I. They discussed how to "thwart Lynch" and devised a plan to advance on Cork. In Cork city, the IRA was similarly routed with virtually no fighting when the Free State launched an amphibious assault in late July. However, the war was far from won. An anti–Treaty newspaper mocked the "ever victorious general," O'Duffy, who prematurely declared in July that the southwest was "practically free of Irregulars."[38] O'Duffy was often tactless, exhibited a dangerous impulsiveness, and sought the media limelight. An example of his tactlessness was seen when he instructed General Brennan to gather regional Free State officers to a conference in Ennis, County Clare. O'Duffy was apparently concerned by a perceived lack of loyalty to the provisional government. He demanded the men "make up their minds which side they were on" and warned that "once they had made their decision there was no going back." Outraged by this patronizing reprimand, a "mutinous mood" broke out among the men until

**Dermot MacManus (left), General O'Duffy (center), and Michael Brennan (right), c. 1922 (courtesy the National Library of Ireland).**

Brennan "was able to smooth their ruffled feathers."[39] O'Duffy had a low opinion of the men under his command, particularly reservists from the Curragh. He wrote frequent intemperate letters which complained of the "absolutely worthless" men in his army, "half of them are now in the clink, or have deserted altogether."[40] The Free State army recruited heavily in "garrison towns," traditional recruitment strongholds for the British army.

In early August, General Collins initiated a nationwide inspection tour of the Free State army. On 12 August, he traveled to Tralee in the southwestern county of Kerry where a unit of the Free State army, the Dublin Guards, was fighting. The

Dublin Guards commanded by Paddy O'Daly had landed in Fenit on 2 August. Collins called them "Ireland's best" and announced that "the people of the kingdom [Kerry] gave our troops a royal welcome. They greeted the national troops as their deliverers from bondage."[41] On the day Collins was in Tralee, Arthur Griffith died suddenly from a cerebral hemorrhage. O'Duffy telephoned Collins to inform him. Collins then interrupted his tour of the southwest to return to Dublin. Griffith's body lay in state in Dublin City Hall under a statue of Daniel O'Connell, the nineteenth-century emancipator of Irish Catholics. The state funeral on 16 August gathered most pro–Treaty officials in Dublin. O'Duffy remained in Limerick. Griffith's widow believed "it was overwork that killed [him]."[42] For O'Duffy, "Sinn Féin was Griffith and Griffith was Sinn Féin." He eulogized Griffith as "the founder and brains of the movement; he was a great reader, clever thinker and clever writer." O'Duffy also praised Griffith's absorption of the ideas of Ferenc Deák and Friedrich List as underpinning the "sound political and economic policy" of SF.[43]

◆ ◆ ◆

The bond between Collins and O'Duffy strengthened in August. Both men became increasingly concerned about the supposed threat of communism. On 19 August, Collins told Horace Plunkett that "after we get over the present trouble, we shall have to fight Bolshevism."[44] Likewise, O'Duffy viewed Labor Party peaceniks as subversives attempting to foment social revolution. He reasoned, if the Free State "can break the back of this revolt, any attempts at revolt by labor in the future will be futile."[45] On 20 August, Collins left Dublin to recommence his tour of the front. He and a convoy of military staff arrived in Limerick the same day he left the capital. Collins and O'Duffy lunched together in Limerick and journeyed as far as Mallow. On parting, O'Duffy recalled Collins was "strong, virile and cheerful … he always found time to be among his soldiers, his gallant little army."[46] Both generals then embarked on respective tours of the southwest. O'Duffy inspected troops in Kerry whilst Collins was set to undertake an inspection of Cork. They planned to rendezvous in Limerick two days later. In Kerry, O'Duffy was subjected to three unsuccessful ambushes by the IRA. He returned to Limerick where he waited until three o'clock in the morning of 23 August for Collins' return. He waited in vain as "little did he know.… Collins was then lying dead on a lonely country road."[47]

In West Cork, Collins' homeplace, the Free State commander in chief was ambushed by a party of anti–Treaty IRA men and killed in action on 22 August. The site of his death is known locally as "Béal na mBláth." An official report from the Free State side described how Collins and members of his personal staff left Cork city on the morning of 22 August. He traveled in a Whippet armored car. Midway between Macroom and Bandon the convoy proceeded along backroads due to obstacles on the main roads. The convoy was attacked by "a large party of Irregulars." Collins insisted on fighting the battle, which lasted for close to an hour. Towards the end of the engagement, he was wounded and "expired in a short time." An Act of Contrition was recited. His last words were recorded in the official report as "forgive them," highly evocative of Christ's words on the cross. The report continued,

> The body was removed under fire to the armored car. The Irregulars were by this time in full retreat, having sustained very heavy casualties and leaving several dead and wounded on the field. The troops were obliged to leave the Leyland Touring Car, and it was in the armored car that the remains were brought to Cork—being conveyed to Shankill Hospital. The sad procession reached the city between midnight and one o'clock on Wednesday morning.[48]

O'Duffy hero-worshiped Collins. Towards the end of his life, Collins apparently considered O'Duffy his prospective successor. He told Batt O'Connor with reference to O'Duffy "there is a coming man. He will take my place."[49] O'Duffy later believed Collins had placed "a sacred trust" upon him, which he would "strive to be faithful to."[50] He traded on his status as the heir to Collins' legacy throughout his political career, telling an audience in 1935: "remember the words of Collins: 'If I fall, you have O'Duffy.' Collins fell and let them have O'Duffy!"[51]

O'Duffy was "stunned" to learn of "the fall of his leader" in West Cork.[52] On 23 August, he delivered a speech to the men under his command which illustrated the deep impact the death had on him personally. "I feel this tragedy of the Irish nation in my very soul within," he declared. The speech was characterized by a flood of emotion: "They who murdered Mick Collins say they were republicans. Republicans! My God! He was the best republican of them all … he was the only man that England feared. He was the only man that could and would secure the absolute independence of Ireland." He forecasted that anti–Treaty republicans, aware "they cannot rule Ireland now," were intent on the ruination of the nation. The death of Collins had a brutalizing impact on many of the fallen leader's closest associates, including O'Duffy and members of his former "squad" who swelled the ranks of the Criminal Investigation Department (CID). O'Duffy declared he was anxious for peace but acknowledged "we don't want peace now and in two months to have another outbreak." He predicted, "it is quite possible before this struggle for freedom … is over, probably more of our best will die, but others will take their place, and please God, the Irish nation will live."[53]

In later years, O'Duffy described letters sent to him by Collins as his "most cherished possessions."[54] Collins' funeral was held in Dublin on 28 August. Following a requiem Mass in Dublin's Pro-Cathedral, Collins was interred in Glasnevin cemetery. Hundreds of thousands of people thronged the streets to mourn the loss of Collins. Perhaps compounding the personal tragedy for O'Duffy, he was unable to attend the funeral due to his sensitive military posting in Limerick. In the southwest, the poor working relationship between O'Duffy and Emmet Dalton frustrated plans for the two forces to link up and sweep for republicans in west Cork and west Kerry. Dalton blamed O'Duffy and in turn O'Duffy blamed Dalton, accusing him of incompetence.[55]

The deaths of Griffith and Collins, the two principal figureheads of pro–Treaty nationalism, left a vacuum in the leadership of the emergent Irish state. The question of succession immediately arose after Collins' death. Despite his anointed status as heir presumptive, few in the provisional government shared Collins' view that O'Duffy should assume political leadership. Nor did O'Duffy present himself as a candidate for the office. Kevin O'Higgins, the minister for economic affairs, proposed Mulcahy's name as a successor to Collins, but Mulcahy declined. On 25

August, the chairmanship of the provisional government fell largely by default to the minister for finance, William T. Cosgrave. The brief totalizing control assumed by Collins of civil-military affairs ended as the provisional government became more civilian in character. The political shift in the administration of the fledgling Free State after Collins' death "virtually ended" O'Duffy's military career, "for a time at least."[56]

◆ ◆ ◆

Kevin O'Higgins became the minister for home affairs in Cosgrave's first cabinet. He was responsible for overseeing the state's police force, the Civic Guard, which suffered several crises under its first commissioner, Michael Staines. Recruits tended to be young, untrained, inexperienced, and were assigned substandard accommodation. Outside Dublin, the force had no clear chain of command.[57] Policing was a contentious issue in Ireland. Historically, the RIC was disliked by nationalists. Whilst ordinary RIC constables tended to be Catholics, the police leadership was almost exclusively Protestant. The RIC was socially atomized as its men lived apart from local communities in fortified barracks. In 1921 Collins founded the Irish Republican Police to work in conjunction with the IRA on policing matters, but there was considerable overlap between membership of the IRA and IRP. The Civic Guards was formed in February 1922 on the initiative of a committee set up by the provisional government. It proposed that the RIC should be transferred to the new force. The Civic Guards operated in 21 divisional areas rather than on a county basis as the RIC had. Other symbolic changes that tried to distinguish the force from the RIC included the adoption of a blue uniform to replace the RIC's green uniform. The basic rank was a "garda" (guard) and it was intended that the force would be considerably smaller in size (4,300) than the almost 8,000 RIC men who patrolled pre-independence Ireland. Initially, the Civic Guards acted as an armed gendarmerie due to the violent atmosphere in Ireland.[58]

Staines, a pro–Treaty SF deputy, had been appointed as the first commissioner in February. Initially, the anti–Treaty IRA encouraged its men to join and destabilize the force. Infiltrators also gathered intelligence and smuggled arms from police depots. Staines erred by appointing former RIC officers to prominent positions in the new Civic Guards to the chagrin of the former IRA men in its ranks. On 15 May 1922, a mutiny broke out in County Kildare. Twelve hundred pro-republican guards successfully seized the Curragh camp. Ernest Blythe recalled "we were told that the bulk of the Civic Guard had mutinied and that they had chased certain higher officers, including Michael Staines, Joe Ring, and others, out of the camp." Blythe claimed Staines "behaved with singular inaptitude" and had ignored evidence that a mutiny was brewing.[59] The mutiny allowed the IRA to raid the Civic Guards' arsenal. The provisional government handled the crisis with kid gloves and tried to reintegrate mutinous officers in the police force, despite recommendations from a government committee that the force be disbanded and replaced by autonomous unarmed police forces established on a regional basis.

In a letter to Mulcahy of 1 September, O'Higgins wrote that "by general agreement" O'Duffy was regarded as "the only one capable of retrieving the Civic Guard mess." He proposed to appoint O'Duffy commissioner of the police to succeed Staines, who had resigned on 18 August. O'Higgins recognized that organizing the police was a formidable challenge and one which would determine "whether we will succeed or fail in laying the foundations of a State."[60] O'Duffy had not been the government's first choice. Seán Ó Muirthile declined the appointment following Staines' resignation.[61] Mulcahy was reluctant to release O'Duffy from active service, realizing he "could ill-afford to lose him" and described him as the army's "right arm." But he understood the appointment was "amply justified" due to O'Duffy's reputation as an excellent administrator.[62]

Blythe recalled that O'Duffy likely canvassed for the commissionership. He remembered "just before the outbreak of the Civil War, O'Duffy and I were in Monaghan electioneering ... and either on the journey to Monaghan or on the journey from Monaghan, O'Duffy spoke to me at great length about his interest in police work and about his belief in his own capacity to do it well." Indeed, during the IRA reunification talks prior to the outbreak of the conflict, O'Duffy's intended role of chief-of-staff was seen as a temporary appointment until he transferred to the police. Blythe recalled, "the opinion of O'Duffy amongst Ministers was very high at the time. His excessive vanity had not manifested itself, and he was thought of as a strict, thoroughgoing, enterprising man, who could tackle such a job as the restoration and maintenance of discipline amongst the Civic Guards very well. In fact, I am satisfied that O'Duffy did a very good job in his earlier days as a police chief."[63] Cosgrave was skeptical of O'Duffy. He told Eamonn Coogan that O'Duffy wanted "to be put in charge of the army" but Cosgrave believed him to be "a wild man" so he "put him in charge of the guards instead." The chairman of the provisional government then asked Coogan to become deputy commissioner "to keep an eye on him."[64]

◆ ◆ ◆

On 11 September, O'Duffy became police commissioner. In a letter of acceptance to Mulcahy, he laid blame on Staines and expressed the view that his own appointment had come too late, as he alone could have prevented the May mutiny. He further blamed Staines for making the force unpopular and complained "it will be very difficult to retrieve its position."[65] As commissioner, O'Duffy chose to overlook past mutinous behavior among the guards. Blythe stated that O'Duffy assured the guards that "as far as he was concerned, the past was the past and nobody was going to suffer for any part he may have had in the mutiny" but he began to "enforce discipline with a stern hand." In upholding his reputation as a strict disciplinarian, he could sometimes be petty. On one occasion, a guard on his first night of duty was overheard by O'Duffy using obscene language and quarreling with another man. The commissioner dismissed him on the spot.[66]

In early October, O'Duffy announced that the guards would be unarmed, although it took until January for this to be fully implemented. This policy distinguished the guards from the army and presented the force as non-combatants in the Civil War. Guards were sent into areas only after the provisional government's authority had been asserted by the Free State army.[67] The strategy of an unarmed police force was to repair the social fabric between the people and police. An unarmed force was entirely dependent on "the moral support of the people." Guards were urged to conduct themselves well to receive this moral support.[68] Indeed, O'Duffy insisted on a policy of passive resistance when confronted by armed men. This was contingent on the guards' own self-discipline and the support of the local people. Because killing guards was unpopular, the IRA largely left them alone.[69] Although the Civic Guards' unarmed policy signaled a clear break with the legacy of the RIC, it retained many of the symbols of the police force which existed during British rule. For example, the Civic Guards was headquartered in Dublin's Phoenix Park Depot, formerly the headquarters of the RIC. On 31 July 1923, the Civic Guards was restyled An Garda Síochána, which translates as "guardians of the peace." The name was proposed by Labor deputy Cathal O'Shannon and reflected an increasingly nationalist identity for the police force. As commissioner for 11 years, O'Duffy imprinted his idealistic vision on the Garda Siochána, or Gardaí. In historian Conor Brady's view, O'Duffy, then in his early thirties, was "precisely the man to organize and direct the novel and ambitious undertaking of creating an unarmed native civil police force for a country whose experience of justice administration had been the contrary of this ideal."[70]

Blythe recalled that O'Duffy "established supremacy over the Guards very quickly, and after a little time no doubt remained as to their discipline and loyalty."[71] Despite still being an elected representative from Monaghan, his primary focus was on building the Civic Guards. Local speculation abounded that he would resign his parliamentary seat. The Irish Farmers Union in Ballybay even selected a candidate for the prospective by-election. He seldom attended the parliament which only began to meet after Collins' death.[72] His vision of the Civic Guards was a "strictly non-political ... police force for all the people, and not for any section of the people." O'Duffy told recruits in November 1922 that it was not the business of a policeman "how the people think politically, everyone is entitled to their own opinions."[73] However, in his later years he frequently strayed outside the bounds of political neutrality by canvassing friends to support his favored candidates.[74]

O'Duffy's removal from active service in the Free State army dovetailed with a brutalization of the Civil War. In his later career, he sought to downplay any culpability in the Free State's controversial execution policy by claiming he was focused on police work during this period. However, in the aftermath of Collins' death, O'Duffy and Dalton each lobbied Mulcahy to allow summary executions. He asked GHQ to allow him to execute prisoners captured with arms as GOC in the southwest. He had a particular animus against "trucileers," demanding that the men under his command in the southwest "act vigorously, especially with those who did not fight against the English." He also advised Dalton on 3 September to set up a military court to try and execute men convicted of murder or attempted murder.[75] August was "the month of ambushes" and saw the deaths of 58 Free State soldiers. Initially, Mulcahy refused to allow summary executions.

O'Duffy was preoccupied with police work from September onwards and did not appear again before the cabinet until after the conclusion of the Civil War in May 1923.[76] By November, Lynch's strategy of a sabotage campaign to bankrupt the nascent Free State prompted the provisional government to support an executions policy.[77] The 7 December IRA assassination of Seán Hales, a pro–Treaty SF politician who supported repressive legislation, caused the Free State to execute four prominent republican prisoners in retaliation. Rory O'Connor, Liam Mellows, Dick Barrett and Joseph McKelvey were executed on 8 December by firing squad. These executions were patently illegal; each man had been imprisoned since July and bore no responsibility for the assassination of Hales. The executions led to an immediate outcry from republicans and has remained one of the most controversial actions of the Civil War. Whilst not directly involved in the notorious executions policy, the moral question of O'Duffy's culpability is open to debate. Mary MacSwiney explained in 1924 that from her "personal knowledge," O'Duffy "insisted on getting a job which would relieve him from the responsibility of any of the acts which civil war entailed and because he had been convinced that Collins meant to use the Treaty as a Stepping Stone."[78]

◆ ◆ ◆

On 18 January 1923, Liam Deasy was captured and subsequently urged Lynch to surrender, disputing the idea that the war could realistically be won.[79] Tom Barry then advised Lynch to make peace with the Free State government. Lynch refused the pleas.[80] He desperately held out hope of an impending shipment of German artillery which failed to materialize. Pakenham wrote that Lynch "displayed a noble-spirited optimism, more and more unrealistic."[81] Although Lynch hoped to compel the Free State into peace negotiations, he was unwilling to countenance an outright surrender. For many, it was evident that the Civil War was unwinnable for the IRA.

O'Duffy presented his assessment on the state of the country in February 1923 to O'Higgins. It was drawn from reports received from police barracks across the country. Dublin's problems, he claimed, were the result of gangs, "city scum ... always alive for any chance to plunder and loot, ready to espouse any cause which undermines order and government." In east Wicklow, the situation was "practically normal." But in the west the IRA had "complete freedom and the people were intimidated." In Kildare there was "an orgy of crime which inevitably follows on decay of ordered government." He praised the work of the Donegal police in northwestern Ireland who experienced "none of the wild and insane orgies of crime common in other counties," but he acknowledged the illicit *potín* trade remained an issue. He was deeply concerned about the *potín* trade in many counties. It was the "greatest evil" facing Mayo whilst 20 men in Longford "in a demented state" were committed to the mental hospital due to the illegal substance. Kerry was "spared the curse" of *potín* but remained a hive of other criminal activity.[82] Viewing the apparent disintegration of law and order prompted O'Duffy to adopt a more conservative outlook than his earlier revolutionary zealotry.

Lynch was killed on 10 April when ambushed by 50 Free State soldiers in the Knockmealdown Mountains in Tipperary. He was replaced as IRA chief-of-staff by Frank Aiken, an associate of de Valera and a political moderate who was originally neutral. On 27 April, de Valera called for a ceasefire. On 24 May, Aiken issued an order for the IRA to "dump arms" which signaled the end of the Civil War. A speech from de Valera acknowledged the republic had been "destroyed" by the Free State army and urged that "further sacrifice of life would now be in vain and continuance of struggle in arms unwise in the national interest."[83] The latter stages of the Civil War were characterized by atrocities. In Kerry, several anti–Treaty prisoners in Ballyseedy were strapped to a landmine by the Free State army and exploded in an act of callous cruelty. Heavy-handed actions in Kerry by the Dublin Guard were justified by its commander, Paddy O'Daly, who reasoned: "nobody asked me to take kid-gloves to Kerry, so I didn't."[84]

In the immediate aftermath of the Civil War, there were approximately 12,000 republican prisoners in Free State jails. The restoration of habeas corpus due to the ceasefire, as affirmed in a court of law on 31 July, legally required the automatic release of all interned republicans. Whilst O'Duffy had estimated it would take until the summer of 1923 to put the Civic Guards on a stable footing, he did not object to freeing the prisoners. But the civilian government took a tougher line. It refused to countenance releasing thousands of IRA men and women and invoked the Special Powers Act to continue the detentions indefinitely. Kevin O'Higgins explained that they would not allow a replay of the Civil War in autumn.[85] Republican-led hunger strikes ensued in October 1923 but the Free State government dragged its heels. Many prisoners were not released until summer 1924.

O'Duffy's role in the Civil War cast a long shadow over his later career. McGarry observed that despite being removed from the army during the conflict's most notorious incidents, O'Duffy became "one of the most vilified figures of the Civil War" in subsequent republican memory.[86] Collins' death profoundly diminished O'Duffy's status in the Free State hierarchy. As Ireland's "lost leader," Collins continues to enjoy contemporary widespread popularity.

Almost immediately after the Civil War, O'Duffy shared a platform with anti–Treaty speakers at the opening of Breffni Park in Cavan. His speech on that day epitomized the moral crusade which became a mainstay of O'Duffy's subsequent career in the police and politics. He called for "all sections of the Irish people" to come together for a common objective to "save the youth of Ireland from the sea of moral degradation into which they were traveling."[87] The crusade to reverse the apparent decay in Irish society, particularly among its youth, became central to O'Duffy's mission.

# 6

# Building the Guards

Shortly before the conclusion of the Civil War, O'Duffy was invited to attend an international conference of police officers in New York. Delegates from the British, German, American, French, Austrian, Italian, and Irish police forces were represented at the conference in May 1923. It was attended by O'Duffy and Patrick Walsh, assistant commissioner of the Civic Guards and O'Duffy's first cousin.[1] O'Duffy's attendance at the conference was important. He was one of the first representatives of the Irish Free State to attend an international event in an official capacity. His mission extended beyond the conference and indicated its wider significance. He was received by President Calvin Coolidge in the White House, where he joined the president and first lady for a private social function. In Ireland, this was considered a "very significant ... indication of the advance which Ireland has made." It contrasted with the curt treatment de Valera had received from the United States government in 1919. O'Duffy was proud to see the equal status afforded to the Irish state, particularly the sight of the Irish tricolor flag placed "at the right hand-side of the Stars and Stripes."[2] As a youthful luminary of the revolutionary generation, General O'Duffy encapsulated the image the fledgling Irish state tried to project abroad. During his diplomatic mission in North America, he visited various major cities on the east coast of the United States and the Canadian city of Toronto. Along the way he paid visits to prominent Catholic clergymen including Cardinal Hayes and Irish-American leaders like John Devoy and Daniel Cohalan.[3]

In New York, O'Duffy was fêted at the international police conference. Cosgrave proudly boasted to an audience in Galway in July 1923 that O'Duffy "got the first place, the highest honor, the best attendance of any police officer who attended that great conference of all the police officers in the world."[4] O'Duffy expressed fondness for the New York Police Department, made up of "seventy five percent" Irishmen. The police band performed a rendition of Irish airs and the Irish national anthem, Amhrán na bhFiann. They also played the "wedding march" to signify the union of the Irish Civic Guard and the New York Police Department. It was perhaps the closest the bachelor O'Duffy ever came to being a bridegroom.[5] The conference appointed O'Duffy a vice president of the organization.

The Irish police chief was profiled by the American press. His revolutionary background and War of Independence exploits captured the imagination of American journalists, a fascination O'Duffy was happy to indulge. Readers of a profile in the *New York Evening Post* learned how O'Duffy, "one of King George's most rebellious subjects," was wounded three times in combat—"you will look in vain for the index finger of his right hand, shot off in one of his numerous engagements." Although he "carried a price on his head for three years," General O'Duffy "never lost the smile in his blue eyes nor the lightning power of his right arm. He has a laugh for a friend, a blow for a foe, and looks at the world straight in the eye." The encomium continued, "standing straight as an arrow, lean and strong, and looking remarkably well set up in his blue tunic and slacks, black Sam Browne belt and scarlet insignia of rank, General O'Duffy inspires confidence in his ability to keep turbulent Ireland in the palm of his hand." American journalists were also fascinated by the novelty of an unarmed police force.[6] In New York, O'Duffy dryly commented that "no one else in Ireland is unarmed except the police."[7]

The 1923 conference birthed a policing tradition in Ireland which has endured until today. In New York, O'Duffy and Walsh met Colonel Walter Scott, an honorary commissioner of the New York Police Department. O'Duffy described him as "one of the most public-spirited and influential, as well as one of the most wealthy citizens" in New York.[8] Scott was impressed by the gardaí and gifted a $1,000 gold bond to finance an annual gold medal for a member of the force. It was decided the medal should be annually awarded for valor. In 1925, he provided $500 for silver and bronze tiers of the same medal. However, the 1929 Wall Street crash devalued Scott's gift.[9] O'Duffy later renewed his acquaintance with Scott during his involvement with the Olympic Games in 1932. He described him as a "good friend of the Force."[10] The "Scott Medal" continues in the Garda Síochána to recognize the valor of its members. It displays a Celtic cross and bears the coat of arms of the United States and Ireland respectively, symbolizing friendship. On the inverse, emblems of the four provinces of Ireland are represented. Its first recipient, Garda James Mulroy, was the victim of an attack by two armed men in May 1923 in Broadford, County Clare. Mulroy and Garda John Donlon were attacked while on a patrol. Mulroy tackled one of the attackers but was clubbed with a shotgun during the struggle and left for dead.[11] Mulroy was awarded the Scott Medal in August 1924 at a lavish ceremony of 4,000 representatives, including President Cosgrave and John Devoy.[12] Historian of the gardaí, Gregory Allen, noted that O'Duffy could be ruthless "in his determination to make heroes." O'Duffy accused Mulroy's companion, Garda Donlon, of displaying cowardice on the night of the attack for having left the scene to seek assistance in the belief Mulroy was dying. This stigma hung over Donlon throughout his career. It was only on the eve of his retirement before the commissioner admitted the injustice done to Donlon.[13]

O'Duffy regularly attended several international events in his capacity as garda commissioner. International observers keenly tracked the development of newly independent countries of the post-war period, including Ireland. O'Duffy and his force "emerged from such scrutiny with the highest possible credit." He was awarded the order of merit in 1924 by New York police commissioner Enright.[14] He attended the conference the next year but met short shrift from a group of "unmarried women" who tried "to pelt the Irish police chief with eggs" and yelled "traitor" in a "tempestuous chorus of cat-calls" as he took the stage at a hall in New York. O'Duffy simply smiled bemusedly towards the source of the barrage of eggs.[15] The egg attack was likely the work of Irish republicans. The *Belfast Newsletter* gleefully reported that its old enemy, Eoin "Use the Lead" O'Duffy had been "the victim of egg throwing."[16] However, O'Duffy denied the incident occurred on his return to Ireland, at least in the manner it was reported in the press.[17]

◆ ◆ ◆

In August 1923, a general election was held in Ireland. O'Duffy retired from his parliamentary constituency in Monaghan, vacating his seat to Patrick Duffy. O'Duffy was glad to leave politics, claiming he had no time for it as he worked a 17-hour day as commissioner of the Garda Síochána.[18] The political atmosphere remained tense in the aftermath of the Civil War. Newly elected TD Patrick Duffy was shot in Ballybay shortly after the poll, although he survived his injuries.[19] The pro-Treaty political party under Cosgrave reconstituted itself as Cumann na nGaedheal (CnaG), which won 63 seats. De Valera's republican party won 44 seats but continued to abstain from the Free State Dáil. The remainder of seats were won by Farmers, Labor and independents. The absence of the republican opposition left Cosgrave's government with a de facto majority in parliament. Although a supporter of the Treaty settlement, O'Duffy's attitude to the government was lukewarm at best. The only member of the cabinet he admired was Mulcahy, who continued to serve as minister for defense.[20]

On 7 January 1924, O'Duffy acted as best man in the wedding of his close friend Dan Hogan at the Holy Family Church in Dublin's Aughrim Street.[21] His first year as Garda Commissioner had brought him considerable "mental strain" but the results were said to be "gratifying in the extreme."[22] His workload was considerable and consumed his life. His home was in the Garda depot in Phoenix Park and his social life mostly consisted of attending Garda functions. However, his focus on building the country's nascent police force was interrupted by a crisis in the Free State which threatened the very survivability of the state. The aftermath of the Civil War resulted in mass-demobilizations from the army and a reduction in rank for those officers who maintained their enlistment beyond wartime service. A clique of army officers with IRA backgrounds, particularly former members of Collins' "squad," believed their status was being whittled away under the Cosgrave government. This disaffection galvanized a faction of the army which styled itself the Irish Republican Army Organization (IRAO). It was formed in January 1923 to agitate for the protection of the status of ex-IRA men in the Free State army and to pressure the government to adopt a more pro-republican policy. The IRAO's chief spokesperson, Liam Tobin, intensely disliked Mulcahy and the IRB, of which he was president after Collins' death. The pressure the IRAO exerted on the Free State government became increasingly troublesome and bordered on mutinous.[23]

The IRAO was backed by Joe McGrath, the minister for labor in Cosgrave's cabinet. A rift emerged in the pro-Treaty movement between the IRAO, IRB-associated figures like Mulcahy and Ó Muirthile, and Cosgrave's civilian government. There was considerable crossover between all three wings of pro-Treaty nationalism. The Cosgrave government tapped the phone of IRAO leaders, suspecting mutinous activity. Tensions came to a head in March 1924 when the contents of phone calls made by the IRAO's Charlie Dalton indicated a coup d'état was in the offing. As minister for home affairs, Kevin O'Higgins ordered the arrest of the alleged conspirators. However, Dalton and Tobin preempted O'Higgins by delivering an ultimatum to Cosgrave on 6 March which demanded the removal of IRB-aligned officers from GHQ (Mulcahy, Ó Muirthile, Gearóid O'Sullivan and Seán MacMahon). It also expressed disaffection with the government's lack of action in implementing Collins' stepping stone theory.

The arrests commenced on 6 March. Even Joe McGrath's opulent home, Cabinteely House, was raided by state forces. Incensed, McGrath promptly resigned from the cabinet and from the CnaG party. Decisive action between 6 and 12 March ended the plot, however, the arrest of many prominent IRAO-aligned officers exacerbated ill-feeling in the army. The events were described in the press as "swift, dramatic and momentous."[24] On 8 March, O'Higgins called on O'Duffy to assume control of the army, replacing MacMahon. Whilst Cosgrave and O'Higgins were concerned about the activities of the IRAO, they were equally troubled by revelations of the IRB's influence over the army. The appointment of O'Duffy may therefore appear bizarre, but O'Higgins gambled that O'Duffy "probably valued personal advancement over any other consideration."[25] It was hoped that O'Duffy had been removed from the IRB's orbit during his absence from the army. The crisis amounted to a struggle for "the supremacy of civilian authority over the military," which echoed the 1921 crisis.[26] O'Duffy shared several of the grievances of the IRAO. He remained strongly republican in outlook and was soon bitterly disappointed by the 1925 outcome of the boundary commission, a fiasco which failed to shift any territory along the border.

On 10 March, O'Duffy became Officer Commanding the Defense Forces of Saorstát Éireann, a post created to enable him to tackle the crisis. He was temporarily replaced as garda commissioner by W.R.E. Murphy. A week later, the crisis ended. O'Duffy was then promoted to inspector-general of the defense forces, a title which confirmed his supremacy over the military.[27] He was endowed with "absolute control over every man in uniform." He announced he would "exact strict discipline" in the military in the wake of the army mutiny.[28] The scale of the crisis should not be underrated. O'Higgins even advised Cosgrave to resign as president of the executive council during the height of the crisis. As inspector-general, O'Duffy tried to cool tensions and restore order in the unhappy force. His personal prestige and reputation as a "model Catholic" led the men under his command to "idolize" him, according to Mary MacSwiney. She continued, "he is far more likely to be a popular candidate for President than either McGrath or Mulcahy. I believe he is extremely unscrupulous and personally I have rather grave doubts about the correctness of his Catholic ideas."[29] It was interesting that MacSwiney foresaw a political career for O'Duffy, whilst possessing severe misgivings about his personality.

As inspector-general, O'Duffy inveighed against the "new but unworkable" reforms of the army proposed by Mulcahy when he was minister for defense. He proposed his own comprehensive reform of the army in close collaboration with Dan Hogan. The proposals were the fifth scheme for the reorganization of the army mooted in the past year. It was considered important to get the organization right so that "the army will not have to stand the shock of another one" in the near future.[30]

The proposals included a decentralization of power to regional generals, defanging the centralizing tendencies of GHQ. The peacetime force was to employ 18,966 men. The scheme entailed forming one GHQ, three command headquarters, nine brigade areas, 27 infantry battalions, and a training camp in the Curragh. Additionally, detailed plans were laid to establish a corps of engineers, an artillery corps, an armored car corps, an air corps, a signal corps, military police, a medical corps, a military school of music, a cavalry corps, a transport corps, extra units and a military college.[31] He pressed the executive council to adopt his scheme without delay, pointing to the "urgent necessity for getting the different Departments going on definite lines, with every Officer knowing and carrying out his own particular duties."[32] In addition to the nuts and bolts of reforming the military, he tried to instill an ideological attitude of service among the men. On 23 August, he addressed a commemoration to Collins in Béal na mBláth, "this sacred spot," where he implored the military to "resolve that we will try, so far as we can, to emulate his great soldierly qualities, and self-sacrifice."[33]

On 17 October, O'Duffy's term as inspector-general ended. Contrary to some claims that he was reluctant to leave the army, it was always intended that his involvement would be brief and restricted to crisis management. O'Duffy and his fellow officers held a banquet at Clery's restaurant in Dublin to mark his return to the guards. He was presented with "a beautiful sword as a souvenir."[34] He left confident that the army was in a better state than he had found it in March, which he

**Garda Commissioner Eoin O'Duffy lays a wreath at the grave of Michael Collins in Glasnevin cemetery, 23 August 1923 (courtesy the National Library of Ireland).**

compared to a mercenary army. Rolling short-term contracts, a hangover from Civil War mass-recruitment, were replaced with permanent commissions and enlistments. Peadar MacMahon, whom O'Duffy had appointed chief-of-staff in March, assumed full authority of the permanent army with the passage of the Defense Forces (Temporary Provisions) Act 1924. MacMahon and O'Duffy were "on good terms" and O'Duffy was godfather to his second son, Peter.[35] The reforms initiated by O'Duffy "effectively made MacMahon the first chief-of-staff of the permanent defense forces." Vestigial aspects of the army's structure dating from the original IV, such as the democratic election of officers, were discontinued.[36] Despite ceasing to perform the duties of inspector-general from October onwards, O'Duffy nominally retained the position until he formally resigned on 13 February 1925.[37]

◆ ◆ ◆

On 27 October 1924, O'Duffy once more became commissioner of the Garda Síochána. He soon became head of a "combined and reorganized force" when the Dublin Metropolitan Police headed by W.R.E. Murphy was disbanded and amalgamated into the Garda Síochána.[38] O'Higgins carefully studied and supported the plan.[39] A follower wrote that in his quest to instill virtues of loyalty in the guards, O'Duffy led from the front and "inspired his men with his own indomitable spirit."[40] The commissioner's daily routine was highly regimented. Each quarter hour was accounted for, whether it was spent studying newspapers, attending to correspondence, visiting training classrooms, or interviewing his officers. After dinner, he worked at his desk until ten or later. Departmental messages from O'Higgins were received close to midnight, which O'Duffy read upon receipt before retiring to bed. Typists were required to live in the depot so as to always be available without delay, even on Sundays. His annual holiday never lasted longer than one week.[41] A poem published in a garda magazine captured his image as a workaholic:

> The Chief of the Force is not sleeping tonight,
> He's awake!
> A phone's at his side and a map's on the wall,
> And his look is intense as he answers a call—
> The General's awake, yes awake! …
> So I stand and I think, then I walk up and down,
> On my beat,
> And the night passes on and the little stars peep,
> Yet the General works on in the silences deep,
> Alert and awake, wide awake.[42]

From the outset, General O'Duffy played a prominent role as the figurehead of the new force. He actively courted press attention. He tried to channel the guards towards pursuits he approved of, including engagement in sport and cultural nationalist pursuits. He regularly delivered sermons against "the drink evil," warning that Ireland was "never more drunken than today." The gardaí's success in clamping down on illicit alcohol embedded the force within local communities, "which began to turn to the Civic Guard with other local problems."[43] But O'Duffy despaired that Irish freedom had been interpreted "by a lot of our people" to mean "freedom to drink more."[44] Comments like this betrayed a pessimism about public morality and pointed to his disenchantment with the outcome of the revolution. The force continued to raid *poitín* distilleries. In one haul they seized 500 gallons of the illegal substance.

In his confidential submission to the Carrigan committee, O'Duffy detailed "the prevalence of rape, incest and child abuse." This, according to McGarry "provided further evidence of his belief in the collapse of the moral order."[45] O'Duffy claimed that the "morally depraved," who would previously have been "exorcized from society," were now "regarded as rather clever and interesting."[46] Perhaps as a reaction to his growing pessimism about Irish society, O'Duffy tried to convert the guards into a force which reflected a "purer" Irish identity. Guards were encouraged to join the teetotaler Pioneer Total Abstinence Association and wear its lapel pin. One poem published in *Guth an Ghárda* envisioned "'a great dawning day for Ireland' when her brave sons no longer are slaves to the drink-fiend, the curse on our land."[47]

Under O'Duffy's commissionership, the Garda Síochána was to be "Irish in thought and action."[48] Guards were expected to learn the Irish language. A mandatory language examination for new recruits was often personally conducted by O'Duffy, although he admitted his command of Irish was "not so strong as I would like it." But guards were expected to "keep pace with the growth of bilingualism, and should really be ahead of it."[49] He hoped the guards would in time become a fully Irish-speaking force.[50] *Gaeilgeoir* guards were encouraged to wear a *fainne*, a gold lapel pin which indicated an individual's linguistic proficiency. Devout Catholicism was another important identity marker for the Garda Síochána. As commissioner, O'Duffy led pilgrimages to Rome and Lourdes. In 1928, 250 guards were received by Pope Pius XI in the Vatican.

From February 1922 to February 1932, 8,230 men joined the gardaí. Of these recruits, three fifths had been in the IRA. Less than two percent of recruits had an RIC background. Half of all guards came from an agricultural background. O'Duffy said, "the son of the peasant is the backbone of the force."[51] This same demographic later swelled the ranks of the Blueshirts. Cosgrave declared that "this new Child of the State—the Garda Síochána—has given intense satisfaction."[52] It was said that O'Duffy could often display "human sympathy" when judging recruits and that "many an act of consideration and help by O'Duffy changed the entire career of a man for good."[53] He considered the guards to be "the flower of the young manhood of Ireland," pointing to his belief in the guards as exemplars of Irish virtue. He told the guards in May 1923, "I want you to be men first, last, and all along the line."[54] McGarry considered that O'Duffy's attitude towards the guards was a harbinger of his later attitude towards the Blueshirts and his efforts in both organizations to promote the values he held to be true.[55] Another central element of O'Duffy's vision for the guards was its status as "an athletic police force." He believed "athletic prowess meant sacrifice, training, abstinence" and produced "alertness, endurance, the willingness to take risks, enterprise—all of which culminated in one word, efficiency."[56] He considered a prospective candidate's "best recommendation … was athletic fitness with a keenness such as a GAA record shows. Gardaí, like the soldiers, subsequently won notable successes at hurling, football, boxing, and handball."[57]

O'Duffy's work in his first few years as commissioner was highly praised. By 1928, it was reported that illegal distillation had "practically been wiped out in the country." Guards received a "severe education ... mentally and physically" and attained a university-equivalent education at the Garda College in Phoenix Park. Promotion in the force was regarded as refreshingly meritocratic. O'Duffy was proud of the youthful image of his force; the average guard was aged just 24. A British journalist praised the commissioner as "a fine sportsman and a good shot" and "an all-round athlete of fine physique."[58]

As commissioner, O'Duffy kept himself in the public eye. He was regularly asked to present prizes to winners of the Irish Hospitals' Sweepstake, a lottery pioneered by Joseph McGrath. General O'Duffy also spearheaded campaigns on issues like animal welfare. In May 1926, he told a public meeting in Molesworth Hall that the gardaí "have done better work in prevention of cruelty to animals than has ever been done before by any organized body of men in any country." He had "very strong feelings" about the practice of cattle houghing in rural parts of Ireland. One newspaper hoped "that through his influence this particularly revolting type of cruelty will be stamped out."[59] He relished his status as the principal figurehead of the Garda Síochána and self-servingly marshaled his appointment to receive public plaudits, an indicator of his considerable ego. Even his closest associates recognized one of the General's weaknesses was his "love of the limelight" and his self-appreciation in his own administrative talent.[60]

◆ ◆ ◆

In the first decade of the Free State's existence, the CnaG government performed "solidly if not always very imaginatively," according to Michael Gallagher and Michael Marsh. "In many ways the administrative system carried on much as before."[61] Aside from a few ambitious projects like the Ardnacrusha hydroelectric scheme, the first independent Irish government was conservative if not reactionary. Pro-Treaty politicians believed the threat of radical republicanism stalked the land. Speculation abounded that the underground IRA had gone "red." Indeed, just two years after its defeat in the Civil War the IRA sent a delegation to Moscow of Seán Russell, Gerald Boland, and "Pa" Murray. By the late 1920s, the IRA was "rhetorically very pro–Soviet Union."[62] O'Duffy inherited a tradition in Irish policing of monitoring "subversive" political elements in Irish society. Whilst the mainstay of such police work under the RIC concentrated on monitoring Irish republicans, the Garda commissioner was preoccupied with the threat of communism. By the late 1920s, he saw the IRA as a "skeleton of the Irregular organization" which struggled to maintain a foothold in Irish political life. He identified key Irish communists like Peadar O'Donnell as particularly subversive. He reported that in September 1927 "the Communist International (Moscow) sent an invitation ... to the members of the Communist Party (Ireland) to attend the decennial celebrations of the Revolution." O'Duffy correctly identified O'Donnell as an influential advocate of a campaign against the payment of land annuities. These were annual payments collected from Irish farmers by the Free State government and paid into the British treasury as debts arising from the Wyndham land acts of the early 20th century. The anti-annuities campaign was regarded by O'Duffy as "one of the first steps laid down in Soviet textbooks for breaking the existing regime and bringing about the Soviet of Working Farmers and Peasants."[63]

Garda surveillance into the activities of alleged communists was sophisticated enough to include detailed descriptions of communist meetings, such as "[Seán] Murray entered the room and said...." It showed "that the Police were in a position to follow closely the activities of foreign and Irish Communist leaders."[64] O'Duffy also worried of the influence of "Soviet money" which "reached the hands of Irregulars and Communists" to establish front organizations like the Anti-Imperialist League, described by O'Duffy as a "Soviet-controlled organization." His anti-communism intensified over the course of his tenure as garda commissioner. He predicted in 1931 that the IRA, just shy of 5,000 volunteers, planned "to stage an open insurrection in 1932" and were recruiting, drilling, and arming towards this end.[65] Fears of politically motivated "illegal activity" led to the formation of garda special branch in 1925, a department of the police commanded by David Neligan tasked with combating political crime. Unlike ordinary gardaí, the special branch was armed and, where possible, quartered separately from the regular force. Its creation undermined the reputation of the Garda Síochána as a fully unarmed police force.

Although the government occasionally fretted about small left-wing groups, it "primarily feared the IRA, and the republican version of communism," according to Emmet O'Connor.[66] However, the IRA under Moss Twomey distanced itself from communism, partly impacted by a bishop's pastoral in October 1931 which criticized the IRA's political front, Saor Éire, as an anti-religious communist group. Aside from subscribing to orthodox Catholic social teaching that communism was atheistic and incompatible with Christianity, O'Duffy held conspiratorial beliefs about the nature of communism. In December 1931, he described it as a "gigantic Judaic-Masonic conspiracy against Christianity, long prepared, carefully launched, and zealously forwarded by the greatest forces in the world to-day." His anti-communism retained a distinctly Catholic flavor. He saw Irish anti-communists as "immediately responsible" to the "instructions of the Pope and the Catholic Hierarchy."[67]

Notwithstanding the paranoia which the specter of communism evoked, active communists remained on the margins of Irish politics. Of burning concern to the Free State government and O'Duffy was the political realignment of the anti-Treaty republican movement under de Valera's leadership. Having broken with SF in 1925 due to their refusal to abandon abstentionism, de Valera founded Fianna Fáil (FF) in November 1926 as a new political party which would challenge the Cosgrave government at the ballot box. Although a republican party, FF was prepared to work the Treaty settlement. As Briscoe noted, FF presented a chance "to compromise with principle for the sake of real political power."[68] In the June 1927 general election, de Valera's party won 44 parliamentary seats to CnaG's 47. FF campaigned on a range of progressive social policies which allowed it to reach voters beyond a core ideological base. Elected FF deputies were initially reluctant to enter the Dáil due to the presence of the detested oath of allegiance.

Many CnaG supporters feared that once in power, FF would settle old Civil War scores. O'Duffy shared this concern. Despite the force's avowedly non-political nature, FF supporters in the guards were occasionally victimized and passed over for promotion. A Monaghan guard, Thomas McQuaid, believed he had been forced out of his job owing to his family's support for FF. O'Duffy's "spies in Clones ... made my retention in an Irish police force untenable," recalled McQuaid. He continued, "during my last years in the force I was subjected to constant supervision, but despite many attempts of my superior officers, I was never fined for disciplinary charges while in the force. This case is one of political victimization purely, and I think the public should be given the facts."[69]

By the mid-late 1920s, O'Duffy treated the gardaí as his personal bailiwick and resisted attempts by the CnaG government to "interfere" in his force. O'Duffy's belief in his own supremacy over the force has been compared with the relationship between J. Edgar Hoover and the FBI. O'Higgins' department of justice regularly locked horns with O'Duffy over his tendency to make appointments without departmental input. In a dispute about pay conditions in the force, General O'Duffy intemperately criticized civil servants who enjoyed "handsome remunerations" and leisurely whittled away their work hours while "my staff work an average of 12 or 13 hours a day" but "do not grumble because they feel they are doing useful work for the Government and the Nation."[70]

The most significant rift between O'Duffy and O'Higgins emerged over the question of the treatment of IRA prisoners. In November 1926, ten attacks against the guards by the IRA across the country provoked members of the police force in Waterford to brutally beat republican prisoners who were in their custody on unrelated charges. Whilst the commissioner made excuses for the police brutality, O'Higgins was adamant that such acts undermined public trust in the Garda Síochána as a genteel, unarmed force. The dispute was "a trial of strength ... between the two men," according to Brady.[71]

O'Duffy was hauled before the cabinet where he admitted to misbehavior by the guards, but pleaded that there was "a measure of justification" and pointed to their good records of service. When the cabinet agreed that the errant guards should be dismissed, O'Duffy challenged the cabinet's authority and claimed it was his prerogative as commissioner to appoint and dismiss guards. He was asked to leave the meeting. In private session, the cabinet affirmed that they "would not tolerate such an attitude on his part." Summoned back, the commissioner was informed in no uncertain terms by Cosgrave that "if he did not dismiss the guards in question ... the government would provide itself with a new commissioner who would dismiss them." He left without making a promise, but the next day begrudgingly complied with the ultimatum.[72]

On 6 December 1926, just weeks after his tetchy meeting with the cabinet, O'Duffy produced a "lengthy, intemperately worded memo" in which he lamented how the Irish people had psychologically become accustomed to violence and resisting state authority due to the impact of British rule, the War of Independence, and the Civil War. He despaired about the condition of the Irish people who "know or care little" about "the rights and responsibilities of citizenship." He appeared to regret not just the political outcome of the revolutionary period but its impact of upending principles such as the rule of law and justice.[73] O'Duffy was not alone among pro-Treaty nationalists in adopting this attitude. Even O'Higgins had grown disdainful of separatism and the fruits of the revolution which prompted him to formulate fanciful plans of an Irish dual monarchy. P.S. O'Hegarty regretted that the Irish revolution had "derided the Moral Law and said there was no law but the law of force." The War of Independence produced "a general moral weakening and a general degradation and a general cynicism and disbelief in either virtue or decency, in goodness or uprightness or honesty," he wrote.[74]

O'Duffy's growing cynicism about the moral uprightness of the Irish people and his paranoia about the threat of republicanism led him to advocate arming the guards. He warned O'Higgins that even his own force believed the CnaG government "has not been as generous as it should have been in its treatment of the force," alluding to 1924 garda pay decreases, and implied the government could not rely on the police force.[75] It was a remarkable report. O'Higgins strongly rejected O'Duffy's proposals to throw overboard the distinctive unarmed policy of the Garda Síochána which allowed it to become embedded in society during a turbulent time in Irish history. Explosive memorandums containing arbitrary proposals from the police commissioner regularly landed on the desk of the minister for justice. Cabinet

**Commissioner O'Duffy poses with Waterford gardaí at a presentation honoring Garda Denis O'Sullivan for his gallant rescue work at a recent fire, 12 July 1925 (courtesy the National Library of Ireland).**

misgivings with O'Duffy's performance led O'Higgins to question his continued service as commissioner. Michael Francis Leahy, an ex-clerk in the British Admiralty, was canvassed by O'Higgins to succeed O'Duffy.[76]

On 10 July 1927 in Booterstown, the second most powerful man in the Free State, Kevin O'Higgins, was shot by the IRA on his way to Mass. He simultaneously held the portfolios of minister for justice, minister for external affairs and vice president of the Free State. Upon learning of the shooting, O'Duffy rushed to the scene of the shooting. He described his final encounter with the critically wounded government minister in characteristically dramatic terms:

> Looking into my eyes as I was kneeling by his side, the Minister said: "Is that you, Owen? I am dying, Good-bye, Owen. You were very good. We have done good work. Continue on the same lines."... Mr [Patrick] Hogan, the Minister for Agriculture, came into the room, and knelt on the other side of our Chief. Looking at Mr. Hogan, the Minister said: "Hogan! My two best friends, Hogan and Owen—Owen and Hogan, goodbye."[77]

Elsewhere, the death of O'Higgins was described similarly. As he lay dying "bravely, fearlessly, Christian-like forgiving his murderers, but unconquerable to the end," he looked into O'Duffy's eyes as the garda commissioner knelt by his side, and said: "Is that you, Eoin? I am dying. Good-bye Eoin. You were very good. We have done good work. Continue on the same lines."[78] The death of the 35-year-old cabinet minister was deeply mourned by supporters of the government. Despite having recently had a war of words with O'Higgins, O'Duffy laid claim to O'Higgins' legacy, much as he had done with Collins. FF deputy Seán Moylan later poked holes in O'Duffy's claim to O'Higgins' legacy, pointing to the commissioner's conduct arising from the Waterford case.[79] Describing O'Higgins as "one of Ireland's illustrious sons," O'Duffy stated immediately after the minister's death that "much remained to be done" to fulfill his legacy.[80] Typical of O'Duffy, he inserted himself into the center of the story and claimed O'Higgins' proudest achievement "was the institution of the Garda Síochána."[81]

O'Duffy attended the funeral and requiem Mass held at St Andrew's Church in Dublin's Westland Row by the Archbishop of Dublin, Edward Byrne. The renowned Irish tenor, Count John McCormack, sang at the funeral. Masses were held across Ireland for O'Higgins.[82] The assassination of O'Higgins hardened O'Duffy's resolve to crackdown on illegal republican activity. FF immediately condemned the assassination and denied any hand in it. However, the Cosgrave government applied the Public Safety Act and introduced a system of military tribunals which targeted republicans. As FF supporter Robert Briscoe acknowledged, "we were all suspect." Briscoe's home was regularly searched by special branch, who warned him, "when you go to bed, sleep in your clothes. We will be back! When we come we will take care of you as we did Noel Lemass."[83] In August 1923, Lemass was abducted by the CID in broad daylight. He was summarily executed and his body was dumped on the Featherbed mountain. He was the brother of FF deputy Seán Lemass. This coercion prompted FF to abandon its half-way policy of refusing to swear the oath of allegiance.[84] On 11 August, FF deputies entered the Dáil. The atmosphere was icy. FF deputies even carried revolvers under their coats. But the entry of FF into parliament "changed the political picture completely" and added democratic legitimacy to the Irish Free State.[85]

State repression in the aftermath of O'Higgins' assassination led to a cat and mouse policy between the gardaí and republicans. O'Duffy explained: "all one can do is hamper and hinder the movements of criminals as much as is humanly possible; make them suffer, make their lives a burden, apply remitting surveillance to their every movement and generally make their connection with the conspiracy and murder a non-paying proposition."[86] In July 1929, in reaction to the IRA's killing of a guard in Clare, it was discovered that the local police planned to retaliate by killing the local IRA leader, T.J. Ryan. De Valera, who represented the constituency of Clare in the Dáil, visited Ryan and read into the parliamentary record forthright allegations of police brutality:

> On refusing to give an account of his movements (he had already been held up three times on the journey from Sallins County Kildare), Mr Ryan was pushed against a wall, threatened, and struck repeatedly on the stomach and chest. He was then ordered into the car, and, as he was entering, one of the detectives rushed at him and kicked him. When in the car he was again assaulted, one detective, taking hold of the iron starting handle of the car, struck him with it on the legs, severely wounding him on the shin. The other detective rushed at him and struck him with his fist on the right eye, blackening it. Before he was let go threats of all sorts were made by the detectives, including threats to murder Mr Ryan.[87]

In September 1928, de Valera launched a pro–FF newspaper, the *Irish Press*, to propagate the party's message. The newspaper was privately owned by his family. FF increased its popularity in the aftermath of the 1929 Wall Street crash. It built a professional organization and established local branches nationwide. By contrast, CnaG was regarded by the public as aloof. It retained an outmoded political structure which failed to keep pace with FF's dynamic style of campaigning.

◆ ◆ ◆

Although O'Duffy regarded the death of O'Higgins as a personal tragedy, it likely spared him the indignity of being sacked as garda commissioner. It was an ironic twist of fate. CnaG politicians like O'Higgins were aware of the General's considerable character flaws. Chief amongst his shortcomings was his heavy alcohol consumption. According to his secretary, O'Duffy only began drinking when he was "well advanced in years."[88] Tim Pat Coogan, the son of deputy commissioner Eamonn Coogan, recalled hearing that O'Duffy's long workdays were followed by "long nights of cards and drinking with an inner circle of senior officers."[89] Indeed, O'Duffy's lifestyle as garda commissioner was highly chaotic. He developed the egotistical habit of referring to himself in the third person as "the commissioner." In addition to his heavy drinking, he was a chain smoker and "sixty cigarettes a day constituted his normal expenditure of tobacco."[90] He was a smoker since at least 1921. Alcohol and tobacco consumption took its toll on O'Duffy's physical appearance. The difference between photographs of the rake-thin and wiry General O'Duffy of the Civil War period and those of the corpulent and prematurely aged O'Duffy of the 1930s is remarkable. Even his supporters commented on his changing visual appearance, but it was explained away as the result of "the service he has given his country."[91]

O'Duffy's drinking was undoubtedly a tragic element of his character. In November 1922, he told the fledgling police force that physical attacks or humiliation would not smash the men's reputation, a lack of self-respect and self-control would. He continued, "once you allow yourselves to give way to drunkenness or any of the evils that follow in its train, you will go from bad to worse until your future career will be blasted. Your records are clean now. There is nothing down against one of you, if a black mark is to be put down against you, you must put it there yourselves. No one else can do it. Your future is entirely in your own hands."[92] O'Duffy failed to practice what he preached, and it has immensely clouded his legacy. However, the seeds of alcohol overindulgence could be seen in Michael Collins' character too. In London in 1921, he and Griffith lived a bon vivant lifestyle and indulged in many excesses. He was said to have heavily imbibed during his last fateful tour of Cork. Collins' premature death prevented any foibles he exhibited during his lifetime from developing into potentially gaping faults which may too have impacted his legacy. In the case of O'Duffy, his descent from a teetotaling moralist into private debauchery has undoubtedly tarnished his memory.

In his final years as garda commissioner, O'Duffy's leadership style was theatrical, ostentatious, and erratic. He regularly waded into the public arena in his self-appointed capacity as Ireland's moral watchdog. In May 1930, he appeared before a select committee on moneylending where he strongly denounced the practice. He inveighed against those who preyed on the "very poor" but also scorned those who lived beyond their means. He demanded "a tightening up of the law."[93] Most moneylenders were in Dublin. O'Duffy heavily criticized exorbitant rates of interest placed on loans, ranging from 60 to 100 percent interest in some cases. He explained that drinking, gambling, and domestic quarrels were the prime causes underlying one's motivation to acquire a high-interest loan. The practice had "been responsible for many suicides," he observed.[94] His public interventions illustrated how he craved the limelight. As a political rival observed, "General O'Duffy is that type of vain man who likes to see his photograph in the newspapers every other day, or his name mentioned somewhere in them."[95]

O'Duffy's awareness of disturbing crimes, particularly child abuse, undoubtedly impacted his growing pessimism about the state of Irish society. He witnessed an alarming increase in sexual crimes against girls aged 16 and younger, including many cases of children under 10 years. He estimated only 15 percent of such cases were ever prosecuted owing to the anxiety of parents to keep the crimes secret, the reluctance of parents to subject their children to cross-examination in court, and "the actual technical embarrassments" such as the difficulty of proof.[96] O'Duffy's testimony to the 1931 Carrigan committee and its subsequent report was buried by the CnaG government, indicative of Ireland's culture of containment.

O'Duffy used his status as Ireland's police commissioner to secure audiences with international statesmen. In May 1929, he welcomed the NYPD commissioner Richard Enright, who praised O'Duffy and the guards as "entrusted with more duties than any police force he knew of, and of executing every one of them well."[97] In October 1928, he visited Benito Mussolini in Rome. They conversed in English about policing matters in their respective countries. The Duce was apparently impressed by what he learned of the Garda Síochána. O'Duffy's secretary recorded that the meeting went positively.[98] However, this account was produced after O'Duffy turned heavily towards Italian fascism. Another account indicated that O'Duffy was repelled by Mussolini's superior attitude and that the meeting was far from successful. Following introductory small talk, O'Duffy was abruptly gestured towards the exit by a goose stepping Blackshirt. As he followed his escort to the door, O'Duffy unconsciously began to mimic the Italian's strides. Humiliated by the entire encounter, he asked an accompanying priest, "did you ever see such a blithering idiot [Mussolini]?"[99] However, there is a flaw in this account of the 1928 meeting, as Mussolini did not introduce the goose step (*passo Romano*) until 1938. O'Duffy became an admirer of Mussolini during the 1930s. He was described in 1933 by a foreign newspaper as "the Irish Mussolini."[100] Elsewhere he was described as "an athletic Mussolini."[101] O'Higgins was also described as an "Irish Mussolini" due to his reputation as the strongman of the Irish Free State.

McGarry observed that during his visit to Italy, O'Duffy was impressed by the "great experiment" of fascist Italy and was "attracted to Mussolini's political agenda of fierce opposition to communism and the dynamic nature of his movement."[102] Marches, uniforms and strong displays of masculinity appealed to the General's tastes. Mussolini, as editor of *Il Popolo d'Italia*, regularly praised SF and criticized British conduct in Ireland in 1920. He was even involved in a scheme to provide the IRA with "a boatful of guns and ammunition for free," an operation canceled by Michael Collins in 1921.[103] Sympathy for Mussolini and fascism also existed within CnaG. In December 1932, the party newspaper published an article which argued against universal suffrage and praised Mussolini as the only leader who "had the courage to restrict the vote to those who give evidence that they can use it properly."[104] Manning argued that prior to 1933 there is "no evidence to suggest that O'Duffy was deeply interested in political ideas" at all.[105]

◆ ◆ ◆

In the gardaí, O'Duffy was a staunch advocate of physical fitness and sport. His reputation as an able administrator dated from his period as an organizer in the GAA. By his own account, O'Duffy received envoys from the National Athletics and Cycling Association (NACA) to become its president. NACA officers hoped he could breathe new life into their flatlining organization. It also faced debts which were twice the size of its annual income. On 19 January 1931, NACA elected the garda commissioner as its president.[106] "Thank God that General O'Duffy is unmarried," said an athletics supporter, as the task which O'Duffy faced in trying to rebuild athletics in Ireland whilst maintaining his heavy workload as garda commissioner was regarded as "Herculean."[107] In his presidential address, O'Duffy promised to "retrieve what we have lost" and to put NACA into the black. He aimed high, aspiring to see an Irish athletics team participate in the upcoming Olympic Games in Los Angeles. "We want self-sacrifice and self-denial; we want more hard work and less petty jealousy and criticism. We must stand out for rigid adherence to the laws and rules of the Association on the part of the athletes, officials, and councils, for strict impartiality, for punctuality, for loyalty and discipline."[108]

O'Duffy's mission to rescue Irish athletics mirrored his burgeoning self-image as a crusader destined to "save" Ireland. In May 1931, he claimed, "their race was deteriorating" but they were "not beaten yet" and that he was "determined to save their people." He extolled the virtues of "the simple life" and warned against smoking and drinking in athletics. "In Germany, the youths who wished to distinguish themselves on the sports field avoided the cabarets and the dance halls." The General felt the Irish "had the material in this country" to train its athletes and to "do honor to their country."[109] He was critical of a perceived cultural malaise in Ireland. In contrast to other countries, the Irish "were too much concerned with the jazz hall, the cinema, and the street corner." His newly launched reform agenda for NACA aimed to create a finance association, to introduce better organizational structures, and to launch a campaign to promote Irish athletics. He appealed for a £10,000 war chest to fund his vision.[110] He appealed to politicians, irrespective of party affiliation, to support the campaign. He explained that as commissioner of police, he knew how the Irish youth were deteriorating, but refused to elaborate. Again, he drew a parallel with German youth, stating that "you could not offer a greater insult to a [German] boy than to ask him to have a drink or a cigarette."[111]

The "decadence" of Irish youth culture greatly perturbed O'Duffy and underpinned his return to sports administration. His efforts won plaudits across the board, including from Archbishop Michael Fogarty of Killaloe. He applied his knack for administration to bring NACA back to a position of solvency. The resources of the guards were utilized to send 30,000 appeal letters.[112] His work for Irish athletics "earned him unstinted praise from all lovers of sport in the country."[113] In September 1931, O'Duffy was elected president of the Irish Olympic Council. The body's remit was not limited to athletics and included several sports organized on an all-Ireland basis. He attended an Olympic convention in New York in January 1932, and from there he and the Irish delegates traveled to Chicago, Denver, Salt Lake City, and eventually to the site of the Olympic Games, Los Angeles. In Hollywood, he recalled the "privilege of seeing moving pictures being shot.... Many of the film stars are of Irish descent, and all are courteous and decent, not at all the type they are sometimes represented to be."[114]

In the first half of 1932, O'Duffy pressed the Irish Olympic Council to adopt the Irish tricolor flag for the Olympic Games. Although it had been agreed that the team's flag would combine the four traditional provinces of Ireland on a ground of St Patrick's blue, at international contests, including the Olympic games, Irish teams would be represented by the green, white and orange tricolor. He dismissed opposition internally and agreed to postpone the decision to a committee hearing of the International Olympic Committee in June. O'Duffy threatened to resign the presidency of the council if the tricolor flag was removed due to the influence of British sporting authorities over Ireland's Olympic team.[115] At the meeting in June, the principle was affirmed in an apparent victory for O'Duffy and those who supported the tricolor's use at international sporting events.

The tenth summer Olympic Games began in July in Los Angeles. O'Duffy was received throughout his tour of the United States as a representative of Ireland, including athletes from Northern Ireland and the Irish Free State. But at the last moment he discovered the Irish team was to be designated Irish Free State and would march under a green banner bearing the name Irish Free State rather than under the tricolor. The change was due to lobbying by the British delegation. When he learned of this supposed snub, O'Duffy threatened to withdraw the Irish team: "We refuse to compete as representatives of a truncated Ireland."[116] He asked for permission to announce on the loudspeakers this unanimous decision to the 100,000 spectators he claimed were of Irish descent.[117] However, the Olympic committee submitted to O'Duffy's demand. A new banner reading "Ireland" was hastily produced. Members of the Irish team won two gold medals in Los Angeles: Bob Tisdall, in the 400-meter hurdles, and Pat O'Callaghan, in the hammer throw. However, the controversy persisted in the aftermath of the Olympic Games.

At a meeting of the Irish Olympic Council in October, more motions were proposed to drop the tricolor in favor of an alternative flag at the instigation of Northern Ireland clubs. O'Duffy reaffirmed that "the tricolor is the only flag we can adopt at international athletic contests." He was particularly aggrieved by the role of British-based clubs in seeking to influence the decision.[118] He detected the hand of "imperialistic Englishmen" who had "always shown an alacrity and enterprise in widening the divisions which inevitably occur among an independent, individualistic people such as the Irish." He considered the involvement of British clubs to be a "brazen attempt at conquest."[119]

His presidency of NACA came to an end in 1933 when he became leader of the Blueshirts, "an organization likely to be construed as political." His loss was greatly felt by the association and tributes flowed in to praise his work. One newspaper concluded, "no matter how his position may be viewed, the services which General O'Duffy rendered to the sport of athletics and cycling in Ireland will never be forgotten, and every sportsman who came into contact with him will sincerely regret that, owing to circumstances, he has felt obliged to sever his official connection with the NACA."[120]

◆ ◆ ◆

In the early 1930s, FF grew in popularity due to its advocacy of radical social policies rooted in autarky and state-led economic intervention. It benefited from the unpopularity of the CnaG government's economic policies, particularly the miserly minister for finance Ernest Blythe. His 1924 budget cut the old age pension by one shilling per week, an act which "remained embedded in memory and contributed to the government's eventual loss of office some years later."[121] Famously, Kevin O'Higgins had characterized his generation as "the most conservative-minded revolutionaries that ever put through a successful revolution."[122] Spending cuts were felt by the army and Garda Síochána. On 28 August 1929, army officer Colonel Hugo MacNeill established the National Defense Association (NDA) to promote the interests of policemen and soldiers. O'Duffy supported the group.

The government was alarmed by the new organization, fearing a repeat of the 1924 army mutiny. In 1930, Desmond FitzGerald, minister for defense, banned serving members of the police and army from joining the NDA. As such, it wound up operations the same year. But the NDA reminded the government that a powerful coalition between the police and army still had the potential to derail civilian government. The NDA wrongfooted the government by making public allegations of misconduct in the defense forces, including claims that the men received virtually no training and that the soldiers were repeatedly the victim of erratic and arbitrary meddling by senior officers and the government.[123]

Blythe's austere final budget before the 1932 general election contained a pay cut for the gardaí. Incensed, O'Duffy went into rebellion against the CnaG government. He wrote to Blythe to ominously remind him that elections were won and lost based on the support of the police. Whilst the gardaí had once been "servants of the government party," he claimed this was no longer the case. The pretense of the force's political neutrality continued to slip.[124] The government's relationship with O'Duffy was rocky during the twilight of the administration. Blythe believed O'Duffy had "gradually become too arbitrary and obstinate."[125] Plans to remove the commissioner were once again proposed, contingent on CnaG being returned to government after the general election, scheduled for February 1932. Cosgrave considered sending O'Duffy to Washington, D.C., as ambassador to the United States.[126] O'Duffy's growing disaffection with the government also stemmed from its repeal of several special powers which had been introduced to allow O'Duffy to tackle the threat mounted to the state by the IRA. As far as he was concerned, "those who proposed to destroy the constitution of the state should have no recourse to protection under it."[127]

During the election, CnaG smeared FF as communist-adjacent in a campaign which would be regarded as highly sensationalist by modern observers. CnaG claimed FF was controlled by the "shadow of the gunman," the IRA. Alarmist propaganda claimed that a de Valera-led government would act as a precursor to a revolution by left-wing republicans. Pro-Treaty politicians like T.F. O'Higgins compared de Valera to Alexander Kerensky, leader of the Russian liberal-left government which preceded the Bolshevik coup d'état. A contemporary CnaG poster declared, "we want no Red on our flag." But FF carefully presented itself as a republican party founded on Christian principles and easily brushed off insinuations of crypto-communism as misplaced. The results saw FF win 44.5 percent of the overall vote and elect 72 deputies to CnaG's 57. After the election, the Labor Party supported FF, which allowed de Valera to become president of the executive council.[128] Cosgrave mistakenly believed CnaG would win the election on a platform of their record in government and because FF was "unfit to govern." As garda commissioner, O'Duffy was responsible for ensuring the election was conducted in an orderly manner. By all accounts, he discharged his duties fairly.

Among some sections of the Free State apparatus, the victory of FF caused concerns that supporters of the Treaty would suffer under the new government. They anticipated mass dismissals of civil servants, army officers, and senior police officers. There was even a fear that an FF government would pursue a punitive agenda to punish those connected to Civil War–era atrocities. Some militaristically minded pro-Treaty officials hastened to formulate a plan which would subvert the ascension of FF to power, including, if necessary, an anti-democratic coup d'état. The pro-Treaty party suddenly found itself handing power over to the defeated side of the Civil War. The leadership of pro-Treaty nationalism had been characterized by mediocrity since the death of Collins. Soon, supporters of the Free State began to look towards Collins' former protégé as a potential leader who could revive the ailing fortunes of pro-Treaty nationalism.

# 7

# Leading the Blueshirts

The victory of FF put O'Duffy's future as garda commissioner on notice. He had predicted that CnaG would lose the general election. It was within this context that he began to canvass support for a coup d'état among the state's security forces. The prospect of a coup was not simply borne from a self-serving desire to retain certain privileges in the Free State regime, it was also influenced by a belief that Irish society was in a tailspin morally and spiritually. This fear could be seen in O'Duffy's efforts to make "a virile race" of the Irish through athletics.[1] He had praised the U.S. for elevating sport to "almost a religion to her young people."[2] He believed a prospective FF government would accelerate this social decadence.

As a coup d'état was not mounted in 1931–2, it is difficult to separate hearsay from genuine conspiracy. David Neligan, the head of the special branch, described how O'Duffy went to great lengths to engineer a pre-emptive takeover before FF came to power. Neligan claimed that he was cornered by O'Duffy at the officers' mess area of the Phoenix Park depot and invited to join a conspiracy. O'Duffy produced a proclamation he had printed which declared a state of emergency and announced the establishment of a military-led provisional government. However, the sincerity of O'Duffy's plans have been doubted. They were described as a "drunken dry run" which were conjured "late at night up in the Phoenix Park," but O'Duffy "got no support there at all and the civil service was totally loyal to whatever government was in, so it wasn't even a starter," argued Manning.[3]

Another indication of what was planned came from Peadar MacMahon, whose conversation with Richard Mulcahy in the 1960s is reproduced below:

> MacMahon: Did you know that Hugo [MacNeill] and a few others were going to take over the government before Fianna Fáil came in?
>
> Mulcahy: Were they? From whom?
>
> MacMahon: From FitzGerald as M[inister] for Defense but I think he was laid up. They were making preparations in the Curragh. Blythe I think was acting Minister [for Defense]. I told Blythe about this. He was going to sack MacNeill before he saw him. Michael Brennan was there too; he was Adjutant General at the time. I don't know what he said to MacNeill but he wasn't sacked. Hugo was very unreliable ... he had made arrangements and had an armored car with Tony [Lawlor] in charge.
>
> Mulcahy: Was Tony in on this too?
>
> MacMahon: Oh yes.[4]

MacMahon misremembered several facts in his account. Blythe was not acting minister for defense at the time for example. Nor was Michael Brennan adjutant general in 1931. Irrespective of these errors, it appeared that a coup was potentially in the offing in late 1931. MacMahon's nephew wrote that "the only proof behind it is Peadar's word. MacNeill was never reprimanded by the Cabinet and Mulcahy had been a member of the Cabinet at that time. Yet Peadar was not the sort of man who spoke lightly of such matters."[5] If there was a conspiracy, support for it collapsed when O'Duffy and MacNeill indiscreetly canvassed senior officers who were staunchly opposed to the idea. This suggests that support for a military takeover was not very widespread, and the idea went nowhere.

From O'Duffy's perspective, he began to see himself as the strongman Ireland needed to stave off moral decay. As McGarry observed, it was a stroke of fate for de Valera that O'Duffy's loyal henchman Dan Hogan had resigned his position as chief-of-staff of the defense forces suddenly in February 1929 following an argument in which he had struck the minister for defense, Desmond FitzGerald.[6] Hogan would most likely have been a willing collaborator in an O'Duffy-led conspiracy. In May 1930, O'Duffy wrote a letter of recommendation for Hogan and drove him and his family to board a boat in Cobh bound for the United States, where they emigrated.[7] Hogan went on to mysteriously disappear in America in the early 1940s.

In late February 1932, the *Irish Press* reported that "two Cumann na nGaedheal ministers and others are to attempt to obstruct the transfer of power to Fianna Fáil."[8] Cosgrave emphatically denied the rumor. CnaG handed power over to FF in a courteous manner, given the bitterness of the election campaign and the unhealed wounds of the Civil War. Some anti-democratic army officers continued to take soundings for a prospective seizure of power even after FF assumed the reins of government. According to Lemass, Paddy O'Daly, by then retired from the army, urged army officers to revolt against the incoming government.[9] MacNeill canvassed for a coup d'état at a civil service *céilí* in the Mansion House on St Patrick's Day, 17 March 1932. When he approached Mulcahy about his plan, he was told "not to be an ass."[10] The peaceful transfer of power helped to cement Ireland's status as a functioning democracy.

FF formed a government on 9 March. Almost immediately, it introduced a bill to abolish the oath of allegiance. The Special Powers Act was withdrawn, which lifted the proscription of radical organizations like the IRA and Saor Éire, emptying the political wing of Arbour Hill prison. The new government was faced with the daunting task of organizing the World Eucharistic Congress in June, a major Catholic event to be hosted in Dublin. Cosgrave had called the election for February to provide his CnaG government with a renewed mandate in advance of the scheduled congress in June and the imperial conference in Ottawa in July.

In March, O'Duffy met with the new minister for justice, James Geoghegan, where they discussed his future service, an indication that de Valera was keen to remove O'Duffy from his position.[11] However, O'Duffy remained as garda commissioner for the short lifetime of the new government. The celebration in June of the real presence of Christ in the Eucharist has been regarded as an important milestone in reconciling both pro–Treaty and anti–Treaty sides of the Civil War on the grounds of a mutual Catholic faith.[12] Logistically, the event required massive preparation. It was recognized that the organizer should be a committed Catholic who understood the magnitude and reverence required in such a celebration of the Catholic faith. O'Duffy, who had acted as chief marshal of the "vast crowds" that attended Mass in the Phoenix Park in honor of the centenary of Catholic Emancipation in 1929, was considered an ideal candidate. His "magnificent organizing ability" was well known.[13] The garda commissioner had already been designated as the chief marshal of the Eucharistic Congress by Cosgrave and had begun preparations before FF entered government in March. President de Valera inherited the appointment.

The Eucharistic Congress attracted half a million faithful Irish Catholics. It was widely considered a successful display of Irish fidelity to the Catholic Church. "Church and State, priests and people, paid eloquent tribute to Commissioner O'Duffy, and through him to each and every member of the Garda for their magnificent work during those wonderful days and hours," his secretary recalled. Cosgrave, recently voted out of office, wrote to thank the chief marshal for carrying out his duties "courteously, efficiently and untiringly."[14] O'Duffy's "splendid work" received the special thanks of the Archbishop of Dublin, Edward Byrne.[15] O'Duffy undoubtedly appreciated the pomp and mummeries of the Eucharistic Congress. Five years later, in the court of General Franco, O'Duffy was asked about his experience of military command. He replied that he had commanded a million men at the Eucharistic Congress in 1932. "Franco merely smiled," recalled one witness.[16] In the aftermath of the congress, O'Duffy was apparently overlooked to receive an honorary papal title. That several FF ministers received such awards aroused suspicion with O'Duffy's secretary that the FF government had deliberately requested that the chief marshal not be bestowed with such an honor.[17]

◆ ◆ ◆

A week before the general election, a new association was founded on 9 February 1932 to represent the interests of army veterans. It was christened the Army Comrades Association (ACA). The society adopted a succinct set of aims; firstly, to uphold the state; secondly, to honor the IV men who died during the Anglo-Irish struggle, and eventually to raise a national memorial to them. Its objectives were completely uncontroversial. A distinguished IRA and National Army veteran, Colonel Austin Brennan from County Clare, was elected the first president of the ACA. He was a brother of Michael Brennan, chief-of-staff of the defense forces. But the figure who drove the fledgling organization was Commandant Ned Cronin from Charleville, County Cork who was elected its secretary. Cronin, the man behind the ACA, "became an absolute constant through all the transformations of the organization's identity."[18] A large farmer and an army veteran, Cronin joined the IRA in 1920, sided with the pro–Treaty faction and became a commandant in the Free State army. Opponents alleged that Cronin joined the IRA for cynical, self-serving motivations on the advice of "a well-known local politician," believing that "victory would bring the spoils of lucrative positions."[19]

On St Patrick's Day, the ACA held a public meeting in Wynne's Hotel in Abbey Street, Dublin. It was chaired by colonel and doctor Thomas F. O'Higgins, in place of Colonel Brennan who was ill. The meeting passed a resolution demanding that the recently elected FF government continue to provide preferential treatment to ex-soldiers.[20] The organization was to remain largely uncontroversial until a new leadership was elected in August 1932 which oversaw a transformation of the genteel veterans' lobby group into a full-fledged political movement. The widening agenda of the ACA was seen in a document it issued during the early period of the FF government. Its mission was now to "meet a National emergency" by opposing the attacks against "free speech" which were principally carried out by FF and IRA supporters. The ACA adopted a further resolution to "organize the young manhood of the country for disciplined public service in such a way as to secure a true expression of the national will in a revitalized State." It appealed to all able-bodied men and particularly the youth to act as "a worthy successor of the heroic soldiers of Ireland who through the generations asserted rights against her enemies within and without."[21] Its remit had expanded considerably since its formation.

The ACA became a rallying point for staunch opponents of the FF government, particularly due to the government's decision to cease the payment of land annuities to the British state. De Valera issued an executive decree, bypassing the CnaG-dominated senate, to withhold payments. However, the state continued to collect the sums from farmers, which were held in a special suspense fund. The anti-annuities campaign had first been mooted by socialist-republican Peadar O'Donnell and was taken up as an issue by de Valera while in opposition. The crippling impact of annuities and pensions payments on the Free State economy should not be understated. The Free State paid more to the British government in annuities and RIC pensions than Germany paid in war reparations. FF regarded it as unjust that the Irish people should repay debts for land which was originally seized from their ancestors by conquest. Lloyd George called de Valera "that pillar of salt who always looks to the past." The new policy was part of a strategy to achieve Irish self-sufficiency and reduce the dependence of Irish agriculture, the mainstay of the economy, on the British market. However, retaliatory British tariffs hobbled the Irish economy and signaled the outbreak of the "economic war." Briscoe, an FF supporter, recalled that "coal became as precious as diamonds" and "cattle roamed the fields not worth the killing, and the farmers could not pay their rates."[22] Struggling farmers opposed to FF's handling of the economic war flocked to join the ACA.

Initially a non-centralized body, the ACA depended on local initiative to grow. It adopted a quasi-military structure and members were expected to swear an oath to the organization. Dale Montgomery argued that the militaristic identity of the organization was "culturally specific," as it continued the militarism which was injected into Irish political culture during the War of Independence.[23] Taking this point further, one could characterize the ACA and the IRA respectively as a reassertion of Civil War culture. Just four men were required to form an ACA company, which was to be led by a captain, a vice captain, a secretary, and a treasurer. Three to four companies formed a district executive.[24] As the ACA developed in 1932–33, it attracted the interest of several CnaG politicians who saw political potential in it.

◆ ◆ ◆

In December 1932, it was reported that O'Duffy would soon resign as garda commissioner due to government pressure. This was denied by all sides.[25] The rumor stemmed from recent findings of an inquiry into O'Duffy's handling of an incident at Kilrush, County Clare. Two IRA officers, T.J. Ryan and George Gilmore, were shot by renegade guards in Kilrush with the tacit support of the upper echelons of the special branch. O'Duffy then tried to cover up the involvement of the local superintendent. Although the government denied it would remove O'Duffy, the department of justice built a corpus of evidence to be used to justify a future sacking of the garda commissioner.[26]

Towards the end of 1932, de Valera planned to call a general election for the new year to secure a mandate for his contentious annuities policy. The British government anticipated the minority FF administration would collapse, which left them stubbornly opposed to entering negotiations. The general election was held on 24 January 1933 under a tense political atmosphere, "one of the most bitter, turbulent, and colorful in the history of independent Ireland."[27] FF won 77 of 153 seats in the Dáil, a razor-thin majority. Cosgrave's party lost eight seats from the previous year's election. The agrarian National Center Party picked up 11 seats. Whilst it accepted the Treaty settlement, the Center Party wanted to move beyond Civil War divisions. As police commissioner, O'Duffy ensured law and order was upheld during the election campaign. On the day the FF government was re-elected, several English newspapers carried reports that O'Duffy would soon be sacked or resign. The IRA had been baying for his resignation for over a year and pressured FF to rid themselves of this turbulent commissioner.[28]

On 22 February, O'Duffy received a telephone call at his office in the Phoenix Park depot from the cabinet secretary who conveyed a request from President de Valera to meet O'Duffy at three o'clock. O'Duffy left in a hurry, leaving his office scattered with files. He went directly to de Valera's office, where Patrick Ruttledge, the minister for justice, was present. The president bluntly told O'Duffy that the cabinet had decided to make certain changes in the coming administration and this would involve a change in commissioner. De Valera told O'Duffy that his decision was irrevocable and urged him to accept another post with the board of public works as controller of prices at a salary of £1,300 per annum.[29] O'Duffy was stunned and rejected the offer of alternative employment. He cited his record during the Eucharistic Congress and his handling of the recent general election as evidence of his service to the FF administration. However, de Valera was not interested in haggling with O'Duffy. He had made up his mind that O'Duffy must go. De Valera acknowledged that O'Duffy's work was perfectly satisfactory, but that "owing to the nature of the duties which he anticipated the Police would likely be called upon to carry out, he thought that O'Duffy's position would be difficult."[30] Colonel Ned Broy was earmarked as his replacement.

At 41 years old, he was made redundant from a role which meant far more to him than any ordinary job. After 11 years in the force, the bachelor O'Duffy was left with little else in life. Decades of overwork had prematurely aged him (his unhealthy relationship with alcohol and cigarettes also took its toll). On 2 March 1933, he left his former residence at the garda depot and moved to an apartment at 2 Wilton Place in Dublin city. His future secretary acknowledged that whilst O'Duffy was humiliated, he was not "broken in spirit."[31] The day after his unceremonious dismissal, Irish newspapers reported on the "sensational decision" which left Ireland "startled." As the *Irish Independent* explained, O'Duffy had been,

> an outstanding figure in the public life of the country.... It is not as a promoter of athletics, or as an officer in the struggle against the British, and later as one of the high command in the National Army, that his name is most familiar to the public. He has been the head of the first police force under an Irish Government. The Garda Síochána has won unstinted praise on all sides for its efficiency and impartiality. The success of that force has been the work of General O'Duffy more than any other man.

The decision to remove him in such an abrupt manner was interpreted as an insult to the legacy of Kevin O'Higgins, who had appointed O'Duffy to head the new force "with characteristic astuteness." It was ironic considering O'Higgins' plans to remove O'Duffy shortly before his death. O'Duffy was described as "highly popular with all members of the Garda, in the welfare of which he took a deep interest." It was noted that "all ranks will deeply regret his removal from office."[32]

The sacking of the man who was viewed as indelibly associated with the Garda Síochána led to "a good deal of uneasiness throughout the country." The erstwhile police chief was "a man to whom the people have learned to trust." An editorial in the *Dundalk Democrat* newspaper, claiming to speak on behalf of the public, reacted to the dismissal on 25 February:

> We thought it was generally recognized that the country had been fortunate in finding a man of his type and quality to fill a difficult and responsible post. As far as the public is concerned, we think it is recognized. What has prompted the Government to remove him from his high office, without any reasons assigned, we do not know. Nobody has suggested that General O'Duffy has failed in his duty. There is a feeling in some quarters that his earlier association with the political party now in opposition may have something to do with his removal....
>
> Nowhere is feeling in this matter stronger than in County Monaghan, General O'Duffy's native place. The people of the county are proud of him as a distinguished son of a county that has produced many distinguished men. The feeling is as strong amongst people who did not share or sympathize with his early political work in the country, as amongst those who did. So far as published information leads them to believe, they feel that a Monaghan man has been harshly treated. And if this feeling is not to influence the political future of the country, the sooner the matter is publicly discussed, in all its bearings and details, the better.

A satisfactory explanation from the government was not forthcoming. This simply added to speculation that "a good servant of the State" had been penalized for the supposed crime of having "served as loyally an earlier and duly constituted Government."[33] His reputation with the public soared. Even some FF supporters like Margaret Mary Pearse, the sister of Patrick Pearse, wrote to O'Duffy to express her regret over his dismissal.[34]

Despite its intention to dismiss the garda commissioner had it won re-election, CnaG saw the sacking as evidence that FF's agenda was to penalize pro-Treaty servants of the state. The Center Party saw O'Duffy's removal as a dark omen of FF's attitude towards law and order. Both the Center Party and CnaG speakers at public meetings were heckled, jostled, and in some cases assaulted by republicans. There was a growing suspicion among the opposition that a blind eye was being turned to forceful suppression of their freedom of speech. In March, James Dillon, a TD for the Center Party, argued that O'Duffy was at least owed an explanation "so that in common justice his name could be vindicated." A motion in the parliament demanding an explanation was defeated by FF, with Labor deputies abstaining.[35]

The ACA began to act as defenders of CnaG meetings. Dr T.F. O'Higgins, a CnaG deputy, was elected president of the association in August 1932. His ascendency brought several CnaG politicians into the ACA, which they hoped could provide sufficient muscle to stave off disruptions of their meetings. As president, O'Higgins oversaw a policy challenging the IRA's activities, particularly their campaign which targeted opposition meetings under the slogan of "No Free Speech for Traitors." He declared:

> As an organization we do not desire to meddle in politics, but we must be permitted to say that we regard as charged with extremely dangerous potential the new fashion of branding as traitors certain public men with whom we happen to have had the privilege of being associated in defense of the state. Should an Irishman come to harm as a result of "traitor pointing" the consequences may be a deplorable condition of reprisal and counter-reprisal which would bring discredit on our race.... We shall deem it our bounden duty to resist any counter-attempts to interfere with free speech or the free expression of opposition.[36]

A former ACA member later explained that his primary motivation in joining the association was to do something about the problem of opposition meetings being broken up by the IRA. "We only wore the blue shirts so we wouldn't be beating the heads off our own if things got a bit lively."[37] The first appearance of the distinctive blue shirt was at a convention of the ACA in County Kilkenny on 8 April 1933. The previous year there had been a confrontation in Trim, County Meath where two groups of ACA members misidentified each other as meeting disruptors, leading to internecine violence. It was decided by the organization's leadership that a uniform of some kind must therefore be adopted.[38] This would also produce comradeship by obscuring class divisions based on the quality of attire worn by ACA members. Part of O'Duffy's agenda was "the abolition of class consciousness."[39] Blue was proposed by Ernest Blythe. The ACA thus adopted its distinctive uniform, "the blue shirt and black beret," the wearing of which would "both stimulate recruiting and improve discipline."[40] Henceforth, the ACA acquired the nickname "the Blueshirts."

Blue was supposedly chosen due to its association with St Patrick. O'Duffy told members of the Blueshirts on 17 March 1934: "You have taken the cross of St Patrick for your shield and his blue as your color ... you will in every act and word be true always to the noble traditions of your race, of which St Patrick is the patron."[41] The symbology spoke to a deeper, Christian Gaelic tradition. Blythe championed the use of St Patrick as a symbol, which was "comparable to [Jacques Doriot's] personification of Joan of Arc in the mythological past of the French *Parti Populaire Français*," according to Mike Cronin.[42] The ACA also adopted the *gormán* as an emblem of the organization, the Irish translation of the cornflower. Blythe admitted the English name was "not so appropriate as its Irish name."[43]

The removal of O'Duffy as garda commissioner dovetailed with an increasingly violent and bifurcated political culture. The opposition frequently pointed to

O'Duffy's dismissal as evidence that the government was running roughshod over the laws of the land. Former attorney general John A. Costello pointed out that "the section of the 1924 Civic Guard Act, under which General O'Duffy was removed from office…, had been repealed in 1925, and that consequently his removal was illegal."[44] After 11 years as garda commissioner, O'Duffy decided in March that he would make preparations for "a long Mediterranean cruise" towards the end of the month.[45] His vacation took him to the Middle East, where he attended the Divine Liturgy of the Greek Orthodox Church on Easter Sunday (Pascha) in Alexandria, Egypt. He then traveled to the Holy Land before coming back to Ireland via Europe, stopping off at Trieste, Venice, and Paris. His secretary recalled his "stories of this delightful tour" proved he was "a sharp observer" of culture and heritage.[46] His month and a half sojourn abroad lasted until 15 May, when he returned to the port of Dún Laoghaire in south Dublin. When asked if he had any plans about his future, he replied that he had not. Those who turned out to greet him were generally supporters from NACA.[47]

In mid–May, the former commissioner conferred with President de Valera over the steps the government would take to provide him with a pension. He did not receive his pension until March 1934, over a year after his sacking as police chief.[48] It was understood that de Valera once more offered O'Duffy alternative government employment, "but the General is believed to adhere to his original decision that if the Government did not want him as Commissioner of the Garda he would prefer to retire from public employment."[49] Having returned to Ireland from his trip abroad, his secretary wrote that O'Duffy was soon "drawn, willy-nilly, into the vortex of politics which he loathed, and of which he had already been a victim."[50]

In July 1933, O'Duffy returned to Dublin from a brief excursion to Bundoran in Donegal. At this stage, O'Duffy was restive and desirous of a new project to sink his teeth into. His reputation and prestige among the Irish public was extremely high. He was invited by several members of CnaG who had already joined the ACA to become a member of the organization with an eye to taking over its presidency. Blythe and T.F. O'Higgins supported the plans to utilize O'Duffy's immense popularity and reputation as a competent organizer to launch a new campaign against FF. The *Irish Press* reported on 18 July that O'Higgins was anxious to allow O'Duffy to become president of the ACA. It claimed the ACA would be reorganized under his prospective presidency to include "a greater reference to the Athletic Revival, in which General O'Duffy has played a big part." It speculated that should O'Duffy reject the offer to become president, that Ernest Blythe was the most likely second choice.[51] Considerable cajoling encouraged O'Duffy to assume the leadership. He later claimed that O'Higgins, Blythe and others "went on their knees to me appealing to me to take over the ACA."[52]

O'Duffy assented to his name going forward for the presidency. On 21 July, he was elected the new leader of the ACA at a special meeting in the ballroom of Dublin's Royal Hibernian Hotel, Dawson Street. He was loudly cheered as he entered the room. He was escorted to the platform by Gearóid O'Sullivan, then an opposition deputy, which caused the cheering to grow in volume and intensity. T.F. O'Higgins, the outgoing president, in his speech stated that he was looking for a successor due to mounting political duties, and "when he was hoping that a miracle would happen and that on the horizon would appear a suitable head of the organization, Providence and incidentally President de Valera took a hand in the game." This prompted an uproar of laughter and applause. Laurence O'Neill, an independent politician aligned with FF, sarcastically echoed the sentiment, telling the Senate in August 1933: "lo! A star appeared on the political horizon, a Daniel come amongst them, and they elected as their chief, General O'Duffy."[53]

At the special meeting which saw O'Duffy elected, the ACA voted to change its name to the National Guard. Before this name was settled upon, O'Duffy made the unusual proposal that the standard spelling of "comrades" could be substituted for "komrades" for added effect and to give the organization the more striking acronym AKA.[54] In choosing the name National Guard, O'Duffy derailed government plans to launch a new volunteer reserve of the army which it intended to call the National Guard. It hoped this reserve force would attract young Irishmen to its ranks who may otherwise be tempted to join the IRA.[55] The National Guard created a new executive leadership position for O'Duffy, that of director-general.

In his speech to the newly rechristened National Guard, O'Duffy stated:

> I am not the nominee of any political party. I never had, and have not now, any association or interest in any political party. As Commissioner of the people's police force, I have administered the laws as passed on to me by the Government chosen by the people. It is because I see in the members of your Association the class of material which can be molded into a great national organization, which can and, please God, will raise the youth of this country above the bitterness of mere party politics, that I have answered the call.

He claimed the National Guard would never become subordinated to a political party, despite its unofficial alignment with CnaG. O'Duffy's non-political stance indicated his disillusionment with the party system generally. As the Blueshirts grew it developed its own distinctive political mythology and associated heroes and martyrs. It organized commemorations for the dead of the Civil War, such as the National Army soldier, Robert Barry, who died in 1922. In his speech, Ned Cronin eulogized Barry as one who was "called a traitor because he donned the uniform of Ireland's first army.... They should remember that the men who called Robert Barry a traitor ... were to-day calling Blueshirts traitors."[56] However, Joe Lee noted that in contrast with FF, the Blueshirts were ineffective in marshaling Irish history for political purposes. O'Duffy was "an amateur compared with so professional a manipulator of the past as de Valera."[57]

O'Duffy announced his priority was to achieve the unification of the country, north and south. He sidelined the issue of whether or not a republic should be declared and confessed that he had been "sorely disappointed by the lack of interest in the Northern position taken in the Free State." He claimed that intra-party divisions were stymying effective action being taken to end partition and explained that "there was only room for one national organization in the six counties, and to be effective, it must be part of a very important part—of an all-Ireland movement extending from Antrim to Cork." He continued, "the partition of Ireland was built on a rotten foundation, and could not very long withstand a steady, concentrated effort from both sides. The hard-headed businessmen of the North would not be fooled indefinitely by politicians and placeholders." He asked the delegates to "go back to your districts, each one feeling that the honor of the National Guard rests on him alone. Work constantly, cheerfully, and fearlessly to build up its reputation. Guard that reputation jealously. My last word to you is to resolve to be faithful to the National Guard and to Ireland." The speech led to a standing ovation and cheering.[58]

The National Guard was a departure from the conservatism of the Cosgrave years. O'Duffy represented a militaristic strand of pro-Treaty nationalism mostly associated with Collins. He openly expressed his disappointment with the CnaG government's lackluster northern policy. His speech's non-political nature was partly an effort to forge a distinctive identity for the Blueshirts. However, it also indicated his growing disaffections with the political party system, which he came to see as a festering wound infecting the Irish body politic.

Under O'Duffy's leadership, associate membership of the Blueshirts was opened to women who eventually made up over a quarter of its membership. They were termed the "Blue Blouses."[59] It continued to restrict membership to "all citizens of Irish birth or of Irish parentage who profess the Christian faith." This precluded Jewish involvement with the National Guard. The Jewish community were concerned by the rise of the National Guard, which appeared to emulate the style if not

**Director-General of the League of Youth (Blueshirts), Eoin O'Duffy, seated at his desk, 14 June 1934 (courtesy the National Library of Ireland).**

the substance of continental anti-Semitic movements. One Jewish leader in Dublin wrote to Blythe to seek clarification on whether the Blueshirts were against the Jews. Blythe "completely disavowed any association" with anti-Semitism.[60] However, Jewish fears increased when O'Duffy was quoted as saying that "Jews were the instigators of Communism" as grounds to restrict membership of the National Guard to Christians. O'Duffy denied the accuracy of the report, claiming the comment was made during a general conversation about Russia and that he "had not the Free State Jews in mind when speaking of Communism."[61] Approximately 60 Dublin Jews called on General O'Duffy on 3 August 1933 to voice their concerns. He assured them "that he was not against Jews generally, and that, with one notable exception, no Jews had anything to do with Communism." The exception was presumably Karl Marx. The Jews were reportedly "quite satisfied" by his explanation.[62] Blythe further denied the Blueshirts were "Nazi or anti-Semite." Whilst he noted that the National Guard was distinctly and identifiably a Christian movement, he wrote "it is not out to persecute, injure or attack those who are not Christians."[63] Members of "secret societies," such as the Freemasons, were also ineligible for membership of the Blueshirts.

The National Guard's newly adopted objectives under O'Duffy's leadership are reproduced below:

> To promote the reunion of Ireland.
>
> To oppose Communism and alien control and influence in national affairs, and to uphold Christian principles in every sphere of public activity.
>
> To promote and maintain social order.
>
> To make organized and disciplined voluntary public service a permanent and accepted feature of our national life, and to lead the youth of Ireland in a movement of constructive national action.
>
> To promote the formation of coordinated national organizations of employers and employed which, with the aid of judicial tribunals, will effectively prevent strikes and lock-outs, and harmoniously compose industrial differences.
>
> To co-operate with the official agencies of the State for the solution of such pressing social problems as the provision of useful and economic public employment for those whom private enterprise cannot absorb.
>
> To secure the creation of a representative national statutory organization of farmers, with rights and status sufficient to ensure the safeguarding of all agricultural interests in all revisions of economic and political policy.
>
> To expose and prevent corruption and victimization in national and local administration.
>
> To awaken throughout the country a spirit of combination, discipline, zeal, and patriotic realism which will put the State in a position to serve the people efficiently in the economic and social sphere.
>
> To promote the Irish language and all that is best in the national tradition.
>
> To encourage athletics and other physical fitness of our people.

The program of the National Guard incorporated elements of corporatism, which was endorsed by the Catholic Church in the encyclicals of Pope Leo XIII's *Rerum Novarum* and Pius XI's *Quadragesimo Anno*. The Blueshirts hoped to submerge class strife to the "national interest." O'Duffy claimed the Blueshirts had "done more to break down class distinction than any existing or previous organization in this country."[64] O'Duffy hoped corporatism could "create unity among the workers" and "would create national unity and enable the whole community to progress towards national prosperity at a rate utterly impossible under present conditions."[65] The strongly anti-communist and pro–Christian aspects of the program were typically right-wing. Whether the Blueshirts was a fascist organization or not has been repeatedly debated and contested. Its leadership aside, the ordinary membership prioritized their agricultural self-interest over adherence to far-right ideology.

In addition to offering an idealized alternative to class strife, corporatism (or vocationalism) was presented as a third way between Marxism and capitalism. It was more than simply a way of ordering a political economy, but also envisioned sweeping changes to society. A definition of both social corporatism and political corporatism is offered by Antonio Costa Pinto. He explained that at the social and economic level, a corporatist system would organize social and economic interests in society into a limited number of singular, compulsory, non-competitive, hierarchically ordered and functionally differentiated categories. Each is recognized (if not created) by the state and ceded a representational monopoly within their respective categories in turn for their observing certain limits on their selection of leaders and articulation of demands. It aimed to promote class collaboration: O'Duffy wrote, "the people of Ireland include the capitalist as well as the worker, the farmer as well as the industrialist, the farm-laborer as well as the factory worker."[66] State-licensed corporations would equally represent employers and workers in particular sectional economic areas with the state as the final adjudicator. At the political level, corporatism envisaged the establishment of a system of political representation based on an "organic-statist" view of society in which its organic units (families, local powers, professional associations and interest organizations and institutions) would replace the individual-centered electoral model of representation and parliamentary legitimacy. This system would become the primary and/or complementary legislative or advisory body of the ruler's executive.[67]

The Blueshirts adopted the trappings of European fascism including military-style uniforms, public marches, a straight-armed fascist salute, and the cry "Hoch O'Duffy!" (Hail O'Duffy!). The Blueshirts have often been considered "para-fascist," according to Roger Griffin's typology of fascism, in the sense that they combined elements of outward fascism but were distinguished by conservatism, authoritarianism and indigenous nationalism.[68]

Historian Mike Cronin profiled the social make-up of the Blueshirts. An archetypical recruit had a Free State army background and was a farmer's son. O'Duffy described the National Guard as "an organization of poor men and boys. Its members were farmers' sons and laborers and town workers, many of them unemployed."[69] Some recruits came from outside the pro–Treaty gene pool. Augustine "Gus" Fitzpatrick from Naas, County Kildare, threw his lot in with the Blueshirts after O'Duffy became director-general. Fitzpatrick soon became "one of the most foremost and most active members" in Naas where he served as second-in-command of the local company. His background was firmly republican. Having served in the anti–Treaty IRA during the Civil War, he later supported FF in the 1933 general election.[70] It was significant that O'Duffy could attract men like Fitzpatrick to his banner. However, he exaggerated his appeal to republicans. He claimed to have brought

500 men from the IRA into the Blueshirts, a claim which was mocked by the minister for justice who retorted that "at that rate of absorption there must be practically no members of the IRA who are not members of the [Blueshirts]," implying the IRA was infinitesimal.[71] According to his secretary, O'Duffy helped bring people into the pro–Treaty movement which CnaG "never dreamed possible."[72] The widespread social phenomenon of the Blueshirt movement was noted by an American journalist in Ireland, who found the streets of Cork in late August 1933 "thronged with hefty young men (and a few old ones, too) wearing Blue Shirts."[73]

◆ ◆ ◆

A poem published in the pro–CnaG newspaper, *The United Irishman*, in August 1933 presents a window into the thinking behind the formation of the National Guard:

> With the Communist leanings of Fianna Fáil
> And the Soviet measures brought into the Dáil,
> It was high time this perilous trend to retard,
> So the nation cried out for the National Guard.
>
> When the right of free speech was endangered last year,
> 'Twas the ACA rescued it, knowing no fear;
> It is needful to check the Bolshie methods ill-starred
> And the ACA now is the National Guard.
>
> It will stand 'twixt the people and Communist teaching,
> All the doctrines that Bolshevik leaders are preaching;
> Which dear Éire's stout struggle for freedom have marred;
> Yes, the Saorstát is safe with the National Guard.[74]

FF supporters and the IRA bitterly opposed the formation of the National Guard. After one meeting a "crowd of a dozen young men" jeered at "the men in blue shirts" and scuffles broke out. Police separated the two groups.[75] Republicans claimed the National Guard was a front for British imperial interests and was funded by "British money to enable them to carry on their anti–Irish activities."[76] However, the Northern Irish government viewed the National Guard as indistinguishable from radical republicans. It was immediately proscribed by Sir Richard Dawson Bates, the minister for home affairs. O'Duffy reported that the National Guard's headquarters had been inundated with enquiries from northern nationalists, who saw "a ray of hope that the movement may bring unity of effort for an all–Ireland organization pledged to end the unnatural boundary." He considered the fact the National Guard had so quickly fallen foul of the Northern draconian public order laws to be an honor, "the young National Guard has received its national baptism." General O'Duffy was pleased to report that the aspect of the National Guard's platform most heavily endorsed by Southern delegates at its conference was its position on partition. On 8 August, northern authorities arrested Richard Mulcahy in Belfast, mistaking him for O'Duffy. When the error was realized, the CnaG deputy was released.[77]

As director-general, O'Duffy aimed to recruit 100,000 members by the end of 1933. By July 1933 he claimed there were already 25,000 Blueshirts. Political education was important for the National Guard and members were expected to be "versed in our policy and will be quite capable of diffusing it amongst our people."[78] However, it was unclear what the exact ideology of the Blueshirts was. An influx of intellectuals soon tried to provide the organization with greater philosophical sophistication. Soon after assuming the leadership of the Blueshirts, O'Duffy commenced an "organizing drive" across the country which focused initially on the south. He was described as being "full of enthusiasm" as he set out on this three-week "period of very intensive organizing work."[79]

His new position required that he relinquish the presidency of NACA. Although he explained that "the National Guard will be run on strictly non-political lines" he acknowledged "it may eventually take political form by appealing to the electorate on its own policy as against that of all existing parties."[80] It was also heavily linked in the public mind to CnaG. However, Frank MacDermot urged Blueshirts to join the Center Party as the only party interested in "giving increased political power to agricultural interests" and promoting the reunification of Ireland "as a question dwarfing all other constitutional questions."[81] O'Duffy was seen by CnaG politicians as "a man who got things done and would be capable of confronting an enemy." In private correspondence between CnaG politicians, positive comparisons between O'Duffy with European counterparts abounded. He appeared to be a prospective leader capable of breathing new life into the ailing party. Even Cosgrave acknowledged in May 1933 there was a "growing belief that Cumann na nGaedheal is finished." Party membership subscriptions were drying up, it had lost seats in the recent election, and their remaining supporters were increasingly demanding the party take a more strident stand against the FF government.[82] The only movement associated with pro–Treaty nationalism with any vibrancy was the Blueshirts.

◆ ◆ ◆

In the Blueshirts, O'Duffy found new allies and collaborators who provided an intellectual gravitas to the new movement. Foremost was Ernest Blythe, the erstwhile minister for finance and the successor to Kevin O'Higgins as Free State vice president. Blythe, an intellectual who became interested in fascist ideas, helped to inject the Blueshirts with his corporatist ideology. Many former CnaG politicians were enthused by the rise of European fascism and adopted elements of fascist doctrine in their own thinking. Desmond FitzGerald, a self-described Thomist, became more militantly anti-communist and far-right during the 1930s.[83] Blythe's ideological crusade was aided by a Blueshirt "brain trust" of James Hogan and Michael Tierney, academics in University College Cork and University College Dublin respectively. They were "more sophisticated" advocates of corporatism than O'Duffy.[84]

Tierney came from a small farming background in Galway and became a scholar of Greek. In his 1920 treatise *Education in a Free Ireland*, Tierney argued an independent Ireland must become "not only the Gaelic state of the past, but the Christian state of the future." He synthesized Catholic social teaching with a respect for modern technology whilst still harkening back to the imagined glories of Gaelic antiquity. The clique of Catholic intellectuals who flocked to the Blueshirts were au fait with the debates on distributism in the Anglophone world as pioneered by G.K. Chesterton and Hilaire Belloc. Tierney, although an early admirer of Mussolini, preferred the Austrofascist system of Dollfuss by 1934.[85] He saw Ireland under FF as succumbing to atomization and class warfare, along the lines of "Godless" cities in England. Desmond FitzGerald agreed that there was a burgeoning crisis in the Irish Free State, contrasting his country with the "spirit of Italy" under Mussolini where "even the humblest road worker felt that he was working for not merely so many pounds a week, but that he was working for the glory of Italy." FitzGerald and Tierney were particularly inspired by the corporatist systems of Italy under Mussolini and Portugal under Salazar.[86] In UCD, he represented a conservative tendency; whilst his antithesis, Daniel Binchy, represented a more liberal tendency.

Even W.B. Yeats was swept up with enthusiasm for the Blueshirts. The Anglo-Irish poet had penned Casandra-like warnings about communism since the time of the Russian Revolution. He was appointed to the Free State senate during Cosgrave's government. An outspoken elitist and anti-egalitarian, Yeats believed de Valera should face a "Fascist opposition" manned by "the despotic rule of the educated classes" which would be "the only end to our troubles." Yeats claimed responsibility for proposing the red saltire on a field of blue as the flag of the Blueshirts.[87] At one point, Yeats hoped to play the role of theoretician in an Irish fascist government along the lines of Giovanni Gentile in Italy. He wrote that "democracy is dead and force claims its natural right.... That Ireland reacts from the present disorder is turning its eyes towards individualist Italy." Like Mussolini, Yeats shared a strong affection for the writings of Italian philosopher Giambattista Vico. In the summer of 1933, Yeats was infatuated with the Blueshirt movement and was enthusiastic about O'Duffy's leadership. He even composed three marching songs for the Blueshirts.[88] One included the lyrics "What is equality? Muck in the yard: Historic nations grow, from above to below."[89]

The poet met General O'Duffy on 24 July 1933 at the instigation of Dermot MacManus, a wounded former British army officer who became a Free State officer. Yeats and MacManus were often seen "gloating in the Kildare Street Club over the prospects of a really virile fascist Irish State."[90] The meeting was not particularly successful or productive. Yeats was far too much of an abstract intellectual for O'Duffy. Meanwhile, Yeats described O'Duffy in the aftermath of the meeting as "an uneducated lunatic."[91] Writing to Olivia Shakespear, Yeats was slightly more generous: "I did not think him a great man though a pleasant one, but one never knows, his face and mind may harden or clarify."[92] Yeats' brief association with the Blueshirts ended and he retreated back to his intellectual castle in the air.

The Blueshirts intelligentsia looked towards the Vatican for philosophical succor. O'Duffy's speeches were often prepared by the traditional conservative right-wing. However, he remained "beyond their control" and occasionally went off script, taking a more stridently pro-fascist and anti-democratic stance.[93] In a press interview after becoming leader of the National Guard, when queried on whether the organization was fascist, he denied it was but added that if there was any good point in fascism, he would be prepared to adopt it.[94]

Examinations of the ideology underlining the Blueshirts have continued to blossom in recent studies. A 2021 article by Seán Donnelly sought to identify the intellectual origins of "Blueshirtism." He identified Michael Tierney, Michael Collins,

Ernest Blythe, and Desmond FitzGerald as "Irish Catholic intellectuals" who were "engaged deeply" in debates surrounding Catholic social teaching and doctrine.[95] The inclusion of Collins among this list is strange as he was not by any means an intellectual. Whilst Blythe undoubtedly impacted the Blueshirts' ideological course and even commended vocationalism as "recommended by the present Pope," he was not a Roman Catholic.[96] Unlike several other republicans from a Protestant background, Blythe never "swam the Tiber." He remained a lifelong Presbyterian.

Perhaps the most important contribution of Blythe to the Blueshirts was his attempt to revive pro–Treaty nationalism as a radical force capable of challenging FF. His political thinking became rather unorthodox in the 1930s. He coined the neologism "diast" to describe his political beliefs. David Fitzpatrick speculated that the "obscure term" may refer to either an acronym for "democratic Irish associative state," or else it was "a corruption of 'diaster,' a double star."[97] Blythe's diast theory included elements of corporatism. It envisioned the establishment of "a great national patriotic organization" termed the "Diastal Union" or "Diastal Association" which would vet prospective candidates in relation to elections. This "organic democracy," Blythe believed, would preserve the right of electors, but 90 percent of elected deputies would be chosen by "an organization constituting a mass communication of defense and guidance."[98] In May 1933, he worked on a publication, *The Diast: An Occasional Bulletin*, which argued "national progress is not possible unless a new type of organic or integrative state is created in the twenty-six counties." The new system of government would be "more suited to modern needs" and would combine "co-ordination and discipline, stability and leadership."[99]

Whilst the chief ideologues of the Blueshirts were clearly inspired by foreign developments, they publicly tried to position the growth of the Blueshirts as an organic phenomenon and one deeply rooted in Ireland's past. Blythe wrote in August 1933 that the National Guard was "purely the product of Irish needs and conditions" and denied it was fascist. Blythe placed the organization in the tradition of the Fenians, the Land League, the Gaelic League, the IV and SF.[100] It was predictable for the National Guard to try to find its own native tradition and trenchantly deny foreign influence. This was a common theme of fascist movements elsewhere. For example, Oswald Mosley claimed his party's use of the straight-arm salute was not inspired by fascism or Nazism but was an ancient form of address "used in early Britain many centuries before a Fascist Party was created in Italy."[101] When O'Duffy voiced opposition to parliamentary democracy, he denounced it as "un–Irish." In a statement of 8 August, he stated: "Every day it is becoming more and more detrimental to the best interests of the Irish people."[102] Criticism of parliamentary democracy was by no means alien to the thought of CnaG. Members of the party later sought to exaggerate their total commitment to democracy. In April 1933, the CnaG newspaper republished an article from the *English Review* by Harold Goad which heaped praise on Italian corporatism, though the "one criticism" from the editor was that the original article disregarded or minimized "the part played by the Fascist Party, which is undoubtedly the life-giving force of the whole system."[103]

Opponents of the Blueshirts strongly criticized its ideology as fascist and reactionary. In letters to the editor signed by Maud Gonne and John Sweetman, the

National Guards' pro-corporatist proposals were dismissed as reminiscent of "the old French system under Richelieu" which sought to "divide the commoners into classes." They urged the government to proscribe the Blueshirts.[104] At a speech in Clare in mid–August 1933, President de Valera criticized O'Duffy and those who claimed that parliamentary democracy was not Irish but who supposed that continental-inspired dictatorship was. He urged O'Duffy to read Irish history if he wanted to know what Irish opinion was on dictatorships.[105] The reference to "continental dictators" drew a rebuke from Mussolini himself, who expressed his disappointment, having "had a very pleasant talk with Mr de Valera when he was here [in May] … but his idea of me as a Dictator is wrong." Mussolini claimed he was "called by the people" and did not "impose myself by force on the people of Italy."[106]

With the arrival of a "well-respected, popular and dominant leader," it was customary within the Blueshirts to greet each other with a cry of "Hoch O'Duffy!" and a "Victory Salute." Detailed instructions were published in the Blueshirts' journal on how to perform the infamous salute:

> The right hand is to be swung up until it is in front and higher than the shoulder, with the palm facing forward and downward and until the arm is at an angle of forty-five degrees from the perpendicular. The fingers will be kept together fully stretched out with the thumb close to the forefinger. Care should be taken to ensure that the arm points straight forward and upward from the shoulder and that the hand is not carried to the left so as to be in line with the face, nor to the right so as to be outside the line of the body. The salute will always be given with the right hand.[107]

A 1934 photograph showed O'Duffy taking the salute from a large cohort of supporters, including Cosgrave and the Lord Mayor of Dublin, Alfie Byrne. Padraig Yeates wrote, in a memorable sentence, that Byrne appeared "more like a little boy asking permission to go to the toilet than a potential Irish strongman."[108] As director-general, O'Duffy engendered a significant personal loyalty within the organization, which Mike Cronin has argued was tantamount to a burgeoning personality cult. Much of O'Duffy's leadership style and substance carried on from techniques he had practiced as garda commissioner. He encouraged Blueshirts to establish a range of social initiatives including cycling, hiking, and sporting groups which carried out their activities in the open "as a way of demonstrating their force."[109]

◆ ◆ ◆

On 25 July 1933, General O'Duffy announced plans to lead a commemorative march to Leinster Lawn on 13 August in homage to Griffith, Collins, and O'Higgins—the holy trinity of Free State nationalism. It is highly disputed whether this march was planned simply as a commemoration or if O'Duffy intended to emulate Mussolini by launching a "March on Dublin." An annual parade to Leinster Lawn commemorating the three fallen Free State martyrs was a feature of public life under the Cosgrave government but was predictably discontinued when FF came to power in 1932.[110] O'Duffy's plans may have amounted to nothing more sinister than to reassert this lapsed element of pro–Treaty political culture. However, de Valera took no chances and moved quickly to prevent a potential putsch.

Two hundred pro–FF recruits were encouraged to join a new wing of the police force, the auxiliary special branch, which was nicknamed the "Broy Harriers" after O'Duffy's successor, Ned Broy. The nickname also referenced a well-known pack of hounds, the Bray Harriers.[111] This ramshackle division was hastily assembled by recruiting former anti–Treaty IRA men in just 48 hours before the planned 13 August march. The force was characterized by ill-discipline, a lack of training and an obstinate refusal to obey orders issued by "non–Harrier Garda officers."[112] *An Phoblacht* described the anti–Treaty IRA veterans who made up the ranks of the Broy Harriers as having been "seduced into accepting the Free State" by emphasizing "the menace of the Imperial-Fascist organization."[113]

Whether a coup d'état was afoot or not has remained unanswered in Irish historiography. De Valera's son, Terry de Valera, took umbrage with "modern revisionists" for allegedly trying to distort the historical record by downplaying the danger the proposed march presented to the youthful Irish democracy. He recollected that his father received intelligence from Captain Seán Brennan of the Broy Harriers and "other trusted sources" which warned that a coup d'état was imminent. The government mobilized the Broy Harriers and drew up plans for a heavy guard to take key positions along government buildings and installations. A "theoretical line" along Merrion Street was envisioned and orders were given for police "to open fire if the Blue Shirts should pass this line." The plans went unimplemented as the march never took place.[114] O'Duffy's secretary stated that Terry de Valera's claim was a "deliberate falsehood" and added that "like his father, he was careful not to try to substantiate it."[115]

Seán MacEntee, FF minister for finance, reflected: "We saw O'Duffy as a real danger to Parliament and State. We also saw it as a dangerous political plot by former Free State forces to overthrow the new Government. Some former [CnaG] deputies were Blueshirts and we saw an attempt at a coup d'état." MacEntee's daughter recalled how one summer afternoon she and her two siblings were "bundled into the State car" and driven to the official residence of the chief-of-staff of the defense forces, General Michael Brennan, in Phoenix Park. "My father and the General were closeted together in the General's study for what seemed hours. Even at the time I thought it was an oddly artificial afternoon; I am now virtually certain that we children were 'cover,' a 'front' for serious discussions relating to … the ACA's efforts in 1932–34 to subvert the (Free State) Army, and bring about the coup to which my father refers."[116]

Reflecting how grave the situation had become, de Valera's government passed a new firearms order which revoked the possibility of renewal for thousands of firearms certificates on the cusp of expiry. Civilian firearms were to be handed into the police. The government believed it faced threats from both the left and right, the IRA and the Blueshirts. The IRA was unhappy with the government's hesitation to declare a republic. Peadar O'Donnell suspected de Valera's "radicalism" amounted to little more than "a dated, narrow distaste for the symbols of political oppression" rather than a genuinely anti-capitalist agenda.[117] In late July 1933, firearms were seized from several prominent figures associated with the CnaG government, including Blythe, Mulcahy, O'Duffy and others. Blythe refused to surrender his firearm. On 29 July, special branch called at the former garda commissioner's home at Wilton Place to collect his Webley revolver and his automatic pistol.[118] When he refused to comply with the order, the guns were seized from him. One had belonged to Michael Collins, "who had it in his hand when he fell in ambush during the Civil War" according to one report. The gun was given to O'Duffy by Collins' sister "as a token of remembrance."[119] Gardaí were satisfied that he "has no good reason for requiring the firearm" and seized the gun.[120] The decision to take the personal firearms of senior pro–Treaty politicians was particularly controversial as they acquired such weapons for self-defense in the wake of O'Higgins' assassination. The president claimed, "that everybody who was not blind" could recognize the order was introduced due to the growth of "two forces [the IRA and National Guard], each of which would be used as an excuse for the growth and increase of the other." He further accused O'Duffy of wanting to install a dictatorship.[121]

De Valera publicly argued that the rationale underpinning the IRA's continued existence had dissolved when the oath of allegiance was removed by FF. "We are getting to the position of general acceptance here in Ireland of the principle that as the people were free to elect any Government they wanted without any barrier, that they could have a Republic if the majority declared for it; that there was no excuse whatsoever for the possession of arms." The IRA responded by accusing FF of being influenced by "pro–British elements." Republicans resented being lumped in with the National Guard, which they considered "a re-assembling of the Imperialists" who wanted to take power "to bind the Twenty Six Counties more firmly to British Imperialism."[122] The government cannily maneuvered to undermine both forces at a time when the IRA was weak and divided while the Blueshirts was new and only just finding its footing on the political terrain. The action was an unabashed effort to centralize state power under the new government's rule.

The state's policy was debated in the Dáil on 1 August. Deputy Frank MacDermot believed the "inquisitions" by FF were launched as a "kind of demonstration" to satisfy the clamoring of their supporters "to show their disapproval and dislike" of the Blueshirts. He asked rhetorically whether "the revolver of General O'Duffy was going to make all the difference as to whether the National Guard is a body formidable to this State or not formidable to this State?" Former agriculture minister, Patrick Hogan, criticized "this envenomed attack on General O'Duffy" and particularly the post-hoc rationalization that whilst the National Guard was "acting within the law at the moment ... they may go outside it." He denounced de Valera's claim to be a vindicator of democracy, stating: "I think there is more real nationality and democracy in General O'Duffy's little finger than in [de Valera's] whole body."[123]

Tensions rose in the lead up to the planned march of 13 August. It was planned that Dermot MacManus would be chief marshal. The marchers were to proceed past the Cenotaph on Leinster Lawn, where wreaths would be laid. They would then march to Glasnevin cemetery, where blue cornflowers would be laid on the three graves. Here, O'Duffy would deliver an oration at Collins' grave.[124] O'Duffy strongly rejected claims that the Blueshirts intended to stage a coup d'état, calling the rumors "obviously absurd."[125] A "humorous" piece of doggerel was published before the march in the National Guard's journal titled *A President's Soliloquy*:

Woe's the day!
My head is gone astray!
Ev'rything is blue!
I think I have the flu!
Blue Shirts light around my bed at night,
And at dawn they dance a fling in Leinster Lawn.[126]

On the eve of "the great National Guard parade," the Blueshirts gave every intention the march would proceed. The same day, the government proclaimed the event, invoking the Constitution (Amendment No. 17) Act 1931 which was passed by the Cosgrave government. The decision to ban the march was taken "after long and careful consideration" due to the National Guard's militarized formations and uniforms. Crucially, their "avowed aim … to destroy the existing parliamentary institutions" amounted to an attempt "to resort to violent means to attain this end," FF reasoned.[127] The left-wing *Irish Workers Voice* newspaper was critical of the government's decision to combat the National Guard by using coercive legislation and to place "the fight against fascism … in the hands of the police—the same whom O'Duffy has organized."[128] O'Duffy complied with the order of 12 August and canceled the parade in an effort to avoid the proscription of the National Guard itself. In an uncharacteristically magnanimous statement, O'Duffy declared that on such a "solemn and dignified occasion" as the anniversaries of Griffith, Collins, and O'Higgins, it would be inappropriate to provoke a "public disturbance which would dishonor our glorious dead."[129]

On the intended morning of the parade, the government ordered a force of Broy Harriers armed with 300 rifles and several machine guns to take positions across the city. This was despite the cancelation of the parade by O'Duffy.[130] The IRA similarly mobilized its Dublin Brigade in anticipation that the Blueshirts would proceed with their march and try to mount a takeover.[131] *An Phoblacht* claimed to have read a captured document which implicated a local division of Blueshirts in a scheme to covertly arm themselves with revolvers. They claimed this cast serious doubts over the Blueshirts' self-description as an "unarmed" and "non-military" organization.[132] The IRA leadership was keenly aware that the FF government had used the threat of the Blueshirts as a pretext to expand their own powers and suppress all "anti-constitutional" movements.

Maurice Manning acknowledged "we have learned little new about the abortive march to Leinster Lawn" in the years since the publication of his 1970 monograph. He acknowledged that "no evidence of any sort has emerged of the existence of plans by O'Duffy to seize power."[133] Fearghal McGarry argued it was "unlikely" that O'Duffy planned a coup d'état in August 1933, but recognized that the disorder and violence which inevitably would have arisen may have prompted the unpredictable General to launch a jumbled effort to seize power.[134] Manning argued there were "no plans for a coup d'état" and even if O'Duffy tried to seize power "it would have failed within days" due to opposition from constitutionalists in CnaG, who had longstanding misgivings about his judgment. Brian Hanley argued that if the march had proceeded successfully, it would have enhanced O'Duffy's reputation and caused his star to rise with all wings of pro–Treaty nationalist opinion.[135] There has been no new evidence to suggest a coup d'état was O'Duffy's intention.

The pro-CnaG *United Irishman* ascribed "the real reason" for the march's cancelation not in a sincere belief by FF "that General O'Duffy meant to seize Leinster House on Sunday, abolish the Oireachtas on Monday, and set up a Vocational Council in the following week-end," but rather an effort to avert public attention away from de Valera's admission that "the English market is gone forever" because of the economic war. "Each month of the Economic War does more damage than the last."[136] For its part, FF saw the Blueshirts as a fifth column which undermined the government's economic war stance. Addressing a public audience, the pro-FF lawyer, Thomas O'Donnell, claimed the opposition had "helped England to continue the economic war and they have made it almost impossible for our own government to carry through their full program of national development."[137] As O'Duffy sought to avoid a collision course with the government, he complied with the government's order. Nonetheless, there were still a few incidents on the day of the planned march. For example, two Blueshirts were attacked on O'Connell Street whilst on Parnell Street there were "several scuffles" between Blueshirts and the public.

Whether his prestige was negatively impacted by his compliance with the ban or not is debatable. O'Duffy estimated that the National Guard's membership had already swelled to 40,000 by August. Historian Mike Cronin described how under O'Duffy's leadership, membership numbers ranged from 30,000 to 50,000.[138] Although the banned parade was a setback, O'Duffy was not overly perturbed and vowed "no ban, no coercion will break us ... we put our trust in the rising generation of youth."[139] General O'Duffy exhibited a conservative streak which shunned the negative publicity associated with putschism. In remarks made near the anniversary of the cancelation of the march, O'Duffy indicated his sensitivity about the onlooking eyes of the international press:

> Notwithstanding the decision to call off the parade which was promptly announced in the public press, the Government pretended to believe that it would come off ... the press of the world were brought here, and press-cameramen to photograph the wild Irish in action, to picture the Blueshirts in bloody conflict with their comrades in the National Army.[140]

The cocksure leader of the Blueshirts predicted to a French journalist just days after the banned march that "we shall be masters of Ireland in three years."[141] It was an overly bold prediction but one which illuminated O'Duffy's growing hubris. Just eight days after the march's cancelation, the National Guard was proscribed by the FF government.

# 8

# In Politics

O'Duffy stubbornly refused to vacate his place in history. He had correctly predicted that the government's ban on the planned parade to Leinster Lawn would likely be followed by a ban on the National Guard itself. Should the government make such a move, he argued, then "every man and woman who remains a member must be arrested."[1] The government moved to ban the organization on 22 August. A military tribunal was set up by the minister for justice, Ruttledge, to prosecute cases related to membership of the "illegal society." The government had simply reconstituted the military tribunal which was last operational under Cosgrave's government. Upon learning the news, O'Duffy was short for words, stating simply: "I have nothing to say except that the National Guard awaits the verdict of the Irish people."[2]

Buoyed by the considerable spike in recruitment under his leadership, O'Duffy planned to defy the ban. He was egged on by the mainstream opposition parties, CnaG and the Center Party, which were both on the verge of agreeing to a political fusion. The Blueshirts embarked on "a winter of intense activity" which generated repeated acts of violence as political turmoil continued to grow.[3] Regular brawls broke out between Blueshirts, FF supporters and left-wingers. O'Duffy saw his political mission in messianic terms, arguing that the National Guard alone was equipped to "raise the Irish nation … out of the ignominy of party politics, out of the sectarianism, and out of the rot of Communism."[4] A contemporary laudatory poem also captured the apocalyptic tone: "Sure, Heaven above in our favor has wrought / we've a man who has suffered, who couldn't be bought! / We'll cleave to O'Duffy—he is God's own decree! / He will lead, and we'll follow—to Hell, if need be!"[5]

By a twist of fate, the banning of the Blueshirts allowed O'Duffy to enter the foreground of national politics. Before its proscription there were already indications that the National Guard was taking an increasingly political stance. The director-general acknowledged that Blueshirts "might be called upon to select candidates for elections" and that whilst no decision had been taken in this regard, the organization's constitution outlined "that elections might be contested where desirable."[6] In mid–August there were rumors that a general election would be called. It was reported that an unspecified "difference" between Cosgrave and O'Duffy prevented the two leaders from cooperating. O'Duffy replied, "there can be no split … where there is no unity."[7] He urged Blueshirts "associated with political parties" not to "drop out of ordinary political work" but instead to "endeavor to secure that the policy of the National Guard shall ultimately meet with universal acceptance."

The National Guard's attitude amounted to lobbying the mainstream parties and, in some cases, infiltrating newly established parties to "see that the new bodies are taken care of." Blueshirts were urged to "get in everywhere" and make their presence felt.[8]

By late August, the political atmosphere had become extremely tense in Ireland. O'Duffy more than Cosgrave appeared to personify the opposition to de Valera and his government. Illustrating the level of political bitterness, one local branch of FF passed a resolution calling on the government to refuse O'Duffy his state pension due to his involvement in the Blueshirts.[9] On the other side, CnaG politicians looked towards O'Duffy as a prospective unity candidate who could oversee the amalgamation of their moribund political party with the Center Party. O'Duffy had longstanding misgivings about how CnaG exercised power in the Free State, particularly Cosgrave's reluctance to exploit the Treaty settlement to achieve unification and greater independence from Britain. In a report from September 1924, he argued that ordinary people believed "now more than" before independence that Ireland was "in the grip of Freemasonry" and believed the country was "being controlled by the old gang in the interests of England." He emphasized that these were not the fringe views of republicans but were widely held among the public. He believed that the credibility of pro–Treaty nationalism had been diminished under CnaG.[10] When he learned of the 1923 ultimate financial settlement agreed between Cosgrave and the British government which "handed over millions of pounds to John Bull," he strongly opposed it.[11] O'Duffy represented a far more radical wing of pro–Treaty nationalism than Cosgrave.

Under FF's watch, the livelihood of farmers was increasingly hampered due to the economic war. Farmers were increasingly drawn to the Blueshirts, which offered a radical opposition to FF. The National Guard demanded immediate steps to relieve Irish farmers "from all liability for rates and annuities in the present year" 1933. The Blueshirts claimed they alone could "save [farmers] before they are overtaken by utter impoverishment and bankruptcy."[12] Inside the amorphous pro–Treaty movement there was a growing fear that FF was rolling back the progress made by the CnaG government in the first decade of Irish independence. They feared de Valera was willfully allowing anarchy to fester and overseeing the transformation of Ireland into a rogue state. The government's heavy-handed attitude towards the National Guard appeared to confirm pro–Treaty fears that de Valera had dictatorial tendencies. CnaG's party newspaper saw the banning of the National Guard as "a clear threat to the liberties of the people and the constitutional stability of the State." They feared the government could take "a small step further" and declare CnaG or the Center Party unlawful organizations. Although they recognized "some differences of opinion" between CnaG and the National Guard, particularly O'Duffy's "ideas on the question of constitutional reform," the newspaper thundered that it was "the duty of all to stand whole-heartedly by General O'Duffy's organization when it is being wrongfully attacked and persecuted."[13]

For politicians engaged in merger negotiations, the sudden arrival of O'Duffy was a wildcard. Those who wished to see "a new leader and a new style of leadership" arise from the talks looked to O'Duffy as one who could fulfill this role.[14] As has been noted in a recent work by Ciara Meehan and Stephen Collins, O'Duffy's reputation as a "patriot and state-builder" enabled him to be considered leadership material.[15] On 24 August, a deputation from CnaG arrived at a Blueshirts rally in Waterford. They urged O'Duffy to accept an invitation to join the negotiations to form a new political party. He claimed it was "only after lengthy deliberations and with great reluctance" that he agreed to participate. He later claimed it was "a serious mistake to have entered the merger."[16]

A meeting was held on 1 September at CnaG headquarters at 3 Merrion Square, Dublin. It involved Frank MacDermot of the Center Party and William Cosgrave, who interrupted a holiday in Connemara to hasten back to Dublin. O'Duffy was described in the press as "perhaps the busiest man in Ireland" owing to his commitment to "not only dealing with his own affairs" but keeping abreast of developments between the parties. During the negotiations, O'Duffy was flanked by his Blueshirt supporters, Dr T.F. O'Higgins and Commandant Ned Cronin.[17] O'Duffy and his allies were delighted with the night's developments. He prepared to continue the talks over the weekend whilst finding time to attend the all–Ireland hurling final at Croke Park on 3 September. Ernest Blythe was a key figure in engineering the inclusion of O'Duffy in the negotiations. Although he lost his Dáil seat in the general election, Blythe was more active in opposing the government outside parliament than when he had been an elected representative from Monaghan. The curious alliance between the former minister and the former garda commissioner was well noted in the press, who recalled "it is not so long ago since they were at daggers drawn on the question of cuts in the pay of the Garda."[18] Blythe's motivations have often been characterized as cynical. In a memorandum, he argued that CnaG would benefit from an influx of youthful Blueshirts who could be employed to engage in thankless electioneering duties. "It will never be possible to get responsible businessmen, middle-aged farmers or busy professional people to do such work."[19]

A merger between the three groups was widely anticipated. On 4 September, the minister for industry and commerce, Seán Lemass, derided the merger as the "cripple alliance," which lacked any substantial policy differences from CnaG except for the proposal that it would have a new leader. Lemass chided O'Duffy's corporatist ideology as reminiscent of the Soviet system in Russia.[20] Seán MacEntee gave full vent to the contradictions within the new movement by declaring he could not decide if Frank MacDermot, James Dillon and Ernest Blythe "were converting themselves into strong Republicans as Gen. O'Duffy said he was from 1917 to 1921" or if General O'Duffy had become a pro–British imperialist or crypto-unionist like his newfound political bedfellows.[21] These contradictions initially left the party bereft of policies and created insurmountable ruptures within the organization. Lemass found it incredible to conceive of how unity could be achieved in such a diffuse party where "a man like Mr Dick Mulcahy, an organizer of the IRB" could sit "side by side with Mr [Maurice] Dockrell, an ex–Unionist."[22]

◆ ◆ ◆

The new party was officially launched on 8 September 1933 when the negotiators agreed to the terms of the merger at a convention at the Mansion House. O'Duffy was to serve as president and leader of the party, despite his lack of a Dáil seat. Cosgrave became chairman of the party, parliamentary leader, and vice president. MacDermot and James Dillon were also included among the party's six vice presidents. Joe Lee argued that Cosgrave may have given way to O'Duffy, cognizant of his erraticism, on the understanding that his blunders would eventually "help [Cosgrave] re-establish his control" in the party.

The new party was to be known as Fine Gael (FG), with the subtitle the United Ireland Party. The confected dual name resulted from a compromise between the groups, as the Blueshirts and CnaG wanted an Irish title while the Center Party preferred the United Ireland Party, which was coined by MacDermot. The Center Party leader even said he would not have been prepared to join a party which used any other name. As leader, O'Duffy more often used the name United Ireland Party than FG. His reputation as a linguistic nationalist aside, O'Duffy displayed a greater interest in using English-language names for his organizations including the Young Ireland Association, League of Youth, and the National Corporate Party. He was criticized by hardline republicans for christening the new entity the United Ireland Party, thus sacrificing the last vestiges of outward Irishness in CnaG, its Gaelic language name.[23] The name Fine Gael drew together a modernized spelling of "Gaedheal," while "Fine" is a slightly archaic word meaning a tribe.[24]

The *Irish Press* reported that MacDermot had been severely outmaneuvered in the negotiations. It described O'Duffy's new role as providing a "means of escape from the awkward situation he had created for himself" as leader of the proscribed National Guard.[25] A pro-republican newspaper printed a joke about how a snake, representing O'Duffy, "was discovered on the roadside of Scotshouse, County Monaghan. When approached it wriggled into a ditch. The reptile is supposed to have fallen from a lorry laden with foreign fruit."[26] This was meant to portray the extent to which O'Duffy had slithered away from illegal paramilitarism towards constitutional politics whilst also alluding to his flirtation with foreign ideologies.

The party's foundation was described contemporaneously by the *Daily Mail* as the most important political development in the Irish Free State for many years. The National Guard was renamed the Young Ireland Association (YIA) and was integrated into FG as its youth wing. The cult of youth was a prominent theme of O'Duffy's outlook. Under an FG government, a state-sponsored youth movement was envisioned, along the lines of the Italian *Balilla* or German *Hitlerjugend*.[27] In addition to being president of FG, O'Duffy remained director-general of the YIA. It was a remarkable ascent for O'Duffy, who had served the FF government as garda commissioner at the beginning of 1933 and by the year's end had assumed the mantle of leader of the opposition to the same government.

Initially, FG was light on policy proposals. Its earliest manifesto spoke of a desire to oversee the "voluntary re-union of the Irish nation" but chastised FF's "double-faced policy of retaining the present constitutional position, and at the same time discarding its advantages."[28] This reflected the party's compromise policy of agitating for a united Ireland but maintaining membership of the British Commonwealth. This sentiment was alien to O'Duffy's longstanding militancy on the question of partition and his instinctive republicanism. His acquiescence to such a policy was the result of an uneasy trade-off. He justified this stance on the basis that "the only real alternatives before the Irish people are the reunion of Ireland on our present status, or the declaration of a republic for twenty-six counties."[29] Differences between the new political bedfellows were incisively identified by the *Irish Press*. Party members held divergent views on the use of the tricolor as the national flag and Amhrán na bhFiann as the national anthem.[30]

Perhaps in exchange for his support on a Commonwealth retentionist policy, O'Duffy ensured that corporatism became part of FG's platform. He described corporatism as based on "Christian truths and teachings" as outlined in papal encyclicals which tried to provide a Catholic solution to the social questions spawned by the industrial revolution.[31] O'Duffy was said to be "the only one who showed enthusiasm" for corporatism; Cosgrave, MacDermot, James Dillon "and other prominent figures displayed much less interest."[32] However, prominent politicians like Blythe and FitzGerald were proponents of corporatism. Outwardly, FG tried to ameliorate internal disagreements and keep its focus on the need for a unity of minds, espousing a shallow hope of "obliterat[ing] the memories of the Civil War."[33] O'Duffy's secretary acknowledged that the new party's vice-presidents, Dillon and MacDermot, "had no stomach for advanced nationalism."[34] Both had favored the appointment of Patrick Hogan to the presidency of the new party over O'Duffy, but he refused the role. The unifying feature of the new party coalition was its trenchant opposition to de Valera and FF.

Intellectuals like James Hogan were deeply critical of FG's lack of comprehensive policies. He derided the political horse trading between various factions which had produced "a zero policy or an amorphous utilitarianism of the Cumann na nGaedheal sort." He lamented, "we never equipped ourselves with a self-consistent political philosophy."[35] Hogan and Tierney sought to inject the tabula rasa FG with a corporatist policy as its central plank. Hogan's major work during his time in the Blueshirts was a booklet titled *Could Ireland become Communist? The facts of the case*.[36] O'Duffy may have leaked confidential garda documents on communism in Ireland to Hogan during the period of his research. The General's views on parliamentary democracy were well known. He wrote that "there is no reason why we should make an idol of Parliament."[37] His views caused some embarrassment for his new colleagues. But they were not unique in the party. The pro–FG *United Ireland* newspaper printed an article which praised Hitler and claimed it was necessary for members of the YIA to study "all new political movements in other lands" as a model to "build up the new Ireland." Although it did not offer a full endorsement of National Socialism, the author equivocated for the Nazi regime and argued that if Hitler's government restored the discipline and principles of the "Teutonic military Order of Chivalry" in modern Germany, it would offer Europe "a sound bulwark against the encroachments of Communism."[38] A key figure who provided a Europeanized conception of corporatism in the new party's upper echelons was John Marcus O'Sullivan, a distinguished academic educated in Germany who served as minister for education during the Cosgrave years. As a front-bench deputy, he gave full rein to the corporatist ideas of Hogan, Tierney and others.[39]

Although the *Irish Press* indicated MacDermot had been the loser from the negotiations and was the victim of political machinations by O'Duffy and Cosgrave, O'Duffy's follower, Liam Walsh, depicted the General as the primary victim of political subterfuge arising from the smoky rooms of 3 Merrion Square. Writing with hindsight, he recorded that O'Duffy "committed one of the greatest mistakes and sincerest regrets of his life" by participating in the negotiations. Walsh speculated that "had the subsequent merger not taken place there would have been a drastic purge of self-seeking politicians [from the Blueshirts]." He continued, "with all his kindness, [O'Duffy] could be ruthless when thwarted by intriguers."[40] But from an outside perspective, O'Duffy's political career appeared to be on an upward trajectory. As part of drumming up publicity for FG, O'Duffy prepared to embark on a nationwide tour in advance of its first electoral test, the local government elections. Originally scheduled for 14 November 1933, they were not held until June 1934. O'Duffy attributed this postponement to "the rapid spread of the United Ireland movement" and fear on the part of FF.[41] The threat of prosecution by the military tribunal still hung over those associated with the Blueshirts. It was reported on 2 September that "it is more than probable that the leaders of the National Guard will find themselves one of these days facing a military tribunal," but the journalist foresaw trouble for the government as "these repressive measures" would provide "a huge advertisement" for O'Duffy's movement.[42]

As leader of FG, O'Duffy surrounded himself with lackeys such as Thomas P. Gunning from County Leitrim.[43] Gunning was appointed as O'Duffy's press secretary in mid–October.[44] Educated at St Nathy's College, Ballaghaderreen and at the University of Fribourg in Switzerland, Gunning was initially a Catholic seminarian who abandoned the prospect of a life of the cloth to pursue a career in journalism. He was attached to the editorial staff of the *Irish Independent* before becoming editor of the weekly *The Standard* (later the *Catholic Standard*).[45] In his capacity as editor of *The Standard*, Gunning printed anti-communist stories in late 1933 which warned of a fusion between the IRA and the Communist Party. The stories were revealed as a hoax perpetrated by an English-based communist, Frank Breen, who "sold bogus information to *The Standard*."[46] Liam D. Walsh also became a staunch supporter of O'Duffy and the Blueshirts. Walsh was active in the IV in Dublin during the War of Independence, but was court-martialed and imprisoned for 12 months on charges of embezzling unit funds. He joined the National Army at the outbreak of the Civil War, leaving the force in October 1923. Following his discharge, complaints emerged of his unpaid accounts.[47] He was described by the gardaí in 1940 as "a shady type" and as one "who would belong to any Society or Organization out of which money would be forthcoming."[48] Both Gunning and Walsh were ardent fascists. During his political career and beyond, O'Duffy associated with ethically questionable characters.

Contemporaneously, the creation of FG appeared to mark the re-emergence of pro–Treaty nationalism as a united force, but as time would tell, the new party represented little more than a continuity of CnaG. O'Duffy's leadership of the new party was a gamble which reflected the desperation among various anti–FF politicians "to defeat the seemingly invincible de Valera."[49] The alliance with the Blueshirts and O'Duffy offered a temporary fillip to CnaG, but as Kevin Rafter observed "the costs of the short-lived alliance were considerable."[50] For the Center Party, his leadership offset the image that they had been absorbed by a larger party. However, former Center Party members had early misgivings about General O'Duffy's leadership qualities and political views.

◆ ◆ ◆

Following the creation of FG, General O'Duffy embarked on a barnstorming cross-country tour to boost support and establish the party on a solid footing which could challenge FF's highly effective political machine. Without the responsibility of representing a parliamentary constituency, O'Duffy felt his time could be better served by turning his attention towards organizational efforts. He rejected a challenge from the government senator William Quirke to fight a by-election in Tipperary. Quirke proposed to resign his seat and force a by-election if O'Duffy promised to personally contest the Tipperary seat. O'Duffy rejected the offer: "I will choose my own battleground."[51] Shortly afterwards, O'Duffy's local rival, Dr Conn Ward, then an FF deputy in Monaghan, challenged him to contest a by-election in his native county. O'Duffy, however, referred to his previous statement and suggested that Ward had deliberately held out on making the offer "until I had definitely decided not to contest any by-election." He reiterated that he would be "of more service to the people" in his national organizational capacity particularly with a possible general election on the horizon.[52] It was speculated that in the event of a general election, O'Duffy would contest a Dublin constituency or "a rural constituency enjoying a big population" where "the number of representations diminishes the demands upon the time of leaders of Parties."[53] O'Duffy's recruitment drive was typical of his theatrical style. Initially, he hoped to recruit three to four full-time salaried inspection officers for

**President of Fine Gael (United Ireland Party) Eoin O'Duffy, portrait photograph, c. December 1933 (courtesy the National Library of Ireland).**

the purpose of organizing Blueshirt companies across the Free State. It was expected these officers would oversee the doubling of membership in their assigned counties by the time they submitted final reports.[54]

On 28 October, O'Duffy returned to his native county where he was greeted by enthusiastic crowds and blazing tar barrels. Addressing a large meeting, he struck a populist tone. He declared that he had no faith in politics or politicians in general, a sentiment he admitted "might appear strange now that he was the new leader of a political party." He obediently repeated the party line on republicanism, arguing that the declaration of a republic in the Free State would "put the seal for-ever on partition."[55] Eager not to be outflanked by FG on the question of support for Irish unification, de Valera contested and won a seat in the Northern Irish parliament at Stormont in early December. He never took his seat in Stormont owing to FF's continued abstentionist policy north of the border. It remains the first and last time FF ever contested an election in Northern Ireland.

As he toured the country, O'Duffy sought to present an outwardly respectable image as he tried to build a broad coalition. He challenged de Valera and the government to prove that the Blueshirts were "out for the overthrow of the Government or the establishment of a dictatorship."[56] His rhetoric focused on the impact of the economic war. O'Duffy mocked "that outside Gilbert and Sullivan comedies no more bizarre war had ever been waged than the so-called Economic War with Britain." FF, he declared, was a decaying organization which had wrecked the country by their own rashness.[57] He also sought to enhance his image as an international statesman in-waiting. In late October, he dispatched a congratulatory telegram to the new French prime minister, Albert Sarraut, with whom he had been "close friends for twenty years."[58] As garda commissioner, he had visited Sarraut in Paris in 1928 when he was French minister for the interior.[59] The Vatican also took an interest in Irish affairs. Leo McCauley, Irish chargé d'affaires in the Vatican, recorded in a memorandum how he was quizzed by the acting Cardinal secretary of state on whether de Valera's popularity was waning in Ireland and "if General O'Duffy appeared to be strong enough to achieve his ambitions."[60]

Public meetings addressed by O'Duffy continued to act as a magnet for violence and disorder. Most notably, he was "savagely attacked and beaten on the head" with a hammer at a meeting in Tralee in October 1933. The attack caused blood to stream down his face.[61] At the same meeting, his motorcar was stoned and ultimately burned by the crowd, having been drenched with petrol. He later received compensation of £240 for the destroyed vehicle.[62] The injured O'Duffy was spirited away on a backroad to Killarney. Twelve members of the IRA were jailed for their role in the incident by the military tribunal.[63] FG meetings continued to be marred by scuffles between O'Duffy's blue shirt–cladded followers and opponents from FF and the IRA. A meeting in Cork on 2 December saw stones and bottles hurled through windows. A veritable siege of the meeting hall by republicans took place until garda reinforcements arrived to clear the street with a baton charge. Tom Barry, a veteran local IRA commander, was injured during the disturbance.[64] Although he condemned such acts of violence, President de Valera regularly commented caustically that it was not the job of the government to make certain causes popular. This implied that violent actions were the natural product of the opposition's unpopularity. FF's stance towards the main opposition party, which it viewed as a threat to stable democracy, was heavy handed. Political violence led to fears that the Civil War was being replayed.

On 8 December, the government invoked article 2A of the constitution to declare the YIA an unlawful organization. O'Duffy had been an advocate of article 2A during his term as garda commissioner. On 7 October 1931, he had asked the CnaG minister for justice, James FitzGerald-Kenney, for a carte blanche to utilize the powers contained in article 2A to carry out a response he admitted was "somewhat extreme" to "deal with extremists—murder gangs."[65] Ironically, this draconian provision was now turned against him. On the day the ban was announced, O'Duffy told a Donegal audience that he was determined to face down the government and would continue to act as leader of the Blueshirts, which he claimed had ballooned to reach a membership of 62,000. He asserted that the government's action had "proclaimed half the Irish race." The meeting was also addressed by Cosgrave and Dillon, who indicated their support for O'Duffy's stubborn defiance.[66] The same day, Ned Cronin was arrested and charged with sedition and membership of the Blueshirts. He went on to be acquitted on the first charge but received three months imprisonment for wearing the blue uniform of the banned movement.[67] Like the National Guard, its carbon copy, the YIA, was banned. John Regan surmised, based on a survey of department of justice files related to the Blueshirts from the era, that "it is possible to conclude with a degree of confidence that there was no evidence to suggest an organized conspiracy against the Fianna Fáil Government in late 1933."[68]

The minister for justice, Patrick Ruttledge, claimed the ban was necessary as the Blueshirts resembled a paramilitary. Its conduct was "purely and simply a copy of military lines," Ruttledge argued. He produced a memorandum signed by O'Duffy as garda commissioner in November 1928 which advocated the banning of political uniforms following a march by 19 members of the British Fascisti in Dublin on Armistice Day.[69] Commissioner O'Duffy had disliked the imperialist overtones of the British Fascisti and the pro-loyalist output of its propaganda officer for "Southern Ireland," C.W. Higginbotham. He rejected claims they were simply commemorating their war dead.[70] On 14 December, the YIA was dissolved and replaced with an identical organization, the League of Youth (LoY). It shared the same address as Fine Gael, at 3 Merrion Square. Maurice Manning acknowledged the tactic of "dexterous name-changing" was reminiscent of Daniel O'Connell's means of subverting British suppression of his organizations in the 19th century.[71]

Historians have suggested that by late 1933 FG's constitutionalist politicians began to experience buyer's remorse arising from their support for O'Duffy as party leader, as he shanghaied them along on a collision course with the lawful government. Anthony Jordan wrote that within the FG parliamentary party it was felt there was "too much confrontation at political rallies" and too much "talk of coup d'états from either side." He argued that whilst CnaG politicians believed they needed a strong man to lead them, they soon became unhappy with O'Duffy's domineering leadership style.[72] However, in late 1933 FG publicly backed their leader to the hilt in his defiance of the government. Moreover, there was not always a strong delineation between constitutionalist parliamentarians and Blueshirts. Many politicians, including Desmond FitzGerald and Gearóid O'Sullivan, appeared in parliamentary buildings wearing the distinctive uniform of the YIA under their coats.[73] Indeed, Blythe, a prominent CnaG political leader, was a regular orator on the Blueshirt speaking circuit. It was not until 1934 that O'Duffy's shortcomings and the party's poor performance in June's local election prompted a leadership heave. This was a major cause for the rupture in FG, not an abhorrence of O'Duffy's views.

Incensed at the second banning of his movement, O'Duffy vented his spleen to an audience of 1,500 in Ballyshannon, County Donegal, on 9 December. Hurriedly taking the podium, without the usual introduction, O'Duffy launched into a garbled speech. He dramatically removed his overcoat to reveal he was wearing the eponymous uniform of the proscribed Blueshirts. John Regan described the speech as "a remarkable performance even by O'Duffy's standards."[74] Its tone was deeply xenophobic. He repeatedly referred to de Valera as a "bloody foreigner." The speech was conspiratorial. He accused the government of planning his assassination. He even took up a defense of republicans, responding to an accusation from Seán MacEntee that a certain section of the IRA was in the pay of John Bull (England), O'Duffy declared:

> I say as a Republican myself ... that in saying that he is a damned liar. You are not in the pay of John Bull, and whenever Mr de Valera runs away from the Republic and arrests you Republicans, and puts you on board beds in Mountjoy, he is entitled to the fate he gave Mick Collins and Kevin O'Higgins. He does not understand the people of this country, because he is a half-breed.

Much like Henry II's allusion to the "turbulent priest" Thomas Becket, O'Duffy's reference to the fate de Valera deserved was immediately interpreted as a threat against the president's life. O'Duffy spurned captatio benevolentiae by admonishing his audience, telling them it was "not to your credit that there are not more blue shirts here to-night." Upon finishing his speech, he left the platform, pushed his way through the crowd and left with a priest for a local hotel. They were followed by a large section of the crowd, including both supporters and detractors. The crowd surged around the hotel's entrance. "The excitement became so intense that the Guards were forced to use their batons to disperse them."[75]

Having slipped away from arrest by the Garda Síochána in Ballyshannon, O'Duffy spent the night on the run in Kiltimagh as the guest of the politician Seán T. Ruane. The General reared his head the next day at a fateful public meeting in Westport, County Mayo. Here, his "adventures" continued. Several miles outside the town, O'Duffy and his supporters were stopped by gardaí. He was told he could not address a meeting while wearing a blue shirt. The General and ten of his supporters then "made a dash across the fields" and split up into groups, which enabled O'Duffy to successfully reach Westport. When he and his supporters reached the town center it was cordoned with police. O'Duffy was forcibly prevented from approaching the platform by special branch. Suddenly, the audience rushed towards their leader and broke the cordon, literally carrying O'Duffy over their shoulders to the platform. One police officer tried to grab his ankle but the hold was broken by the crowd. Upon taking the podium, General O'Duffy launched into a speech until he was waylaid by the garda superintendent who told the General he would not allow him to speak. "Ah, Superintendent. I must speak to my people," he replied, before resuming his speech. He explained that he had just been arrested "by two of your county representatives," FF deputies Conor Maguire and Patrick Ruttledge, "and I hope when they next come before you–" But O'Duffy's speech was cut short as nine Gardaí rushed the platform to arrest the rabble-rouser. O'Duffy resisted arrest, pulling his arm from the policeman to get out of his hold, telling him: "You are assaulting me, I will charge you with assault."[76] Suddenly the crowd began to rush the platform, which looked in near danger of collapsing. After a brief scuffle, O'Duffy appealed to the audience for peace and announced he would comply with the police. A witness reported that O'Duffy told the arresting officer: "I hope my arrest in the county which gave birth to [Michael] Davitt will mean that the followers of our policy will be increased by thousands."[77] A large section of the crowd then followed as he was marched to the local police station, shouting "Up O'Duffy" and "down with the Spaniard!"[78] He was transported to Mountjoy jail "under a heavy escort of police and soldiers" the next day. In May 1935, O'Duffy was awarded £200 in damages connected to the incident arising from false imprisonment and assault by the arresting policemen.[79]

Immediately after the arrest of O'Duffy and some of his supporters in Westport for wearing a blue shirt, John A. Costello, Paddy McGilligan and Vincent Rice lodged an application for an order of habeas corpus. They successfully argued before the supreme court that the applicants were being detained unlawfully; that they were unlawfully arrested without warrant; and that they were unlawfully arrested and were being unlawfully detained for the unknown legal offense of wearing a blue shirt.[80] The supreme court deliberated in the case for two days before ordering that O'Duffy be released without charge. Patrick Morrisroe, the bishop of Achonry, sent a telegram to O'Duffy congratulating him on the "victory of justice over shameless partisanship and contemptible tyranny."[81]

Although released from Mountjoy jail, five charges still hung over O'Duffy for which he was to be tried in January by the military tribunal. They related to his involvement in the Blueshirts and the alleged incitement to murder President de Valera. While celebrating his victory in the Dolphin Hotel, O'Duffy received a summons for his impending appearance before the military tribunal two days later. The detective inspector recalled his interaction with the General, whom he considered to be under the influence of alcohol:

> Eventually at 12.45 a.m. he came from the room and addressed me by saying "Good Night, young fellow" and shook me by the hand. I then gave him the document which he read and having done so addressing me he asked "What is next? What follows this? What is next?" I replied that the last paragraph explained. He then read the last paragraph again and said "I suppose you will be Commissioner some day." I replied "I will try to perform the duties allotted to me." He then said "I suppose you would assassinate if directed, you would assassinate if directed." I said "It is a very unfair remark, General, especially coming from you"... He said "The Irish People will pronounce their opinion of you. This is assassination."[82]

The speech which O'Duffy intended to deliver in Westport was reproduced in full in the *United Ireland* newspaper on 23 December and included a warning that Ireland was slipping into "Russian, Mexican and Spanish conditions."[83] The speech further alleged how he was impressed upon during the Treaty debates in 1921–22 to support the Treaty by some who later became FF deputies.[84]

In late October, a young Blueshirt, Hugh O'Reilly of Innishandon, Bandon, County Cork, was dragged from his parents' home by masked men, beaten, and subsequently died from his injuries in December. O'Duffy and 1,000 men from the LoY attended the funeral Mass presided by Bishop Cohalan of Cork.[85] Tom Barry was considered the "chief suspect" by the police in the controversial murder case.[86] O'Reilly became a martyr for the cause: "His sacrifice will not be forgotten and his bones will not be un-honored. His burial place will for generations to come be a center of pilgrimage."[87] On Christmas day another Blueshirt, Cornelius Daly, a vintner from Drimoleague in Cork, was beaten to death in Dunmanway.[88]

As the year drew to a close, Irish society was increasingly riven by political divisions. The animosity between de Valera and O'Duffy was loaded with Civil War bitterness. Although O'Duffy was the extra-parliamentary leader of the opposition, his erratic behavior had been displayed during his incendiary speech at Ballyshannon. His colleagues evidently began to prepare O'Duffy's speeches in an effort to stage-manage the unpredictable General. FF critics had regularly mocked O'Duffy's dramatic and contradictory speeches. Seán T. O'Kelly even implied O'Duffy was under the influence of alcohol.[89] However, he remained a popular leader among a great swathe of the population. De Valera would, in the words of Alexander Pope, "bear, like the Turk, no brother near the throne."

On New Year's Eve 1933, O'Duffy appeared at a LoY dance in Cashel, County Tipperary, where he received a check of £50 before he returned to Dublin in advance of his trial date of 2 January.[90] His defense barrister, John A. Costello, successfully obtained an order from the high court which challenged the jurisdiction of the military tribunal in O'Duffy's case. The complicated legal stand-off between the civil and military authorities prompted the president of the tribunal to adjourn the case for several months. Costello successfully muddied the waters when he challenged the attorney general's claim that article 2A of the constitution conferred upon the military tribunal equal status to the civil courts.[91] The perception was that O'Duffy had scored another victory against the government, whose case against him was crumbling.

◆ ◆ ◆

Despite rumors that the government would be forced to call a snap general election and appeal to the country the suggestion was emphatically denied by the government.[92] In the event, no general election was held. The government's ham-fisted efforts to proscribe the Blueshirts was seen as "slightly ridiculous" from the first proscription on the National Guard onwards. Attention was drawn to the taxpayers' money being spent trying to quell the Blueshirts.[93] O'Duffy exploited his legal battles to present himself as defiant in the face of FF persecution. He joked FF had issued an "SOS" ("save our seats") as for "every speech I made brought a hundred new supporters."[94]

As the first FG ard fheis (party convention) approached on 8 February 1934,

O'Duffy's public engagements were carefully planned by a background team of party advisors. He was required to attend FG headquarters every Thursday to give an account of the Blueshirts' activities to Cosgrave, Dillon and MacDermot who kept a watchful eye on their unpredictable leader. His speeches were prepared by Ernest Blythe and others, which O'Duffy later claimed was tantamount to censorship.[95] Questionable references to abolishing parliamentary democracy and other incendiary remarks disappeared from his speeches. Criticism of the government focused on its handling of the economic war and broken promises to farmers: "You were promised prosperity. The land was to flow with milk and honey."[96] But beneath the surface of this moderate image, O'Duffy's fascist proclivities burgeoned. FF politician Thomas Derrig presciently warned Cosgrave that "the O'Duffy movement began in a frolic, but it might well end in a tragedy."[97]

The ard fheis, held in Dublin's Mansion House, was highly orchestrated and stage managed. Liam Walsh recalled that the first ard fheis was "a never-to-be forgotten scene." He described the FG leader in characteristically glowing terms: "A sincere nationalist, a man of the people—flesh of their flesh and bone of their bone—General O'Duffy fought for and served Ireland and had no responsibility for any of the political or economic policies of the previous 12 years, and he could, in consequence, advocate a policy which was sincere and honest."[98] O'Duffy was asked by the FG association in Carlow-Kilkenny to accept a nomination to become its prospective parliamentary candidate, though O'Duffy still had hopes to win a seat in his native Monaghan.[99] Between 1,600 and 4,000 delegates thronged into the Mansion House on 8 February among "animated scenes" as "old stalwarts" from the War of Independence era rubbed shoulders with the youthful members of the Blueshirts. "There was nothing like this since the Eucharistic Congress," a delegate recalled.[100] Manning observed that this convention saw "a striking display of Blueshirt strength, and morale generally was high."[101]

FG formally adopted corporatism as party policy. The central thrust of General O'Duffy's speech at the convention focused on corporatism. He was most likely assisted in its drafting by Blythe, who later felt O'Duffy's ideas about the corporate state were "vague" but cleaved between an admiration for European fascism and an understanding that corporatism had "the blessing of the Church."[102] It was for this reason that Mike Cronin considered Blueshirt ideology to essentially represent clerical fascism. He further noted that whilst O'Duffy was enamored by the successes of European fascism, the purveyors of clerical fascism in an Irish context were intellectuals like Tierney, Hogan, Blythe, FitzGerald, and John Marcus O'Sullivan. Aside from the papal encyclical *Quadragesimo Anno*, O'Duffy cited the 1931 encyclical *Nova impendet* ("On the economic crisis") as "the way forward" for the Blueshirts.[103]

O'Duffy was keen to appeal beyond the bourgeois and wealthy voters who made up CnaG's traditional voting bloc. "I yield to no man in my solicitude for the welfare of the workingman," he wrote.[104] It was an attempt to challenge the emergent class divisions between the two major parties. It represented an effort to remobilize the original cross-class pro–Treaty coalition. Early working-class support had gradually atrophied since the death of Collins, as the pro–Treaty movement became sectional and increasingly associated with the middle class. In a classical Marxist sense, it could be argued that Collins represented a Bonaparte figure within Irish society, as a leader who was not completely beholden to class forces. O'Duffy may have exhibited a similar tendency had he achieved power. This would tally with Gregor's observation of the shifting Marxist understanding of Mussolini's dictatorship in Italy.[105] Collins has also been characterized by Marxists as a comprador capitalist and a counter revolutionary.

The Labor Party, which offered tacit support to FF, was deeply critical of O'Duffy's "ready-made Italian system" which would revoke "the dearest right of the workers, the right to withdraw their labor" by banning strikes.[106] Although advocates of corporatism argued that strikes were not prohibited under the system as "the workers are placed in such a position of security that the necessity for strikes as a weapon against injustice does not arise," this failed to convince many on the left.[107] The party newspaper reported that the part of O'Duffy's speech which outlined his policy on the corporate system was, "contrary to what might have been expected," listened to "with the most rapt enthusiasm and ... received with the heartiest and most frequent applause."[108] O'Duffy concluded with a rallying call to prepare for an electoral victory, which satiated those who may have felt concerned by aspects of the new corporatist policy.

Although corporatism can retrospectively be seen as a touchstone of fascist ideology, at the time such ideas were popular in a diverse array of political movements which bore no trace of fascism, such as supporters of Franklin Delano Roosevelt's New Deal.[109] Some Irish adherents of corporatism believed in it as an abstract principle which would eventually replace the need for traditional politics. Tierney argued that Mussolini would be replaced "not by another dictator" but by "a new entity suited to the needs of modern civilization—the Corporate State," which suggested the need for conventional political leadership would wither away in due course.[110] Blythe saw the creation of a planned economy through "various Vocational and Corporation Councils" as a means to create a flourishing economy. He flatly acknowledged that the Irish economy had failed under the Free State, which was an interesting admission considering he was its former minister for finance. He argued, rightly, that the Irish economy was indelibly linked with agriculture, and proposed that in order for native Irish industry to flourish that agriculture must first be put on a sound basis. The Blueshirts would have "complete and absolute" involvement and authority in the corporate system, particularly in the realm of agriculture.[111]

In his speech to the first FG ard fheis, O'Duffy argued that it was high time that people recognized "the limitations of the present parliamentary system" which retarded efforts to implement "any Christian social program." Navigating an uneasy line between anti-parliamentarianism without expressly denouncing democracy, he announced that in corporatism "we have a new type of democracy—economic democracy. It does not replace political democracy—it completes it."[112] But significantly, as Eugene Broderick observed, the focus given to corporatism in the party newspaper and elsewhere was likely "out of all proportion to the interest in the policy among the general membership of Fine Gael and the Blueshirts."[113]

Elements within FG promoted an exclusivist definition of Irish nationality. In an article of 10 February 1934, Blythe promoted a racialized view of Irish nationality and citizenship. He argued that during Ireland's struggle for independence, when the country was "enslaved by outsiders," those who were prepared to identify with the oppressed nation and were "willing to fight for it and share in its sufferings" would be accepted as Irish "with little question." However, he argued that with the advent of native government the situation had changed and "stricter consideration must nowadays be given to the question of who is entitled to be regarded as an Irishman in the full sense of the term than was necessary in the past." Referencing the qualification of being a natural born citizen to be eligible to become president of the United States, Blythe wrote it was "weak and foolish" to permit "a foreigner with no trace of Irish blood in his veins and with no ancestral connection with his nation" to become president of the executive council of the Irish Free State. Although there was no such provision in the constitution forbidding even "a full-blooded African negro from becoming President of the Executive Council," he was convinced that public opinion was out of step with the law on this matter.[114]

In academic literature on identity in Ireland, it has been asserted that although a former colony, the Irish nation state has "imagined itself as based on a racialized notion of identity" and a desire to prove the "Irish nation was not different from other European nations and did therefore differ from subaltern non–European peoples."[115] Blythe argued that a nativist provision should be included in the constitution to apply to all occupants of all government ministries, judges of the superior courts and members of the defense council.[116] O'Duffy also believed that "no foreign [should] become a President or Government Minister of the State in Ireland."[117] The unsubtle subtext which drove such reassessments of the essential nature of Irishness was the insinuation that de Valera was not fully Irish owing to his birthplace in New York and his non–Irish father. De Valera was frequently referred to as a "Spaniard" by detractors. However, a range of views existed on such matters, and it would be disingenuous to characterize early FG policy as essentially racist. Some party statements took a more liberal view. For example, an article published in July 1934 denounced the mistreatment of the majority black population by white South Africans as "little better than that of slave owners." In scorning the Boers, which had been a cause célèbre of Irish nationalists of yesteryear, the author displayed a far more progressive view on race than Blythe.[118]

Anti-communism remained a preoccupation across all ideological wings of FG, from those tangentially aligned with fascism like Blythe and Tierney to more moderate politicians like Dillon and MacDermot. "Red" baiting was a centerpiece of party propaganda. The imagined threat of communism in Ireland was significantly exaggerated by FG politicians at podiums and by priests at pulpits. When the British socialist politician James Maxton, a supporter and admirer of de Valera's government, requested that Leon Trotsky be afforded asylum in the Irish Free State, MacDermot seized the opportunity to launch a brouhaha in the Dáil where he implied the government were fellow travelers of the exiled Russian Bolshevik leader.[119]

Intellectuals like James Hogan lent "this strident anti-communism … a credible and plausible foundation" through their public intellectual pursuits.[120] However, the party's distinctively anti-communist flair soon lost its luster as the FF government demonstrated its own anti-communist and pro–Catholic bona fides. Claims that the "dictatorship of the Fianna Fáil Cabinet" would pave the way for a communist dictatorship of the IRA became discredited, particularly as the government clamped down on the IRA with harsh draconian measures.[121] FF further oversaw the deportation of James Gralton, a Leitrim communist who held American citizenship. O'Duffy's secretary, Thomas Gunning from Leitrim, claimed Gralton had given Leitrim "the undeserved nickname of the Bolshie county."[122] The Gralton case illuminated the widespread prevalence of anti-communism at all levels of Irish society. Mel Farrell wrote that under O'Duffy's leadership, FG "foregrounded their opposition to communism."[123] If this was the case, he was pushing an open door.

◆ ◆ ◆

Hot on the heels of the ard fheis, O'Duffy felt indestructible. Despite setbacks like the censorship of the party newspaper in mid–February, which generated a heated Dáil debate, a party editorial of 24 February optimistically predicted that should a general election be called the government party would lose 20 or 30 parliamentary seats.[124] The nationwide tour began to resemble a political crusade. O'Duffy told an audience in Newbliss, County Monaghan on 16 February that "Fine Gael had now a majority in the country" and threw down the gauntlet to de Valera to call a general election.[125] On the last day of February, the Minister for Justice introduced the Wearing of Uniforms (Restriction) Bill 1934 which was debated in the Dáil. Ruttledge sought to outlaw the wearing of blue shirts at political rallies by statute. During the parliamentary debate, O'Duffy's barrister and the future FG Taoiseach, John A. Costello, made an infamous speech which included the memorable and oft-quoted sentence: "The Minister gave extracts from various laws on the Continent, but he carefully refrained from drawing attention to the fact that the Blackshirts were victorious in Italy and that the Hitler Shirts were victorious in Germany, as, assuredly, in spite of this Bill and in spite of the Public Safety Act, the Blueshirts will be victorious in the Irish Free State."[126] The comment came back to haunt Costello in his post-war political career. However, perhaps indicative of O'Duffy's posthumous status as a lightning rod for FG politicians of the period, Seán Lemass's daughter retrospectively misremembered O'Duffy as the originator of the quotation.[127]

Although the uniforms bill was railroaded through the Dáil on 14 March, when it was referred to the Senate, the upper house of the parliament, it was denied a second reading. As such, it could not become law for 18 months. In a fit of pique, de Valera introduced legislation the very next day to abolish the Senate.[128] O'Duffy warned his audience in de Valera's own constituency that the abolition of the Senate spelled the imminent creation of a dictatorship and that the stacking of the judiciary would naturally follow.[129] Predictably, the Senate rejected the attempt to abolish the upper house. As such, it prolonged its own abolition by 18 months.

The supreme court delivered its ruling on the controversial constitutional question of the authority of the military tribunal on 22 March. Its judgment recognized that the powers of the tribunal were limited and copper-fastened its status as an inferior court to the civil courts, lest its powers "might become like those of the Star Chamber" of Tudor England. The court found that the military tribunal was empowered to consider the issue of whether O'Duffy remained a member of organizations proscribed under article 2A, namely the National Guard and the YIA, after the ban. But it ruled that the charges of sedition and incitement to murder were not triable by the military tribunal.[130] Patrick McGilligan, an FG deputy, ridiculed the series of "hysterical, futile and nonsensical attempts" of the previous four months "to get General O'Duffy waylaid and put into jail."[131] The saga began to take on the appearance of a comedy of errors on the government's part.

The first major test of O'Duffy's leadership loomed in the form of the local elections, scheduled for 26 June 1934, which the party intended to fight as if it were a general election. O'Duffy prematurely predicted victory and predicted the downfall of the government.[132] Even if FG had won a majority of local government seats, it was absurd to suggest this would have precipitated the collapse of the government. Externally, FG appeared to be on a steady footing and well primed to score an electoral advance under O'Duffy's energetic leadership. He regularly delivered two to three speeches per day.[133] At the time of the ard fheis in February, FG could boast 1,078 branches to FF's 1,800.[134] Although the party was clearly growing, the question remained as to whether its growth was sufficient to compete with FF in a general election. O'Duffy ordered that selection conventions for local candidates should be held before 18 April.[135]

In Charleville, County Cork, 10,000 people turned out for a public meeting. They were mostly supporters of Ned Cronin, a native of the town, who had recently been released from Arbour Hill prison. O'Duffy outlined that his party would "appeal to the Irish race everywhere for financial support during the coming summer" to electorally challenge FF. He denied reports that a brief absence he took from Ireland was connected to "studying fascism in Italy" or that he was "over looking for money from John Bull" in England.[136] At the same rally O'Duffy suggested his "youthful" movement may be at a disadvantage due to age-based restrictions on the franchise in the upcoming local elections. FF jumped on this statement, as FG senators had stalled government efforts to expand the franchise the previous year. They again introduced a bill in parliament to lower the voting age following O'Duffy's statement.[137] The minister for lands, James Connolly, reminded the Senate that even General O'Duffy "feels that it will be to the advantage of his Party to have the widest extension of franchise."[138] Despite such appeals, the measure was again rejected by the opposition party and would not become law for another year. This highlighted the extent to which O'Duffy's "cult of the youth" sentiment clashed with his conservative colleagues in parliament. FF criticized the apparent hypocrisy of FG who "profess a great interest in the young people" yet "deprived about 800,000 [young people] of a vote."[139]

O'Duffy optimistically predicted that FG would capture 20 of the 23 local government councils at the forthcoming local elections. In seeking to establish councils "which would be bulwarks against the follies of Fianna Fáil," he was clearly angling towards a massive campaign of opposition to the government. Whilst he recognized it was regrettable to add such an intensely party-political tenor to the local elections, he warned that "desperate diseases required desperate remedies."[140] FG hoped to capitalize on the growing anger of farmers against government seizures of cattle from local farmers for non-payment of land annuities. Seized cattle were sold at auctions which came on foot of the government's cattle slaughter scheme in April. Under the same scheme, free beef was distributed to workers and the poor. This generated a significant following for FF among the working-class, whilst farmers viewed the FF government as penalizing hard-working farmers who got up early in the morning. They accused the government of doling out their produce to ne'er-do-wells. This added a significant class dimension to the Blueshirt phenomenon.

Cattle auctions became a site of confrontation between local farmers and buyers from elsewhere, often from Northern Ireland. Garda intervention was regularly needed to maintain order. Dr James Ryan, minister for agriculture, became a polarizing figure among Irish farmers. However, the government retained the support of a significant number of FF-voting farmers which helped the government to weather the storm.[141] FG deputy for North Dublin, Patrick Belton, organized a "Farmers Convention" in early April in opposition to the continued payment of annuities to the government, which they alleged amounted to a double payment.[142] The Irish exchequer continued to collect annuities payments but withheld them rather than transfer the money to Britain. Belton considered the special duties placed on cattle by Britain to effectively mean that Irish farmers had already paid their annuities. He warned the government that farmers would "fight in defense of our homes."[143] In late May, O'Duffy appointed Belton, a firm supporter and an ardent clerical fascist, to the party's front bench as spokesperson for agriculture replacing Patrick Hogan, the minister for agriculture in Cosgrave's government.[144]

In a statement issued to the press, Cronin and O'Duffy tried to restrain the LoY from engaging in illegal agrarian attacks and urged members in possession of unauthorized firearms to hand them in to the police.[145] In 1934 and 1935, individual Blueshirts were frequently convicted for illegal activities including the obstruction of roads, membership of unlawful associations (such as the radical "Annuities Defense League"), cutting telegraph wires, or possessing firearms.[146] O'Duffy's rhetoric at public meetings often endorsed violent responses. At a meeting in Drogheda, he urged Blueshirts that if they had to fight "to give ten blows for their one. We do not mind if we have to go to jail—we are going to jail in a good cause."[147] At a speech in Kinsale on 12 April, O'Duffy urged that "we must make life intolerable for those who will not yield to our demands."[148] His militant language drew private rebukes from his conservative allies, who pleaded with the General not to wander off script. Damning his leader with faint praise, James Dillon told O'Duffy: "When you stick to your notes, General, you're the greatest speaker there is. But let some old women in the audience shout 'Up Dev' and God knows what you will say next."[149]

Although FG hoped to mobilize the Blueshirts as part of a mass electoral campaign, the LoY was increasingly sidetracked with fighting an anti-rates campaign as agrarian unrest continued across the country. Colonel Jerry Ryan, a senior Blueshirt and member of the FG national executive, was charged by the military tribunal with leading a conspiracy to shoot a rate-collector from Upperchurch, County Tipperary.[150] O'Duffy assured protesting farmers that they had "the whole strength and resources" of FG behind them.[151] He became increasingly cocksure of victory, telling voters that he expected the "certain" local election victory would be followed by an equally certain general election victory.[152] Slogans such as "O'Duffy Abú!" and "Up Cronin" were painted across street corners in the run up to the vote.[153] At a final rally in Cashel, County Tipperary, O'Duffy told thousands of supporters that they faced a choice between a "Fianna Fáil dictatorship" or a slew of FG-controlled councils which would "impose some check on the mad and reckless policies" of the government.[154]

The results of the local election in June proved that O'Duffy's predictions of a large victory were drastically off mark. Instead of winning control of 20 councils, as he had predicted, FG won control of just six to FF's 14. On three councils the parties were equal in strength.[155] The total number of elected councilors by party affiliation is reproduced below:

| | |
|---|---|
| FF | 728 |
| FG | 596 |
| Labor Party | 185 |
| Others | 371 |

Although he claimed he was "very pleased" with the result, he had grossly over-promised what would be achieved during the campaign.[156] As leader he bore the chief responsibility for the significant electoral shortfall. His efforts to spin the result as meaning the opposition had "won the Local Government elections" and that FG "had Mr de Valera beaten to the ropes" was unconvincing.[157] As one local newspaper in Mayo recorded, the local election result had "pricked and deflated the Blueshirt balloon."[158] The *Irish Workers' Voice* heralded "another smashing of O'Duffy and his Fascist imperialists" and urged the creation of a "nation-wide united anti–Fascist movement."[159] O'Duffy's internal opponents now had cause to move to oust him from the leadership. The relationship between O'Duffy and his fair-weather friends in FG soured in the run up to the local elections. On 14 June, a memorandum was read out to the parliamentary party in O'Duffy's absence which recorded his "dissatisfaction with the activity of the party generally in the Dáil and in the country."[160]

O'Duffy's leadership of FG had been unorthodox from the beginning. Due to not holding a Dáil seat, he was largely removed from day-to-day opposition in parliament and could not defend himself against attacks from government or Labor deputies. O'Duffy characterized the Labor Party as "only the tail of the Government."[161] His nationwide organizational tour resembled a cross between a permanent election stump and a traveling apocalyptic preacher. FG's anti-communism quickly lost its appeal as it became obvious that FF was anything but soft on communism. FF still warned the IRA that if FG came to power, they would experience a much harsher crackdown.[162] In 1934, the IRA leadership expelled prominent left-wing officers such as Frank Ryan, George Gilmore and Michael Price. Each was dedicated to "the fight against Irish fascism" and subsequently founded the Republican Congress in April 1934. Many in the Republican Congress felt that "the IRA leadership had failed to give a lead to the struggle against the Blueshirts."[163] However, Frank Ryan took little active part in anti–Blueshirt violence and even indicated that such actions were counter-productive.[164]

Regan compared O'Duffy and his traveling band to "Chicken Licken and

Goosey Loosey who went around prophesying the sky was going to fall down." However, their chimerical quest to find communists and their prophecies of the skies falling down "were beginning to sound less convincing."[165] His tour racked up a considerable bill. James Dillon indicated that O'Duffy's popular appeal was beginning to dry up as early as February 1934 when he suggested that attendance at FG meetings "was becoming almost embarrassing."[166] Conversely, some anti–Blueshirt politicians, such as Labor TD Richard Anthony, expressed concern that many on the left-wing had allowed themselves to "get into a blue funk about the Blueshirt movement" and that his party should focus on other issues.[167]

It has often been suggested that O'Duffy's critics in FG became restive due to their leader's increasingly extremist rhetoric and pro-fascist views, which he began to express again in public during the summer of 1934. F.S.L. Lyons uncharitably viewed such "wild language and false positions" as evidence that O'Duffy acted like "a child in politics."[168] The General's own personal foibles and unhealthy relationship with alcohol further accelerated disaffection with his capacity for leadership. On 9 July, while convalescing in a nursing home in London Frank MacDermot wrote to O'Duffy to "make a more formal protest than I have yet done" against the tendency of the leader and others to "imply that it is our official policy to replace [parliamentary government] by a Blueshirt ascendency modeled on Fascism."[169] Lemass told the Dáil that O'Duffy's bungled understanding of fascism was "picked up on a holiday cruise in the Mediterranean."[170] James Dillon claimed in 1940 that his disillusionment with O'Duffy's "Hitlerian convulsions of speech" caused him to feel "something dangerous was getting loose." He recalled that he experienced a Damascene moment about O'Duffy's true nature when he accompanied the General to an event in Cork:

> One day in west Cork, I was standing behind him on a balcony when he addressed a rally of several thousand young Blueshirts. He was speaking very rapidly. It dawned on me that they were hanging on his words in a kind of obsessed way and I suddenly realized that he was speaking without any verbs. It had no discernible meaning. It dawned on me that if this fellah told them to go and burn down the town, they'd do it. I thought: "We've got to get rid of this man. He could be dangerous." I remembered Hitler.

Historian Robert Fisk added that Dillon and Cosgrave "valued parliamentary democracy more than they did the possibility of overthrowing de Valera." This sentiment allegedly undergirded their determination to jettison O'Duffy from the leadership of FG.[171]

The ideological gulf inside FG was not merely reducible to a tussle between democrats and fascists. The national question also featured as a significant bone of contention. O'Duffy adhered to a dynamic, militarist strand of pro–Treaty nationalism which briefly held sway under Collins' leadership, but gradually dissipated under Cosgrave's conservative government. The unresolved questions of 1922 reasserted themselves within the FG of 1934. O'Duffy articulated more aggressively pro-nationalist policies than his moderate colleagues could stomach. In a letter to MacDermot, Dillon even referred to O'Duffy and the Blueshirts as "our left wingers" due to their perceived radicalism.[172] At a speech in Cork on 5 July, O'Duffy strongly denied charges by Patrick Ruttledge that an FG government would "mop up the IRA" and instead offered an olive branch to the staunch republicans, calling them "good men."[173] O'Duffy hoped to outflank FF on republicanism. He even goaded de Valera to declare a republic and stated that the Blueshirts "would be delighted to support him" if he did. It was a reversal of his earlier position of supporting Commonwealth membership as a trade-off for Irish unification. If he were president of the executive council, O'Duffy said, he would have no hesitation declaring a republic in 24 hours of taking office.[174] He further pronounced that he and "95 per cent of the Blueshirts" would be prepared to participate in a war against Britain if the economic war spilled into an armed confrontation.[175]

Pro-republican pronouncements were anathema to the conservative wing of FG, made up of nationalists, ex-home rulers, and ex-unionists. In an interview with the northern nationalist newspaper, *The Irish News*, the interviewer pinpointed the divide between O'Duffy and his colleagues over the question of Northern Ireland as signaling that "the break cannot be far off."[176] O'Duffy proposed appointing a LoY commissioner in Northern Ireland, with a brief to help end partition and create a new all–Ireland capital city in the historical site of Tara, a site in County Meath with deep roots in Irish mythology.[177] The heightened agrarian agitation of the Blueshirts, which bordered on defiance of the law, was another area of discomfort for constitutionalists. In the aftermath of the local elections, O'Duffy took a swipe at the prosperous rancher class of large farmers, who were traditional CnaG voters. He rejected the idea of FG as a pro-rancher party.[178] As such, a range of issues contributed to precipitating a split within the party approximately a year after its foundation.

◆ ◆ ◆

Some moderates in FG despaired about O'Duffy's fascist tendencies, mostly from the ex–Center Party wing. In mid–August 1934, it was revealed that General O'Duffy held a conference in Dublin with "Terje Ballsrud" [sic], a representative of the Norwegian "Greyshirts."[179] Baalsrud was a minor figure in Norwegian fascism, soon to be outshone by Vidkun Quisling, Norway's wartime puppet leader. Baalsrud was editor of the party organ of the *Fedrelandslaget*, a right-wing anti-communist organization which became a political party in 1933. It refused to describe itself as fascist, despite being influenced by Italian fascism and corporatism. Some members adopted a gray shirt.[180] During his service as a cabinet minister in the short-lived government of Peder Kolstad in 1931–32, Quisling was drawn towards Mussolini and domestically became closer to Baalsrud's movement.[181]

Republicans alleged that O'Duffy was in contact with Mosley's British Union of Fascists (BUF) and that the two leaders had reached a "secret arrangement," presumably related to the status of Northern Ireland in a scenario where their respective parties each came to power.[182] "The company he was keeping … was increasingly fascistic," wrote Mike Cronin. However, members of the BUF were banned from membership of the Blueshirts from July 1933 onwards. Mike Cronin cast doubt on the suggestion that the Blueshirts worked with Mosley's movement. Neither Ned Cronin's son, Richard Mulcahy's son nor Lady Diana Mosley could recall "any links between the two movements" when interviewed by Mike Cronin. He concluded that "the BUF and the Blueshirts kept themselves separate."[183] A brief correspondence was later entered into by Liam Walsh, O'Duffy's secretary, with the BUF's Alexander Raven Thomson, nicknamed the "Alfred Rosenberg of British Fascism." A heated debate over the thorny issue of Ireland's constitutional status (commonwealth or republic) prevented a meeting of minds between the Irish and British fascists.

The campaign by O'Duffy's opponents to remove him as FG leader was attributed by Walsh to their "envy, fear, greed, ambition and the desire to equal if not surpass General O'Duffy." He laid blame on Frank MacDermot and James Dillon, whom he castigated as crypto-unionists whose support for the British Commonwealth was unacceptable to a patriot like O'Duffy.[184] General O'Duffy claimed that his irksome vice presidents regularly threatened to resign, he considered "all these resignation bomb-shells would be too much for the League of Youth to bear."[185] A major reason for the rupture in FG arose from O'Duffy's support for an illegal campaign urging farmers to refuse to pay land annuities to the government. The LoY ratified a motion endorsing this call at its conference in mid–August. Although a motion calling for the Blueshirts to split from FG was withdrawn, the fact it had been proposed at all illustrated the depth of the divide between the Blueshirts and the politicians.

The intensification of anti-government feeling among the Blueshirts came in the aftermath of a bloody incident on 13 August 1934 at an auction of seized cattle at Marsh's Yard in Cork. Local anger was palpable in the local farming community following the seizure of cattle from farms in Bishopstown and Ballincollig due to the farmers' failure to pay land annuities. On the morning of the auction, 3,000 protestors turned out at Marsh's Yard to express their opposition to the seizure. A cordon of 300 members of the Broy Harriers faced down the protesting farmers. A lorry loaded with men drove into the locked gate of the cattle auction which led the police to open fire on the crowd in a sordid attempt to restore order. Nine were wounded in the shooting, including one fatally: the 22-year-old Michael Patrick Lynch of Carrignavar. The dying Lynch was attended to by the wife of Eamonn O'Neill, a West Cork FG deputy, before he was given the last rites by a priest. He was moved to a nearby hospital where he died later that night. Immediately after the shooting, hand-to-hand fighting between the farmers and gardaí broke out, which left two policemen injured. Although the flare up lasted for less than half an hour, "excitement prevailed for the remainder of the day" and several thousand farmers followed the armed military and police escort which transported the cattle to the nearby railway station.[186] Michael Patrick Lynch remains the only person ever killed by the gardaí in a civil disobedience.

Incidents like Marsh's Yard animated farmers' grievances and accelerated the Blueshirts' demand for radical direct action against the FF government. They looked towards O'Duffy to lead a campaign against annuities payments whilst tariffs endured. An article by Dale Montgomery recorded the longstanding overlap between Blueshirt activities and criminality. A police report attributed 718 incidents of violence to the Blueshirts between 1 July 1934 and 31 May 1935. Seventy percent of these incidents occurred in counties Cork, Kilkenny, Limerick, and Waterford.[187] O'Duffy planned a shakeup of FG, which included elevating agrarian radicals like Belton to high office within the party. Blythe was to become the party's propaganda officer, under O'Duffy's proposed scheme.[188] At a secret session of the LoY's governing body, a resolution was passed which committed the organization to supporting farmers who would not pay annuities to the government for as long as the government refused to refer the question of the farmers' liability to a special tribunal. O'Duffy was now committed to implementing an illegal policy. It was reported that this created "acute differences" in policy between O'Duffy and Cosgrave, and that a split was on the cards. Although O'Duffy instantly dismissed the rumor as "nonsense," Cosgrave initially declined to comment.[189] His silence was telling.

On foot of the Blueshirts' new radical policy, its director-general sought to receive the same imprimatur from his FG colleagues. At the meeting of the national executive on 30 August, O'Duffy proposed that FG should support a strike by farmers to withhold their annuities to the government. The motion was seen as "striking at the financial foundations of the state" which, if passed, would "unequivocally sanction the use of unconstitutional methods."[190] Aside from the obvious legal ramifications attached to slipping into unconstitutional methods, the pro–Treaty party had fought the Civil War to establish a functional democratic state. They would not risk destabilizing the Free State by engaging in agrarian lawlessness. Republican Congress gleefully hoped to foment a split within FG by painting a lurid picture of the official opposition declaring "guerilla warfare on the government" if the motion were passed, arguing that large scale "blocking of roads, wire cutting and interference with cattle seizures" would soon be endorsed by FG.[191] Indeed, one newly appointed member of the national executive even advocated derailing trains, to the consternation of Michael Tierney and James Hogan. Tierney complained about the impact of the tangled FG-Blueshirt relationship on policy formulation, arguing that permitting "every lunatic in the country [to] decide their policy for them" must end.[192] Although no clear view was arrived at, a "furious row" broke out between O'Duffy and Hogan, who resigned on the spot from his position. Shortly after the meeting ended, Tierney privately informed O'Duffy that he too planned to resign.[193] Hogan went to the press to publicly express his opposition to General O'Duffy's "destructive and hysterical leadership."[194]

In addition to his rejection of the proposed campaign to withhold annuities, Hogan also opposed O'Duffy's militant statements against partition and his plans to appoint a Blueshirt organizer north of the border. Hogan stated that he failed to see any difference between O'Duffy's policy and the policy of the IRA.[195] He later criticized Cosgrave for having "sat still and let [O'Duffy] run amok for a whole year, while I was a crank and a lot worse because even in council I dared to oppose the mad mullah in some of his most outlandish suggestions."[196] For his part, O'Duffy denied he wanted "foolish spectacular activities in the North" but nor did he want "cynical abandonment." He continued, "I only want the Blueshirts to keep the thought of the North warm in their hearts." O'Duffy charged that Hogan "knows nothing and he cares less about our Nationals in the North who have so long been treated with indifference."[197]

A divide between the "the militant and the Parliamentary sections" of the opposition was widely acknowledged before and after the national executive met. Although General O'Duffy declared that amicable relations continued to exist within the party after the stormy conference, his statements were characterized by the press as "many, lengthy and contradictory."[198] There was speculation that a formalized fissure would see O'Duffy lead the Blueshirts out of FG, on foot of which he would launch a new political party. *An Phoblacht* erroneously reported that O'Duffy, Cronin and Blythe were preparing to launch a new party in early September following the impending split.[199] In fact, Cronin and Blythe helped to drive a stake into O'Duffy's leadership of the Blueshirts.

Despite the resignation of Hogan and Tierney, there appeared to be an unsteady unity in the party as O'Duffy attended a commemoration flanked by Dillon and Cronin to honor Collins at the scene of the lost leader's assassination in Béal na mBláth. Eight thousand supporters turned out to the event on 3 September. Standing on the site "made sacred by the blood of Michael Collins," O'Duffy launched a plea for his supporters to remain loyal and dedicated to achieve Collins' unfinished vision. He assured his audience that there was "no split in the Blueshirts" and referred to Lynch's recent death at Marsh's Yard. He finally concluded with a moving tribute which synthesized the Blueshirt movement with the powerful memory of Collins: "The spirit of Michael Collins is abroad today; the nation is once more upon the march; who dares cry 'Halt' to us?" The speech produced prolonged cheering.[200] It was an incredible performance and the presence of most FG figureheads indicated there was a chance O'Duffy could survive yet another crisis.

The faux unity displayed at the Collins commemoration was short-lived. O'Duffy was presented with a four-point ultimatum by his vice presidents (Cosgrave, Dillon and MacDermot) setting out the terms of his continued leadership of the party. They demanded that he attend weekly meetings with the vice presidents. They also urged that a meeting should be scheduled in the Mansion House to finally iron out any remaining ambiguous elements of policy, in an effort to prevent O'Duffy from making policy on the hoof. They were particularly concerned with preventing the erratic General from making extreme comments about republicanism or forthrightly expressing his admiration for European dictators. The ultimatum required that all his future speeches would be prepared in advance and would be screened by party staff. Finally, they demanded that O'Duffy would only interact with the press by writing and would refrain from providing oral statements.[201] The ultimatum was nothing short of a ritual humiliation. Although he briefly acceded to the demand, he soon reneged on the deal. The ultimatum illustrated the complete lack of faith among the party's vice presidents in their leader's judgment and competency. Others like Blythe awoke to O'Duffy's manifold shortcomings "as leader, thinker, speaker, and organizer." According to David Fitzpatrick, from Blythe's perspective, "O'Duffy had failed in his performance as a charismatic puppet, so he snapped the strings."[202]

On 13 September, O'Duffy and Cosgrave appeared together at the funeral of Alderman John Jinks, a former politician in County Sligo, whose absence at a 1927 Dáil vote had saved the CnaG government.[203] It was one of the last public appearances the two men made as political allies. In one of his final speeches as FG leader in mid–September, O'Duffy reaffirmed that the Blueshirts were "composed largely of farmers' sons and of agricultural workers" who saw the political turmoil of the economic war as a threat to their inheritance. He argued that the new Blueshirt policy encouraging its members to withhold annuities payments to the government was similar in tone to "Fianna Fáil speeches from 1931, where they advised the people not to pay."[204] A brief newspaper strike in September may have slightly prolonged O'Duffy's leadership as his bombastic statements no longer had any output in the daily press which was "to a large extent his shop window."[205]

On 18 September, O'Duffy arrived at 3 Merrion Square with a resignation letter which he handed to the party's general secretary, Liam Burke. Dillon viewed the letter as an effort by O'Duffy to blackmail his party colleagues into accepting his will.[206] It was a tactic he had used in the past and would use again in the future. However, on this occasion it backfired. At the FG national executive meeting of 21 September, he read out the contents of his resignation letter. He claimed policy differences were paramount in provoking his resignation, "I stand for an independent and undivided Ireland … whether it be a Republic, the restoration of the ancient Kingdom of Ireland, or an All-Ireland Free State." He argued that the Irish people had a sovereign right to withdraw from the Commonwealth. This implicitly pro-republican sentiment conflicted with the views of the FG vice presidents. But his main grievances were concerned with agriculture and the land annuities. He believed it was "immoral and unjust to ask a farmer to pay in these hard times a bill which he has already met" due to tariff increases; he praised the Blueshirts in their "struggle against the gross injustice of the Government's demands," declaring:

> I will whip no man on to do anything which I would not have the "guts" to do myself; I will egg no man on with my right arm while making a show of restraining him with my left.… The prisoners in Arbour Hill and Mountjoy are either right or wrong. The UIP, according to the speeches of the leaders of that party, hold they are guilty of deplorable breaches of the law, that they have embarked on an unjustifiable campaign of destruction … yet the official organ of the UIP appeals for funds for these prisoners. Was such hypocrisy ever heard of before? … My belief is that the present struggle is a national struggle, a continuation of the Land League struggle.[207]

The FG national executive accepted O'Duffy's resignation. He was replaced by Cosgrave as acting leader of FG.

O'Duffy told the press he was "glad to be out of politics" but alluded to a political comeback: "my services will always be with the Irish people in circumstances and under conditions which, in my opinion, make those services effective and valuable."[208] It is likely that O'Duffy hoped to engineer a split between the LoY and FG, remaining on as leader of the Blueshirts and contesting the next general election as a separate force. He castigated an alternative resolution to his anti-annuities campaign proposed by the national executive of FG as being "so completely futile and ambiguous" as to render it worthless. He added, "I brought a useless discussion to an end declaring that the Blueshirts and farmers might expect no lead from the National Executive and would simply have to carry on as they thought best themselves, and abide by the consequences."[209] In his resignation letter, he offered to remain as leader of the LoY, apparently hoping to strengthen his position by winning a vote of confidence among the Blueshirts. Dillon detected the hand of Belton in backstairs machinations in trying to divorce the Blueshirts from FG.[210] Dillon also blamed Thomas Gunning for his role in the controversy, whom he referred to as "a bad lad."[211]

Siphoning the Blueshirts away from FG would have provided O'Duffy with the freedom to lead the 47,923-strong LoY into open defiance against FF over the land annuities issue and to organize greater activities north of the border despite a ban from the Northern Ireland government.[212] Given O'Duffy's penchant for fascism, it is likely he wished to shake off the constitutionalists in FG, particularly the ex–Center Party wing. O'Duffy's hopes that he could continue to lead the Blueshirts were dashed when Cronin and Blythe joined in the chorus of denunciation of O'Duffy's leadership at a meeting of the LoY which immediately followed his resignation from FG. Blythe's early involvement in the O'Duffy debacle severely hampered his reputation and left him a marginal figure within FG.

Since summer 1934, the LoY required a cross-membership with FG, which threw a legal question mark over O'Duffy's ability to remain leader of the LoY while not a member of FG. The invitation to attend the LoY meeting stated that attendance was "absolutely essential" as "business of vital importance" would be discussed. It was only upon arriving at FG/LoY headquarters that all committee members learned of O'Duffy's resignation. At the meeting, O'Duffy discussed the issues which had arisen between him and the party's vice presidents. He read out a proposed message of farewell, "undated and unsigned," which he proposed to publish if the LoY agreed to his resignation. He then left the meeting and allowed the LoY to deliberate without him. One delegate, Colonel P.J. Coughlan considered this "very manly and honorable."[213] However, it was discovered that Gunning had been "telephoning to O'Duffy, every quarter of an hour for instructions." Belton also traveled to O'Duffy's home at 2 Wilton Place for similar purposes.[214]

Despite efforts by the General to micromanage his continued leadership of the Blueshirts, his efforts failed. When Ned Cronin realized that Gunning was under instructions to split the Blueshirts, he made the bizarre but apparently true accusation that Gunning had urged him, after his release from Arbour Hill to murder O'Duffy. "Gunning was unable to deny this and shortly afterwards the Central Council unanimously accepted the resignation."[215] One senior officer claimed he had "lived in hell for the past three months with that man [O'Duffy]" and picked up the draft resignation statement before saying "what he would not give to have that dated and signed." A Blueshirt loyal to O'Duffy, Captain Tom Hyde, entered the room of the FG national executive where he listened to Dillon talk disparagingly of his former leader. Hyde "could not stand it any longer; his very blood was starting to boil. He stood up and told Dillon how dare he criticize a man of General O'Duffy's national record."[216] These early tensions between some in the LoY and the political operatives indicated a split in the Blueshirts would follow.

A pro–FG faction of the LoY central committee ruled that O'Duffy was ineligible to remain as director-general and immediately elected Cronin as his replacement. The manner in which Cronin was quickly chosen was characterized by O'Duffy and his supporters as irregular, because it was not voted on by all LoY members. A protracted stand-off ensued between the O'Duffy-led faction and the Cronin-led faction over the legitimacy of the new leadership. Manning acknowledged that "the haste with which Cronin was given charge of the Blueshirts had all the appearances of both being irregular and of being an attempt to forestall some possible split."[217]

The director of the LoY in Dublin, Michael Stack, rejected the claim that O'Duffy's resignation was accepted by the Blueshirts' central council.[218] An unedifying dispute arose over who was the legitimate director-general of the Blueshirts, O'Duffy or Cronin. The affair helped to "hopelessly discredit the Blue Shirt movement and to damage the prestige of the parliamentary Opposition," according to one historian.[219]

The nature of O'Duffy's resignation prompted a flurry of rumors. There was unfounded press speculation that O'Duffy would contest the upcoming Senate elections for FG. This failed to materialize as the scale of the breach between O'Duffy and the party was insurmountable.[220] He described his gladness to be leaving politics but undermined this by immediately agitating against Commandant Cronin's leadership and attempting to launch his next political initiative. O'Duffy's brief leadership of FG came to an end on 21 September 1934, just over a year since the party's formation. Unelected, he was restricted to traversing the country attempting to ready the FG organization for an electoral test. He claimed the 200 public meetings he attended and the creation of over 1,100 FG branches was "all Blueshirt work, for without the Blueshirts, Fine Gael would never have got anywhere."[221] However, his predictions for what could be achieved in the June local elections proved overly ambitious and caused internal rumblings about his ability to deliver an electoral victory.

Perpetual policy differences between O'Duffy and his party colleagues mounted over issues including land annuities, corporatism, Northern Ireland, republicanism, parliamentary democracy, and even the youth franchise. O'Duffy's instincts were frequently radical and, in many respects, bore more resemblance to FF than the conservative FG. He openly endorsed FF's industrial policy of protectionism over liberal free trade, but he disagreed with aspects of the government's implementation of protectionism with regards to its impact on agriculture.[222] Ruttledge caustically asked in a speech why O'Duffy would not simply join FF if he was such a republican. Although ideologically there may have been some overlap between FF and O'Duffy on some issues, he had a personal antipathy towards Éamon de Valera. In a report submitted in August 1927 as garda commissioner, O'Duffy observed that FF had a deleterious impact on national security: "Since the entry into the Dáil of the Fianna Fáil party the situation has become worse. The Police have been made to learn that it is dangerous to impede the liberties and progress of these would-be murderers, a halo of righteousness surrounds them and their followers."[223] Freed from the overbearing pressure of his colleagues in FG, O'Duffy set out to create a new political party which would more accurately and honestly reflect his values. The next chapter investigates O'Duffy's establishment of the National Corporate Party, which hoped to break the mold of Irish politics.

# 9

# National Corporate Party

The LoY experienced a significant internal split following O'Duffy's disputed resignation. The affair generated severe confusion and ill-will among ordinary Blueshirts. Dillon stated that following the split O'Duffy was "on the rampage and already showing signs of self-destruction."[1] O'Duffy claimed not to have resigned as director-general of the Blueshirts but merely as leader of FG. In response, on 25 September, Ned Cronin produced the unsigned and undated farewell address. This muddied the waters and appeared to contradict O'Duffy's version of events. In it, O'Duffy stated he would stand down and begged that the new leader would receive "that loyalty and obedience you so cheerfully gave to me."[2] O'Duffy strongly repudiated Cronin's suggestion, claiming that he alone remained the sole director-general of the Blueshirts and that Cronin's leadership was "null and void."[3] Liam Walsh repeated O'Duffy's narrative: that FG had artificially created a "new" Blueshirts under Commandant Cronin which tried to usurp O'Duffy's organization. According to Walsh, the "old guard under General O'Duffy ... continued and thrived despite the campaign of calumny and falsehoods waged upon it and upon their leader by the chips of the Fine Gael Party."[4] In truth, O'Duffy's faction was very much the rump group. The split marked the rapid decline of the Blueshirts.

Although a protracted period of jostling for the support of the membership ensued between the two factions, Cronin had significant advantages owing to the institutional support of FG and its newspaper, the use of party offices, and access to party funds. He also retained the support of the major Blueshirt leaders, including Ernest Blythe, T.F. O'Higgins, Colonel Jerry Ryan and Commandant Denis Quish.[5] O'Duffy largely financed his faction from his own coffers. He personally funded the establishment of a political news sheet. Cronin set about expelling several O'Duffy loyalists, including Thomas Gunning, who was prevented from entering his office at 3 Merrion Square in the wake of O'Duffy's resignation.[6] True to form, O'Duffy started a campaign in early October to traverse the country to shore up his support from the fractured LoY. His rhetoric hardened and he encouraged criminality in the form of tree felling to disrupt cattle seizures.[7] He forecasted that the Blueshirts would "march through the present crisis more glorious, more virile, and better citizens than ever before."[8] However, Colonel Ryan warned against such a campaign, which he presciently forecasted "will cause bad blood among old comrades ... and it will bring about utter confusion and the complete collapse of the League of Youth."[9]

At a dance in Carrickmacross on 1 October, O'Duffy delivered a dramatic speech. He informed delegates: "I am still your leader. Anybody who stands in our way will be sent back in very short time to the obscurity in which I found them." It illustrated his hubris and inflated ego. He claimed that he would "disappear from public life" if one vote was cast against him by local Blueshirt leaders in Kerry.[10] The split was highly acrimonious. O'Duffy referred to Blythe as a "damnable traitor" who "was going around Roscommon saying that Monaghan was against me."[11] Repeatedly, the General tried to position himself as a peacemaker interested in finding a compromise. This likely pointed to his weakened position, as one newspaper put it "General O'Duffy was cutting no ice, and if he should succeed in rallying to his standard any substantial number of Blueshirts it would cause surprise." The report claimed that O'Duffy was trying to undo his admitted blunder in resigning as leader of FG by seeking control of the Blueshirts.[12]

Patrick Belton, by then a renegade FG TD, broached a compromise peace offer between the two rival Blueshirt leaders. Although O'Duffy responded positively to his proposed round table, Cronin rejected the proposal out of hand on 6 October.[13] Belton was expelled from FG the same month owing to his support for O'Duffy and his perceived efforts to split the party.[14] P.J. Coughlan wrote, "his only crime was to demand fair play for the man who built up the greatest organization this country has ever known."[15] A right-wing demagogue in his own right, Belton initially supported O'Duffy and announced his plans to form a new party with O'Duffy at the helm.[16] This failed to materialize, and the two men later fell out. O'Duffy was a poor judge of character and regularly clashed with former allies. He wrote to a pro–Cronin Blueshirt from Kilkenny to complain "[I] find it hard to believe that my comrades of yesterday should try to ruin my reputation."[17]

Various local branches of the LoY were polled to determine where they stood on the leadership question: Cronin or O'Duffy. In late October, the Clonmel branch of the Blueshirts declared unanimously for Cronin. At a meeting of the Navan branch only 35 out of 100 units were represented at a conference which voted to adopt a neutral position.[18] The low quorum illustrated the high levels of disaffection and a declining membership. In early November, a meeting of Blueshirts in Limerick became violent as supporters from the Cronin faction challenged O'Duffy's right to preside over the meeting. Disorder intensified as several young Blueshirts "jumped on the seats and tables arguing and gesticulating" against General O'Duffy. A bitter argument ensued between O'Duffy and Denis Quish, until O'Duffy in a "stentorian voice" accused Captain Quish of "being a well-paid official of the other side" which prompted Quish to level counter charges of financial unscrupulousness against O'Duffy. Finally, the row ended when O'Duffy's supporters forcibly removed their factional rivals from the meeting.[19] Similar scenes happened two weeks later in Ballyshannon, County Donegal. Although the meeting was closed to the press, audible loud noises came from within the meeting hall. Suddenly, Commandant Cronin and 12 of his supporters erupted from the room in a fit of rage. The local convention declared in O'Duffy's favor.[20]

On other occasions, Blueshirts regarded as belonging to O'Duffy's faction were prevented from addressing meetings. At a meeting of Leitrim Blueshirts in October, Gunning was prevented from speaking as he belonged to the "opposition."[21] Cronin's faction spurned all attempts to compromise, including middle-ground attempts to select a compromise candidate for director-general. The name of General Seán MacEoin, an FG deputy, was suggested.[22] O'Duffy was best man at MacEoin's wedding in June 1922. O'Duffy wrote that "these meetings of Cronin and these engineered snow ball resolutions of confidence are absurd."[23] McGarry acknowledged that by late 1934 his challenge to Cronin was more significant than had been previously acknowledged in the historiography. O'Duffy continued to draw audiences of thousands of supporters for his speeches.[24]

O'Duffy's faction was in urgent need of finances if it hoped to have any chance of success. A new headquarters was opened at 97 Middle Abbey Street in Dublin, which bore a heavy cost on O'Duffy's personal wealth. In an appeal letter, O'Duffy stated he was "not anxious to raise huge funds and spend them wastefully" but recognized "we need a considerable amount of finance to carry on."[25] In a letter to supporters he wrote "if we can get cash now success is absolutely assured. There is no other barrier in the way."[26]

◆ ◆ ◆

In an editorial published by the *Kilkenny People* newspaper, it was acknowledged that General O'Duffy had "many excellent qualities and certain outstanding limitations." Whilst recognizing that "democracy may have its faults," the article challenged the assumption that a dictatorship was a preferable alternative. It argued, "we prefer [democracy] to any system of Dictatorship that modern Europe has thrown up whether it is centered in Rome, Berlin or Moscow."[27]

O'Duffy was faced with the need to outline clear policy differences between his faction and Cronin's. In FG, discord grew between O'Duffy and his colleagues over three key differences: land annuities, republicanism, and fascism. In late November 1934, Frank MacDermot explained that under O'Duffy's leadership there was "too much of what I call flirtation with Fascism." He "saw no reason to introduce Mussolinis or Hitlers into this country."[28] Freed from paying lip service to the parliamentary sensibilities of his constitutionalist colleagues, O'Duffy became more open about his fascist sympathies. He attended a private showing of a film entitled "The Rise of Mussolini" on 2 December in Dublin.[29] His successor as garda commissioner, Colonel Broy, also attended the screening.[30] In late November, it was announced that following the reorganization of the League of Youth, "a scheme for a new party" would be presented by Belton and O'Duffy.[31] Early in 1935, Belton had a hand in setting up the "New Land League," which O'Duffy offered his initial support to. Gradually, O'Duffy's attitude to the New Land League cooled, as he saw it becoming too aligned with FG.[32] O'Duffy's intentions were certainly political; he wrote to supporters in December 1934 that "we find it necessary to contest elections and undertake the functions of a political party."[33]

In late December 1934, O'Duffy became more heavily involved with international fascist networks. Irish-centric literature has referred to O'Duffy's attendance at international far-right conferences, particularly the 16–17 December 1934 "Fascist International Conference" held in Montreux, Switzerland. In public, O'Duffy intermittently wavered between open sympathy for and identification with fascism and a tendency to "put the green jersey on" and claim his political views were authentically Irish and infused with Catholic social teaching. Irish historians have generally highlighted O'Duffy's attendance at such conferences to illustrate the extent to which his politics mirrored continental trends. However, detail about the particulars of O'Duffy's involvement with international fascist cliques has been lacking. The broader international context of the rivalry between Nazi Germany and Fascist Italy has also been overlooked.

Several Irish historians have claimed that O'Duffy attended a December 1934 Nazi-sponsored conference in Zurich held by the "International Action of Nationalisms." The origin of this claim is found in Michael A. Ledeen's 1972 book *Universal Fascism*, which anachronistically labeled the group a "neo–Nazi organization" despite its pre-war existence.[34] Cronin explained that it was founded to spread the "ideas of international National Socialism and a universal racist doctrine." Details about the "International Action of Nationalisms" or the backgrounds of several of its attendees were not found in Ledeen's study. This organization was in fact the "Internationale Arbeitsgemeinschaft der Nationalisten" (IAdN), referred to in English as the "Nationalist International," but more literally translated as the "International Working Group of Nationalists." The IAdN was founded in April 1934 by the German jurist Hans Keller, with the active financial support of Joseph Goebbels' propaganda ministry. Its slogan was "nationalists of the world, unite!" an inversion of the Comintern slogan "workers of the world, unite!" Its headquarters was in Zurich, in neutral Switzerland, where it presented itself as an alternative to the League of Nations. In January 1935, the Swiss authorities denied Keller reentry to Switzerland as an "undesirable foreigner," which prompted his organization to move its headquarters to London that year and finally to Berlin in 1936.[35]

However, the suggestion that O'Duffy attended an IAdN conference is incorrect. The IAdN organized its first conference on 5–7 December 1934 in Berlin, not Zurich. It was held in the opulent Hotel Kaiserhof. Contemporary newspaper reports placed O'Duffy in Bandon, County Cork, on 6 December, the mid-point of the Berlin conference, where he delivered a speech encouraging a campaign of tree felling to disrupt cattle seizures.[36] Each of O'Duffy's absences from Ireland were regularly reported and speculated upon in the Irish media. It would have been unlikely for O'Duffy to have journeyed to Berlin without at least one journalist catching wind of the story. A further reason which explains O'Duffy's non-attendance was that he fell firmly within the Italian orbit in late 1934. This alignment with Italy also explains why Oswald Mosley did not attend the IAdN conference, contrary to Ledeen's claim. Mosley was then in the pay of Mussolini's Italy.[37]

There was an Irish delegate at the IAdN conference in Berlin: the FG deputy from Louth, James Edward Murphy. The Irishman praised Nazism as the solution to the Versailles crisis and the upheavals of the 1929 Wall Street Crash, dubbing Nazism "the most interesting movement in the world at present." He also claimed that the press in England was "controlled by Jews" and posited that "the English are the oldest nation of Europe, this is why they are very internationally minded."[38] Murphy was a Drogheda businessman first elected as a SF deputy to the Second Dáil in 1921; he and O'Duffy were then parliamentary colleagues. He supported the

Anglo-Irish Treaty and served in parliament until 1937. He was a "devout Catholic" who was a senior Knight of Columbanus and a member of the Dominican third order.[39] Murphy was associated with the Blueshirts and paraded behind a banner which read "O'Duffy leads; we follow" at Trim in March 1934.[40] In May of that year he welcomed O'Duffy to a rally in Drogheda.[41] As most of his Dáil contributions focused on agriculture and parochial issues, his attendance at a Nazi conference was peculiar. Another Irishman involved with the IAdN was Walter F. Starkie, reputedly the chairman of the Irish national committee of the Akademie für die Rechte der Völker. He wrote to Heller in 1938 praising the Munich Agreement.[42]

On 16–17 December, O'Duffy left Ireland to attend a conference of the Comitati d'Azione per l'Universalità di Roma (CAUR) at the Palace Hotel in Montreux, Switzerland. The meeting was dubbed a "secret fascist congress" in a "palatial hotel." CAUR was founded in 1933 by an Italian government functionary, Asvero Gravelli, who edited the journal, *Ottobre*. Gravelli was one of the Italian delegates in Berlin two weeks previously who bickered with Keller and the German Nazis over anti-Semitism and race. The IAdN can be seen as a "counter-reaction to the Italian CAUR."[43] This was illustrative of the worsening relations between Europe's two most prominent dictators. Following Hitler's assumption of power in January 1933, Mussolini disliked the upstart leader of Germany and feared his Nazi government had designs on German-speaking areas in northern Italy. Relations between the two demagogues reached a low ebb when the Austrian dictator Engelbert Dollfuss, an ally of Mussolini in an important buffer state between Italy and Germany, was assassinated by the Austrian Nazi Party in July 1934. The prospect of Italy launching a war to prevent an *Anschluss* became a distinct possibility. Each regime tried to act as the far-right metropole which would influence personalities and movements abroad. Mussolini considered Nazism to be "the revolt of the old German tribes of the primitive forests against the Latin civilization of Rome."[44] Although O'Duffy was a very minor figure in the international disputes which moved parallel to the Italo-German rivalry, he sided firmly with the Italians.

The Montreux conference, the "Fascist International Congress," brought together 14 movements from 12 countries including O'Duffy, Vidkun Quisling from the Norwegian Nasjonal Samling, and representatives drawn from the Spanish Falange, Salazar's party in Portugal, Romania's Iron Guard, and several other minor extreme-right parties. Swiss police were sent to the small town to protect the Romanian foreign minister, Nicolae Titulescu, who lived in the hotel, because the Iron Guard had issued a death threat against him. In Montreux, O'Duffy outlined a set of targets for the conference, including to recognize "the general principles of fascism" and to arrange to host annual meetings in different countries. He made an appeal to Britain on Ireland's behalf, arguing that Ireland must first be given its full independence before goodwill could exist between the two nations.[45] O'Duffy supported a motion initiated by the Italian delegation which condemned racial persecution. He spoke forcefully against any motion which would "recommend international action against the Jews," in opposition to the virulent anti-Semitism of the Iron Guard.[46] He said, "they had no Jewish problem in Ireland" and that he "could not subscribe to the principle of the persecution of any race."

Speaking to journalists upon his return, O'Duffy clearly pinned his colors to the mast, opting for the more "genial" Italian variety of fascism: "the Nazi policy is not compatible with the corporative system."[47]

O'Duffy supported Mussolini's efforts to "export Italian Fascism as a revolutionary solution to the crises affecting Europe," centered on the concept of the corporate state and the "universality of Rome." It was ironic considering Mussolini's one-time aphorism that fascism was "not an article for export." Mussolini rebuked Hitler's racism and argued "anti-Semitism had no place on the Italian agenda," pointing to the presence of a disproportionately high number of Jews in the National Fascist Party when compared to the total Italian population.[48] O'Duffy's newspaper loftily argued there was "no justification for singling out Jews for persecution just because they are Jews" and that anti-Semitism was "the rock on which both Hitler and Craigavon will perish."[49] A seven-member committee was elected at Montreux to oversee the new Fascist International, to which O'Duffy was elected.[50]

Following the Swiss conference, O'Duffy traveled southwards to Italy where he conferred with Benito Mussolini.[51] Here they discussed "freely and frankly" the operation of the corporate state in Italy. O'Duffy's secretary noted that whilst O'Duffy took inspiration from Mussolini's corporatism, he recognized such a model "would not be suitable for Ireland" and that the system must be adapted "to a purely Irish mold."[52] After his return, he praised the Duce and corporatism as the savior of Italy's agricultural problems. Clearly, he hoped a parallel would be drawn with Ireland's agricultural crisis. He adopted a parochial view on the meaning of fascism, publicly stating that it was simply an Italian expression of the corporatist system, which had been endorsed by the Catholic Church.[53] Mussolini invited O'Duffy to return to Italy two months later. In January 1935, O'Duffy was elected to the International Center for Corporate Studies in Rome.[54]

Support for CAUR dwindled as Mussolini's fair-weather allies in the various European political parties began to falter in their loyalty to Rome, beginning with Frits Clausen from Denmark, who had been elected chairman of the seven-man council in December. Clausen's movement fell increasingly under "the long hand of Hitler," according to CAUR officials. The raison d'être of the rival international far-right internationals largely disappeared with the advent of the Rome-Berlin Axis 1936. With the "meteoric rise" of Galeazzo Ciano, who became Italian foreign minister in mid-1936, the death knell of CAUR was sounded as he reorientated Italian foreign policy towards closer relations with Germany. Ciano had been a long-time critic of the pan-fascist initiative.[55]

During the early stages of O'Duffy's involvement in CAUR and the attempt to forge a "Fascist International," his erstwhile colleagues in FG expressed dismay with their former leader for recklessly aligning with unabashed continental fascism. An article published in the FG newspaper acknowledged that although several political figures (Blythe and Cronin) in the Free State had received the invitation to the "secret congress," only O'Duffy had been so foolish as to accept. Interestingly, FG reaffirmed its support for corporatism, which had been adopted as party policy at the February 1934 ard fheis. However, it stressed that corporatism was adopted "not on the suggestion of General O'Duffy ... [but] in accordance with the principles laid down in the Encyclical *Quadragesimo Anno*."[56] Although the party still praised "the guiding genius of Signor Mussolini" in implementing corporatism, it claimed that "fascism and the Corporate system are by no means necessarily associated with each other."[57] This resembled O'Duffy's own hair-splitting pedantry. Throughout 1935, O'Duffy continued to build his repertoire of international links but remained mostly within the orbit of Italian fascism rather than the German Nazi government. In late March, O'Duffy and Gunning attended a meeting hosted by Anton Mussert's National Socialist Movement in Amsterdam.[58]

In 1935, Liam Walsh, O'Duffy's secretary, entered correspondence with Alexander Raven Thomson, policy director of the BUF. Thomson sent his well-wishes to O'Duffy's movement in its "difficult struggle" but adopted a largely condescending stance on Ireland. He explained that a Mosley-led Britain would not insist on the payment of land annuities, "as a bitter hatred of usury is a vital part of our policy." But he hoped that a corporatist Ireland would remain inside the British Empire, where they "had great need of Ireland as a source of rich foodstuffs."[59] In reply, Walsh explained he could not endorse Thomson's full views and explained "there can never be a united Ireland again within the Commonwealth." Walsh implored his British counterpart not to "take my letter as a criticism of your policy, far from it" and explained that "like most corporate movements our struggle is a different one." He bragged to Thomson that O'Duffy's movement would win ten to 12 seats at the next general election, thereby holding the balance of power in parliament.[60] Thomson replied by informing Walsh he would see it as a "catastrophe" if Ireland left the Commonwealth. Condescendingly, he asked whether it was "still not possible for you people to look beyond the Parish Pump to the wider destinies that Irishmen have made their own?," by which he referred to Irish involvement in British imperialism.[61]

In reply to Thomson, Walsh emphatically answered "Yes! It is possible for us people in 'Southern Ireland' to 'look beyond the Parish Pump.' We look to 'Northern Ireland' as part of our territory, both nationally and geographically." His letter continued to discursively quote O'Duffy's more inflammatory pro-republican statements in an assertion of Irish irredentist principles.[62] Thomson's curt reply demonstrated his exasperation, "What can I say? … I must admit I shall never fully understand the Irish, North or South; and I feel that a further discussion of our differences can scarcely lead to any useful result."[63] The correspondence between the two men, although classed as private and unofficial, illuminated the unbreachable differences between Irish nationalists and British imperialists despite their mutual affinity for continental fascism. Thomson's condescending tone was evident throughout the exchange. The letters contradict a claim by John Rodden and John Rossi that O'Duffy "sent out feelers to Oswald Mosley… (Mosley rebuffed him)."[64] This suggestion is unfounded. Whilst Walsh occasionally sent letters to Mosley, formal cooperation was absent. O'Duffy was particularly sensitive to avoid an association with the BUF, links which socialist-republicans scoured for.

Further illustrating the imperialist and anti–Irish mindset of British fascism, Arnold Leese's Imperial Fascist League called for the return of Britain's "oldest" and "lost" colony, Ireland. In June 1939, Leese argued for the reoccupation of the Free

State, demanding that the British government "end the Irish State; and do it now and quickly."[65]

◆ ◆ ◆

As 1935 began, O'Duffy promoted his faction's independent political line. He declared they were "the only Blueshirts." The impact of his continental junketeering was evident in the prosaic pro-corporatist policy he proposed for his organization. His "policy was to introduce the corporative system in this country and put it in a prosperous position, as had been done in Italy."[66] In a lengthy speech at Creggs, County Galway, O'Duffy outlined the supposed benefits of corporatism for Irish agriculture.[67] At the opening of his organization's new headquarters in Pearse Street, which was named St Patrick's Social Club, O'Duffy railed against parliamentary democracy and denied that the FF government represented authentic democracy.[68] It was announced in February that General O'Duffy intended to hold an ard fheis of his supporters on 8 June, which seemed to tease the reconstitution of the pro–O'Duffy Blueshirts into a political party.[69]

By early 1935, the campaign against the payment of annuities was petering out as an end to the economic war appeared on the horizon. In January, the coal-cattle pact was signed between the Irish and British governments which increased the British quota on cattle imports from Ireland by one-third, in exchange for an Irish increase in coal imports from Britain. It foreshadowed the eventual Anglo-Irish Trade Agreement of 1938.[70] The government adopted a hard line against recalcitrant Blueshirts who refused to pay land annuities, which led to hundreds of arrests. Cronin's Blueshirts moved away from direct action while O'Duffy's faction was not in a strong enough position to take advantage of the residual disquiet. Gradually, the desire for radical action against the government dissipated and O'Duffy's place in Irish public life fell with it. The horny handed sons of the toil who swelled the ranks of the original Blueshirts cared little for corporatism, and thus failed to follow O'Duffy into his latest political venture. Cronin's role from 1935 onwards was to oversee the winding down of the Blueshirts and to fold the movement into FG.[71] Although Cronin had ambitions to become leader of FG, his hopes were dashed at a party convention on 21 March which confirmed Cosgrave's leadership.[72] Once bitten, twice shy, FG's political operatives were unprepared to offer the leadership to another unelected Blueshirt strongman. By October 1936, Cronin's Blueshirts were disbanded by the FG national executive and he was locked out of the party's headquarters. "The League of Youth, a pale shadow of its former self, was laid to rest behind the stuffed keyhole of the Georgian head office," wrote Uinseann MacEoin.[73] Cronin later emigrated to England to work as a printer, having squandered much of his personal finances on the Blueshirts.[74]

At a St Patrick's Day rally on 17 March at Tara, County Meath, a speech was read out on O'Duffy's behalf by Gunning which urged the Blueshirts not to rest until "the great goal had been achieved—the Irish corporate state." In a significant announcement of policy, Gunning articulated that four-province federalism with each province having a "legislative council" may be an acceptable solution to the problem of partition, with "some center such as Tara" as the capital of the new Ireland.[75] Despite such lofty pronouncements, O'Duffy's importance in Irish politics had melted away. Although he could posture as the leader-in-waiting of the Irish nation on the international stage with fellow fascists, his domestic position was poor. Former supporters like Dr O'Higgins and Blythe had abandoned O'Duffy during the acrimonious split, leaving him in the lurch with just a small cohort of supporters like Belton and Gunning. O'Duffy planned to launch a new political party in June which would outflank FF on republicanism while promoting corporatism as the panacea to Ireland's woes. The *Irish Workers' Voice* claimed that it was "too late" for O'Duffy to "hide himself in the folds of the Tricolor" owing to his Civil War record. "He was English imperialism's agent for ten years; he is Italian imperialism's agent now."[76]

General O'Duffy argued there was little difference between CnaG and FG, and attributed its lack of overall success in the local elections to the fact that "not one of their TDs had referred to the national question or the Ulster question" during the campaign.[77] He explained that he was "not prepared to lead the League of Youth with the Union Jack tied to his neck," by which he meant supporting a pro–Commonwealth policy.[78] This signaled a new departure towards alignment with republicanism. As a prominent Civil War general, O'Duffy's reputation with republicans was not particularly high. During the zenith of his leadership of the Blueshirts, many in the IRA opposed O'Duffy because he made "Kerry a graveyard in 1922" and because they held an instinctive anti-fascism.[79] His record as garda commissioner similarly antagonized veteran IRA men. Despite his poor relationship with republicans, O'Duffy launched a quixotic effort to engineer a rapprochement with the IRA. Martin White described "a surprise move" on the General's part to seek an alliance in spring 1935 with "the anti-democratic forces of republican extremists." Although the plan may not have been realistic, it illustrated how O'Duffy continued to identify as a republican. His acceptance of the Treaty in 1921 was largely pragmatic and influenced by his devotion to Collins. He was a militarist during the War of Independence and remained a militarist throughout his life. O'Duffy sought to make inroads with the IRA by opening a line of communication with an IRA supporter, Anastasia Nevin of Cashel, County Tipperary. His hopes to use Nevin as an intermediary to contact the republican movement proved fruitless when she rebuffed his plans.[80]

In Northern Ireland, his movement failed to gain any ground. The Royal Ulster Constabulary reported that "a few copies" of O'Duffy's newspaper had been found in Northern Ireland, "but it would not appear to be in circulation in the North" aside from "occasional copies ... being brought into the Six Counties by persons traveling to and fro." The police recommended it was not necessary to prohibit its circulation.[81]

By 1935, the IRA had expelled many of its left-wing elements, including Frank Ryan and Peadar O'Donnell, who left to create the Republican Congress. O'Duffy likely saw a political vacuum within the IRA, which he believed was now cauterized of communism. The IRA was in a quandary at the same time. In April, Seán Russell met President de Valera to discuss prospective cooperation between the IRA and the FF government. Russell promised IRA support for de Valera for a five-year period if he promised that his government would declare a republic towards the end of its period of government. De Valera was unimpressed by Russell, telling him "you want it both ways," and angrily dismissed the IRA envoy.[82] Ironically, the IRA became largely directionless due to the disappearance of the Blueshirts as a force of any significance. Its army council was "increasingly aware of the glitter and temptations of Fianna Fáil" for its members, many of whom joined the party.[83]

Although it was naïve for O'Duffy to expect that the IRA would be willing to contemplate cooperation with him, he may have hoped the state's repressive actions against both the IRA and the Blueshirts would engender mutual sympathy. Indeed, there is evidence of co-operation between imprisoned members of both organizations.[84] Significantly, O'Duffy rebuked de Valera's statement that Ireland would not allow itself to be used as a base by foreign powers for an attack against Britain.[85] The IRA shared the view that Britain becoming embroiled in a continental war would be to Ireland's benefit, following the nationalist aphorism that England's difficulty is Ireland's opportunity.

Aside from trumpeting his republican credentials, O'Duffy paradoxically tried to launch a cross-border initiative for Irish unification under a fascist regime with Job Stott from the Ulster Fascists (UF). Stott was a Yorkshire Catholic who relocated to Belfast where he re-enlisted in the British army during World War I. He later became a B Special and played a prominent role in establishing the UF with Captain T.W. Armstrong.[86] O'Duffy had previously encountered the UF in September 1934 when he claimed to have conferred with a delegation of 26 UF members, including 24 Protestants, in Cork.[87] The UF were willing to work with the Blueshirts and voiced their conditional support for Irish unity but "within the British Empire of FASCIST NATIONS."[88]

O'Duffy and Stott held a meeting in Wynn's Hotel, Dublin, where they founded the "32 Club" on 19 February. In May, the 32 Club published a four-point program: that the organization's central aim was the reunification of Ireland; that the Club's title symbolized the 32 counties of Ireland; that the Club would foster "friendly relations" between North and South, including through social, cultural, business, and other activities; and that membership was open to all Irishmen and women regardless of religious confession or political affiliations. Its members were to be called Pioneers and were entitled to wear a silver badge.[89] Belton, then an independent TD, and Alexander McCabe, a former FG TD, joined the Club.[90] By throwing his lot in with O'Duffy, Stott recognized the disintegration of the UF as a political force by March 1935. He established the Ulster Center of Fascist Studies with himself as "Director of Studies."[91]

North of the border, the 32 Club was fronted by Captain The O'Donovan, an eccentric well known to the police.[92] At an ill-conceived meeting of just ten attendees on 10 April, a motion was proposed by William McKeaveney to establish a Belfast branch of the 32 Club. A "direct negative" motion was proposed, which was carried by four votes to three. Despite a report in the *Blueshirt*, the proposal to establish a Belfast branch was outvoted. The Royal Ulster Constabulary produced a frank assessment:

> From what can be ascertained, the meeting resolved itself into a huge farce, no one apparently taking the proceedings very seriously. McKeaveney is described as a "mental case" and The O'Donovan may be described as falling within the same category. No attempts have been made to hold further meetings.[93]

Significantly, O'Duffy acceded to a policy of establishing an "independent monarchy" for all–Ireland, the status of which "should be equal in every respect to that of Great Britain."[94] McGarry ascribed the entire curious incident to the growing desperation of O'Duffy to find allies capable of replenishing his depleted ranks of supporters.[95] If this was his intention, it was a monumental error as the UF were a microscopic group of no political significance.

◆ ◆ ◆

It was reported in May 1935 that O'Duffy's Blueshirts planned to field candidates in every constituency at the next general election. In characteristic bullishness following a tour of County Tipperary, General O'Duffy announced his position was just as strong in South Tipperary as before the split and predicted that they would win two to three seats in the constituency at the next general election.[96] O'Duffy's faction held their ard fheis at the Mansion House on 8 June. In attendance was the father and sister of Hugh O'Reilly, the martyred Blueshirt who died in December 1933. The family remained loyal to O'Duffy's faction after the split. The General's address returned to the familiar themes of corporatism and republicanism, which became the cornerstones of his new party. He balanced his growing identification with international fascism by arguing that "if Sinn Féin from Hungary was a good idea, a Corporate system from Italy was not necessarily bad."[97]

Most significantly, the 350–600 delegates at the convention approved a motion by O'Duffy to launch a new political party. Several proposed names were bandied about including the National Front and the National Association before finally the National Corporate Party (NCP) was settled on.[98] In Irish it was translated as Cumann Corpruiteac Naisiunta. O'Duffy's faction of the LoY thus formally evolved into a political party.[99] *The Blueshirt* newspaper was renamed to *The Nation*, evoking the newspaper of the same name edited by Thomas Davis of the Young Irelanders. The NCP was an oddity in Irish politics. It retained elements of the militaristic structure of the LoY, including its use of uniforms and organizational units. Members were required to swear an oath of loyalty to O'Duffy as director-general.[100] Colonel P.J. Coughlan from Cork was elected as deputy director-general. It planned to set up a youth wing called the Young Comrades' Association.[101]

From the beginning, O'Duffy intended the NCP to reflect his own personal political views rather than a compromise between various competing elements as was the case in FG. The Proclamation of the Irish Republic from 1916 was adopted as "the basis of national policy" for the newly christened political party, which positioned itself firmly on the bedrock of republicanism. He announced, "We will establish a Republic de jure for 32 counties and de facto for 26." Interestingly, this largely presaged developments in Ireland's constitutional status between 1937 and 1948, from the introduction of the new constitution to the declaration of the Republic of Ireland.

Throughout the Blueshirt period, O'Duffy had been sensitive to claims by the IRA and FF that he was soft on unionism. O'Duffy rejected the notion that any group had "a monopoly of patriotism." In July 1936, a branch of the NCP in County Westmeath passed a resolution calling for the immediate release of all republican prisoners. Lieutenant Duffy, a local party official, queried why the government had proscribed the IRA and closed republican offices yet would not close the Masonic Lodge on Molesworth Street.[102] General O'Duffy's heightened republicanism was reflected across the movement's symbols, including in the decision to alter the traditional "blue shirt" uniform by adopting green ties and replacing the beret with the traditional IV slouch hat. Ordinary members of the organization were also dubbed "Volunteers."[103] By December 1935, the NCP shed its use of the blue shirt altogether and replaced it with a green shirt. This led the organization to be dubbed the "Greenshirts," although it never had the same popular currency as the original Blueshirts.[104] One commentator wrote that "many people rubbed their eyes ... when they read in the daily papers that Gen. O'Duffy had declared for a Republic."[105] The NCP's stance on the riots in Northern Ireland during 1935 was typically republican. It condemned the "unprovoked and brutal attacks" against the nationalist minority. Northern violence reached its zenith in July during the traditional Orange marching season.[106]

The party's leadership structure was dictatorial, with O'Duffy exercising sole authority over its direction. The Führerprinzip is a common hallmark of fascist parties. But, as Eunan O'Halpin noted, O'Duffy was not strongly ideological, "so long as he was in unchallenged command he was relatively indifferent to the direction pursued."[107] O'Duffy was candid in his rejection of parliamentary democracy, which he claimed was "doomed."[108] In addition to adopting the ideology and structure of a fascist organization, the NCP also emulated the liturgy of fascism. At the ard fheis on 8 June, upon entering the meeting hall, O'Duffy was "received with the Blueshirt salute" and was escorted to the podium by a guard of honor.[109] However, there were initial teething problems in the party. At the ard fheis, Dr Conway, a supporter from Cork, argued against basing the NCP on the Easter Proclamation. He claimed that only those properly recognized as delegates by the constitution of the LoY were entitled to vote, which would have disenfranchised two-thirds of the attendees. This "resulted in a certain amount of disorder." Following his election as director-general, O'Duffy "monopolized the congress and threatened to resign if all his motions were not carried." One newly elected member of the national executive threatened to withdraw from the congress in response, but Gunning prevailed upon him to remain. The motions were voted on in rapid succession "as a great deal of time had been wasted during the early part of the congress." O'Duffy then brought the ard fheis to an abrupt end and asked delegates to prepare for the evening's dance. A special branch agent in attendance recorded "the congress, as such, appeared to be little better than a huge farce as immediately O'Duffy was again elected Director-General he assumed the role of Dictator and had things his own way. There would be little to fear from this Movement."[110]

The *Tipperary Star* opined that the newly formed NCP was "a sincere attempt to steer the welfare of the country on new lines and to maintain the national tradition." After decrying the "high temperament of the Celt" which historically produced internecine splits and disagreements, the editor expressed sympathy with O'Duffy's desire to sublimate intra-party conflict to the interest of the "national advance" and dismantling the "out of date" party system. "General O'Duffy is, we believe, voicing the deeper feelings of a goodly number, certainly many sensible people within and without the existing parties." It prevised the end of the party system and its replacement by corporatism but acknowledged that O'Duffy may be ahead of his time in advocating such a solution. It concluded: "The present effete system places many people with much in common in opposing ranks, it smothers the inner, honest opinion of the individual representative and tends almost inevitably to put party interests before all others."[111] Evidently, there was a measured enthusiasm for the new movement in some quarters.

The party had a populist set of policies including the adoption of a charter of rights for workers, profit sharing for workers along cooperative lines, the introduction of a minimum wage, the introduction of a 40-hour work week, the lowering of the old age pension age to 65, and the creation of a second chamber of parliament which would represent vocational interests. The NCP further positioned itself as equally opposed to communism and capitalism, rejecting "alien influence" in national affairs.[112] He claimed that as leader of FG "the big money had ceased to come in" because he refused to "venerate the moneybags or trim his national policy to suit them."[113] O'Duffy also had kind words to say about the social credit theories of Major C.H. Douglas, but he "did not pretend to be an authority on it."[114] His choice of a green shirt may have been to emulate the green shirt of the non-fascist Social Credit Party led by John Hargrave.

Although he attended the ard fheis in June, Belton opted not to join the NCP, continuing to sit as an independent TD. O'Duffy found supporters elsewhere, such as John Hassett, a former CnaG TD for County Tipperary until 1933. Hassett was announced as an NCP candidate to regain his seat.[115] A local speaker in Cashel appealed to traditional supporters of FG, FF, and even the IRA to support Hassett's candidacy at the next election.[116] Although there was rumor of an early general election, whereby O'Duffy would be in contention for a Dáil seat in Monaghan, no such general election was held until 1937 by which time O'Duffy's party had withered away.[117]

In his study of the NCP, Martin White stated the greatest concentration of members were in the province of Munster, particularly counties Cork and Tipperary. Dublin and the Free State border counties were also considerable strongholds for the party, particularly counties Monaghan and Cavan. O'Duffy's local appeal in Monaghan is understandable, given the parochial nature of Irish politics. The party's membership fee was just one shilling per year, a low sum which suggested the leadership's desire to rapidly build a mass membership among the working class. However, total membership remained low. Party meetings were poorly attended. When special branch troubled themselves with sending an agent to NCP meetings their reports indicated low attendance; for example, just 12 attended a meeting in Ferns, County Wexford, in September 1936 and 18 members were present at a meeting in Cashel, County Tipperary.[118] "Small attendance" of the new party was recorded at a conference in Navan, County Meath. James Cooney, county director in Meath, told the meeting he was "disappointed" by the low turnout from the public.[119]

Social functions like dances and annual liturgical events such as commemorative speeches at Béal na mBláth and an annual memorial for Hugh O'Reilly

Eoin O'Duffy and an unidentified Blue Blouse holding a baby (godparents?), c. 1933–4 (courtesy the National Library of Ireland).

continued to attract thousands of spectators. It should not be inferred from such turnouts that the NCP was particularly popular. Political speeches and commemorations attracted curious locals and offered a departure from the monotony of rural life. Separate commemorations to Collins were held on different Sundays in August by O'Duffy's followers and Cronin's followers. Spectators were invited to "come and hear a message from the man whom Collins singled out from amongst his many faithful soldier-comrades to be his successor when death threatened."[120] Overall, the party stagnated. Notably, White found that a mere seven percent of the party's membership were women, in contrast with 26 percent of the Blueshirts' total female membership.[121]

◆ ◆ ◆

In October 1935, Italy invaded Abyssinia. The East African country bordered Italy's colonial possessions in Somaliland. Reacting to the attack, the League of Nations stated that Mussolini's invasion breached articles 12 and 16 of its Covenant. It introduced a range of economic sanctions against Italy for committing an act of aggression. The response could have been anticipated, but Mussolini departed from his usual cautious foreign policy and instead "behaved like an incompetent amateur" by seeking to realize his imperialist ambitions in Africa.[122] Internationally, there was considerable speculation that Britain stood to selfishly gain by the imposition of sanctions against Italy. Britain had its own imperialist ambitions in the region. The Italian ambassador in Berlin told Irish diplomat Charles Bewley in November that initially the war was not particularly popular among the Italian public, "but that since England had intervened the Italian people were unanimous in favor of carrying it through." The Italian ambassador continued, "there was now only one opinion in Italy, namely that a rich power was using its resources to prevent a poor nation from having enough to survive."[123]

Despite the prevalence of the view that the United Kingdom was self-servingly manipulating the conflict, President de Valera resolutely stood behind the League's program of sanctions from the outset. Bewley, Irish diplomatic representative in Germany, reported concern that in Germany the Irish pro-sanctions policy was interpreted as the Free State simply succumbing to English influence.[124] De Valera's policy was roundly supported by many in the opposition, including Patrick McGilligan, an FG deputy and former minister for external affairs in Cosgrave's government. However, several other prominent FG members including Cosgrave, T.F. O'Higgins and Ned Cronin argued that de Valera had naïvely jumped the gun in declaring his unconditional support for sanctioning Italy. It was felt that de Valera should have used the issue of the Free State's support at the League of Nations as a bargaining chip to extract concessions from Britain in the economic war. Despite the Dáil voting nearly unanimously for the sanctions bill in November, MacDermot was so incensed by Cosgrave's advocacy of a cynical quid-pro-quo that he resigned from FG.[125] With the departure of MacDermot, alongside his own resignation a year previously, O'Duffy claimed that FG was now nothing more than a revived CnaG.[126]

Prior to the invasion, O'Duffy participated in a CAUR conference in Montreux in September. Far-right political leaders from 17 European nations were present, including Belgium, Czechoslovakia, Denmark, France, Norway, Switzerland, and Ireland. Mussolini chaired the conference. The leaders unanimously endorsed Mussolini's policy on Ethiopia and condemned the League of Nations. Towards the end of the meeting, O'Duffy promised the Italian dictator a detachment of 1,000 Irish volunteers to fight alongside Italian troops in Ethiopia when the time came.[127] "They are aware that the Italian war against Ethiopia represents the struggle of civilization against barbarianism with which all the hidden forces of retrograde materialism and anti-Fascism are today allied," observed the Italian newspaper *Il Messagero*.[128] Liam Walsh, then acting as NCP secretary, declined to confirm or deny the Italian report when asked by an *Irish Press* reporter on 14 September. Ned Cronin strongly opposed the prospect of Blueshirts of either faction embarking on such a "reckless policy" and becoming embroiled in a conflict "which is not, and should not, be any concern of this country."[129]

Following the conference in Switzerland, O'Duffy took a detour through Germany where he inspected the "labor camps for young people" and "the military camps for the Storm Troopers" in Cologne and Dusseldorf. He then concluded that, while he "did not approve entirely of Hitler's policy," he believed "Hitler was very much misrepresented." Upon his return to Ireland, the General discussed the details of his offer. He explained that "several Blueshirts" had proposed the initiative to him and he had "received letters from various centers asking for particulars" on how they could enlist to help Italy in its impending war. "Irishmen have been in many armies in the past and may now volunteer for service with either side as individuals, but the question of Blueshirts volunteering as such is a matter for the National Executive," he teased. He concluded by conspiratorially declaring that the forces of Marxism and capitalism had united against the Duce.[130] In presenting the offer as stemming from the proposal of grassroots Blueshirts, O'Duffy tried to offset the perception that he had made the improbable offer in a fit of excitement. Reactions in some quarters to O'Duffy's offer were sharply critical. A meeting of communists was told by one speaker that "the dockers of Dublin would have something to say if it came to transporting O'Duffy's Blueshirts to Abyssinia."[131] The *Evening Echo* reported that the Emperor of Abyssinia claimed to have received offers from 5,000 Irishmen to volunteer for his cause.[132] A letter published in the *Irish Independent* argued that General O'Duffy had disgraced his "great part in Ireland's fight for freedom" by supporting Italy's brutal war of conquest.[133]

Addressing an NCP meeting in Listowel in late October, O'Duffy denied he invented the offer and insisted that hundreds of Blueshirts had independently volunteered their services. By then he had switched his position from one of offering Italy "our physical support" to one of providing "our moral support." He argued that Irishmen would not be prepared to fight for Italy or against Abyssinia, but for "the Corporate system." He believed that FG was hopelessly lost on the question of Abyssinia while de Valera had been "deceived by the British" into providing unequivocal support to the Abyssinian Emperor who was "only a catspaw of the British," contrasting the much reported plight of Ethiopia with war propaganda from 1914 centered on "Catholic little Belgium."[134]

Interestingly, one Irishman, 18-year-old Barry Cagney from South Mall in

Cork, applied directly to the Duce for a commission to fight in the Abyssinian conflict. Cagney's family were supporters of the NCP and O'Duffy provided the young man with a personal recommendation. Although Mussolini declined on the grounds that foreigners were ineligible to obtain commissions, he offered Cagney a place on a three-year course at the Royal Air Academy in Caserta, funded by the Italian government. The young Corkman departed for Italy in November 1936.[135] The Italo-Ethiopian War was over by 1937. Although he had achieved a military victory, the consequences left Mussolini diplomatically isolated. Italy increasingly fell within the sphere of influence of Hitler's Germany, which presaged the formation of the Rome-Berlin Axis in 1936 and the eventual Pact of Steel in 1939.

Were it not for O'Duffy's involvement in the Spanish Civil War, his 1935 offer to raise a detachment of volunteer Blueshirts to fight alongside the Italians in Ethiopia would largely be seen as a quixotic incident of little significance. However, it foreshadowed what was to come. Of further significance, the incident illustrated O'Duffy's growing realization that he was unlikely to achieve power in Ireland by conventional political means. Having a seat at the table at conferences of European fascist leaders as a national leader-in-waiting likely buoyed O'Duffy's ego. This could be seen in a self-indulgent remark by O'Duffy to Gunning in April, "I'm the third greatest man in Europe."[136]

In December 1935, the General admitted to an audience of supporters that "for some time past" the NCP "had been somewhat in the shade." Underlying this recognition was an understanding that to rejuvenate his political career he must latch onto a new popular cause. One such prediction was that a war would break out between Italy and Britain, under which circumstances "there would be conscription in the North of Ireland."[137] Undoubtedly, he remembered the Irish conscription crisis of 1918 and how it acted as a catalyst in propelling SF to victory at the December 1918 general election. Additionally, O'Duffy would have been aware of the precedent of Irish nationalists looking abroad for support from England's enemies. O'Duffy was well-known as Italy's most enthusiastic cheerleader in Irish politics. The General recognized that a major paradigm shift was needed before his shrinking political movement could ever hope to seize power. Although this pattern of thought betrayed his growing desperation, it was to remain his primary political strategy for the rest of his life.

◆ ◆ ◆

As 1936 approached, the NCP was failing to make an impact on the Irish political landscape. He was unable to coax a single elected representative to join his ranks, leaving the distinct impression that the NCP was a one-man band. In transforming his rump of the Blueshirts into the Greenshirts, General O'Duffy implicitly realized that his wing of the movement had been the loser of the factional dispute with Cronin. He reasoned that continuing to use blue would generate an embarrassing confusion between his latest venture and FG at a general election. O'Duffy personally chose the shade of green used. It was planned the green shirt would be in place by the time of the NCP's conference in summer 1936.[138] O'Duffy penned a mawkish justification for the change: "All over the world green is, and ever shall be recognized as the symbol of the Emerald Isle. Make no mistake about it, this country shall always be known as Green Erin."[139] The NCP was careful not to disrespect members who were "beaten in their blue shirts—in fact, three were killed." But, the party reasoned, "it was for a cause, and not for a color, that they suffered and died."[140] Blythe expressed his gladness with the decision: the "factionalists ... have now abandoned the name, the policy and the shirt."[141]

In December 1935, O'Duffy forecasted that if a general election was held in May his party would win 25 parliamentary seats.[142] He predicted that "a change is coming" and that mainstream parties would soon be swept away, presumably following a mass disenchantment with the political establishment.[143] In late 1935, O'Duffy delivered a speech where he claimed peace negotiations had taken place in Geneva between de Valera and the British government aimed at ending the economic war. He alleged that the Irish president proposed Document No 2, which caused so much trouble in 1922, as a solution. De Valera dismissed O'Duffy's claim as mere "fairy tales."[144] O'Duffy repeatedly criticized the League of Nations, which de Valera was a staunch supporter of. He argued that Ireland should follow Germany's example and leave the League, which he said was led by "a Jew named Litvinov, a leading figure in Communist and anti–God organizations in Russia."[145] If someone was Jewish, even if he mistakenly believed they were Jewish, O'Duffy gleefully pointed it out. He referred to the French prime minister Léon Blum as a "wealthy Jew and Freemason."[146] O'Duffy saw the League of Nations as stacked against Irish interests and Italian interests (which were interchangeable to O'Duffy) "because Mussolini stamped out Freemasonry and Bolshevism in Italy."[147]

When the Dáil voted almost unanimously to sanction Italy, O'Duffy despaired. If Britain were to turn loose the Black and Tans in Ireland again, he argued, the League of Nations would not allow the Free State to even raise the matter.[148] His political views, particularly on international affairs, generally showed him up as an ultramontane fascist who obediently followed Italy. He even proposed Italy as an alternative market to Britain for the export of Irish agricultural produce. Mussolini personally wrote to O'Duffy to express his surprise and disappointment at the attitude of the Free State towards Italy, but thanked him and the NCP for its "brave stand ... on behalf of the Italian people."[149]

For the first half of 1936, O'Duffy trundled on hosting countrywide semi-regular NCP meetings. His public pronouncements continued to praise Mussolini while occasionally seeking to distance himself from fascism. Ludicrously he told an audience of the Historical Society of Trinity College Dublin in May that "I don't know anyone in this country who advocates Fascism."[150] His speeches were highly repetitive. FF's Seán T. O'Kelly referred to him as "the ablest master of blatherskite I ever listened to."[151] The party's views on international affairs were mostly rooted in anti-communism, with a tinge of anti–Semitism. On Palestine, the NCP stated that "the Arabs are being shot down as were the Irish Volunteers from 1916 to 1921. The Jews are over-running the country since the Balfour Declaration and large cities like Tel-a-viv populated exclusively of Jews are quickly springing up.... The Arabs have our complete sympathy."[152]

At a dinner held in O'Duffy's honor at Dublin's Central Hotel in March, the unremarkable list of attendees illustrated the General's diminishing prestige. Instead of sympathetic politicians, senior civil servants, and high-ranking former colleagues from the army and Garda Síochána, O'Duffy was increasingly associated with a ragbag of hangers-on like his new secretary Liam Walsh and Captain The O'Donovan, who was described as a "mental case" by the RUC.[153] O'Duffy said he was happy with the event thanks to the presence of close friends and because discussion of politics was banned. Speakers lauded O'Duffy for his past achievements including his involvement in the GAA, athletics, the Olympic committee, the Eucharistic Congress, the Volunteers, the army and of course the Garda Síochána. The focus on reminiscences showed how increasingly O'Duffy, although only 46 years old, was already seen as yesterday's man.[154] Speculation that he would contest a by-election in West Cork in October 1936 proved unfounded, although it was felt "he has a fairly representative following in the constituency."[155]

The NCP hosted its first official ard fheis as a political party at Rathmines Town Hall on 25 July. Approximately 400 delegates attended, "many of them women" according to a report.[156] Although the Gardaí reported turnout was as low as 250,[157] the party claimed a total of 650 delegates had participated.[158] In his keynote speech, O'Duffy predicted a general election that autumn would leave the NCP in the role of kingmaker. But in such a scenario, he was ambivalent about supporting either major party, "they don't care a thraneen about the country." O'Duffy was greeted with a standing ovation and a fascist salute, which the General gladly returned.[159] Various motions were passed at the convention. They included an expression of "grave concern" at the number of foreigners employed in Irish industries, particularly an influx of Germans; support for the creation of a government ministry for the Gaeltacht; an extension of greetings to Mussolini, whose government has "shaken the prestige of the old world"; that the former constitutional provision allowing for the initiation of referenda should be restored, having been abolished in 1928; that the Irish Free State should withdraw from the League of Nations; that O'Duffy, on account of "his popularity, personality and organizing ability," should undertake a fundraising tour of the United States. A further resolution advocating the removal of all monuments and statues commemorating British rule was passed by the ard fheis but was subsequently referred to the national executive for further examination. O'Duffy was returned unanimously as director-general, with Colonel Coughlan re-elected as deputy director-general. Walsh was formally elected the NCP's general secretary. Major Hume Sleigh from Scotland, from the strongly anti–Catholic Scottish Democratic Fascist Party, spoke at the meeting as a foreign dignitary.[160]

Despite General O'Duffy's bold predictions of impending success, contemporary assessments of the party's future remained bleak. "The National Corporate Party does not seem to impress the general body of the electors with its program and for that reason I cannot see many successes coming its way," wrote one newspaper observer.[161] The coming of the Spanish Civil War provided a fillip to the ailing NCP.

# 10

# The Spanish Civil War

For General O'Duffy, the outbreak of the Spanish Civil War in July 1936 signaled his potential rehabilitation as a serious political leader. The coup d'état launched on 17 July by a coalition of rightist interests in the Spanish army against the left-wing Republican government began the protracted civil war. The conflict lasted for three years and saw an intense polarization of Spanish society. Significantly, the Catholic Church sympathized with the Nationalist or "Patriot" forces. The conflict was frequently portrayed in Ireland as a war between the forces of communistic atheism and the defenders of the faith. It became an intensely ideological struggle, which was heightened by the involvement of international powers. Germany and Italy backed Franco's forces to the hilt, while the Soviet Union offered its support to the beleaguered Spanish Republicans. At the outset of the conflict, the fascist powers airlifted Franco's troops from Morocco to mainland Spain where they "advanced unchecked" from Seville to Madrid.[1] Meanwhile, Britain and France engineered an international non-intervention pact aimed at preventing the Spanish conflict from spilling across borders and sparking a world war.

The Irish public initially responded with an outpour of sympathy for the "Patriot" forces soon to be dominated by General Francisco Franco. This was influenced by the various reports of acts of violence and atrocities committed by Republican leftists against innocent Catholics in Spain. Some reports were highly sensational. The *Irish Independent* was a major purveyor of articles which portrayed the war as "a Catholic crusade against communism." Between July and September 1936, the newspaper published 22 lead articles on Spain, in contrast with 16 in the *Irish Times* and just three in the *Irish Press*. The *Independent* urged de Valera to sever diplomatic ties with the Spanish government and recognize the Nationalists as the legitimate government.[2] Even a young Conor Cruise O'Brien was swept up in pro–Nationalist fervor. The student had to be defended from attack when he supported a pro–Franco motion at Trinity College Dublin.[3] Throughout the conflict, the *Irish Times* went against the grain by expressing reservations about Franco's cause and raising awkward questions like why the Catholic Spanish nation had freely elected the Republican government.[4] The American writer Paul Blanshard observed that the *Irish Times* represented "not so much any leftist tendency as the last stand of the Anglo-Irish Protestant Ascendancy on behalf of freedom."[5]

Many local authorities adopted the Clonmel Resolution which urged de Valera to recognize Franco's regime.[6] Although de Valera's international policy was one of strict neutrality, he publicly indicated that his sympathies lay with the Nationalists in Spain, "a great old Catholic nation" where "the vast majority of the people" wanted to see "Christian truths" triumph.[7] As the Red Terror intensified in Spain, the demand that Ireland should play a more proactive role in aiding the Spanish rebels became popular. Cardinal Joseph MacRory strongly condemned the Republican Congress and other Irish socialist groups which expressed support for the Spanish Republicans. To do so, Cardinal MacRory stated, was "a scandal and an outrage."[8] The Irish hierarchy strongly swung the full weight of its moral support behind Franco.

Responding to an appeal by the *Independent* in August for greater action, the Irish Christian Front (ICF) was established to support "the stricken people of Spain in their fight against the forces of international Communism." Among its chief organizers was Alexander McCabe and Patrick Belton. Immediately, it initiated a scheme to raise funds to provide ambulance units and other humanitarian aid.[9] The ICF claimed the aims of communism were to launch a war on religion, class war, and the abolition of private property. "Its weapons are intrigue, hatred, violence, intolerance, dictatorship."[10] At a large rally on 30 August at College Green, the ICF, a "non-sectarian, anti–Communist movement," whipped up a frenzy among the audience. However, Belton was clear that Irish aid to Spain would exclusively take the form of humanitarian support and would not include lethal aid.[11] The ICF organized monster rallies with a reported turnout of 30,000 in Cork, evincing a popular support not seen since the days of Daniel O'Connell.[12] An ICF rally in Dublin reportedly attracted 100,000 attendees, who raised their arms above their heads in a quasi-salute which made the sign of the cross.[13] Left-wing republicans like Frank Ryan openly sympathized with the Spanish Republic, an action which put them at loggerheads with former colleagues in the IRA who tried to steer a neutral course. Ryan denounced the pro–Franco activities of the ICF, arguing there was "more Christianity in any one Spanish worker than there is in the whole of the miscalled 'Irish Christian Front.'"[14]

Although O'Duffy and Belton used similar dramatic language to describe the conflict's horrors, the General was prepared to go beyond the provision of mere humanitarian support. O'Duffy claimed on 15 August that Madrid priests "are battered to death on the altars, and their heads stuck on the railings outside the churches by the howling mobs of women and youths armed by the Government."[15] He argued that if such alleged acts of anti–Catholic violence constituted democracy "then the sooner Fascism triumphs, the better."[16] The horrific tales O'Duffy described were par for the course in the daily press. He firmly backed the justness of the rebel cause, arguing it was consistent with the Catholic conception of a just war. The Republican government had violated the rights to free exercise of religion and the right to property, which had "no moral binding force whatsoever."[17] Aquinas' dictum that when a law is contrary to reason it is called an unjust law and thus ceases to be law and becomes instead an act of violence was invoked by O'Duffy and other cheerleaders of the Nationalists. He described Francisco Franco as being "raised up" by God, "a patriotic and God-fearing man to deliver Spain out of the hands of Satan and his Communist legionaries."[18]

◆ ◆ ◆

In early August, O'Duffy was contacted by Count de Ramírez de Arellano, a Carlist from Navarre living in London. He was advised by Cardinal MacRory to contact O'Duffy regarding a proposal to form an Irish Brigade to fight for the "Patriot" forces.[19] His tale of woe was reproduced in O'Duffy's Spanish memoir:

> My country ... is in the thrall of the most terrific death struggle, trying to free itself from the horrible and vile Communist and Marxist rule and the ghastly influence of Soviet Russia.... Do you think it might be possible to raise in Ireland a volunteer force to come to aid us? ... What a glorious example Ireland could give the whole of Christendom!

O'Duffy claimed "the idea of an Irish Brigade for Spain had not entered my mind until then, but this letter set me thinking."[20] Having previously mooted the idea during the Abyssinia crisis, it is unlikely the suggestion was completely alien to his thinking. In addition to harboring a sincere solidarity with the Spanish Nationalists undergirded by his Catholic worldview, raising a volunteer force was seen as a way to revive his moribund political career.

He tested the reception for such a proposal by penning a letter to the *Independent*. His kite-flying appeal was published shortly before he embarked to the continent, a departure which generated considerable speculation that he was in Europe "to make contact with representatives of the insurgents."[21] In fact, he was taking a ten-day holiday in the Hague. Upon his return, he issued a statement to the press on 20 August which formally advocated the formation of a Brigade. While he argued the Irish government should immediately break off diplomatic links with the Spanish government, he asked: "Should we not go further and raise an Irish Volunteer Brigade for service in Spain? ... I believe there are thousands of young men here who would cheerfully answer the call to join the crusade." Keen to promote his own cause, O'Duffy announced he was prepared to lead such a brigade personally. He added, "if two men go to Spain, I will be one of them."[22] At his party's commemoration to Collins in late August, O'Duffy argued it was what Collins would have wanted. "If he were alive ... he would not be content with talking and deploring what was happening in Spain."[23]

NCP headquarters in Pearse Street was inundated with expressions of interest in the venture. "Every post now brought me hundreds of letters from all over Ireland and from Irishmen in Britain and other countries offering their services for a volunteer brigade," he wrote.[24] It was reported that some northern Protestants even planned to join the effort, possibly associates from the Ulster Fascists.[25] O'Duffy claimed over 6,000 men volunteered to join the Brigade. Reactions from the left were predictably hostile. *The Worker* referred to the arch–Catholic O'Duffy joining forces with Franco and Mola who were "at the head of the Mohammedans against the Spanish Government and people."[26] Belton disagreed with the wisdom of Irishmen going to Spain, urging that Ireland did not need "more wild geese." IRA leader Tom Barry prohibited IRA members from participating in the foreign conflict for either side.[27]

The question soon arose if it was legally permissible for O'Duffy to recruit Irishmen to serve in Franco's rebel army. One constitutional lawyer speculated that O'Duffy could violate article 73 of the Foreign Enlistment Act 1870. O'Duffy claimed he was unaware of any Act passed by the Free State parliament "which prohibited a body of Irishmen from joining up to assist in the fight for Christianity against the forces of darkness."[28] The legality of the venture remained ambiguous, but O'Duffy was determined to proceed with it regardless. Privately, the attorney general admitted it was doubtful that the 1870 Act was applicable, and that even if it were, it "does not prohibit persons from taking part in a civil war such as this ... it was obviously passed for the purpose of preventing Englishmen joining either side in the Franco-Prussian War."[29] The FF government ironed out any potential legal ambiguities when it enacted the Non-Intervention Act in February 1937 to specifically forbid Spanish Civil War recruitment. Enlistees without special permission would henceforth be punishable by up to two years in prison and a £500 fine.[30]

After receiving a public response "so prompt, so generous and so spontaneous," O'Duffy initiated contact with the Spanish Nationalists by meeting the Carlist count in London in early September 1936. They agreed he would lodge a formal request with Franco's headquarters, explaining the proposal in detail. O'Duffy duly produced a memorandum which included particulars on prospective conditions of service, uniforms, volunteers, transport issues, and international complications.[31] In London, O'Duffy awoke to the complicated realities of factionalism within the amorphous Nationalist movement. Ramírez specifically intended the Irishmen to fight alongside Carlist forces. It also became clear that the entire project would fail to materialize without the support of Franco. In the early stages of the scheme O'Duffy recruited the services of his erstwhile colleague from the Blueshirts, Thomas Gunning, who had worked in Spain as a correspondent following his redundancy as the General's secretary.[32] Gunning, a Spanish speaker, became his personal secretary in Spain.[33]

O'Duffy was in his element as a planner and organizer. The Irish Crusade Against Communism was launched as a front group to gather recruits who were asked to provide their own valise and to be ready at short notice to travel "with the first batch" to Spain.[34] It was intended that the brigade would be organized into three battalions, each consisting of four companies.[35] On 20 September, the Spanish expressed "general agreement" with the scheme but requested a personal interview with O'Duffy first. He left the next day for Spain, traveling via London, Paris, St Jean de Luz, Pamplona, and Burgos before finally reaching Valladolid. Dublin opinion expected that O'Duffy's plans would reach a dead-end, like many of his previous schemes. The *Irish Press* gleefully reported that General Cabanellas had politely declined O'Duffy's project but that the General and his secretary were being fêted by the Spanish insurgents during their stay at the royal suite of the Plaza del Castillo in Pamplona.[36] Judith Keene noted that Franco tended to flatter foreign guests and treat them to displays of military pomp. O'Duffy's personality was highly receptive to such a charm offensive.[37]

In Valladolid on 22 September, O'Duffy met Emilio Mola, the general responsible for Nationalist forces north of and including Madrid. The two generals conferred for an hour, discussing Ireland's historical ties to Spain. They also shared a background as former police chiefs in their respective countries (Mola served as chief of police under Alfonso XIII). It was a day of high tension for the Nationalist forces as

Mola awaited news from the siege of the Alcázar, in which a trapped force of cadets led by José Enrique Varela withheld a siege by Republican forces. As O'Duffy and Mola spoke, they were interrupted by his chief-of-staff who saluted and announced that Generalissimo Franco wished to speak to General Mola by telephone. O'Duffy saw Mola lift the telephone, speak a few words with Franco, and lay down the receiver. Franco had relieved the beleaguered forces, broke the siege, and scored a highly significant victory for the Nationalists. Mola rushed towards O'Duffy, embracing him "in an ecstasy of joy." Standing on a balcony from the military headquarters, Mola announced the news of the victory to cheers from the crowds below. That night, O'Duffy was permitted to broadcast a message "as a Catholic and an Irishman" from the same headquarters. He had "never been so carried away with enthusiasm" as he was when he saw the "spirit of a great and historic nation standing like tested steel to preserve again ... the glory of Christian civilization against the onslaughts of a heathen foe." O'Duffy promised that Ireland would "leave nothing undone to help her historic friend and ally." His listeners chanted "*Viva Irlanda*!" in lieu of "*Viva España*!"[38] The next day, Mola traveled to Caceres where he received Franco's imprimatur for the Irish Brigade, allowing preparations to begin in earnest. Franco had greenlighted the proposal despite hesitation from his diplomatic staff.[39] General Mola briefed his staff to expect the arrival of a "Green Shirt Legion" from Ireland in due course.[40] It was the only time O'Duffy met Mola, who died on 3 June 1937 in an air crash in northern Spain. Mola's death helped to solidify Franco's hold over the leadership of the rightist coalition.

◆ ◆ ◆

The Irish public learned in early October that Franco and Mola had "enthusiastically accepted" O'Duffy's offer.[41] Special branch reported that O'Duffy and his Spanish associates "have received monies through the Spanish Agent in London which are sufficient for their purpose."[42] But the General still faced the formidable task of recruiting and organizing a private army. The administrative infrastructure of the NCP was promptly converted from overseeing the daily running of a political party into creating a brigade, beginning with sifting through the 6,000 interested applicants. Medical examinations of prospective candidates were carried out by Dr Patrick Cagney, an NCP supporter from Cork.[43] The NCP's activities were suspended to lend the Irish Brigade the pretense of being non-political. However, O'Duffy ordered 1,000 NCP green shirts for the brigade from a manufacturer in Dublin, which cast immediate doubt on the effort's non-political character.[44]

"The organization of the Brigade was, perhaps, the most difficult job I have ever undertaken," wrote O'Duffy. "But with the help of willing workers at headquarters all obstacles were gradually surmounted."[45] Manning wrote that "the lethargy which had characterized O'Duffy's leadership of the NCP now disappeared and was replaced by a burst of frenetic activity."[46] Special branch recorded in October that "there does not seem to be any loss of enthusiasm on the part of O'Duffy and his officers."[47] O'Duffy's rival, Ned Cronin, issued a statement in early September which mocked O'Duffy's proposal as "moonshine" and predicted the Brigade "had as much chance of reaching [Zaragoza] as it had of reaching the moon."[48] He would soon change his tune, realizing the threat of a politically resurgent O'Duffy.

A formal contract was agreed between O'Duffy and Franco. A total of 5,000 Irish volunteers were to form eight Banderas in the Tercio of the Spanish Foreign Legion (Army of Africa). This branch of the Spanish army was notorious for its brutality. It relished in the glorification of death, as seen in the motto popularized by its first commander, José Millán-Astray, *¡Viva la Muerte!* ("Long live death!"). Eventually, just one Bandera was formed from the Irishmen who reached Spain. The eight Banderas were to be under "Hispano-Irish command," with each commander an Irishman and his adjutant a Spaniard. It was intended that Spanish officers attached to the Banderas would have knowledge of English and should "be tactful and courteous in their relations with their new comrades." It was hoped the Banderas would form a unit to operate jointly in the field. The Irish would furnish their own medical staff, chaplains, nurses, and cooks. O'Duffy believed the Banderas would receive ample field-kitchens and table utensils from sympathizers at home.

As men gradually made their way to Spain it was already believed by mid–October there were enough men to form the first Bandera. O'Duffy added there would be "no difficulty in bringing out several thousand more men." A Spanish quartermaster was to be assigned to the Banderas. Irish soldiers would receive pay equal to equivalent ranks in the Tercio. O'Duffy was to be bestowed the rank of Brigadier-General in the Spanish army in addition to acting as inspector-general of the Irish Banderas, directly responsible to General Franco. He would have both an Irish and a Spanish aide-de-camp.[49] Although O'Duffy appeared to have secured an early commitment from Hugo MacNeill to take a leading role in the brigade, he soon backed out. The generous contract between Franco and O'Duffy demonstrated how seriously the Generalissimo took the venture. It also helped Franco to secure Carlist backing for his leadership.

Interestingly, O'Duffy asked that the Irish Bandera not serve in engagements against Basque nationalists, co-religionists of the Irish and a fellow small nation. Later, O'Duffy reversed his instinctive sympathy for the Basques and adopted an orthodox Nationalist anti–Basque sentiment, characterizing them as "Reds" and "destroyers of religion." He drew a parallel between "absurd" Basque nationalism and proponents of Northern Ireland's existence.[50] A Basque newspaper despaired that while there was a "black Spain" there was also a "black Ireland." "The odious blackness is represented today by O'Duffy. He is a bad Irishman and his is a bad Ireland," opined the *Euzkadi* in August 1936.[51]

Recruits tended to be drawn from rural areas and small towns. This mirrored the geographic profile of members of the Blueshirts. One volunteer, Matt J. Doolan, later wrote that the Irish Brigade "was a very fair cross-section of Irish life of the period, including a number of prominent members of the Old IRA." He expressed surprise at the high volume of volunteers who were politically uncommitted but "earnestly believed in the nobility of our cause in fighting for the freedom of religious expression." He further claimed they were "of unimpeachable character."[52] From a sample study of 61 members of the Bandera, McGarry determined that 27 were members of the NCP and a further 22 were Cronin-aligned Blueshirts.[53] An early contingent of volunteers included "men of all ranks of life, including doctors, chemists, ex-army men, farmers, mechanics, an urban district councilor, and an engineer," according to O'Duffy.[54] Denis McGuinness, a Dubliner who joined the effort at 20 years old, explained their motivation was to fight against communism rather than to fight for fascism. McGuinness initially hoped to send remittance to his family but was disappointed to discover they "only earned an average of 15 pesetas every five days and so it was hardly worth his while."[55] O'Duffy utilized the power of cinema, appearing in a newsreel where he appealed to the viewers' sense of adventure and invoked historical Irish military themes. One cinemagoer was "hooked" and enlisted in the brigade.[56]

Several ex-officers from the Irish army joined the Bandera, including Colonel Patrick Dalton. He became O'Duffy's second-in-command but effectively led the Bandera. Men with past military experience also enlisted, particularly from the Civil War. Some had been cashiered out of the defense forces for misconduct. One ex–IRA man had been sentenced to death by the IRA for his involvement in a 1921 robbery, but this was reduced to an expulsion from the revolutionary force following an intervention by Michael Collins.[57] Overall, the average member tended to be young, without military experience, and motivated by a confessional zealotry. In one case, eight young men from Enniskillen, County Fermanagh were recruited by their parish priest. Contemporary assessments of the caliber of men who joined could often be scathing. One priest observed that the recruits were primarily interested in securing a paycheck and would otherwise have enlisted in the British Army. He viewed other recruits as essentially corner boys who enlisted for a change of scenery.[58] In some cases, anxious mothers wrote desperate letters to the Irish government expressing their concern that their young sons had signed up to the Bandera without parental approval and begged for some intervention. The Irish government received representations "from the parents of four boys under 21 years of age who have joined the O'Duffy Brigade."[59] The Irish government later lobbied Franco's regime to repatriate underage recruits. This mixed bag of recruits and the caliber of officers appointed by O'Duffy negatively impacted the Bandera.

The daunting task of transporting potentially thousands of Irish recruits to war-torn Spain remained a major logistical problem for General O'Duffy and his staff. Although quotes were received from British shipping firms, they were astronomically high. At any rate, O'Duffy was concerned a British crew would be unreliable. A solution beckoned when Juan de la Cierva, a Spanish aeronautical engineer and "one of General Franco's right-hand men," summoned O'Duffy to London where, "beaming with delight," he informed the General that he would oversee the transport of the Irishmen to Spain. De la Cierva had overseen the transport of Franco from the Canary Islands to Morocco at the outbreak of the conflict. The Spanish aviator informed O'Duffy he had chartered the *SS Domino* which was fitted with quarters to cater for 1,000 men. Nicolás Franco, brother of the Generalissimo, supervised the preparation of the ship. Minute details even included preparations that the food would be suitable to the Irish palate. Nicolás Franco planned to travel aboard "as a gesture of appreciation" to the Irish brigade. The ship was to be captained by a Spanish admiral and a staff of English-speaking Spaniards on its voyage to Passage East, five miles from Waterford, on the afternoon of 16 October. It was to arrive in port at Vigo in the northwest, where the force would be blessed by the cardinal primate of Spain. It all seemed too good to be true. General O'Duffy issued orders across the country for volunteers to assemble at the precise time and location, prioritizing discretion and punctuality. O'Duffy's staff arranged for signalers and experienced nautical officers to await the arrival of the *Domino*.

On 14 October at 7 p.m., O'Duffy was at home in Mount Merrion packing his luggage when a caller arrived. The caller, a courier dispatched by Franco, informed him that the sailing of the *Domino* was postponed until further notice owing to concerns that the voyage would undermine the international Non-Intervention Pact. O'Duffy was devastated, "I had got some hard knocks in my time; this was the most severe of all." He scurried to the home of his secretary, Liam Walsh, where, at the eleventh hour, they issued notices of cancelation to key organizers across the country.[60] It was a major setback for the fledgling Irish Brigade.

Disappointed by the failure of the *Domino*, O'Duffy hastened to Spain to meet Franco at his headquarters. O'Duffy intended to leave Salamanca with "a final decision as to whether his brigade of 2,000 men will leave Ireland for Spain or not."[61] A London newspaper reported that O'Duffy had abandoned the project and that an official statement was forthcoming. His secretary in Dublin, Walsh, denied the report's veracity.[62] At the bishop's palace in Salamanca, Franco received O'Duffy. It was their first meeting. O'Duffy expressed his "intense disappointment" with the cancelation of the operation but was successfully cajoled by an apologetic Franco who encouraged his Irish guest to stay for a while longer in Spain "to await developments." O'Duffy and Gunning were afforded every luxury and traveled to various fronts while visiting ornate Spanish cathedrals with Spanish aristocrats. Upon his return to Salamanca, O'Duffy conferred for a second time with Franco and his staff. Franco acknowledged that the Soviets were actively running roughshod over the Non-Intervention Pact, which encouraged the Generalissimo to press ahead with the scheme. However, O'Duffy was advised to funnel his men into Spain in small numbers.[63]

O'Duffy's skeleton crew in Ireland faced significant burdens in organizing the brigade. Liam Walsh, general secretary of the NCP, assumed the burdensome task of managing volunteers and their transport. Gardaí reported that O'Duffy considered Walsh's "power of organization and mobilization" to be "faulty," which later led him to dispatch Diarmuid O'Sullivan and Thomas Carew back to Ireland to "speed up arrangements."[64] Special branch believed the "financial affairs of the organization were not very carefully managed" by Walsh, who had a history of embezzling funds dating back to his days in the IRA and Free State army.[65]

In a letter of 3 January, Captain Walsh replied to complaints by Colonel Coughlan of disrespect against him by General O'Duffy. Walsh was at pains to defuse the situation, but the tone of his letter displayed the significant strain he was under. He explained to Coughlan how he knew fully "what you have to put up with in Cork" and asked that the Colonel appreciate "what I have to put up with all over the country in my capacity as Secretary." He continued, "I am not complaining, but my job is not by any means an easy one and is daily becoming harder. I am really tired and your letter Colonel certainly does not ease matters." He reiterated his fatigue towards the end of the letter: "As I said before Colonel I really am tired."[66] Perhaps due to the significant personal role played by Walsh in organizing the Brigade, the chapter on the Bandera in his unpublished biography of O'Duffy is remarkably brief.

◆ ◆ ◆

Irish enlistees were directed by O'Duffy's staff to travel in small groups by the Yeoward Line from Liverpool to Lisbon. The first party of ten men left from North Wall in Dublin on 13 November aboard the *Lady Leinster*. With this small departure, the Irish Brigade now became "an accomplished fact" which O'Duffy took pride in. The advance party was made up of men with military experience including Diarmuid O'Sullivan, P.J. Gallagher, Thomas Carew, and David Tormey.[67] On 20 November, O'Duffy left with 40 men for Spain, including Dalton, his second-in-command; and Gunning, his private secretary.[68] Gunning taught two daily Spanish classes while an evening *céilí* dance was held. The next day, a further 32 men left Liverpool. The majority were reportedly under 25 years old, some with military experience while others were students.[69] In Lisbon, the men were welcomed by priests and government officials from the Salazar regime. One Irishman was impressed by the "beautiful blue color of the sea and picturesque coloring of the houses on the hills above the Bay." He remembered the journey to Spain was "uneventful," but that during the journey they passed a village ravaged by war. It had changed hands several times between Republican and Nationalist forces. He recalled seeing "bloodstained walls, scribbled mottos on buildings, some of which were just shells." The local church "had been used as a stable for mules during the red occupation" and was "badly smashed and statues burnt and defaced."[70]

The first contingent of Irish recruits to reach Spain received training at a military base in Caceres from a monolingual Spanish speaker, Captain Capablanca, which led to obvious difficulties. A further 80 men drawn from "every county in the four provinces" traveled to Spain on 27 November. Accompanying this contingent of men was Fr Joseph Mulrean from Moate, County Westmeath who served as the brigade's chaplain. Mulrean previously ministered in Gibraltar and spoke fluent Spanish.[71]

The Irishmen were constituted as the XV Bandera in the Foreign Legion, following a brief stint as the XIII Bandera which was changed due to superstition that 13 was an unlucky number.[72] It was staffed with Irish officers and cooks but with Spanish adjutants and interpreters. Fr Alexander McCabe, rector of the Irish College in Salamanca, recalled that the Bandera was "too top-heavy, perhaps. It was a bit ridiculous to have over fifty officers, between Irish and Spanish, for seven hundred men."[73] O'Duffy chose the flag of the Bandera: a red cross on a field of emerald green, bearing the inscription *In Hoc Signo Vinces*. It also used a Wolfhound as a mascot. The men's tour of duty was to last for six months or the duration of the war, whichever came sooner.[74]

A glowing profile of O'Duffy appeared in the *Independent* as the first groups of Irishmen departed for Spain. "For nearly 20 years he has been a familiar personality In Irish life," now General O'Duffy was entering "probably the most eventful period in a life of intense activity."[75] He formally received his commission as a major-general from Franco on 28 November, although he declined to accept a salary. From Salamanca, he traveled to Caceres to "supervise the training of the volunteers" before he would lead them into action. Speaking to the press, O'Duffy strongly rebuked "armchair critics" of the endeavor. He refused to be drawn on questions about whether Ned Cronin planned to journey to Spain.[76] Although initially skeptical of O'Duffy's brigade, Cronin soon tried to capitalize on the overwhelming public support for the Spanish Nationalist cause. He hoped to secure a meeting with Franco where he would propose to form a separate brigade drawn from the ranks of his Blueshirts. He journeyed from Liverpool to Lisbon aboard the *SS Aguila*. During the voyage, members of the NCP demanded that Cronin should apologize for causing the 1934 split.[77] Cronin canvassed other passengers for potential recruits and spread disquiet among the ranks by suggesting they had "no hope of return."[78]

Cronin arrived in Lisbon in early December. Eager to stop Cronin from stealing his thunder, O'Duffy dispatched Gunning to Lisbon where he succeeded in having the Portuguese secret police steal Cronin's passport. Gunning warned him he would be shot if he crossed the border into Spain.[79] In Lisbon, Cronin lobbied Mariano Amoedo, the Nationalist representative in Portugal. Amoedo wrote to O'Duffy that Cronin "told me he would like to join the Irish Corps under your command.... He mentioned that he did not know whether it would be agreeable to you that he should join the Irish Legion, as he belonged in Ireland to a different political party to that which you direct and lead." Unaware of the deep hostilities between the two men, Amoedo presumed O'Duffy and Cronin would set aside any differences "to help Spain to fight the common danger from Russia and communism." A

**Major-General Eoin O'Duffy wearing the uniform of the Irish Bandera, Spanish Nationalist army, c. 1936–7 (courtesy Monaghan County Museum).**

handwritten note by Dalton accompanied the letter and urged O'Duffy that Cronin's presence would cause most of the Bandera to ground arms.[80] Colonel Coughlan, deputy director-general of the NCP told Walsh that during a party meeting in Cork the local members agreed "that Ned Cronin should have been let land in Spain." Regarding Cronin's treatment, Coughlan worried that "the politicians were using it against us."[81] War correspondent Francis McCullagh recalled that Franco's archives were "simply bursting with letters from Irishmen denouncing other Irishmen."[82]

By December, O'Duffy was eager to transport more men to Spain. A commitment by the Spanish fell by the wayside when yet another planned voyage was canceled. Meanwhile, de la Cierva died in a plane crash on 9 December. By sheer luck, O'Duffy narrowly avoided sharing the same fate as they were scheduled to journey together. O'Duffy changed plans at the last minute due to the possibility of an extended delay in Hamburg.[83] Owing to the scattered arrivals of volunteers, an increasingly unhappy O'Duffy evidently gave up on waiting for a Spanish ship to materialize. He dispatched Walsh to Berlin to sound out the German government about providing transport for large quantities of men from Ireland to Spain.[84]

The Nazis agreed to provide the steamship *Urundi* for the mission, which was scheduled to transport 500 men from Galway Bay on 13 December. Late that night, hundreds of volunteers mobbed into Eyre Square in Galway city. At one o'clock in the morning, most of the volunteers boarded the *Dun Aengus* in stormy weather conditions, in preparation for a mid-sea transfer to the *Urundi*. Three locals impulsively jumped aboard as the *Dun Aengus* disembarked. For a while, the *Dun Aengus* "cruised around in the open sea at the mouth of the bay, but there was no sign of the mysterious ship." Several men began to complain of hunger and thirst, although "the majority bore their position with cheerfulness." A heavy downpour drenched the men on the upper deck, while those below began to suffer from sea sickness. The German vessel failed to arrive until 10:30 a.m., at which stage most men were exhausted and many were ill. Thirty-five would-be Bandera soldiers changed their minds, opting to return home. To prevent others from following suit, the rope ladder was pulled up.[85] One of the men who was in Galway that evening had just a few days previously been convicted by a Monaghan court of drunk driving and possession of five rounds of revolver ammunition.[86]

By 3 o'clock, the men aboard the *Dun Aengus* began a scramble up the swaying rope ladder to the *Urundi* in a process O'Duffy admitted was a "lengthy and dangerous task." The *Dun Aengus* swayed near the German vessel. "The men had to jump and catch the rope ladder, when they got to the top the German sailors pulled them in."[87] The *Urundi* flew the German Swastika ensign, giving rise to the lyric "they sailed beneath the swastika to Spain" from Christy Moore's *Viva la Quinta Brigada*. The voyage was plagued by gales until the *Urundi* reached Ferrol Bay where they were transferred to the *Domino*. "Here they enjoyed their first comfortable night's rest and the first good meal since leaving their homes almost a week before," wrote O'Duffy.[88] The Irish government was frustrated. They despaired that there was "no breach of the law except possibly the overloading of the Irish tender (*Dun Aengus*)."[89]

Although O'Duffy expected that successive missions would follow the *Urundi*, it was the first and last major operation to transport pro–Franco Irishmen to Spain.

Plans for the transport of an additional 500 men in January failed to materialize. "It was subsequently admitted by the Officers that they had not left Ireland. It was now generally realized that few, if any, further reinforcements would arrive."[90] It was reported that "somebody blundered" and O'Duffy's plans had "gone agley," leaving 500 men waiting at Passage East all-night in poor weather for a German ship which never arrived.[91] Gardaí reported that the 500 men "spent the night moving about the village in groups" until Walsh ordered the men home due to a "slight accident."[92] This severely hamstrung the Brigade's effectiveness, which with only 700 men formed just one Bandera. In February, the Irish government formally criminalized Irish volunteering in the Spanish Civil War, an action which O'Duffy decried as a "betrayal of Irish and Christian principles" and accused de Valera of dancing to Moscow's tune.[93] The *Round Table* correspondent argued that the Irish government was hardly likely to enforce the foreign enlistment legislation against "General O'Duffy and his merry men, as they probably realize that Spain is the most suitable place for our Irish Don Quixote."[94]

Reporting from the Irish Bandera's headquarters in Caceres in early 1937, the journalist Gertrude Gaffney provided a "first-hand, authentic account of conditions behind the war-fronts in Spain" for a serial in the *Irish Independent*.[95] Escorted around the barracks by her colleague, Gunning, whom the *Independent* also employed as a war correspondent,[96] Gaffney "was at pains to describe how well the men looked": "they looked so much bigger, broader, and more rugged than the small-boned, slender Spanish soldiers with their girlish faces and big dark eyes, most of whom looked so young and immature." She diligently repeated the Bandera's own romantic self-image, describing them as a "Bandera of crusaders ... men who had come to Spain to fight for Christianity—and for nothing else." She ruled out her initial assumption that the men she would find were likely to be mere adventurers. A criticism Gaffney raised was that the men were disappointed as they failed to receive letters from home. Upon investigating the discrepancy, she was assured that the mail had been "mislaid en route" and was seemingly satisfied with an explanation that the mail had been discovered in Lisbon.[97]

Gaffney's impression contrasted starkly with Irish government reports that the brigade was "composed of a poor type of soldier, deficient in physique and character" with "at least two lunatics in the ranks." The same report continued, "most of the officers were ill-trained and inefficient."[98] While some recruits were deemed to be of good character, others had questionable backgrounds and motivations. Patrick Joseph Skehan from County Clare was said to have "traveled to Spain mainly in search of employment and adventure" following a short teaching career and unsuccessful attempts to gain a commission in the British army.[99] John Cross from Limerick was described as unemployed, apolitical (although he was a supporter of O'Duffy) and "addicted to drink."[100]

In contrast to O'Duffy's brigade, a smaller number of Irishmen enlisted to join the International Brigades fighting for Republican Spain. Many were drawn from the ranks of the Communist Party of Ireland, the left-wing of the IRA and its socialist breakaway group, Republican Congress. Between 150–240 Irish volunteers fought for the Republican forces. Nominally led by Frank Ryan, the disparate collection of

Irish volunteers has subsequently been dubbed the "Connolly Column." Most were attached to the Abraham Lincoln Brigade which also included British and American volunteers. A reaction against O'Duffy's Brigade was a strong motivation for Irish socialists to participate in the war effort. Some hoped to exploit the ability to "take a few legitimate potshots at O'Duffy and his followers."[101] Socialist-republicans regularly characterized O'Duffy and Irish fascism as indistinguishable from British imperialism. The International Brigade Association claimed Ryan had "his first encounter with Fascist thugs when he fought the Black and Tans on Irish soil."[102] However, the English leader of the XV International Brigade in Spain, George Nathan, had been a Black and Tan during the War of Independence and was personally responsible for the murders of George Clancy, Mayor of Limerick, and former mayor Michael O'Callaghan. Stradling noted how "the man who first led the Irish into battle" could hardly be considered "a lesser enemy of the Irish republican cause than General O'Duffy himself."[103]

The Irish who fought in the International Brigades are popularly regarded as having distinguished themselves as a force. Sixty-nine of the men died, with a further 26 captured by Spanish Nationalist and Italian troops, including Ryan.[104] Irish volunteers on different sides were briefly close to one another on the Jarama front in February 1937. Frank Ryan sent mocking messages by speaker in response to rumors that the Irish Bandera was nearby: "Irishmen, go home! Your fathers would turn in their graves if they knew that you'd come to fight for imperialism. This is the real Republican Army. The real, real men of Ireland."[105] 30 Irishmen fighting for the International Brigades were killed at the Battle of Jarama while a further 25 were wounded.[106]

◆ ◆ ◆

Life in Spain was a difficult adjustment for the Irish. O'Duffy's complaints were chiefly culinary. He bemoaned the lack of "authentic" tea in Spain, "even in cases when you supply your own tea to the Spanish cook it is always served cold and weak in a beer glass, and always without sugar or milk" but he noted "the coffee, however, is quite good." He particularly disliked being served meals in hotels only to discover that "everything [was] swimming in olive oil." He disagreed with the lengthy intervals between six to eight courses, which he considered "a great waste of time" as "nearly half the day is usually spent between eating and the mid-day *siesta* that follows a long and heavy meal." Instead, the General had food delivered to his office where he "finished it off in about ten minutes."[107] The Irish representative in Spain, Leo Kerney, recorded that "complaints about the food" among the ordinary volunteers "were made from the first day, and despite promises, little had been done to improve rations."[108]

Somewhat trivial cultural clashes became a bone of contention for the men. They failed to take to the Spanish custom of the siesta. When the men were brought to a bull fight, many were horrified by the pastime which "did not appeal to the Irishmen's sense of sportsmanship." Many left early in disgust. O'Duffy acknowledged that most men rooted for the "unfortunate animal" against the matador. When O'Duffy's views on bullfighting were reported, republicans retorted that perhaps O'Duffy found the 1923 Ballyseedy massacre "rather a cruel sport" too.[109] The Irish failed to take to the Spanish custom of spending hours over a single glass of beer or wine. Beer was "rather dear" but wine was "very cheap" which led to many intoxications.[110] Fr McCabe was worried about "the drink problem," believing the men had "grown too fond of 'vino.'"[111]

Until February 1937, the Bandera remained in the barracks at Caceres, undergoing training and awaiting orders. The seeds of dissatisfaction were sown from the outset. Although O'Duffy denied it, he filled appointments to the Bandera's officer corps with his own lackeys from the NCP who "knew nothing of war" and were "unfit to be even lance-corporals."[112] He remained detached from the men, being quartered "in the principal hotel in Caceres" rather than at the barracks. His diary is replete with entries of "celebrations" after victories such as the capture of Málaga, sightseeing trips to historic and religious sites, and attendance at Masses.[113] The brigade acted as a magnet for eccentrics and adventurers with dubious intentions. One such hanger-on was Aileen O'Brien, an American anti-communist formerly active in the ICF, who was suspected of conducting numerous romantic affairs. She was despised by Fr Mulrean and the Irish hierarchy, who were "displeased that O'Brien had been representing the interests of Irish Catholicism in Spain."[114] Considerable press scrutiny was directed at O'Duffy and Belton for living large during their respective trips to Spain. O'Duffy shamelessly admitted to the press and in his memoir how he was lavishly entertained by his Nationalist hosts. Belton and O'Duffy were reported to have received £30,000 collected by Irish Bishops.[115] Belton was criticized by FF in November 1936 for "enjoying himself" on his "Mediterranean cruise" where he shamelessly admitted that he drank many "creamy pints."[116] Such outings generated the impression that Ireland's most prominent cheerleaders of the Nationalist cause were enjoying luxury and excess in Spain.

It was not until a month after their arrival before the men received uniforms, which were ill-fitting and made from shoddy material. Soon the uniforms were "threadbare" and "in rags" due to constant wear. They were never replaced. Morale plummeted due to the absence of parcels and letters from home. Gunning was responsible for collecting the mail from Lisbon, but for weeks on end he returned empty handed or with only a handful of letters. O'Duffy personally traveled to Lisbon where he discovered an abundance of unprocessed parcels. He left for Caceres with "two lorry loads of letters, newspapers and parcels," which he personally handed to each addressee. Some men received delayed notice of family deaths.[117] Illustrating the poor mental state of some soldiers, accelerated by poor conditions in the Brigade, upon receiving letters from home expressing envy at the men's presumed daily routine of "picking oranges in the sunshine," the men became upset and "anxious to get into a fight." The weather was frequently poor. One man, upon receiving such a letter about "the fine time we were having in Spain," flew into a fit of rage and "took a grenade from his back and threatened to blow himself and the billet up." Initially, his comrades laughed at the presumed joke but suddenly it dawned on them that "he meant trouble" and they "edged away from him towards the exit."[118]

Irish brigade member Luke O'Rourke recalled some of his compatriots in the brigade were "quare fellows" who were confined to the cells for reasons not adumbrated. But he was confident these men were not "soldier material" and were "not able for the action when it came." The brutal treatment meted out by the foreign legion to its own soldiers such as punishment whippings disturbed the Irish. O'Rourke remembered witnessing the execution five Nationalist defectors.[119] Denis McGuinness recalled seeing the summary execution of prisoners in Badajoz. The disturbing sight set him thinking "of their families as they struggled on the ground.... When it was over, they were thrown onto a cart. I don't know where they were buried."[120] These unsettling scenes had a profound impact on the Irishmen. One deserter described how there was a "cool-house mutiny" among the Irish, where there was always "a lot of fighting."[121]

The Irish diplomatic representative in Spain reported that due to heightened complaints from the men all letters sent home were "now strictly censored and very few letters got through." In the case of a single volunteer who wrote over 20 letters home, not one reached the intended recipient.[122] The mystery of the unsent letters was solved when it was discovered that Gunning was pilfering money for stamps and other postage costs from the Bandera, a petty crime which reflected his low character. Fr Mulrean also indicated that Gunning had contracted venereal disease from his wife "whom he had induced to misconduct herself with Germans and Italians for money."[123]

◆ ◆ ◆

An inspection of the Irish troops was conducted by Franco on 6 February where he expressed his confidence in the Bandera. Ten days later, Franco ordered them to the Madrid front. O'Duffy recorded that while "many" in the Bandera had experience from the War of Independence, most "were about to go under fire for the first time."[124] Around the time the brigade departed for the front, Frank MacDermot told the Dáil "that if General O'Duffy's military capacities are at all on a par with his political capacities, I do not envy anyone the state of his conscience when he contributes to sending the flower of Irish youth to serve under General O'Duffy's banner." Although rebuked by Belton, MacDermot's prediction of impending disaster proved prescient.[125] The growing social divide between O'Duffy and his men could be seen by the fact the General traveled ahead by car while his men were to travel by train and then march the remainder of the journey by foot. The Irish representative in Spain claimed that until the date of their departure, O'Duffy only visited his force on two occasions; when he first arrived in Spain, and two weeks later when he addressed them about their enlistment.[126]

As O'Duffy left for the front, the journalist Francis McCullagh described him as being "in the best of health and humor, and as pleased at getting to the Front as a schoolboy at getting home for the holidays." Although usually suspicious of McCullagh, the General was friendly and invited him for coffee before continuing the next leg of his journey.[127] Meanwhile, the Bandera boarded a train bound for Torrijos. From there the men were to march to the Madrid front. Trouble immediately broke when it was discovered that the train driver was a Republican spy "with plans to blow up the train."[128] The train left the station "at break-neck speed" until it was halted, at which point the driver and a companion jumped and made a run for it before being captured.[129] Denis McGuinness recalled, "I believe they shot the driver in the back of the head. We heard the shot."[130] What should have been a five-hour journey became a 26-hour one. Upon arriving at the disembarkation point, nobody was there to meet the Bandera and inform them which direction they should march to Valdemora.

As the Irish advanced to Ciempozuelos, 15 miles from Madrid, on 18 February, they experienced their first combat engagement. While setting up camp, the Irishmen came under fire—not from the "Reds" but from a detachment of Franco's army from the Canary Islands. Dressed in the "strange uniform" of the Irish Bandera, complete with "the Irish harp emblem on each lapel of the tunic,"[131] the Spanish fascists mistook the obviously foreign soldiers for volunteers of the International Brigades.[132] Two Spanish officers attached to the Bandera stepped forward to greet their comrades. The opposing officer "stepped back a pace, drew his revolver, and fired point blank" at the Spanish officer attached to the Irish brigade. The two Spanish officers were killed by their own side.[133] Fighting lasted for an hour before the awkward realization came that they were on the same side. However, it was too late for two Irish soldiers, Tom Hyde from Cork, and Dan Chute from Kerry. Hyde was a longtime member of the Blueshirts who subsequently became an NCP keyman in County Cork. McGuinness recalled that the Canary Island troops then "left the way open for us to enter Ciempozuelos." As they marched, the unfortunate men experienced an air raid (from the Republicans) which left some men with wounds from ricochets. McGuinness was deeply upset by Hyde's death and from then on became stoical about his own fate. Hyde had told his comrades he did not expect to return alive from Spain and had executed a will before leaving Ireland.[134]

O'Duffy learned of the deaths of Hyde, Chute and the two Spanish officers the next day. Immediately, he left to confer with Colonel Juan Yagüe, head of the foreign legion. "All agreed that fault lay with officers [of the] Canary Islands Battalion," O'Duffy wrote in his diary.[135] Their commander was shot dead by the Irishmen during the skirmish and the Canary Islands Bandera was soon disbanded. The significant delay of the Irish force's arrival due to the train incident may also have contributed to the misunderstanding. Marcelo Gaya y Delrue blamed the Irish for the incident, claiming that under the influence of whiskey the Irishmen "unleashed a bewildering attack at our own troops."[136] Despite this claim, blame appeared to lie with the Canary Islands troops.

The news of the deaths was reported at home. Chute's mother, upon learning of her son's death, told the press: "My boy is an only son who went to fight for Christ. Although there is a load on my heart, I offer him to Christ, for Whom he fought."[137] The *Irish Press* acknowledged that even those who doubted the wisdom of the entire endeavor expressed "the most general regret and sympathy" for the two fallen soldiers.[138] O'Duffy arranged for elaborate military funerals to be held in Caceres, attended by local dignitaries and the bishop. In Ireland, a memorial Mass was celebrated in Dublin's Pro-Cathedral for the two Catholic martyrs.[139] McCullagh met O'Duffy at breakfast the day after the funerals, where he greeted the General. "Quite well, General," O'Duffy replied, "how's yourself?" McCullagh inferred "from his sarcastic use of the word General, and from his whole attitude, that he was in bad humor and meant to be deliberately rude."[140]

General O'Duffy resolved "to take advantage" of his senior rank and remonstrated to his superior, Franco. He soon became a thorn in the side of the Generalissimo. The Irish subsequently stayed in Ciempozuelos, along the Jarama Valley, for five weeks. Described by O'Duffy as "a town of the dead," here the morale of the troops further nosedived. One of their first duties was to discard decomposing corpses which were strewn across the town. The men lived under daily shell fire. The trenches were described by O'Duffy as "shallow and badly constructed, affording little or no protection from wind and rain."[141] Conditions were predictably bad, with cases reported of trench foot, backache, and lice everywhere "on your head, on your eyebrows, by the fistful on your crotch." Moss Fennell described his experience of a shell attack: After the smoke and debris cleared away, he felt "a sickening sensation" as he experienced "the stench of rotting human flesh. There were three dead and decaying bodies partially covered, one only inches away and seemingly looking straight at me, the glazed and sightless eyes partially falling out of their sockets."[142]

O'Duffy's second-in-command, Patrick Dalton, received a "slight wound" and suffered from sciatica which prompted him to return home.[143] His decision showed his disenchantment with the entire effort, and betrayed a guilty conscience over the deaths of Hyde and Chute. One left-wing newspaper claimed that O'Duffy did not fight but "took the publicity," leaving "the work to be done by Dalton." It continued, "Dalton left Spain at the end of March. No wonder!"[144] He was replaced by O'Sullivan, a functionary from the NCP.[145] Garda intelligence believed O'Duffy was deliberately promoting his political followers to officer roles with an eye towards fielding them as candidates at the next general election. The Irish department of external affairs reported that the men were "to a large extent discontented with their lot. They complain of the bad food, poor clothing and of their treatment generally."[146] The pro-Republican *Irish Democrat* newspaper reported that the men were disenchanted with the lack of Catholicity among their co-fighters: "Moors, Germans, Italians everywhere and no Spaniards?"[147]

Gunning was next to leave the Bandera, making off with a sum of money and several of the men's passports.[148] He remained in Spain, where he found work as a correspondent for Reuters.[149] An Irish visitor described Gunning in December 1937 as being "surrounded by henchmen who seem to be survivors from the Irish brigade, and he seems to reign over them like a gangster chieftain."[150] While holding court in a bar in St Jean de Luz, Gunning was overheard by Kerney's secretary "talk[ing] loudly" about encouraging the Spanish authorities to execute Frank Ryan, whom Gunning accused of committing seven assassinations in Ireland: "for two months I have been trying to get him shot; I've gone to them with tears in my eyes to get them to shoot him, and they won't shoot him."[151] Despite Gunning's best efforts, Ryan was likely spared such an end by the fact his capture was reported in the international media. Even O'Duffy signed a letter to Franco requesting clemency for Ryan.[152]

Gunning came to detest O'Duffy, writing to Desmond FitzGerald in July 1937: "O'Duffy and his entourage of bosthoons have given us a black eye here that will last for generations.... I was very stupid, I did a poor day's work for both Spain and Ireland when I helped the insane, uncultured lout to put his flat and smelly feet across the frontier." Gunning personally appealed to FitzGerald to undertake a propaganda tour of Spain to salvage some of the prestige of the Irish pro-Franco lobby, which he believed was undermined by O'Duffy.[153] Gunning claimed he had "thrown up a job" to attach himself to O'Duffy, believing him to be sincere "when he dissolved his organization before leaving for Spain" but became "disillusioned with fascism as he had seen it in Spain" and "had trouble with O'Duffy." Gunning and O'Duffy each tried to have the other shot.[154] Gunning later traveled to Breslau with his mistress Ingeborg Lorenz for a recuperative holiday and to work for Nazi Germany's propaganda department. He died in a German sanatorium from tuberculosis in June 1940.

O'Duffy's behavior hardly helped to alleviate tensions within the Bandera. A Norwegian journalist told Leo Kerney that O'Duffy was a "queer fellow." In a hotel in Salamanca, the General was in the habit of "calling round him any journalists he saw, standing them drinks and telling them yarns, with the injunction not to repeat them but, apparently, with a contrary intention."[155] It was a curious activity for a Major-General in the Spanish army to engage in, particularly while his troops suffered daily shell fire. International journalists had a low opinion of O'Duffy, believing him to be a "bum politician" who, "having become extinguished in Ireland, had come out to light up again at the flames of the Spanish Civil War." McCullagh recalled that O'Duffy would buy journalists "a double peg of Irish [whiskey] to which he sternly refused to add any water."[156] He was "rarely to be seen, either in public or private, without a bottle of whisky."[157]

On 13 March, the Irish Bandera was ordered "over the top" to capture Titulcia as part of the Battle of Jarama. The first assault resulted in four casualties—three men from Kerry and Sergeant Gabriel Lee from Offaly.[158] O'Sullivan ordered a retreat and the men "ran like hares" from the engagement. The next day, an order arrived that the Irish must launch a second attack on Titulcia. General O'Duffy declined to obey the order, due to pressure from his own men, particularly Captain Tom Cahill of A Company who threatened to mutiny.[159] He issued counter-orders that his men were to remain at the barracks while he departed for field headquarters to confer with General Andrés Saliquet, where he asked the Spanish general to rescind the order. Saliquet agreed to the unprecedented request.[160] O'Duffy later met with Franco that week in Navalcarnero. O'Duffy claimed the Generalissimo agreed with his executive decision to refuse to obey the orders.[161] Historians have cast doubt on this version of events. It was unlikely Franco would have accepted O'Duffy's excuse for disobeying his orders. Even if the town were impregnable, the primary objective of the assault was not necessarily to capture Titulcia but to relieve pressure on Italian troops defending Guadalajara.[162] Franco inspected the brigade on 17 March, St Patrick's Day. A week later, they were moved to the small village of La Marañosa, outside Madrid.

O'Duffy's reluctance to launch a second offensive against Titulcia, believing that half his Bandera would be killed, contrasted starkly with his pugnacious stance as a field commander during the Irish Civil War in marching on Limerick in the summer of 1922.[163] The contrasting examples illustrate the differing motives underlying his involvement in the two conflicts. Whereas during the Irish Civil War, O'Duffy was actively engaged in a serious military confrontation with his former IRA comrades to uphold the Treaty settlement, during the Spanish Civil War he was largely pursuing a propaganda objective to symbolically provide Irish support for Nationalist Spain but he hoped for minimal casualties. Moreover, General O'Duffy in 1922 was temperate, youthful, and focused. A contemporary in 1937 described him as vain, incompetent, and irritable. "This temperamental unevenness is probably," wrote McCullagh, "one of the greatest defects in a great race."[164] His objective was to "be in [Spain] for the celebrations without taking part in the main hostilities," according to a garda report.[165]

The Nationalist leadership soon transferred "a score of Spanish officers" who spoke English to the Irish brigade, to prevent further skirmishes with their own side, to interrogate prisoners and deserters, to facilitate relations between the Irish and the Spanish adjoining forces and the local townspeople, to supplement the lack of military experience in the brigade "including General O'Duffy himself," and to facilitate contact between the Irish brigade and GHQ. O'Duffy was unhappy about this transfer, but his credibility among the Spanish was marginal.[166] The Duchess of Tetuan, a Spanish noblewoman of Irish descent, thought O'Duffy was somewhat "fantastique." She informed the Irish representative that the Spanish were increasingly unhappy with the Irish Bandera, whose men were "much given to drinking." The Spanish were concerned by "cases of shooting amongst themselves" in the Bandera.[167]

◆ ◆ ◆

In La Marañosa, at least 150 of the Irishmen appeared on sick parade. One volunteer later claimed, "we never saw the Reds, but were often under Red artillery fire."[168] In fact, perhaps the sole success of the Bandera came after their transfer from the front. At Maranosa, they participated in a raid against a Republican-controlled armored train, helping to capture several prisoners of war. Séamus McKee recalled their collective horror at the summary executions of prisoners by a detachment of Moorish troops: "[they] shot them like dogs." According to McKee, following this ghastly incident "only a handful expressed any desire to remain."[169] Considering that the German army's representative in Spain, Baron Hans von Funck, advised against the deployment of regular German soldiers to Spain due to the battlefield barbarism of the Army of Africa, the psychological impact of witnessing such ferocity on unseasoned young Irish volunteers must have been severe.

Disenchantment in the brigade was furthered by the overbearing enforced piety of Fr Mulrean, who demanded each man attend weekly confession. Fr McCabe explained, "they feel that he sits down in the Box and begins to listen eagerly, just to satisfy his morbid curiosity. They see that he is constantly doing this outside the Box, and it's very hard to trust a Confessor, who is, at the same time, an inveterate and unscrupulous gossip and slobberer."[170] Among the men, there was growing disillusionment with O'Duffy's absentee leadership. They began referring to him as "General O'Scruffy" and "Old John Bollocks."[171] Special branch reported that "there was dissension in the ranks ... chiefly due to O'Duffy's selection of officers" with an eye to forming a "secret organization of a Fascist nature" upon his return.[172]

Poor discipline was rife in the brigade. McKee recalled that fracas broke out between the Irish and Moorish troops, resulting in the death of one Moor, for which the Irish were fined.[173] The *Irish Democrat* contrasted the experience of the pro-Republican and pro–Franco volunteers: "While Ryan's men were fighting on all fronts, O'Duffy's band contented itself with policing Salamanca and fighting intermittent skirmishes with their Moorish, Italian and Spanish allies in Salamanca bar-rooms."[174] An inspection of the barracks by Yagüe left him deeply unimpressed. Described by Gunning as "a man of violent disposition," Yagüe demanded that a Spanish commander be appointed to put manners on the Irish, although remaining under O'Duffy's nominal generalship.[175] Yagüe wrote to Franco to air his grievances that the Spanish were "making themselves pawns of a political maneuver by this Operetta General," indicating that O'Duffy was cynically using the war to rebuild his domestic career.[176] Seán Cunningham, a company commander in the Bandera, had an altercation with Yagüe. In the heat of the moment, Cunningham threatened to defect to the Republicans. He was arrested.[177] Yagüe dismissed O'Sullivan following his appointment by O'Duffy. Friction soon grew between O'Duffy and Franco. O'Duffy stridently opposed Yagüe's proposed imposition of a Spanish commander. He also resented the transfer of Noel Fitzpatrick and Gilbert Nangle, two English officers (of Irish extraction), to the Irish Bandera. O'Duffy sneered at these "Protestant Englishmen" and claimed they suffered from venereal diseases. The dislike was mutual. Fitzpatrick declared in March, "I've just done a stint with that shit O'Duffy and now I'm here trying to arrange a posting back to my old Bandera." Both men survived the war. Fitzpatrick took French leave in the summer of 1937 following his ill-advised admission to being a Freemason. Nangle left Spain in December.[178] Irish newspapers reported there was "much bad feeling" inside the brigade.[179]

Leopold Kerney reported to Dublin that the Spanish Nationalists were remorseful of ever having had any dealings with the hard-drinking but battle-shy Irish general. Initially wooed by O'Duffy's panache, the Spanish believed he possessed "the military experience and science of a general," but soon learned "his military knowledge is very limited." The Irish diplomat commented, "O'Duffy seems to have completely lost his credit with Franco, who now looks upon him as a bluffer, if not a duffer." The Spanish believed O'Duffy "has bluffed much and promised much whilst performing little."[180] The Irish leader was regularly incommunicado, to the chagrin of his men and the Spanish military. Eager to remove O'Duffy and the Irishmen from Spain, Kerney, Yagüe and Franco conspired to see the Bandera dissolved and the men repatriated to Ireland.[181] The Free State lobbied Franco's regime to begin to repatriate minors who enlisted without parental consent. Thomas Carew recalled an occasion when O'Duffy threatened to send the entire Bandera home if Franco allowed Yagüe to remove certain Irish officers, to which Franco replied, "Send your Bandera home."[182] Gunning claimed O'Duffy was scolded by Franco that he "knew nothing of military matters and that he was poking his nose into affairs that did not concern him." Franco insisted on the Irish Bandera "clearing out" if O'Duffy would not agree to three of his subordinates being Spanish officers.[183]

The men were balloted and voted by a margin of 654 to nine to return home. On 9 April, O'Duffy wrote to Franco requesting the disbandment of the Bandera.

He complained that his authority as "Chief of the Irish force" had been undermined by Spanish officers, particularly Colonel Yagüe. O'Duffy was "obliged ... to accept that unfortunately Your Excellency no longer has confidence in the Irish Bandera. We cannot remain here without your full support, neither can we ask other Irishmen to join us on such a basis." He explained that he had "no alternative" but to request arrangements would be made "to return the Bandera to its homeland."[184] O'Duffy claimed the men had "done their duty" in fulfilling the six-month contract originally set for them and could leave Spain with honor. He blamed the Free State government for upholding the Non-Intervention Pact and meddling with Spanish diplomats to prevent a reserve Bandera from being formed. This, he claimed, left the Bandera below the threshold for the minimum number of men needed to form a brigade. As such, its disbandment was a foregone conclusion and O'Duffy felt honor-bound to return to Ireland.

◆ ◆ ◆

Some intermediaries intervened to save the Bandera. On 21 April, a conference was initiated by the bishop of Gibraltar, Richard FitzGerald, and the Irish-Spanish noblewoman, the Duchess of Tetuán, to reconcile the Spanish generals with O'Duffy. The bishop was unaware of the contempt the Spanish high command had for the Irish Bandera. Fr McCabe relayed the full story to FitzGerald, including how the Spanish leaders could not understand the brigade's "tom-fooling." Although Franco received FitzGerald's pleas, he could not prevent O'Duffy's eventual return to Ireland. McCabe learned a few days later that O'Duffy was fully committed to returning to Ireland and had merely humored the bishop. He was scornful of the Irish general who "never intended to die in Spain or for Spain," but only wanted to form a "Blueshirt" regime by armed force, "if there was no other way."[185]

The rector, the duchess, and the bishop continued in their attempts to repair the damaged relationship between the Irish and the Spanish. On 29 April, Captain Meade, a Spanish officer of Irish extraction and O'Duffy's driver, reiterated to Fr McCabe the Spanish command's view that the brigade would only be allowed to continue if it was commanded by a Spanish officer. Meade was disillusioned with the behavior of the Irish. He had even lent his personal car to O'Duffy, which he wrecked. Fr McCabe and Meade devised a compromise formula whereby the Bandera would be led by a Spanish officer of Irish descent. The Duchess of Tetuán was asked to persuade O'Duffy to return to the negotiating table. The Spanish demanded the imposition of serious discipline, an end to O'Duffy's tendency to consult endlessly with his staff which led to indecision, and closer collaboration between O'Duffy and high command. On the Irish side, Fr McCabe suggested that the Irish should fight on a new front with the Carlists and made requests for the assignment of specific officers. As negotiations were ongoing, O'Duffy arrived and joined them for supper. Fr McCabe was fed up with O'Duffy's foibles and complaints of the Spanish cuisine, "the General has a silly horror of eggs cooked in olive oil. It is little trifles and 'fads' like this, to which the Irish should be quite accustomed to by this time, that are helping to create mountainous troubles in the Brigade."

Despite the best efforts of McCabe and sympathizers, O'Duffy had made up his mind. He exasperatedly said that the brigade would be better off reforming itself as a musical band and enacting a propaganda tour of Spain. He defended charges of drunkenness in the brigade by pointing to the IRA service record of its men, some of whom were "national heroes," and claimed many were pioneers. Fr McCabe wrote that the latter were probably the heaviest drinkers. Overall, he found O'Duffy's excuses "rather puerile." After Mass in the Irish College on 2 May, Fr McCabe made another plea to O'Duffy to accept a Spanish commander and to remove O'Sullivan.

> O'Duffy got quite thick and obstinate, and began to splutter, something about O'Sullivan's merits, and then he shouted out violently, "No, I'll take the Brigade home. I wouldn't stop here for the Duchess of Tetuán, or all the O'Donnells in Ireland. And we'll close the Irish College, too." I was not prepared for this outburst, and I remarked drily, "We'll see about the College later on." He almost jumped about in his rage, and he looked a coarse, rough type, that reminded me of a "pub" on Saturday night.

That night, the duchess and Fr McCabe once again asked O'Duffy to reconsider his position. Fr McCabe even engaged in uncharacteristic flattery, promising the General he would be remembered as a "second Sarsfield." Although O'Duffy was less animated than earlier, he was equally unpersuaded. Two days later, the Duchess of Tetuán spoke to Nicolás Franco's secretary, who politely informed her nothing could be done. Fr McCabe recognized she became strongly disillusioned and lost her "romantic interest in Ireland," her ancestral homeland.[186] Fr McCabe was also fed up with O'Duffy. He joined the almost overwhelming consensus that General O'Duffy had cynically exploited the Spanish Civil War in the sordid hope of reviving his moribund domestic political career.

◆ ◆ ◆

The men returned to Caceres on 10 May. Their departure was delayed by several weeks as the sick and wounded needed time to recover. They set off by train to Lisbon where they set sail for Dublin aboard the *SS Mozambique* on 17 June. Franco spared no expense in ferrying the Irishmen out of Spain. The Generalissimo had kind words to say in a final letter to O'Duffy before his departure:

> I shall always hold a grateful memory of the young Irishmen who for the justice of our cause did not vacillate in offering their services, and their lives, and many made sacrifices in defense of the high ideal that animates the Spanish people in the fight for independence of the Fatherland and for Christian civilization against Moscow Communism.[187]

Most Bandera members left Spain deeply disillusioned with the whole endeavor. In a statement to the press, Eamon Horan laid the blame for "the loss of our national prestige" squarely on the shoulders of O'Duffy and "a few of his followers." "We were not long in Spain until we were convinced that it was a political campaign." Horan recalled that in Caceres, O'Duffy gathered his men and asked that they avoid giving statements to the press. He advised them that "on their return, there would be an election campaign in his favor in Ireland, for which he had his candidates picked."[188]

In the event, O'Duffy did not contest the 1 July general election. He acknowledged it was "possible" there would be "a few Independent candidates who would advocate the ideals for which the Brigade stood and would lead the campaign against

Communism, who would advocate a State based on the Papal Encyclicals, and who would be prepared to recognize General Franco."[189] O'Duffy desperately encouraged his remaining allies in Ireland to contest the general election as independent candidates. The brigade announced to the press that the late Tom Hyde's brother-in-law, Edmond Carey, a former CnaG deputy, would be an independent candidate in East Cork. When approached, Carey stated the announcement "was the first he had heard of the matter" and ultimately declined to contest the election. Elsewhere, O'Duffy tapped James Daly, who was elected in 1934 as an FG local councilor in Navan, to stand in the constituency of Meath-Westmeath.[190] Daly answered O'Duffy's call but polled worst out of all candidates in his area, gaining a mere one percent of the vote. In Cork West, P.J. Coughlan announced the NCP would support the candidacy of John L. O'Sullivan, an imprisoned FG candidate who supported Cronin during the Blueshirts split.[191] But endorsing a slew of semi-sympathetic independent and FG candidates was a far cry from the NCP romping to victory on foot of a successful foreign crusade. The General malingered from yet another campaign.

On 22 June, the men arrived in North Wall looking "tired and worn ... their shirts and shoes appeared worse for wear." Some sported fezzes, badges in the Irish and Spanish colors, and carried small photographs of Franco. Reflecting the social divisions which arose in Spain, O'Duffy's sartorial habits were far different to those of his men: "General O'Duffy ... wore a smart blue suit, brown shoes, and a clean white collar." He "presented a great contrast to the volunteers as he directed the embarkation," a journalist noted.[192] One foreign newspaper described the scene: "Ireland's modern crusaders returning from the Spanish war presented a motley and bedraggled appearance. They might have been the riff-raff of any mercenary army. Their clothes were shabby and unkempt, but their faces were bright and cheery."[193] The gardaí agreed the men looked "disreputable" and like they had "gone through a severe time in Spain."[194] Before the Bandera departed from Lisbon, a spiteful Fr Mulrean contacted the Irish authorities to claim typhus had broken out onboard the *Mozambique*.[195] When the vessel reached Dublin, the men were quarantined and their quarters inspected by immunization staff. They were deemed healthy and allowed to embark.

For a greeting party the veterans were subjected to searches by special branch, with nine cases recorded of confiscated weapons and consequent arrests. O'Duffy protested to the detective sergeant about the treatment of his men. When he was ordered to submit his own luggage to inspection, he claimed the search was politically motivated and denied his bags contained any ammunition. He told the guard, "I have been a long time keeping the law in this country—for eleven years and I am not going to break the law now. I will be keeping the law after this man [de Valera] is gone."[196] Following this ordeal, the men proceeded to march from Alexandra Quay to the Mansion House. Led by St Mary's Anti-Communist Pipe Band, the Bandera marched along Dublin's quays to measured public enthusiasm. However, several men from Kerry led by Eamon Horan marched separately in a show of opposition to O'Duffy.[197] As the main procession reached the Mansion House, O'Duffy was hoisted by the crowd onto their shoulders amid cheers and applause.[198] The Lord Mayor of Dublin, Alfie Byrne, graciously received the returned veterans in his official residence, an action for which he has been much criticized in subsequent assessments. By April 1939, Byrne declined to attend a Mass in the Pro-Cathedral offered in thanksgiving for Franco's victory.[199]

Despite the warm reception for the men at the Mansion House, public enthusiasm for the Bandera had dissipated during its time in Spain. Rumors of defections, poor conditions, and the trickle of internal gossip to the media (particularly reported in the *Irish Press*) tarnished the venture in the public eye. This reputation has largely endured. During an interview in the 1960s, Brendan Behan, the Irish playwright and republican, mocked the Bandera as "the only military expedition in history that came back with more fucking men than they went away with."[200] The sentiment underlying Behan's quip bore some accuracy. The Londoner Fred Thomas and the Canadian "Tug" Wilson "slipped out of Spain with O'Duffy's Irishmen."[201] Although O'Duffy received some minor plaudits for his expedition such as the Freedom of the City of Kilkenny,[202] it offered little comfort when faced with the re-election of FF on 1 July. In all likelihood, the General and his men being waylaid in Spain for over two months following the Bandera's official disbandment frustrated the possibility of the NCP being revived and fielding a slate of candidates. The Bandera returned in the middle of the election campaign. Although he may have taken some solace in the overall loss of seats for FF, FG, and the poor performance of his old rival Ned Cronin as an independent candidate in Cork North, General O'Duffy's own political career was finished.

An unedifying public dispute with the ICF left O'Duffy isolated even among the Catholic right-wing. Belton accused O'Duffy of seeking to "discredit and destroy" the ICF from its foundation. The dispute centered on a claim by O'Duffy that the ICF never financially supported the brigade, which led to counter-charges from Belton.[203] This clash of gargantuan egos continued for months, with each hurling "innuendos, slanders, exhortations" at the other.[204] One provincial newspaper despaired about the "squabbling between Belton and O'Duffy," which was not conducive to helping the "young men … who went out from Ireland to fight for Spain" and were "now without work." It concluded: "Between them, Belton and O'Duffy have not made the new conjunction of Ireland and Spain a thing to be remembered with pleasure."[205] As McGarry noted, the popular "pro–Franco lobby imploded under its own internal tensions before inflicting any substantial political damage on Fianna Fáil."[206] The ICF, led by "political chameleon" Patrick Belton, "left no permanent mark" on the Irish political scene apart from "a series of remarkable public meetings" and encouraging "a residue of anti-republican and anti-communism, a residue that had always existed," according to Michael O'Riordan of the Communist Party.[207]

The government party successfully undermined depictions of the Spanish conflict as a pitched battle between Christianity and communism. Irish Catholic support for the Nationalists dissipated with the bombing of Guernica in April by the German Condor Legion. The Nazis were implicitly denounced as "neo-pagan" by Pope Pius XI in *Mit Brennender Sorge* in March 1937, a condemnation which featured prominently in the *Irish Press*. This helped to muddy the waters of popular support for Hitler's Spanish ally.[208]

Concluding his memoir on the experience of the Irish brigade, O'Duffy wrote:

"We have been criticized, sneered at, slandered, but truth, charity, and justice shall prevail, and time will justify our motives. We seek no praise. We did our duty. We went to Spain."[209] Manning viewed O'Duffy's last word on the Spanish Civil War as uncharacteristically free from exaggeration and extravagance.[210] However, the General's hope for a positive evaluation of his deeds has certainly not borne fruit. The aphorism that history is written by the victors has been inverted in the case of the Spanish Civil War. In Ireland today, an ever-growing number of murals and plaques commemorate the deeds of the Irishmen who served in the International Brigades. By contrast, just one dedication to the memory of the pro–Franco Bandera exists: a plaque in Dublin's pro–Cathedral marking the death of Gabriel Lee. In Spain, a plaque to the Irish Bandera can be found in the church of Santo Domingo in Caceres.

Heightened modern sympathy for Republican Spain reflects the cultural shifts in Irish society. While contemporaneous charges of atheism and communism damaged the reputation of the Spanish Republicans, today such charges reek of a bygone hysteria. As McGarry keenly observed, in "post-nationalist" twenty-first century Ireland, O'Duffy and his followers appear to have "fought not only on the wrong side of the Spanish civil war but on the wrong side of Irish history."[211]

In the immediate aftermath of the brigade endeavor, the special branch suspected that O'Duffy had a "secret plan" to "establish Fascism in Ireland on his return." The report claimed that several of O'Duffy's disillusioned officers "firmly believed ... that O'Duffy has entered into an alliance with German and Italian statesmen with the object of getting aid to foster Fascism in Ireland."[212] A growing reliance on the fascist powers became the dominant feature of the remainder of his career.

# 11

# The Emergency

General O'Duffy largely exited frontline politics in the wake of the Spanish debacle. He sought to curate the Bandera's reputation by establishing the Irish Brigade Association, of which he was elected president. The expedition had negatively impacted his health. "In mind and body," observed Walsh, the General was "now a tired man." He became uncharacteristically timid and indifferent to the daily affairs of the world.[1] Living since 1935 in a house he named "Farney" situated in the Dublin suburb of Mount Merrion, O'Duffy mixed well with his neighbors. He acted as chief marshal of the Mount Merrion Fete and was elected to the executive of the local resident's association.[2] His chauffeur, Robert Butler, originally from Cashel, County Tipperary, lived with him from approximately 1936 until he married in August 1938.[3] O'Duffy's attention mostly focused on managing the activities of the brigade association, writing a self-serving memoir of his time in Spain, and gardening. He kept an uncharacteristically low profile in the media. With the NCP effectively dissolved, O'Duffy failed to make the annual excursion to Béal na mBláth in August 1937. Instead, he attended a requiem Mass in memory of Collins and Griffith and laid wreaths on their graves in Glasnevin cemetery.[4]

In 1937, de Valera shrewdly utilized the British abdication crisis to present a new constitution before the electorate which represented a significant step closer to republican status. The General's opinions on the replacement of the Irish Free State Constitution with a new constitution in December 1937 failed to grace the pages of newspapers. It should have satisfied O'Duffy's own pro-republican sentiments, while implicitly vindicating the "stepping stone theory." Moreover, the provision in the popularly endorsed constitution to re-establish the upper house of parliament, elected on a vocational basis, bore the hallmarks of a watered-down corporatism.[5] O'Duffy and the NCP had supported "the formation of a Senate on vocational lines."[6] Under the new constitution, the President of the Executive Council became the Taoiseach or prime minister. The new head of state, the president, was a largely symbolic position. Dr Douglas Hyde, the founder of the Gaelic League, was nominated by all parties to become president. O'Duffy sent his congratulations to the president on the day he opened the new Senate, which indicated his personal support for Hyde.[7] Once published, O'Duffy sent President Hyde a copy of his memoir. Hyde expressed his "sincere appreciation" for sending him the "very interesting book."[8]

There was no mention of the British Commonwealth of Nations throughout the new constitution. The External Relations Act, passed by the Dáil, became the new foundation stone of Anglo-Irish relations. Ireland's relationship vis-a-vis the Commonwealth was now ambiguous but for the most part, the last remnants of British constitutional authority in southern Ireland became a dead letter. Although de Valera's concept of external association was more nuanced than O'Duffy's desire to immediately exit the Commonwealth and declare a republic, it represented a shift in an incrementally pro-republican direction.

O'Duffy's memoir of the Spanish campaign was published on the anniversary of the return of the brigade. *Crusade in Spain* offered a heavily sanitized image of the brigade's role in the conflict. According to Walsh, O'Duffy penned it "mainly from a desire to see justice done to the Volunteers" and to "dispel the wrong impression created by misleading and mischievous writings, statements and gossip at home and abroad."[9] It was glowingly reviewed in some Irish newspapers. The *Irish Independent* argued that political biases prevented the public from viewing the "true light of the gallant venture." Described as "compact and well written," *Crusade in Spain* was "marked neither by a spirit of vainglory nor by any bitterness towards those who placed obstacles in the path of the Brigade."[10] Elsewhere the book was described as "well-written, well-balanced, restrained, dispassionate, exciting, and at times profoundly moving."[11] The *Irish Press* took a predictably less sympathetic view. It argued the Bandera was a failure and that "despite all the propaganda he heaps over it," its failure is still evident. The reviewer believed it was "evident that General O'Duffy was not frequently with his men" and spent most of his time sightseeing. "The book ... is full of denunciation ... [it] must make every reader feel that instead of adding to the glory of Ireland, the 'Irish Brigade' has only added to the misrepresentation of our nation abroad."[12] The English writer George Orwell, a former volunteer in the Trotskyist POUM militia, reviewed *Crusade in Spain*: "General O'Duffy's adventures in Spain do seem in one way to have resembled a crusade in that they were a frightful muddle and led to nothing in particular."[13]

Quarterly meetings of the brigade association were chaired by O'Duffy. Issues such as the discharge of two veterans from the Irish army for their Spanish activities and the perpetual problem of unemployment among the ex-brigade members illuminated the sorry position of the returned men.[14] In late 1938, the General made tours of Northern Ireland and Cork; however, the cold weather in the north badly inflamed his right eye. In Cork he stayed with a supporter, Dr Cagney, whose son Michael joined the Bandera.[15] O'Duffy was disappointed by the failure of a fund-raising appeal for the brigade association. He believed talk was cheap. Those who proudly expressed their support for "the victory of Catholic Spain" yet failed to reach into their own pockets "for those unemployed, destitute, and maimed members of the Brigade" were lacerated by O'Duffy.[16]

By early 1939, it was apparent that the Republican forces in Spain had been vanquished. In February, the secretary of the Irish department of external affairs advised de Valera to offer de jure recognition to Franco's regime before the inevitable fall of Madrid. This would differentiate Irish policy from that of Britain and France and would secure "whatever special kudos or credit is to be got from advanced recognition."[17] When Ireland recognized Franco's government, the anonymous suggestion was made in an Irish newspaper that O'Duffy should become Irish ambassador to Spain. He enjoyed the "full confidence of General Franco," the proposer claimed.[18] Unsurprisingly, the appointment was not made.

In April 1938, de Valera's government concluded three separate agreements with the British government which formally ended the economic war. The Taoiseach felt that intervention by President Franklin D. Roosevelt was decisive in causing the British to make concessions. Briscoe credited the administration led by Neville Chamberlain, "a flexible diplomat," and the "much more reasonable" secretary of state for dominion affairs, Malcolm MacDonald, with impacting the success of the negotiations. Having learned from the 1921 Treaty negotiations, de Valera personally led the negotiations to London and surrounded himself with loyal lieutenants including Seán Lemass, Seán MacEntee, and James Ryan.[19] The British dropped their claim to the three "Treaty ports" in southern Ireland and agreed to settle the outstanding annuities issue for a lump sum payment of £10 million by the Irish government. British tariffs on Irish imports ended, while the Irish agreed to review their own excise on British imports.[20] The Anglo-Irish Trade Agreement brought a finale to an extremely contentious episode in the history of independent Ireland. The return of the Treaty ports has been credited with providing Ireland with sufficient sovereignty to remain neutral during World War II.

◆ ◆ ◆

Despite his star having fallen dramatically in Irish politics, General O'Duffy remained the most well-known proponent of Irish fascism at home and internationally. As war between the fascist and democratic powers loomed on the continent, O'Duffy represented the other side of the ideological coin in Ireland. Whilst he was primarily a devotee of the Italian strain of fascism, he began to make statements praising Nazi Germany. In May 1939, O'Duffy drew a parallel between pan-German expansionism and Irish irredentism, "there can be no peace at home until we get back our Six Counties, our Alsace Lorraine, our Sudetenland." He further claimed the press was "controlled largely by Jews and Freemasons" and that Hitler was "regarded as a great German by his people." A message of thanks to Hitler was agreed by the brigade association "for his calling of world attention to the mutilation of Ireland by England and the continuous oppression here." It also noted its "appreciation" for Hitler's "keen sense of humor."[21]

Whilst undoubtedly anti-Semitic, O'Duffy's suspicion and hostility towards Jews was distinct from the genocidal ideation of Hitler and his Nazi associates. A Swiss solicitor and former police officer who remembered O'Duffy from an international police conference in Berlin in 1926 wrote to the General in October 1938 asking him to help secure the emigration of Jewish refugees to Ireland. He believed O'Duffy to be "a friend of the Jews" and promised that the refugees were "first rate people" and would "be a great advantage to the country that would allow them to settle there."[22] O'Duffy's anti-Semitism ebbed and flowed. His belief in a Judeo-Bolshevik conspiracy was by no means unique and should be judged without the bias of "presentism." As Dermot Keogh noted, the Catholic press and periodicals regularly carried "radical anti-Jewish articles … about the subversive influence of Moscow, linking Jews to the spread of communism in many articles and editorials."[23] O'Duffy's vacillating anti–Semitism could be compared to Franco's own complicated views on the Jews.

O'Duffy's contact with the German Legation in Dublin placed him under increased surveillance from G2, Irish military intelligence. He consorted with Germans living in Dublin, many of whom supported Hitler's government. During the economic war, Ireland attracted a significant number of German professionals who found employment in universities and industry. Many Germans in Ireland, sympathetic to the IRA and Irish nationalism generally, later worked for the Nazi government. Ironically, the NCP had campaigned against the influx of German migrants during its heyday.[24] In 1934, Germans living in Dublin founded a branch of the NSDAP/AO, the Nazi Party's foreign wing. It was headed by Adolf Mahr, the director of the National Museum of Ireland, and included important German industrialists and company directors living in Ireland. Helmut Clissmann, head of the German Academic Exchange Service, was a member. German Nazis frequented the Red Bank restaurant in Dublin, owned by Mr. and Mrs. Schubert. It became a regular haunt of the Irish far-right.[25] British intelligence estimated that of the 550 German citizens resident in Ireland, 300 were supporters of the Nazi Party. The remainder were "mainly Jewish refugees awaiting naturalization." British intelligence considered these German expatriates the first and foremost "fifth column" in Ireland.[26]

The Irish government adopted neutrality in the wake of the outbreak of World War II in September 1939. It further introduced an emergency powers act, press censorship, and rationing. The term "the Emergency" was applied to refer to the period of the war years in Ireland, indicating the solipsism and parochialism of the Irish government. A pro–Axis underground sprung up around a collection of small societies which repeatedly dissolved or changed their names. In January 1939, the Celtic Confederation of Occupation Guilds (CCOG) was founded by William James Brennan-Whitmore, an Easter Rising veteran and participant in the War of Independence who supported the Treaty. Brennan-Whitmore was an ardent anti–Semite who harbored strongly pro-fascist views. He became a journalist, publishing memoirs of his wartime experiences.[27] Brennan-Whitmore's daughter recalled that the CCOG "didn't take off the ground," that "it was alive and then suddenly it died."[28] In November, it was renamed Saoirse Gaedhal ("Freedom of the Irish").

According to McGarry, a speech by O'Duffy to the CCOG shortly before the outbreak of World War II showed that the General's "admiration of Mussolini had predictably paled" and he now fulsomely embraced Nazi Germany.[29] However, the speech was delivered by Liam Walsh, not O'Duffy. This undermines the claim that O'Duffy had become an enthusiastic supporter of Nazism. He continued to shy away from politics in the wake of the Spanish expedition. Although instinctively pro–Axis, he was principally a devotee of Mussolini's fascist regime. Special branch recorded that Walsh's speech was "so definitely pro–German" that he received "a personal letter of thanks from Dr Hempel, the German minister in Dublin."[30] Despite being on the payroll of the Italian Legation, Walsh explained that "events in Europe move swiftly. Yesterday it was Mussolini and Fascism; today it is Hitler and Nazism."[31] He strongly aligned with Nazi Germany. Walsh and Brennan-Whitmore met the German agent Oskar Pfaus in early 1939, which prompted Pfaus to arrange for Walsh to visit Hamburg where he secured funds from the Deutscher Fichte-Bund to launch a pro–Nazi newspaper, the *Irish World Review*.[32] In his speech to the CCOG, Walsh advocated "perpetual peace," which could be achieved by allowing each nation to develop by its own mode. Essentially, he argued that German expansionism should be tolerated and divided the world into two Manichean camps, democracies (including the Soviet Union) and the Axis powers. He proposed creating a "truly national movement" in Ireland which would include corporatism as a central policy.[33]

Following the outbreak of World War II, Walsh set up the Cumann Náisiúnta ("National Club") to gather Nazi sympathizers in a single organization. Many of Walsh's pro–Axis activities were highly indiscreet and attracted police attention. Flagrant gatherings of Nazi sympathizers were regularly convened in the Red Bank restaurant. In February 1940, Brennan-Whitmore gathered supporters to set up a new pro–Axis political party, Clann na Saoirse ("Family of Freedom"). Whilst Clann na Saoirse was being founded, a meeting was held around the same time in O'Duffy's home at Mount Merrion which included Walsh and Alexander McCabe. In addition, the meeting included Séamus Hann, a County Wicklow businessman of German descent described as "the brains of the organization"; John A. Holden, a Nazi sympathizer and journalist with the *Irish Press;* Thomas F. O'Gorman; and Dr Patrick McCartan, a senior SF emissary during the War of Independence and pro–Treaty TD.[34] The meeting constituted the Irish Friends of Germany (IFG), which evolved from Walsh's Cumann Náisiúnta. Although O'Duffy hosted its inaugural meeting, he kept his distance from the group. Able to see around corners, O'Duffy understood that as a well-known Irish political figure his involvement in an overtly pro–Nazi organization would lead to his arrest for subversive activities.[35] However, he continued to clandestinely maintain contact with pro–Axis networks. On 14 April 1940, O'Duffy attended a "sherry party" hosted in Walsh's Dundrum home. Other guests included Séamus Burke, a former CnaG cabinet minister; Andrew Cooney, anti–Treaty IRA chief-of-staff in 1925; and Alexander McCabe. Special branch observed that "two young girls" accompanied McCabe to the social gathering.[36]

Although O'Duffy tried to remain publicly at arm's length from such organizations, many Nazi sympathizers undoubtedly saw O'Duffy as their natural leader. Unlike some of his associates, O'Duffy was more agnostic towards Nazism. Whilst he was initially attracted to continental fascism due to its uniforms, pomp, and masculine exuberance, Manning argued this was probably "emotional and instinctive rather than intellectual."[37] In the aftermath of the Spanish expedition, O'Duffy largely retreated from public life. He certainly viewed Hitler in a positive light. In his memoirs written in the early 1940s, he echoed the opening of *Mein Kampf*: "the decision of Providence that I should be born in Co[unty] Monaghan has always pleased me well."[38] Hitler's book began: "It seems to me providential that Fate should have chosen Braunau on the Inn as my birthplace."[39] However, O'Duffy was not alone in viewing Hitler positively. Various politicians associated with CnaG and FG harbored pro–Nazi sympathies, including incumbent TDs and former cabinet ministers.

Some traditionally anti–Treaty figures also displayed an admiration for Hitler, such as Dan Breen who thought highly of the German Führer.

Several Irish pro–Nazi sympathizers hoped a German invasion would propel General O'Duffy to power as a puppet leader. John Holden wrote to Walsh to explain he was working "to raise the prestige of O'D[uffy]" and to put him "on the map everywhere—because I am convinced that with a few good men at his side, he will lead the whole outfit to unity and victory."[40] Discreetly, O'Duffy encouraged the notion that he was a prospective Quisling waiting in the wings. Having failed to succeed in Irish politics independently, O'Duffy was aware that an Axis victory offered the last possibility for him to ever achieve his dictatorial ambitions.

◆ ◆ ◆

Many Irish nationalists viewed the outbreak of World War II through the prism of the traditional republican aphorism that "England's difficulty is Ireland's opportunity." Although an uncomfortably large proportion of mainstream politicians longed to see a German victory, or more accurately a British defeat, only a fringe minority ever took steps to initiate a collaborationist relationship with Nazi Germany in the sordid hope of achieving a 32-county republic. During the war years, the IRA maintained a murky relationship with Nazi Germany, particularly under its chief-of-staff Seán Russell. An article in *Republican Review* asked "are we going to allow our natural dislike of dictatorships make us forget that England still refuses to grant our freedom and unity?"[41]

Historian David O'Donoghue wrote that O'Duffy was "in political terms diametrically opposed to the 1939 IRA leadership."[42] However, the tone of some republican propaganda in the late 1930s began to strongly echo much of O'Duffy's rhetoric. In April 1939, the *Wolfe Tone Weekly*, edited by former SF leader (1931–33) Brian O'Higgins, published an article which railed against "Godless, soulless, murderous and hypocritical international finance" and extolled Hitler for having "kicked out international finance." It asked rhetorically when Ireland would follow suit, before concluding that it was "high time to restore the Republic and give life to the people."[43] The same newspaper in December 1937 carried a conspiratorial article which mirrored O'Duffy's own sentiments: "The Bankers—Jews and Freemasons and their allies—the makers of war, of Communism, of Capitalism, of Imperialism, of every anti–Christian force in the world. They own Ireland."[44] In 1937, another republican newspaper espoused a parochial Catholic nationalism underlined by an evident anti–Semitism. Although it eschewed Hitlerism, Marxism and Stalinism as part of the "anti–God horde," it railed against the ascendency in Ireland of "these Jews and Freemasons."[45] Political differences between O'Duffy and some radical republicans were no longer insurmountable. The chief obstacle from the IRA's perspective appeared to be a deeply rooted hang-up over O'Duffy's past misdeeds. IRA man Dan Keating explained, "our utter detestation of O'Duffy was not simply because of the Blueshirts; he was hated because of his past ... in the Civil War in Limerick."[46] Hitherto, O'Duffy's efforts to repair his reputation among republicans by making strongly pro-republican pronouncements had been met with derision. But the prospect of a European war prompted an IRA rethink of its attitude towards its old adversary.

Special branch recorded in December 1938 that O'Duffy was taking soundings from members of republican organizations on potential support for an armed action in Northern Ireland. He apparently healed his relationship with Colonel Thomas Carew, who had criticized the General upon the Bandera's return from Spain. The Colonel was dispatched to Tipperary to investigate "the possibility of securing men and war material" for a northern campaign. Local gardaí felt it was unlikely Carew would receive a hearing from the Old IRA Association in the area, as he was seen as "somewhat shady."[47] Carew, after an inactive spell over Christmas due to "a drinking bout" renewed his enquiries in January. Although the IRA launched a military campaign against England the same month, Gardaí believed O'Duffy's activities were unconnected.[48]

Following a leadership heave in the IRA orchestrated by Seán Russell and the Irish-American Joseph McGarrity, Russell took over the reins of the secret army in 1938. He secured support largely on a commitment to launch a bombing campaign against England which would reinvigorate the ailing force. Uinseann MacEoin wrote that the IRA throughout the 1930s had "a galaxy of talent" but "no clearly defined objective," which left it rudderless.[49] Tom Barry, one of the ousted IRA leaders, complained that Russell's internal coup d'état was financed by the German-American Bund, one of the foremost pro–Nazi groups in the United States.[50] However, Barry was reported by British intelligence to have visited Germany with an agent for the same purpose of discussing "the future action of the IRA in the event of a European war."[51] Russell, a staunch militarist, criticized the IRA for being "too involved in politics" during the 1930s. He proposed a straight-forward objective which whetted the appetite of many militarists. IRA officer Seán MacBride disagreed with Russell's "unrealistic and irrational" policy, which led him to leave the organization.[52] He later founded Clann na Poblachta which enjoyed ephemeral success in the immediate post-war period.

The new IRA chief-of-staff brought Séamus O'Donovan back into the fold. A chemicals expert and veteran republican, O'Donovan created plans for the bombing campaign against England. He was described by G2 as someone who "was in touch with the Germans ... from 1937 on" and one who "tried to indoctrinate the IRA with Nazi ideology."[53] O'Donovan is an interesting historical character who had complex views. He was far from being a prosaic pro-fascist—his magazine supported the Spanish Republican forces.[54] Russell's S-Plan was enacted in January 1939. The IRA bombed properties across English cities with the intention of inflicting financial ruin and precipitating a British withdrawal from Northern Ireland. Although the campaign lasted until 1940, the 25 August 1939 bombing of Coventry (which left five people dead and many more injured) effectively derailed the ill-fated campaign.[55] However, the advent of Russell's aggressive IRA leadership, which was prepared to cooperate with Nazi Germany for the single-minded purpose of ending partition and establishing a republic, provided German intelligence with a potential Irish ally which could wreak havoc on their soon-to-be British enemy.

Before the outbreak of World War II, German intelligence expressed indifference about "whether Ulster was ruled by the British or by the Irish" as it sought to avoid antagonizing Britain. But as war approached, the Abwehr (military intelligence unit of the Wehrmacht) began to take an interest in "encouraging minority movements abroad." The Nazis hoped to utilize such movements for either "military sabotage" or their "political nuisance value."[56] The IRA could certainly provide the former by bombing English cities. The Abwehr sent a German-American agent, Oskar Pfaus, on a mission to Ireland in January 1939 to make contact with the IRA. Initially, Pfaus was provided with several addresses, "mainly those of the Irish Blueshirts, Irish Fascists of the notorious General O'Duffy's organization."[57] On 3 February, Pfaus reached Ireland and stayed in a boarding house. He soon met O'Duffy. Pfaus requested that the General introduce him to the IRA. O'Duffy was taken aback by the request. Manning described the request as "almost comical" and claimed that the IRA turned down the request.[58] Manning added that "the meeting between O'Duffy and some of the IRA leaders in the former Red Bank restaurant in Dublin when O'Duffy sought to act as intermediary is still remembered with amusement by some older members of the IRA."[59] However, recent literature has demurred from the view that O'Duffy was rebuffed by the IRA.

O'Duffy's secretary, Walsh, facilitated a meeting with Moss Twomey, the former IRA chief-of-staff. Twomey subsequently drove Pfaus to a house in Clontarf where he was interrogated by six members of the IRA's army council, including Russell and O'Donovan. Satisfied that Pfaus was a genuine German agent, the IRA dispatched O'Donovan to Hamburg in February where he conferred with the Nazis on the role of the IRA "in the event of war between England and the Reich, and the possibility of Germany supplying the IRA with arms."[60] Also in early 1939, Russell left for the United States to drum up support for the campaign among members of the Clan na Gael. Stephen Hayes was appointed acting chief-of-staff in his absence. Although the appointment was initially intended to last "just a few weeks," the outbreak of World War II trapped Russell in the U.S. where he was temporarily arrested by the FBI.[61]

O'Duffy's involvement in the burgeoning IRA-German relationship did not begin and end with facilitating the Pfaus meeting. In late July 1939, the German diplomatic representative in Ireland, Dr Eduard Hempel, held a "personal meeting" with the IRA leadership in the remote village of Inver, County Donegal to discuss cooperation if war broke out. The "preliminary arrangements" for the meeting were made by O'Duffy and Séamus Burke. British intelligence speculated it "would seem probable" that O'Duffy and Burke "acted as intermediaries between the German negotiators and the IRA," particularly owing to O'Duffy's "contacts with the Axis powers made while he was fighting in Spain for General Franco, the Germans may look upon him as a very suitable man for such a task."[62] G2 reported that O'Duffy attended the meeting in Donegal. State fears grew that O'Duffy planned to engineer a previously unthinkable alliance with the IRA by facilitating and overseeing contact with the Germans.[63] Stephen Hayes subsequently claimed he was the victim of internal machinations by a faction of pro–German militarists in the IRA from Northern Ireland: "They passed me and turned towards the Fascist remnant of the Blue Shirts and O'Duffy's brigade where they found their own views shared to the full."[64]

◆ ◆ ◆

In June 1939, it was reported in the press that O'Duffy had been participating in conferences with former allies to stage a political comeback. It was believed that a new political party involving O'Duffy would be launched by late 1939. Indeed, O'Duffy appeared not to have given up his political ambitions, telling a private audience in December 1938 that the National Corporate Party "would come into being again."[65] An anonymous source described as a former Blueshirt told a journalist that O'Duffy was "not finished yet." He elaborated, "General O'Duffy is not finished, from the point of view of public service. Certain things have been happening in this country, and the general will take part in them. In the new organization that is arising you will have an alignment of parties, in the course of the next six months or so. The General is playing a prominent part in that, and there are things happening behind the scenes at the moment. That is all I will say."[66] O'Duffy claimed his principal aims were not political but rather to expand the Irish Brigade Association's scope and membership. This press report may have referred to the involvement of some O'Duffy associates in launching the Anti-Partition Party. Primarily Cork-based, the organization was founded in June and sought to unify various political allegiances under the common objective of ending partition. At its inaugural meeting, Dr Patrick Cagney joined the organization. He was noted by gardaí to be "a personal friend of General O'Duffy" who had "supported all movements founded by him in recent years."[67]

The Anti-Partition Party organized a well-attended protest at College Green in Dublin on 16 July which was chaired by Simon Donnelly, president of the Old IRA Association.[68] Donnelly chaired another meeting on 9 December which involved 140 senior officers of the Old IRA with a view towards founding a new republican movement.[69] On foot of that meeting, in March 1940 Córas na Poblachta ("Republican System") was launched as a political party which included among its leadership men who fought on both sides of the Civil War. O'Duffy attended its inaugural meeting. A prominent party leader was Roger McCorley, a key IRA leader in Belfast who accepted the 1921 Treaty on the basis that it could be used as a ploy to renew the war effort and consequently joined the Free State army. Others included Roger McHugh, a lecturer at University College Dublin, and Michael O'Mullane, a former de Valera supporter. Donnelly was elected party chairman. Córas has occasionally been characterized as a mere political front of the IRA. It argued for Ireland to exploit the opportunity presented by World War II to establish a sovereign republic. It soon attracted a range of pro–Axis members linked with the IFG and other far-right groupuscules. Its policy was anti–Semitic, pro-republican and pro–Axis.[70] Although O'Duffy attended its first meeting, his involvement in the party appeared to have been limited or non-existent beyond an early point.[71] The party failed to achieve electoral success. Hempel recorded that its failure at the 1943 general election "show[s] that Eire is not likely to move in the direction of an authoritarian state."[72]

There are several reasons why O'Duffy's return to politics failed to materialize. By 1939, the General's health was on the wane. He underwent surgery for "eye and nose trouble" at the Adelaide Hospital in Dublin in October.[73] Walsh believed "the campaign of a quarter century had told its tale."[74] O'Duffy's excessive smoking and drinking also contributed. Another major factor which likely left him reluctant to publicly front an unabashedly pro–Axis party was the likelihood of state repression and arrest. As the foremost Irish fascist, a political "fifth column" led by O'Duffy would be a red rag to a bull. On 23 May 1940, Walsh's house was searched by special branch under suspicion that he was in breach of the Firearms Act 1925.[75] During the raid, the police found compromising papers which linked him to the IFG. The next month, an order was issued under the Emergency Powers Act by Gerald Boland, the minister for justice, for the detention of Walsh "in the interests of public safety."[76] Gardaí noted that Walsh was "in very bad financial circumstances" and that he "is trafficking in espionage on behalf of one or more outside States for gain and not for any higher motive."[77] IRA men were also interned by de Valera's government, with two eventually being executed in September 1940. Another O'Duffy associate, Séamus Hann, was interned in the Curragh camp alongside IRA men, where he wrote poetry in German, English and Irish to the amusement of interned IRA men.[78] The arrest of his closest associates alarmed O'Duffy. Walsh's arrest was the result of his own recklessness.

In 1940, O'Duffy declined a remarkable offer by the IRA to join its leadership as an intelligence officer. In summer 1941, he was invited by former IRA chiefs-of-staff Andy Cooney and Moss Twomey to join a protest against the "Yankee Invasion of the Six Counties."[79] He most likely wanted to avoid internment in the inhospitable conditions of the Curragh. But the fact such offers and invitations were extended by the IRA is highly significant. It demonstrated the extent to which O'Duffy was reconciled with the militarist wing of extreme republicanism towards the end of his life, with objectors like Hayes accused of "preserving old sores."[80]

In late April 1940, Seán Russell arrived in Genoa from the United States. He then traveled to Berlin with the assistance of the German high command. In Berlin, he was recognized as "the diplomatic representative of the Irish Republic" and provided with "every privilege possible," including: "an excellent library, fitted out with special war maps to enable him to follow the course of events, radio-gramophone, etc. and he enjoyed all the privileges of a diplomat with regard to special food, petrol and other rationed commodities."[81] Dr Edmund Veesenmayer, a "coup d'état specialist," was assigned to Russell personally. The IRA leader outlined an overoptimistic plan for a mass German landing in Northern Ireland, which Veesenmayer believed was fanciful and indicated Russell was out of touch with the present condition of the IRA.

The Luftwaffe's failure to assert control over the air in the Battle of Britain during the summer of 1940 diminished the strategic value of Ireland to Nazi war aims. But the Germans still had use of Russell and his organization as saboteurs. In August, the IRA chief and his former comrade, Frank Ryan, were dispatched to Ireland by U–Boat as part of Operation Taube. Their brief was to foment unrest north of the border.[82] The operation plan fell apart when Russell unexpectedly died of a gastric ulcer on 14 August aboard the *U-65*, 100 miles off the coast of Galway, prompting Ryan to return to Berlin. Even if Russell had reached Ireland, he likely would have been met with swift internment. From a post-war republican perspective, it was argued the prospective arrival of Russell and Ryan "could have been a set-back, indeed unwelcome, for the Movement."[83]

In the aftermath of the arrest of 15 IFG members in June 1940, O'Duffy met Maurice O'Connor, the new chairman of the IFG, on 28 July. He advised O'Connor that it would be imprudent to found new pro-Axis organizations as it would simply present fresh targets for police infiltration and lead to more arrests. He said that the German minister in Ireland, Hempel, was "fully aware of all those who supported him." He secured employment for his henchman Tom Jolly with Hempel. He believed there was not enough time to organize a pro-Axis political party but recommended that O'Connor continue networking as "the military situation might change overnight." However, he declined to attend a meeting proposed by O'Connor, instead sending "two trusted men."[84]

O'Duffy remained circumspect during the war years and successfully staved off internment. He was briefly arrested by the Northern Irish government in July 1940 for breaching his exclusion order by crossing the border for the funeral of the wife of Cahir Healy, a former MP for Fermanagh and South Tyrone. O'Duffy was shortly afterwards released into the south. The incident generated a protest in Stormont by the nationalist parliamentarian T.J. Campbell.[85] Healy himself was interned by the British government during World War II under Regulation 18B. While interned, he met Oswald Mosley and the two became close friends. Healy has been credited with persuading Mosley to espouse a United Ireland as part of his post-war program which advocated for a federalized Europe.[86] From O'Duffy's perspective, his closest friends and associates were regularly being interned.

McGarry explained that O'Duffy was privately posing as "a Quisling in waiting, while being careful to deny the authorities a reason to intern him."[87] This was certainly G2's view. He put the German Legation in Dublin on notice that "he expected future German action in Ireland and that when it came he wanted to be part of it." But he was careful to explain that while his public statements may appear to praise neutrality, "he would work for an official policy similar to that of the Axis." Hempel wanted to utilize O'Duffy's military contacts but warned Berlin not to rely on him in a "careless manner," as he believed the General's ideas were vague.[88] During his political career he identified with Mussolini's fascist regime and advocated corporatism on the shallow understanding it was endorsed by the magisterium. Although German spies in Ireland, principally Hermann Görtz, maintained contact with O'Duffy throughout the Emergency, the strategy of the Abwehr was to harness the power of the IRA for sabotage activities. Without the advent of a full-scale German invasion, O'Duffy was not in a position to mount a challenge to de Valera's government with even a reasonable chance of success.

From the outbreak of the war until mid-1940, Ireland remained a target of strategic interest for Germany. The Abwehr cared little for the historical divisions which plagued Irish nationalism and hoped to meld all shades of radical nationalism together to unleash mayhem against the Allies. German intelligence expected Irish POWs from the British army who displayed nationalist or anti-British sympathies to work with the IRA, who in turn were expected to work alongside O'Duffy. Meanwhile, the Germans pressured the IRA's militarist leadership to reunite with Frank Ryan, who broke from the organization in acrimony to help found Republican Congress in 1934 and was transported from Burgos to Berlin in July 1940. The Germans harbored further hopes that a corrupt cadre of pro–Axis Irish army officers could be reached. As a former defense forces chief-of-staff, O'Duffy maintained contact with several senior officers with pro–Axis sympathies like Major-General Hugo MacNeill and his cousin Major Niall MacNeill, a self-professed Nazi.[89] The nature of this scheme was to produce contingency plans that in the event of an Allied invasion of Ireland, the Germans would support a coup d'état orchestrated by a faction of the Irish defense forces.

Many counterfactuals exist about the prospective shape of a collaborationist Irish government in the event of a German invasion or an overall Axis victory. In Berlin, Frank Ryan told Francis Stuart, an Irish nationalist from the literary world who lectured in Berlin, that "in the event of a German victory, he expected to receive a ministerial rank in the postwar Irish government."[90] The IRA hoped to form a revolutionary government in advance of a German invasion, even drawing up a list of Irish "Stalinists and Trotskyites ... to be dealt with on the eve of a German landing."[91] For what it was worth, both G2 and MI5 identified O'Duffy as the prime "potential Quisling." G2 believed his prospective dictatorship would be flanked by "outstanding men" like J.J. Walsh, a former Minister for Posts and Telegraphs and ardent protectionist who quit his role in 1927 over disagreements on trade liberalization[92]; and Ernest Blythe, who would "use" O'Duffy. G2 believed Blythe was "100% Nazi" and stood "head and shoulders above any other pro–German in Ireland" in 1941, although the credibility of the report is diminished by its erroneous description of Blythe as a "wealthy businessman."[93] Cecil Lavery, a former FG politician, was also identified as a potential Quisling. As such, O'Duffy faced several better placed rivals in the event of a puppet dictator being appointed.

◆ ◆ ◆

O'Duffy's flirtatious relationship with the IRA was slightly contradicted by his efforts to secure a state appointment from the Irish government during the Emergency. He called for a coalition government and even proposed in July 1940 that if Dr Hyde resigned the presidency due to ill-health, de Valera should assume the office, leaving W.T. Cosgrave to become Taoiseach in a coalition government.[94] As for himself, he privately asked de Valera for a state appointment. In a letter of 6 June 1940, de Valera curtly thanked O'Duffy "for your offer of services" and acknowledged his name would be placed "on our list" and "it will not be overlooked should the opportunity arise for making use of your service in any special capacity."[95] In August, O'Duffy requested that de Valera appoint him as Chief Local Security Officer, overseeing the 100,000 strong "semi-military body of civilians charged with the safety of their own district against possible invasion or attack."[96] However, de Valera declined the offer on the grounds that authority over the Local Security Force was to be exercised by the garda commissioner.[97] De Valera's reference to the functions of a post he coveted being transferred to the post he famously held likely rose O'Duffy's hackles.

In the winter of 1940–41, the prospect of a new appointment for the General beckoned. An Irish Red Cross Society was founded by statute in August 1939, with its first general meeting called shortly after the outbreak of World War II. The army's general staff were "a bit perturbed" by the lack of consistency in the Red Cross' relationship with the permanent defense forces and Local Defense Force (LDF) units. It was believed the Red Cross lacked a centralized leadership which could ensure its activities (chiefly medical services) were coordinated with those of the defense forces and that the two bodies complemented each other, rather than duplicating the same responsibilities. O'Duffy likely asked his friend, Hugo MacNeill, to lobby the government for the appointment. General staff suggested to the minister for defense, Oscar Traynor, that O'Duffy was a suitable candidate for such a task and advised Traynor to appoint him to the vacant post of director-general of the Red Cross Society. The general staff "was given to understand that the Government were favorably disposed towards the proposal." In Walsh's version of events, Major-General Hugo MacNeill asked him to take soundings from O'Duffy to ascertain if he would accept the position if an offer was made. Walsh reported that O'Duffy was initially doubtful but soon came around to the idea, authorizing Walsh to inform MacNeill that he was prepared to accept the position if an official offer were made. It is more likely that O'Duffy actively lobbied for the appointment. MacNeill asked Daniel McKenna, chief-of-staff of the Army, to inform Traynor that O'Duffy would accept the post.

Enthused by the prospect of once again serving in a position of national importance, O'Duffy undertook a comprehensive study of the whole position of the relationship between the Red Cross and the defense forces. He "started to work out an outline scheme of organization." Walsh saw "a new lease of life" appear in O'Duffy. But despite repeated enquiries, the army's general staff never elicited a government response other than that the matter was "under consideration." The appointment was never made. Walsh wrote that this rebuff "hurt the General very much." He continued, "there was apparently a place for everyone else in the Nation's critical hour, he was not wanted."[98] It was entirely reasonable for the government not to appoint the man whom military intelligence believed to be a "potential Quisling" in the event of a German invasion to either of the highly sensitive posts he sought. The Red Cross vacancy was eventually filled by Joe Sweeney, the former pro–Treaty general from Donegal.

In the event of an invasion, the Red Cross and the Local Security Force would each have been activated in earnest and their importance would have increased tenfold. The fact O'Duffy sought an appointment to head either is highly questionable, given his openness towards collaborationism. It is thus worthy of further reflection. General O'Duffy had little to lose in heeding de Valera's call for national unity during Ireland's Emergency, offsetting his reputation as a would-be puppet dictator. But he was likely aware that his requests to de Valera would be declined. If so, he could later exploit such rejections to present himself as one who was unfairly wronged by a deeply bitter de Valera, allowing him to recreate the sympathy he achieved in the aftermath of his dismissal as garda commissioner. However, the FF government also declined offers of wartime service from several former notables such as Ernie O'Malley, whose sympathies "seem to have leaned towards the German side."[99] If O'Duffy had received such an appointment his importance in Abwehr machinations would have increased dramatically. Walsh even urged his associates to join the Red Cross Society "with a view to gaining control" and ensuring "the

Germans got their share of moneys disbursed by the Society."[100] This may imply O'Duffy's sudden interest in the Red Cross was part of a wider nefarious scheme.

By November 1940, O'Duffy was advising German agents on the identity of would-be collaborators in the defense forces. At the same time as he lobbied the Irish government for a state appointment, he maintained active contact with the German spy, Hermann Görtz, who had parachuted into Ireland in May. The General explained to Görtz that he "could not do much … with the IRA."[101] It was a correct assessment on O'Duffy's part as the IRA's utility to German machinations dwindled following the death of Russell. The organization was riven with internal difficulties, a lack of direction, and faced an intense government crackdown. Hempel warned Berlin that the IRA was "riddled with spies and persons of venal or weak character."[102] In June 1941, acting IRA chief-of-staff Stephen Hayes was kidnapped by the northern faction which he regarded as being "in the grip of the Friends of Germany." Imprisoned on a remote farm in County Wicklow, Hayes was tortured and made to sign a preposterous confession that he was a FF spy.[103] Hempel reported that of 400 IRA prisoners interned in the Curragh camp, "a sharp division" had arisen between "one group sympathetic to National-Socialist Germany, the other anti–German and with a leaning towards Communism."[104] Frank Ryan died in June 1944 in Dresden, a guest of the German regime, from heart failure due to an inflammation of the lungs, caused by pleurisy.[105]

O'Duffy explained to Görtz in November 1940 that he understood "Germany had interest only in a really independent Ireland" and advised that this objective "could be reached only by means of a military dictatorship." He proposed to Görtz that "it was with the army that Germany should get in touch—this was realized by leading heads within the army."[106] Hempel reported that the "chief officers" of the defense forces "are in principle in favor of an incursion into Northern Ireland."[107] In a transmission to the Abwehr, Görtz argued it would be possible "through O'Duffy" to "organize circles among army officers, many of whom are sympathetic and not content with the situation in occupied Ireland (Northern Ireland)."[108]

A major diplomatic incident between Britain and Ireland nearly broke out over a faulty intelligence report which suggested the existence of a vast pro–German conspiracy involving O'Duffy and two FF ministers, James Ryan and Tom Derrig. British intelligence alleged that Görtz had been left at liberty deliberately; with James Ryan planning to use him as an intermediary to form a "secret military agreement" with Nazi Germany in the event of "the forcible seizure of ports and airfields by the British and American Governments." Although the British believed this plot was "the most extreme treachery," a similar operation was agreed between the British and Irish governments in the event of a German invasion (Plan W). This inaccurate report stemmed from Hayes' confession, which was reported to the Abwehr by the IRA and intercepted by British intelligence. It included the claim that James Ryan deliberately allowed the Coventry bombing to go awry, providing a pretext for the introduction of internment.[109] Immediately after narrowly escaping his ordeal, Hayes explained the entire affair to the Garda Síochána.

British intelligence characterized a meeting between Görtz, MacNeill, and O'Duffy as a "most sinister" event. O'Duffy was described as the "late head of the

Irish Brigade who fought for Franco in Spain and always regarded by us as one of the most likely Quislings in Eire."[110] Between December 1940 and December 1941, "a well-known Irish officer [Hugo MacNeill]" had "several conversations" with Henning Thomsen, a counselor in Germany's embassy. MacNeill "had been prepared to declare himself for a policy of military collaboration between Germany and Ireland." He mistakenly believed Operation Barbarossa, Hitler's invasion of the Soviet Union, would come to a swift conclusion and the Germans would shift their attention back to inflicting a defeat against Britain. O'Duffy was also acknowledged as someone "who cultivated regular contacts with the German Embassy at this time."[111]

When Görtz was finally arrested alongside the IRA's new chief-of-staff Pearse Kelly on 27 November 1941 after two years on the lam, the German spy blamed his capture on the "loose talk" of MacNeill and O'Duffy. British intelligence reported that MacNeill and O'Duffy were "firm friends" and that MacNeill was "an admirer of German methods and efficiency."[112] Séamus O'Donovan was interned shortly after Görtz. During the German agent's interrogation by G2, he was urged to identify his collaborators. His interrogator appeared particularly interested in pressing Görtz to single out O'Duffy, explaining: "We want to get at these arch-traitors." McGarry described Görtz's decision to refrain from implicating O'Duffy as "a lucky break" for the General, likely allowing him to avoid internment.[113] In Arbour Hill, Görtz concocted various unsuccessful schemes to break out. In an intercepted secret note, he advocated using General O'Duffy's driver, Robert Butler, "who is a corporal here." He continued, "It is for you to decide whether the General is trustworthy. You know how one can get in touch with the General. I have received a mysterious report here that the General may be willing to help me."[114] Nothing materialized from the supposed offer, leaving Görtz to give up his plans to escape. In 1947, he committed suicide rather than face deportation to Germany.

It has been claimed that one of O'Duffy's final interactions with the Germans was a proposal to organize a "green division," presumably the Irish answer to the Spanish Blue Division, which would "fight against Bolshevism" on the eastern front. Even for O'Duffy this was a most bizarre proposal. The origin of the request was in a March 1943 transmission sent from a cook named Mr. Eastwood aboard the Irish freighter, *Edenvale*, using Görtz's code. At the time Görtz was imprisoned and the transmission intimated it was sent by associates of General O'Duffy. The message requested that arrangements be made for a representative to travel to Germany on O'Duffy's behalf for the purposes of discussing the planned endeavor. Although a previous message from the same source had been received by the Abwehr in February, it was ignored. However, the Abwehr inexplicably believed the March communication to be authentic. In Berlin, Dr Veesenmayer deliberated how the Abwehr could harness the potential propaganda value of O'Duffy's proposed "green division" without arousing suspicions that the General was following orders from Germany and thus antagonizing the Irish government.[115] However, O'Duffy's purported anti-communist misadventure bears all the hallmarks of a hoax.

The communication originated from Joseph Gerard Andrews, an "enterprising and adventurous Irishman," who instructed Eastwood to send the telegram. British intelligence claimed Andrews' primary interest appeared to be in selling the Germans "information about the sweepstake organization." Görtz encountered Andrews in 1941 "when the house of another shady friend of his was used for a very short time to shelter [Anthony] Deery," a sympathetic ex-post office technician who operated Görtz's radio. Andrews successfully gained Görtz's full confidence, to the displeasure of the German agent's associates. Andrews, when not attempting to secure a commission for himself in the defense forces, was associated with a pro–Nazi groupuscule, the People's National Party. Before his imprisonment, Görtz told his associates that the only person in Ireland who knew his code was a woman. MI5 believed this to be Andrews' wife. Andrews was unemployed but living "a rather high life," and his motivation in sending the coded message to the Abwehr was simply "to obtain a sum of money from the Germans," according to British intelligence.[116] Although O'Duffy was prone to extravagant and unrealistic scheming, he did not propose to lead a division of Irish volunteers to fight alongside the Wehrmacht on the eastern front. McGarry referenced the putative incident, apparently believing it to be authentic, to illustrate O'Duffy's supposed lost grasp of reality.[117] However, O'Duffy showed considerable restraint and toed a careful line during the Emergency. This allowed him to avoid internment during the war years in contrast with many of his more careless colleagues.

As World War II progressed, Hempel repeatedly offered Berlin the mature advice to forego further espionage schemes which were largely futile and only served to antagonize the neutral Irish government. As Ireland's strategic importance receded, the German representative demanded that Germany prioritize the preservation of Irish neutrality. Hempel believed the discovery of Görtz had stiffened the government's attitude towards Germany. Aware that the Allies were exerting considerable pressure on Ireland to break off diplomatic relations with Germany, the German representative pleaded with Berlin to desist from counterproductive meddling in Irish affairs.[118] Ireland maintained an official policy of neutrality throughout World War II, while unofficially demonstrating a strong sympathy with the Allies through many of its actions as likelihood of an Allied victory increased.[119]

◆ ◆ ◆

In April 1942, O'Duffy confirmed that he was finally "finished with politics." Freed from the obligations of political leadership and even from the nagging thought of orchestrating a political return, O'Duffy was elected as president of the National Athletics and Cycling Association of Ireland.[120] Upon taking the chair, O'Duffy stated he had severed his former connection with NACA because "politics and sport do not mix." He now intended to "tackle the problems, financial and otherwise, which confronted them."[121]

During the intervening years between his first and second stint as president, Irish interest in athletics had waned. No Irish team participated at the 1936 Berlin Olympics due to continued controversy over NACA's refusal to compete internationally as a partitioned team. The organization's unflinching stance on this issue "restricted the growth of Irish athletics for a further 30 years." The issue prompted a split in Irish athletics in April 1937 which was formalized in 1938, resulting in the creation of a new body known initially as the Irish Amateur Athletic Union

(IAAU).[122] Although he outlined that he "would be prepared to concede much ... to have a team representing all Ireland at the next Olympic Games," O'Duffy remained steadfastly committed to an anti-partitionist policy: "the continuing of partition would never be accepted by the Irish people, and they could not submit to athletic dismemberment." O'Duffy told an audience in Dundalk, "it would take time to readjust national boundaries after the war ... and already many small nations which were represented at the last Olympic Games are absorbed by bigger nations."[123] His attitude to the IAAU was contemptuous. He would not negotiate but would seek to "break [the] rival Association."[124]

At its 1943 congress, NACA secretary Jim Conaghan reported that O'Duffy's "magnetic personality" was largely responsible for an apparent groundswell of renewed interest in Irish athletics. Despite his recurrent bouts of illness and travel restrictions due to the Emergency, O'Duffy traversed Ireland in typical form to drum up support for athletics. A personal appeal by the never-say-die General raised significant funds for NACA, which began to show signs of green shoots ahead. Its debt was cleared, and it even built a nest egg.[125] He soon launched a new crusade, this time against bicycle thieves in Dublin who were a "menace" to people's livelihoods. He set out to tackle the "black market" stolen bicycle trade.[126] The *Irish Independent* reported in late 1942 that O'Duffy's "return to the athletic sphere coincided with a welcome revival."[127]

A further stimulant in the revival of athletics was a campaign O'Duffy launched to build a national stadium in Dublin. The proposal generated significant attention and excitement. It was typical of O'Duffy's penchant for the grandiose. As president of NACA, he conferred with the Irish Tourist Board and assisted in the tentative selection of a potential site by Dublin Corporation and the government. "Dublin was the only capital city in the world without an athletic stadium. There was not even a cinder track, and their public baths were the most primitive in the world," the General announced. He argued that the construction of the stadium would bring employment and leave "a lasting memorial to the country's enterprise."[128] Aware of his declining health, O'Duffy maintained that even if he did not live to see it, Ireland "would one day have a fitting place, central and convenient, in which she could host the Tailteann Games or even an Olympic Games."[129] The Tailteann Games were an ancient Gaelic sporting tournament. J.J. Walsh spearheaded efforts to revive it in 1924. O'Duffy was involved in the project as garda commissioner.

General O'Duffy's health took a further downturn in 1943. In August, he was hospitalized in Cork in a private nursing home.[130] In January 1944, it was reported that a "seriously ill" O'Duffy had entered the Mater Nursing Home.[131] His illness was so severe that he missed the 1944 NACA congress. He even struggled in formulating a short message to delegates from his sickbed, an action which took "super-human will power."[132] He suffered from myocardial degeneration for the final five years of his life.[133] He was not a good patient and grew frequently restive due to enforced inactivity, but towards the end he became "resigned to the will of God that his illness was fatal and his end approaching."[134]

During the months of July, August and September in his final year of 1944, Eoin O'Duffy remained present in Irish national life through a series of talks he presented on the state broadcaster, Radio Éireann. One broadcast was sandwiched in the radio schedule between a recording of the soprano Violet Lynch and music played on the theater organ.[135] His themes were familiar, extolling the virtues of sportsmanship and physical fitness as the antidote to "juvenile delinquency" and national decay. "The athletic prowess of the Irish race has seldom been surpassed by any other nation," he told listeners in July. A considerable emphasis was placed on organizing Irish athletics along Christian lines.[136] Even in his final weeks and days, Liam Walsh recalled O'Duffy's mind was on sport and "he spoke frequently to me of NACA matters." Many of his closest friends came from the world of athletics, "loyal and true colleagues with whom he was proud to be associated."[137] It was a dramatic change from the cut-throat world of politics. O'Duffy's final crusade illustrated the core nature of his public image, as a stalwart promoter of physical health as a mirror to the health of the nation. In one of his final broadcasts, he stated: "If we had a properly organized athletic club in every parish we would have a brighter, healthier and better country."[138]

A flavor of the last days of General O'Duffy was recorded by Walsh, who lived at O'Duffy's home for a time following his release from internment. Other than gardening, General O'Duffy had no other hobbies. Greygates in Mount Merrion, one of Ireland's first suburbs, was built in the early 1930s by developer John Kenny. O'Duffy's home spoke to modernist tastes.[139] He lived frugally as a "typical bachelor," conducting his daily business in a "regular, methodical system." His lifestyle was "unostentatious," he generally ate "only three simple meals a day" and seldom ate after six o'clock. He kept a tight watch over his expenditure, having a lifelong abhorrence of debt. He was a compulsive saver, preferring to "skimp and scrape and deny himself of many things" to avoid drawing from his savings. Walsh denied that O'Duffy was an alcoholic: "As with smoking, he did not take intoxicating liquor until well advanced in years, and notwithstanding the base accusations of some erstwhile political friends he drank in moderation.... He never drank beer but seldom drank wines; he preferred Irish whiskey which, in his last years, he had made into punch."[140] G2 records of O'Duffy's lifestyle indicated he was still a heavy drinker and even kept records of his off-license tab.[141]

In many ways, the contradictions of Eoin O'Duffy were revealed by his habits. Although surrounded by books, he seldom read. Although a champion of the virtue of physical exercise and the crusading president of NACA, he never exercised. Although he basked in the limelight and relished social functions, he was deeply reserved and kept to himself. His days began by answering the morning mail, which often included referee requests for military service pensions from old comrades, recommendations for jobs, invitations, reports from organizations he was involved in, and so on. Afterwards he consulted the morning papers. Despite being out of politics he read newspapers religiously with a pencil to hand, marking off items of interest, cutting them out, and filing the clippings away for future reference. Radio announcements were also noted. He had "an excellent filing system" with one entire wall of his study occupied with a pigeon-holed, roll-shuttered mahogany press which contained thousands of his personal files related to his lengthy career.[142] During the Emergency, efforts to save paper led O'Duffy to hand over "a garage full of old papers and books" to a paper collection team.[143]

It was only after this morning ritual that he lit his first cigarette of the day. He was described as a "chain smoker" and a "heavy smoker" who smoked 70 to 80 cigarettes per day. Much of his day was spent answering correspondence, receiving visitors, and taking calls on the telephone which "never seemed to cease ringing." Despite having a litany of friends and contacts, those who knew him best felt General O'Duffy cut a rather "pathetic and lonely figure at the end" with "few intimates" and he "rarely received a relative into his household."[144] Towards the end of his life, O'Duffy mourned how "hundreds of thousands of the world's manhood have already lost their lives with the irreparable havoc of war," but expressed gladness that Ireland was "one of the few nations blessed with peace."[145] It was probably a genuine sentiment, although one influenced by a recognition that the Axis war effort was doomed following the successful Allied landings at Normandy in June.

As his illness worsened, General O'Duffy moved into the private Pembroke Nursing Home. Here he spent his final days as a bedridden patient. Described by Walsh as a "good practicing Catholic," O'Duffy prayed the Rosary every night "with unfailing regularity." When he became too frail to hold the beads, Walsh placed them in his hand, describing this as "almost the last service I did for him on this earth." With a nurse and Walsh at his bedside, even in his last moments of life the Rosary beads remained wrapped around his fingers.[146] At eight o'clock in the morning of 30 November 1944, at the age of 54, General Eoin O'Duffy died from heart failure.

# Epilogue

General O'Duffy was afforded a state funeral with full military honors befitting a prominent servant of the state.[1] A requiem Mass was celebrated in St Mary's Pro-Cathedral before the coffin was brought to Glasnevin cemetery by a gun carriage draped with the Irish tricolor flag. Mourners thronged the streets to pay their respects to the late General O'Duffy. Six colonels from the defense forces acted as pallbearers while the chief mourners were represented by his brother Patrick, several nephews, cousins, and other relatives. At the graveside the Last Post was sounded by the army buglers and three volleys were fired over the grave. Mourners included de Valera and several prominent government ministers, representatives from the German and Spanish legations, members of the Oireachtas, police, defense forces, GAA, and NACA.[2] He left behind his house, which was sold by public auction in February 1945,[3] and a sum of £9,377 (€361,450 in November 2022). His will stipulated a portion of his estate would be spent on Masses offered for deceased members of the Bandera and for the creation of an athletics cup to be known as the O'Duffy Perpetual Challenge Cup. The remainder was divided between legacies to personal friends but the bulk was inherited by his brothers and sister.[4]

Obituaries tended to respectfully recount General O'Duffy's career and list of achievements. However, the *Irish Times* demurred from the panegyrics and the consensus of not speaking ill of the dead by publishing a critical obituary of O'Duffy. His name was one which "had ceased to mean much to the Irish public … in recent years," according to the obituary. The writer recounted the late General's "quarrell[ing] with the other leaders" of FG and his leadership of the National Guard, "a sort of Fascist movement." But its most serious criticism was leveled at O'Duffy's "final adventure" in Spain which "cost him his reputation." The Bandera's "principal battle was with the Canary Island detachment on their own side" and they subsequently "fought among themselves" on their way back from Spain.[5] The obituary was contemporaneously criticized by the rival *Irish Independent* for having "traduced the dead man and his associates" who "gave expression to what was in the hearts of the masses of the Irish people and history will vindicate them."[6]

What, then, of a legacy? At an October 1949 meeting of Castleblayney Urban Council, local politicians clashed over a proposal to name a new row of terraced houses after the late O'Duffy as a "small tribute" to the Monaghan native. A proponent of the motion argued that, if O'Duffy were alive, "his sole aim would be to end Partition." But the FF chairman of the council, while paying respects to O'Duffy, stated he could not support the motion as O'Duffy voted for the 1921 Anglo-Irish Treaty. When the motion was carried by four votes to three, the dissenting chairman described O'Duffy as one who had "caused so much trouble" and believed he was morally culpable for Civil War executions. Efforts to rescind the motion failed.[7] O'Duffy Terrace near Ballybay remains one of the few things named after him. Other testaments to his legacy include a memorial trophy, the General O'Duffy Cup, a "magnificent trophy, one of the nicest in Irish athletics."[8] It was first established by NACA in 1944, in accordance with his will.[9] Gaelic football spectators in Clones still look on from the O'Duffy Stand, named in his honor. As Tim Pat Coogan noted, having one's name memorialized by the GAA in the naming of a cup, stand, or club is "often the most eloquent statement of the named person's contribution to the history of both sport and politics."[10]

A survey of his posthumous legacy indicates there is still some regard in County Monaghan for one of its favorite sons of the revolutionary period. The GAA in Monaghan erected a plaque to O'Duffy in 2009 in the Aughnamullen Sarsfields Community Center. Local GAA officials at the unveiling ceremony praised O'Duffy as "a courageous man," "a special man," "a great organizer" and "a man whose thoughts when committed to paper were inspiring even though outside of the GAA he had provoked different reactions."[11] The absence of controversy surrounding the plaque was notable. However, a decade later, the inclusion of O'Duffy on a mural at Coláiste Oiriall alongside other notable Monaghan natives generated a backlash. As opposition grew, a spokesperson for the school confirmed the representation of O'Duffy had been removed from the mural.[12] This likely reflected a global cultural shift towards actively opposing monuments which commemorate historical figures deemed problematic. The significance of "decommemoration" was examined by Guy Beiner, particularly efforts by Irish nationalists to replace monuments which represented the heroes associated with the Protestant Ascendancy in independent Ireland.[13] Indeed, O'Duffy's NCP passed a motion at its ard fheis which called for the removal of statues that commemorated British imperialism.

During his lifetime, O'Duffy offered the advice to guard one's reputation jealously. In this, he abjectly failed. It is hard to argue that Gore Vidal's quip that dying may sometimes be a good career move would not have been applicable in O'Duffy's case—if he died in the War of Independence period, he would be commemorated by all sides as a hero; if he died or retired in the middle of his term as garda commissioner, he would be regarded as a patriot and a state builder. In modern FG, his place within the party's pantheon of former leaders has naturally been swept under the carpet. Given his reputation as Ireland's foremost fascist leader, it is understandable that "the party of the progressive center" would be reluctant to adopt his legacy. A search of recent parliamentary debates demonstrates the charged term "Blueshirt" is still regularly hurled across the Dáil chamber to imply that FG has a flawed political pedigree. Marshaling Irish history in political debates is not a new phenomenon. Noël Browne recalled when he was first elected to the Dáil in the late 1940s that parliamentary debates often saw deputies use "trigger words" like "Ballyseedy," "Dick [Barrett] and Joe [McKelvey]," "The Treaty," and "a damn good bargain." Browne recalled the chamber was "filled with shouting, gesticulating, clamoring, suddenly angry men." He found such scenes to be farcical.[14] As such, the continued use of Blueshirt could be seen simply as a continuation of this "tradition."

Regarding O'Duffy's personal political legacy as distinct from that of the Blueshirts, there has been no mainstream interest in adopting him as an ideological forebearer. Only on the political fringes has there been some minor renewed support for O'Duffy. The National Party held a 2017 "historical presentation" at the grave of Michael Patrick Lynch, a figure once regarded as a Blueshirt martyr.[15] A separate far-right website sells a blue t-shirt of O'Duffy's face emblazoned with the text "Unrepentant Fascist Bastard."[16] Irish anti-fascists occasionally continue to utilize the negative memory of O'Duffy, such as a 2021 event hosted by the Connolly Youth Movement titled "Celebrating the Death of Eoin O'Duffy," which included a discussion "on racism and fascism in Ireland, whether from Fine Gael or the National Party."[17]

Divorcing O'Duffy the able IRA commander from O'Duffy the failed fascist leader is as difficult as splitting the atom. However, the Irish government's Decade of Centenaries program (2012–23) has drawn attention to the important role played by O'Duffy during the revolutionary period. Assisted by an advisory group chaired by Maurice Manning, the Decade of Centenaries emphasized regional and local aspects, which in Monaghan and Ulster generally foregrounded the agency of O'Duffy during the War of Independence and Truce period. In January 2022, on the centenary of the ratification of the Truce by Dáil Éireann, a television program aired by the state broadcaster, *Treaty Live*, presented "how modern TV might have reported the Dáil's vote on the Anglo-Irish Treaty on January 7, 1922."[18] In one scene after the seminal vote, O'Duffy and Brugha were jointly interviewed. Viewers noted that O'Duffy came across as calm, coherent, and respectable, whereas Brugha was portrayed as angry, emotional, and irrational. Some took to social media to complain about RTÉ's "softball" portrayal of O'Duffy. Comedian Paddy Cullivan tweeted, "here's lovely reasonable Eoin O'Duffy and frothing madman Cathal Brugha."[19] Whether the renewed emphasis on O'Duffy's revolutionary service will generate a more widespread reappraisal of his legacy is yet to be seen.

Traces of a latent respect for the former commissioner still exist within the Garda Síochána, particularly for his early years of service to the force. Journalist Sarah Carey wrote in 2022, that as "despicable as he was," the gardaí "can be grateful" for its "maverick commissioner."[20] But the General's involvement in the Spanish Civil War has been widely regarded as toxifying his posthumous reputation. Elsewhere, involvement in the Spanish Civil War on the pro–Franco side was not necessarily a graveyard for political careers. In Romania, the deaths of two prominent Iron Guard legionnaires in the service of Nationalist Spain helped to cement Corneliu Codreanu's party as "the pre-eminent right-wing movement in Romania."[21]

An aim of this study has been to contextualize O'Duffy's political career. O'Duffy was an early and thoroughgoing ally of Michael Collins, whose death in August 1922 profoundly impacted O'Duffy's status within the pro–Treaty hierarchy. The afterlife of Michael Collins is outside the scope of this study but suffice to say it has reached a popular apotheosis in recent decades, particularly aided by the release of Neil Jordan's 1996 eponymous film. For many, Collins represents the road not taken. Yet in one of the few primary sources which sheds light on Collins' political philosophy, a collected edition of his writings (*The Path to Freedom*), his fundamental belief system is largely unoriginal. It envisaged a free and Gaelic Ireland, laden with folkish sentimentality. Ironically, this is essentially the popular conception of Dev's Ireland. The amorphous nature of republican ideology during the revolutionary period has been well noted. During the early Free State period, former revolutionaries became ardent defenders of the conservative status quo, culturally, economically, and politically. For example, O'Duffy's neighbor and Monaghan IRA ally, Brian MacMahon, became secretary to the censorship board. One of the few documents he left behind was a "robust defense of the Censorship Board."[22] However, pro–Treaty lickspittles of the 1920s were suddenly alarmed by the advent of FF to power. This allowed a festering anti-democratic anxiety within pro–Treaty nationalism to assert itself.

In the 1930s, many leading political figures aligned with CnaG began to flirt with fascism. The party newspaper regularly published articles which expressed pro–Mussolini, pro-corporatist, and anti-democratic views. Pro-Treaty luminaries like Desmond FitzGerald, father of Taoiseach Garret FitzGerald, proudly wore the Blueshirt in parliament. Even W.T. Cosgrave, the grand old man of Free State nationalism, has been photographed extending the fascist salute of the Blueshirts. The repeated suggestion that FG constitutionalists like Cosgrave balked at the illegality of O'Duffy's plan in August 1934 to lead a new Plan of Campaign against the government over the land annuities issue contrasts with FG's endorsement of lawlessness when defying the bans placed on incarnations of the Blueshirts. Moreover, hysterical anti-communism was a centerpiece of pro–Treaty speechcraft, even among supposedly level-headed politicians like James Dillon. Intense support for Franco's forces was also ubiquitous across most of Irish society and reached a particularly shrill crescendo among FG politicians.

In FG, former members of the National Center Party were the most prominent and principled voices which admonished O'Duffy's fascist views. His views were otherwise tolerated or even shared by many in the former CnaG wing. Meehan and Collins acknowledged that O'Duffy "moved in the right circles" which enabled him to become a prominent pro–Treaty leader, but this was "before his descent into fascism" and that "as O'Duffy's extremism grew, it was those members … who were dedicated to democracy" who ousted him.[23] Narratives which continue to present O'Duffy as a totally unrepresentative and unparalleled figure in Irish nationalist history implicitly perpetuate congenial myths of the Irish state's formation and early years.

The term "scapegoat" has its origins in the Book of Leviticus, which described a ritual in which the Jewish chief priest would symbolically place the collective sins of the people upon a goat and cast the animal out into the wilderness. Although the term is loaded and its application to O'Duffy may imply equivocation, in its original sense it is perhaps an apt metaphor. O'Duffy is a lightning rod who continues to deflect attention away from the problematic views shared by various pro–Treaty leaders, many of whom have enjoyed posthumous acclaim. This book has tried to zoom out from the convenient narrative of O'Duffy's "exceptionalism," and instead has emphasized how he emerged from and existed within the political ecosystem of the pro–Treaty nationalist coalition.

# Postscript

A significant claim to emerge from recent scholarship and documentaries is that O'Duffy was a closeted homosexual. This book, as principally a political biography, has only discursively referenced O'Duffy's private life as a bachelor. The first widespread dissemination of the claim about his homosexuality was in the 1999 broadcast of the RTÉ documentary *Dear Boy*, which concentrated on the life of Micheál Mac Liammóir, with whom O'Duffy was said to have had a secret relationship. The claim originated with a theatrical clique that included Mac Liammóir and Hilton Edwards, the couple who founded the Gate Theatre in Dublin. The alleged relationship remained the stuff of rumor and innuendo for 70 years.[1] In McGarry's study of O'Duffy, he scrutinized the claim and concluded, on balance, that O'Duffy likely was indeed homosexual. The fact the rumor was created and remained secret for so long led McGarry to conclude it was likely genuine. But as relayed in Don Basilio's calumny aria in the *Barber of Seville*, a rumor can begin as a gentle zephyr before it explodes like a cannon. Mac Liammóir and Edwards would undoubtedly have understood the subtle art of creating a damaging rumor. Indeed, Mac Liammóir is perhaps the ultimate unreliable narrator. Even his identity as Irish was fabricated; despite his English birth and origins, Alfred Willmore constructed a faux-Gaelicized name and claimed he was born in Cork. Mac Liammóir's propensity to deceive does not necessarily invalidate the claim of a relationship with O'Duffy. The sources which corroborate the rumor tend to be second or third hand and originate with the Mac Liammóir clique.

McGarry further speculated that "the fact [O'Duffy's] concerns centered on the threat to the virility, manliness, and morality of young men raises questions about his own sexuality" and drew parallels with Robert Baden-Powell, the founder of the Scout Movement, and J. Edgar Hoover, director of the FBI; the sexuality of both men has frequently been commented upon.[2] Historian Aidan Beatty responded that "no proper attempt" was made by McGarry to explain O'Duffy's anxieties around male virility and its connection to national virility, "other than to engage in ultimately unsatisfying (perhaps even pointless) speculations on O'Duffy's possible homosexuality."[3]

O'Duffy's sexual orientation was discussed in Mary Kenny's *The Way We Were* (2022). A reason for the absence of the Irish hierarchy at O'Duffy's funeral, she posited, "could have been that the bishops had heard on the grapevine that Eoin O'Duffy may have been homosexual."[4] It is a highly speculative theory. The hierarchy were also conspicuously absent from the funeral of Patrick Belton, who died two months after O'Duffy.[5] Moreover, the simplistic image of O'Duffy as a cloying appeaser of the Irish hierarchy should be challenged. As Stradling noted, the Catholic Church in Ireland failed "to offer any recognition of the effort made by its crusaders" in Spain, "they washed their hands of the whole affair; no blood was upon their conscience."[6] In addition, Hempel reported during the Emergency that the "sympathies of the higher clergy are for the most part strongly against us."[7] If the Irish hierarchy were as informed about the latest gossip as Kenny suggests, there is little reason to think they were not aware of and disapproved of O'Duffy's pro-Axis views. Despite the lack of corroborating contemporaneous evidence from either friend or foe, a modern consensus is emerging that O'Duffy was indeed a repressed homosexual.

Aside from oral testimony, there is a dearth of evidence about O'Duffy's private life. Although he participated in many weddings as best man, he remained a lifelong bachelor. He displayed some tact about the need for discretion in romantic relationships. He was one of the few people aware of Kevin O'Higgins' affair with Hazel Lavery. Following O'Higgins' assassination in 1927, Lavery wrote a series of letters to the garda commissioner asking him to lay "even a tiny blossom" of white heather beside O'Higgins' body. She appreciated his "help and swift understanding" that "seemed to melt the ice around my heart."[8] Historical speculation about the sexual orientations of Irish nationalist figures is not a new phenomenon. The "Black Diaries," purportedly written by Roger Casement, contained accounts of liaisons with young men (and, indeed, teenage boys) and were used to smear his reputation during his trial in 1916. O'Duffy was aware of the allegations and claimed to have been present at an incident when the original copies were supposedly burned by Lord Birkenhead in the presence of Griffith and Collins in the aftermath of the signing of the Treaty.[9]

In public, O'Duffy rarely spoke about his private life. An exception was in June 1934 when he told an audience of Blue Blouses in County Cork: "Although I am a bachelor, I am not a confirmed bachelor, and I am going to a dance in Youghal to-night."[10] Another remark from O'Duffy was that he "made two great mistakes" in his life: "I did not marry, and I entered politics."[11] Obviously such expressions do not tell us much about O'Duffy's innermost private attitudes, but they are notable nonetheless. In a handwritten note appendaged to a chapter in his unpublished biography of O'Duffy, Liam Walsh wrote:

> There is hardly no aspect of O'Duffy's life or personal character with which gossip was busier than that of his relations with the opposite sex; in fact even an ex minister of state on more than one occasion associated his name with a prominent lady in the Senate. He was no woman-hater, but he allowed no outside influence to interfere with the fulfillment of his work, and marriage to him would be a perpetual preoccupation.[12]

The question arises of the identity of the female senator whom the unnamed former minister alleged was "associated" personally with O'Duffy. From the limited number of unmarried female senators during this period, it is possible to speculate that the reference was most likely to Kathleen Browne (1876–1943). The daughter of a notable Wexford Parnellite, she became a supporter of the Gaelic revival and Irish republicanism. First elected to the Senate for CnaG in 1929, Browne later became a "very active" member of the Blueshirts. She attended the ACA's inaugural dance in the Metropole Ballroom in Dublin on 16 December 1932.[13] She regularly wore the provocative blue-blouse uniform inside the Senate chamber. She defended O'Duffy's character when it was alleged by an FF parliamentarian that O'Duffy organized the Blueshirts along military lines and styled himself "commander-in-chief." Except for Ernest Blythe, she told the Senate she was "the only Senator who took an active part in the organization of the Blue Shirts."[14]

Mary McAuliffe stated that Browne's views on O'Duffy are "unknown." Browne's nephew recalled that she and her sister Maisie defended O'Duffy's involvement in the Spanish Civil War during arguments with their pro-Republican brother James Browne, "the whole thing would break up in disorder and they'd be shouting at each other."[15] In an article on Kathleen Browne, Bernard Browne noted that "O'Duffy had served time as an apprentice engineer in Wexford [in 1913] before returning to Monaghan," implying they may have had some contact.[16] O'Duffy and Browne moved in the same circles; both being heavily involved in the Gaelic League (she served as secretary of the Wexford Gaelic League). At the time, she was 37 and he was 23. It must be stressed that no surviving evidence exists which links O'Duffy to Browne on a personal level. This angle has been explored to scrutinize Walsh's cryptic and vague reference, not to suggest the definite existence of a relationship.

Overall, details about O'Duffy's private life remain elusive. Bachelorhood was not then and is not now an uncommon fate for rural Irishmen. Indeed, several of O'Duffy's siblings never married. The excessive workload he undertook with gusto in his thirties likely took its toll on his private life and offers some explanation for his bachelorhood.

# Acknowledgments

My first thanks are owed to the staff of McFarland & Co. for their work in publishing this book.

I am grateful to the support of the Irish Research Council in funding my PhD at Trinity College Dublin. I am additionally thankful to the Universities Ireland for awarding me the History Bursary (2021) which enabled me to conduct MA research which has influenced the production of this book.

I am also grateful to the staff of several institutions including the National Library of Ireland; the National Archives of Ireland; the Monaghan County Museum; the University College Dublin Archives; the Irish Military Archives; the UK National Archives; the Public Records Office of Northern Ireland; the Cork City and County Archives, and the Cardinal Tomás Ó Fiaich Library and Archive.

Further thanks are owed to my family and friends for their support and encouragement.

# Chapter Notes

## *Chapter 1*

1. Although O'Duffy often recorded his birth date as 30 October 1892, his birth and death returns demonstrate he was born on 28 January 1890. It is unclear why. Notably, Seán MacDiarmada similarly gave his age in the 1911 census as "XXVI" (26), though he was 28.

2. An Charraigeach Dhubh, *logainm.ie*, (https://www.logainm.ie/en/39861), (28 Jul. 2022).

3. 1911 Census Returns data, Cargaghdoo, County Monaghan, National Archives of Ireland (NAI).

4. Eoin O'Duffy, "Reminiscences, Chapter 1: Early Years" [hereafter, *Reminiscences*], Eoin O'Duffy Papers (EODP), National Library of Ireland (NLI), MS 48,300/2/1, p. 3.

5. Anne O'Dowd, *Meitheal: A Study of Co-operative Labour in Rural Ireland* (Naas, 1981), pp. 15–25.

6. Edward MacLysaght, *Irish Families: Their Names, Arms and Origins* (Dublin, 1973), pp. 130–1.

7. Desmond Greaves' journal, Vol. 12, 15 Sep. 1956, (DesmondGreavesArchive.com), (accessed 16 Jan. 2023).

8. *Reminiscences* 3 (Surveyorship), EODP/NLI/MS 48,300/2/3, pp. 9–10.

9. Terence Dooley, *Monaghan: The Irish Revolution, 1912–23* (Dublin, 2017), p. 61.

10. *Reminiscences* 1, p. 13.

11. 1911 Census Return of Owen Duffy, Cargaghdoo, Monaghan, NAI.

12. *Reminiscences* 1, p. 4.

13. Dooley, *Monaghan*, pp. 1–3.

14. *United Ireland*, 7 Jul. 1934.

15. *Reminiscences* 6 (The Language Movement), EODP/NLI/MS 48,300/2/6, p. 6.

16. Hugh MacMahon, *A Fist to the Black-Blooded: The MacMahons of Coas* (Dublin, 2015), p. 7.

17. *Reminiscences* 1, pp. 1–7.

18. Liam D. Walsh, *General O'Duffy: His Life and Battles* [hereafter, Walsh biography], EODP/NLI/MS 48,302, p. 231.

19. In contrast with the census return for 1901, by 1911 Owen Duffy professed to be able to read and write. See Census Returns of Owen Duffy, Cargaghdoo, County Monaghan, 1901 and 1911.

20. *Reminiscences* 1, pp. 7–10.

21. "Saint Peter's Church, Laragh, County Monaghan," Sep. 2017, *National Inventory of Architectural Heritage*, (https://www.buildingsofireland.ie/building-of-the-month/saint-peters-church-laragh-county-monaghan/), (accessed 30 Jul. 2022).

22. Walsh biography, p. 3.

23. *Reminiscences* 1, pp. 10–12.

24. *Reminiscences* 2 (Choosing a Career), EODP/NLI/MS 48/300/2/2/, pp. 1–4.

25. *Ibid.*, p. 6–7.

26. *Dundalk Democrat*, 31 Dec. 1904.

27. O'Duffy to Monaghan County Council, 22 Jun. 1912, Rushe papers, Public Records Office of Northern Ireland (PRONI), MIC/426/1.

28. J.E. Devlin to O'Duffy, 15 Apr. 1912, PRONI/MIC/426/1.

29. Reference from Hannigan, 22 Jun. 1912, PRONI/MIC/426/1.

30. Reference from Bp. McKenna, 23 Jun. 1912, PRONI/MIC/426/1.

31. "O'Duffy, Eoin," *Dictionary of Irish Architects 1720–1940*, (https://www.dia.ie/architects/view/7359/O%27DUFFY-EOIN), (accessed 30 Jul. 2022).

32. O'Duffy to Monaghan County Council, n.d., PRONI/MIC/426/1.

33. Dooley, *Monaghan*, p. 62.

34. *Reminiscences* 3, p. 7.

35. *Northern Standard*, 16 Feb. 1934.

36. Tim Pat Coogan, *The GAA and the War of Independence* (London, 2018), p. 40.

37. *Reminiscences* 4 (GAA), EODP/NLI/MS 48,300/2/4, p. 3.

38. *Reminiscences* 5, (GAA cont.), EODP/NLI/MS 48/300/2/5, p. 7.

39. Séamus McCluskey, *The Monaghan Gael: Eighty Years a Growing, 1887 to 1967* (Emyvale, 1967), p. 9.

40. *Ibid.*, pp. 2–6.

41. Dónal McAnallen, "The Radicalisation of the Gaelic Athletic Association in Ulster, 1912–1923: The Role of Owen O'Duffy," *The International Journal of the History of Sport*, 2014, 31 (7), pp. 705–6.

42. *Anglo-Celt*, 20 Feb. 1915.

43. Richard McElligott, "'An Abundance of

First Class Recruits,' The GAA and the Irish Volunteers 1913–15," *TheIrishStory.com*, (https://www.theirishstory.com/2014/05/23/an-abundance-of-first-class-recruits-the-gaa-and-the-irish-volunteers-1913-15/), (accessed 16 Jan. 2023).

44. George Dangerfield, *The Strange Death of Liberal England* (London, 2012), pp. 83–106.

45. *Anglo-Celt*, 30 May 1996.

46. Séamus McCluskey, *The GAA in Co. Monaghan ... a history* (Monaghan, 1984), pp. 41–3.

47. McAnallen, "Radicalisation of the GAA," p. 708.

48. McCluskey, *GAA in Monaghan*, p. 37.

49. Dorothy Macardle, *The Irish Republic* (Dublin, 1951), p. 180.

50. P.S. O'Hegarty, *The Victory of Sinn Féin: How it won it, and how it used it* (Dublin, 1924), pp. 8–9.

51. O'Duffy to the INAAVD, 22 Jun. 1916, Irish National Aid and Volunteer Dependants' Fund papers, NLI, MS 24,321/2/27.

52. McAnallen, "Radicalisation of the GAA," p. 705.

53. Eoin O'Duffy, "Days That Are Gone," in Seán O'Ceallaigh (ed.), *Gaelic Athletic Memories* (Limerick, 1945), p. 161.

54. Dooley, *Monaghan*, p. 63.

55. Walsh biography, p. 21.

56. McAnallen, "Radicalisation of the GAA in Ulster," pp. 711–2.

## *Chapter 2*

1. *Anglo-Celt*, 20 Oct. 1917.

2. Maryann Valiulis, *Portrait of a Revolutionary: General Richard Mulcahy and the Founding of the Irish Free State* (Dublin, 1992), pp. 14–5.

3. Michael Hopkinson, *The Irish War of Independence* (Montreal, 2002), pp. 15–6.

4. O'Duffy, "Days That Are Gone," p. 177.

5. Richard Mulcahy, "Conscription and the General Headquarters Staff," *Capuchin Annual*, 35 (1968), pp. 385–7.

6. Valiulis, *Mulcahy*, p. 25.

7. O'Hegarty, *Victory*, p. 10.

8. Michael Laffan, *The Resurrection of Ireland: The Sinn Féin Party 1916–1923* (Cambridge, 2004), p. 214.

9. *Irish Times*, 2 Jun. 2018.

10. Eoin O'Duffy, "Account of the History and Policies of Sinn Féin," Mar. 1938, EODP/NLI/MS 48,283/1/2, pp. 2–3.

11. *Anglo-Celt*, 1 Sep. 1917.

12. *Reminiscences* 3, p. 7.

13. Francis Tummon Witness Statement (WS) 820, Irish Military Archives (IMA), Bureau of Military History (BMH), p. 8.

14. *Anglo-Celt*, 8 Dec. 1917.

15. Alice McSloy interview, 21 Jul. 1967, Cardinal Tomás Ó Fiaich Library and Archive (CÓFLA) Fr Louis O'Kane collection (LOK), IV/A/16.

16. Coogan, *GAA and the War of Independence*, pp. 125–7.

17. Tummon WS/820, p. 19.

18. *Anglo-Celt*, 25 Jan. 1919.

19. Jail Diary of Eoin O'Duffy (hereafter, Jail Diary), NLI/EODP/MS 48,280/1.

20. Fearghal McGarry, *Eoin O'Duffy: A Self-Made Hero* (Oxford, 2005), p. 36.

21. *Meath Chronicle*, 21 Sep. 1918.

22. Jail Diary (My thanks to Siobhán Traynor for her translation).

23. *The Anglo-Celt*, 28 Sep. 1918.

24. McGarry, *O'Duffy*, p. 26.

25. *Reminiscences* 5, p. 1.

26. Jail Diary.

27. Proinnsias Ó Dubhthaigh WS/654/IMA/BMH, pp. 14–5.

28. *Reminiscences* 3, pp. 7–8.

29. John Shields WS/928/IMA/BMH, p. 4.

30. Patrick Caldwell WS/638/IMA/BMH, p. 19.

31. Ó Dubhthaigh WS/654, pp. 14–5.

32. Brian MacMahon transcript (1986), 6P1, Monaghan County Museum (MCM).

33. *The Police Gazette* (Hue-and-Cry), 5 Nov. 1920.

34. Walsh biography, p. 236.

35. *Ibid.*, p. 241.

36. *Ibid.*, p. 227.

37. *Fermanagh Herald*, 29 Mar. 1919.

38. Dave Hannigan, *De Valera in America: The Rebel President's 1919 Campaign* (Dublin, 2008), p. 32.

39. Francis M. Carroll, *Money for Ireland: Finance, Diplomacy, Politics, and the First Dáil Éireann Loans, 1919–1936* (Westport, 2002), p. 25.

40. Dooley, *Monaghan*, p. 74.

41. Walsh biography, p. 227.

42. Philip Marron WS/657/IMA/BMH, pp. 1–2.

43. James McKenna WS/1028/IMA/BMH, pp. 1–3.

44. *Ulster Herald*, 21 February 1920.

45. Thomas Donnelly WS/519/IMA/BMH, pp. 4–5.

46. *Irish Independent*, 16 Feb. 1920.

47. 2nd Monaghan Brigade report, IMA, Military Service Pensions Collection (MSPC), A/55; *Anglo-Celt*, 28 Feb. 1920.

48. Dooley, *Monaghan*, p. 82.

49. Hopkinson, *War of Independence*, p. 147.

50. *Irish Times*, 15 Oct. 2019.

51. *Irish Press*, 10 Mar. 1934.

52. *Anglo-Celt*, 24 Apr. 1920.

53. McCluskey, *GAA in Monaghan*, p. 38.

54. 2nd Monaghan Brigade report, IMA/MSPC/A/55.

55. Michael Welch, "Political Imprisonment and the Sanctity of Death: Performing Heritage in 'Troubled' Ireland," *International Journal of Heritage Studies*, 22 Apr. 2016, p. 23.

56. Paul Mulcahy WS/1434/IMA/BMH, p. 6.

57. *The Liberator* (Tralee), 29 Apr. 1920.

58. *Anglo-Celt*, 8 May 1920.

59. McGarry, *O'Duffy*, p. 49.

60. P.V. Hoey WS/530/IMA/BMH, pp. 5–6.

61. Alan Parkinson, *Belfast's Unholy War* (Dublin, 2004), p. 33.

62. O'Duffy to Fr O'Daly, 18 Sep. 1920, EODP/NLI//MS 51,270/1/2.
63. *Anglo-Celt*, 22 May 1920.
64. *Reminiscences* 3, p. 9.
65. *Dundalk Democrat*, 12 Mar. 1921.
66. *Ibid.*
67. McKenna, WS/1028, p. 4.
68. MacMahon, *A Fist to the Black-Blooded*, p. 74.
69. Hoey WS/530, p. 9.
70. Patrick V. Hoey, "Farney in the Fight for Freedom," Ernie O'Malley Papers, NLI, MS 10,973/14, p. 10.
71. John McAnerney WS/528/IMA/BMH, p. 2.
72. *Belfast Newsletter*, 16 Jul. 1920.
73. Hoey, "Farney," pp. 8–10.
74. Tummon WS/820, pp. 19–20.
75. *Ibid.*, p. 20.
76. "What is poitín and how was it made?," (https://anpoitin.weebly.com/what-is-poitiacuten.html), (accessed 15 Aug. 2022).
77. Hoey WS/530, p. 5.
78. Laffan, *Resurrection of Ireland*, p. 257.
79. Joost Augusteijn, *Patrick Pearse: The Making of a Revolutionary* (London, 2010), p. 76.
80. Peter Hart, *The IRA at War, 1916–1923* (Oxford, 2003), p. 246.
81. John McGahey WS/740/IMA/BMH, p. 13.
82. Dooley, *Monaghan*, pp. 88–9.
83. McKenna WS/1028, p. 7.
84. *Enniscorthy Guardian*, 2 Jul. 1921.
85. *Belfast Telegraph*, 29 Jun. 1925.
86. Frank Aiken to Mary MacSwiney, 28 Apr. 1924, EODP/NLI/MS 48,283/6/2.
87. *Irish Times*, 22 Aug. 1921.
88. Dooley, *Monaghan*, p. 91.
89. McGarry, *O'Duffy*, p. 66.
90. *Dundalk Democrat*, 23 Apr. 1921.
91. John McGonnell WS/574/IMA/BMH, p. 6.
92. McKenna WS/1028, p. 7.
93. MacMahon, *A Fist to the Black-Blooded*, p. 119.
94. Marron WS/657, p. 5.
95. McGahey WS/740, p. 5.
96. Tim Wilson, "The Strange Death of Loyalist Monaghan, 1912–1921" in (ed. Senia Pašeta), *Uncertain Futures: Essays about the Irish Past for Roy Foster* (Oxford, 2016), p. 141.
97. 2nd Monaghan Brigade report, IMA/MSPC/A/55.
98. Pat McDonnell, Philip Marron papers, MCM, p. 4.
99. Dooley, *Monaghan*, pp. 84–5.
100. Richard Bennett, *The Black and Tans* (Staplehurst, 2001), p. 82.
101. David Leeson, "Death in the Afternoon: The Croke Park Massacre, 21 November 1920," *Canadian Journal of History*, 38 (1), pp. 43–68.
102. Quoted in Séamus O'Ceallaigh (ed.), *The Gael in Action*, 1943, Cotter GAA Collection, Cork City and County Archives, PR23/17.
103. Ronan Fanning, *Fatal Path: British Government and Irish Revolution 1910–1922* (London, 2013), pp. 240–1.
104. O'Duffy to Monaghan Battalion O/Cs, December 1920, Marron Papers, MCM, p. 5.
105. John T. Connolly WS/598/IMA/BMH, pp. 3–4.
106. Wilson, "Strange Death," p. 183.
107. McGonnell WS/574/IMA/BMH, p. 7.
108. McKenna WS/1028, p. 10.
109. Connolly WS/598, p. 4.
110. Coogan, *GAA and the War of Independence*, p. 174.
111. Art O'Brien to Michael Collins, 12 Dec. 1920, Éamon de Valera papers, University College Dublin Archives (UCDA), P150/1900.
112. Nevil Macready, *Annals of an Active Life Vol. II* (London, 1924), p. 542.
113. Florence O'Donoghue, *No Other Law: The Story of Liam Lynch and the Irish Republican Army* (Dublin, 1954), p. 154.
114. Enda Staunton, *The Nationalists of Northern Ireland* (Dublin, 2001), pp. 49–50.
115. Robert Lynch, *The Northern IRA and the Early Years of Partition 1920–1922* (Newbridge, 2006), p. 48.
116. O'Duffy to GHQ, 28 Apr. 1921, Richard Mulcahy Papers, UCDA, P7/A/18, 104–7.
117. 2nd Monaghan Brigade report, IMA/MSPC/A/55.
118. Seán Corr WS/458/IMA/BMH, p. 11.
119. William J. Kelly WS/893/IMA/BMH, p. 6.
120. McGarry, *O'Duffy*, p. 75.
121. Corr WS/458, p. 12.
122. Patrick Maguire WS/693/IMA/BMH, pp. 6–7.
123. Kelly WS/893, p. 20.
124. Maguire WS/693, pp. 7–9.
125. Lynch, *Northern IRA*, p. 54.
126. O'Duffy file, The UK National Archives (TNA), War Office (WO), 35/206.

## Chapter 3

1. *Anglo-Celt*, 21 May 1921.
2. Corr WS/458, p. 12.
3. Ernest Blythe WS/939/IMA/BMH, p. 95.
4. *Dundalk Democrat*, 14 May 1921.
5. Michael Foy, *The Ancient Order of Hibernians: an Irish political-religious pressure group 1884–1975* (Belfast, 1976), Master's thesis, pp. 152–3.
6. Walsh biography, p. 45.
7. Máire Comerford interview, quoted in Uinseann MacEoin, *Survivors* (Dublin, 1980), p. 45.
8. Michael Hopkinson, *Green Against Green: A History of the Irish Civil War* (New York, 1988), p. 17.
9. MacEoin, *Survivors*, p. 505.
10. John M. Regan, *The Irish Counter-Revolution 1921–1936: Treatyite Politics and Settlement in Independent Ireland* (Dublin, 2001), p. 9.
11. Ernie O'Malley, *On Another Man's Wound* (London, 1961), p. 104.
12. Oscar Traynor interview, Ernie O'Malley notebook interviews (OMN), UCDA, P17b/98.
13. William Sheehan, *Fighting for Dublin, The*

*British battle for Dublin 1919–1921* (Cork, 2007), pp. 125–30.

14. Frank Henderson WS/821/IMA/BMH, p. 115.
15. Joseph Murray WS/412/IMA/BMH, p. 22.
16. *Freeman's Journal*, 30 Jun. 1921.
17. Charles Townshend, *The Republic: The Fight for Irish Independence* (London, 2013), pp. 307–9.
18. Laffan, *Resurrection of Ireland*, p. 236.
19. *Derry Journal*, 13 Jul. 1921.
20. Ernie O'Malley, *The Singing Flame* (Dublin, 1978), p. 15.
21. Tomás Ó Maoileóin interview, quoted in MacEoin, *Survivors*, pp. 97–8.
22. John O'Beirne-Ranelagh, "The IRB from the treaty to 1924," *Irish Historical Studies*, 20 (77), 1976, p. 28.
23. Regan, *Counter-Revolution*, p. 8.
24. Thomas Jones, *Whitehall Diaries III* (London, 1971), (ed. Keith Middlemas), p. 180.
25. Kieran Glennon, "Facts and Fallacies of the Belfast Pogrom," *History Ireland*, 28 (5), (Sep./Oct. 2020), pp. 28–31.
26. Roger McCorley interview, OMN/UCDA/P17b/98.
27. Paul Bew, *Ideology and the Irish Question Ulster Unionism and Irish Nationalism 1912–1916* (Oxford, 1994), p. 60.
28. Matthew Lewis, *Frank Aiken's War: The Irish Revolution 1916–23* (Dublin, 2014), p. 106.
29. Dan Breen, *My Fight for Irish Freedom* (Dublin, 1981), p. 166.
30. David McGuinness WS/417/IMA/BMH, p. 19.
31. *Fermanagh Herald*, 10 Sep. 1921.
32. Lewis, *Aiken's War*, p. 104.
33. RIC County Inspectors' Report (Armagh), Jul. 1921, PRONI/CO/904/116.
34. *Fermanagh Herald*, 10 Sep. 1921.
35. Glennon, "Facts and Fallacies," p. 31.
36. Walsh biography, p. 61.
37. *Fermanagh Herald*, 10 Sep. 1921.
38. *Ibid.*
39. Macready, *Annals*, p. 598.
40. Walsh biography, p. 55.
41. *Fermanagh Herald*, 10 Sep. 1921.
42. Walsh biography, p. 46.
43. Frank Pakenham, *Peace by Ordeal* (Edinburgh, 1935), p. 85.
44. *Irish Times*, 4 Dec. 2021.
45. Pakenham, *Peace by Ordeal*, pp. 93–4.
46. *Ibid.*, p. 130.
47. Biographical entry for O'Duffy, EODP/NLI/MS 48,320/7.
48. Walsh biography, p. 67.
49. Townshend, *Republic*, p. 316.
50. Robert Briscoe, *For the Life of Me* (London, 1958), p. 117.
51. David McCullagh, *De Valera, Volume I: Rise 1882–1932* (Dublin, 2017), p. 218.
52. Dáil Éireann debate, 22 Aug. 1921, Vol. S (4).
53. *Irish News*, 4 Sep. 1921.
54. T. Ryle Dwyer, *Collins and the Treaty* (Cork, 2007), p. 55.
55. *Belfast Newsletter*, 29 Sep. 1921.
56. Walsh biography, p. 46.
57. Dáil Éireann debate, 4 Jan. 1922, Vol. T (11).
58. Seán Ó Murthuile memoir, Mulcahy Papers, UCDA, P7a/209, p. 151.
59. Biographical entry, EODP.
60. Lewis, *Aiken's War*, p. 108.
61. Hopkinson, *Green Against Green*, p. 17.
62. Dwyer, *Collins and the Treaty*, p. 70.
63. Mulcahy letter to the editor (*Irish Times*), 14 Oct. 1962, Mulcahy Papers, UCDA, P7/D/1.
64. O'Malley, *Singing Flame*, p. 23.
65. Cathal Brugha to Charlie Daly, 17 Nov. 1921, quoted in (eds. Síobhra Aiken, Fearghal Mac Bhloscaidh, Liam Ó Duibhir, Diarmuid Ó Tuama), *The Men Will Talk to Me: Ernie O'Malley's Interviews with the Northern Divisions* (Newbridge, 2018) p. 55.
66. O'Duffy to Brugha, 24 Nov. 1921, EODP/NLI/MS 48,281/2/1.
67. Dwyer, *Collins and the Treaty*, p. 182.
68. Differences between Brugha and Stack and other members of the Volunteer Executive and Cabinet, Mulcahy Papers, UCDA/P7/D/96.
69. O'Duffy to all Divisional Commandants, 30 Nov. 1921, quoted in *The Men Will Talk to Me*, pp. 55–6.
70. Regan, *Counter-Revolution*, p. 9.
71. McCullagh, *De Valera*, p. 229.
72. Michael Collins, *The Path to Freedom* (Dublin, 1922), p. 35.
73. Regan, *Counter-Revolution*, pp. 5–6.
74. Notes on the British Memo, 27 Oct. 1921, NAI/DE 2/304/1.
75. *Fenian*, 17 Oct. 1922.
76. Walsh biography, p. 190.
77. Collins, *The Path to Freedom*, pp. 65–6.
78. Dáil Éireann debate, 19 Dec. 1921, Vol. T (6).
79. Lewis, *Aiken's War*, p. 113.

## *Chapter 4*

1. Jim Ryan interview, OMN/UCDA/P17b/103.
2. Undated memoir, Frank Aiken Papers, UCDA/P104/1308.
3. F.S.L. Lyons, *Ireland since the Famine* (London, 1971), p. 438.
4. McCullagh, *De Valera*, pp. 246–8.
5. Briscoe, *For the Life of Me*, p. 129.
6. Lewis, *Aiken's War*, p. 115.
7. Briscoe, *For the Life of Me*, pp. 133–4.
8. Kenneth Griffith & Timothy O'Grady, *Curious Journey: An Oral History of Ireland's Unfinished Revolution* (London, 1982), pp. 264–5.
9. O'Malley, *Singing Flame*, p. 85.
10. Seán MacBride, *That Day's Struggle: A Memoir 1904–1951* (Dublin, 2005), p. 59.
11. Mel Farrell, "'Stepping Stones to Freedom': Pro-Treaty Rhetoric and Strategy During the Dáil Treaty Debates," in (eds. Liam Weeks & Mícheál Ó Fathartaigh), *The Treaty: Debating and Establishing the Irish State* (Newbridge, 2018) p. 35.
12. Walsh biography, p. 71A.
13. Dáil Éireann debate, 17 Dec. 1921, Vol. T (5).
14. Walsh biography, p. 67.

15. Dáil Éireann debate, 17 Dec. 1921, Vol. T (5).
16. *Irish Independent*, 10 Jun. 1935.
17. Mary MacSwiney to Aiken, 22 Apr. 1924, EODP/NLI/MS 48,283/6/1.
18. Dáil Éireann debate, 17 Dec. 1921, Vol. T (5).
19. Macardle, *Republic*, p. 624.
20. Patrick Murray, *Oracles of God: The Roman Catholic Church and Irish Politics, 1922–37* (Dublin, 2000), p. 37.
21. O'Duffy, "Account of the History and Policies of Sinn Féin," p. 11.
22. *Irish Times*, 24 Dec. 2021.
23. *Irish Examiner*, 31 Dec. 1921.
24. *Freeman's Journal*, 30 Dec. 1921.
25. John M. Regan, "Review of Eoin O'Duffy: A Self-Made Hero," *Reviews in History*, 2007, (583).
26. Lyons, *Ireland Since the Famine*, p. 445.
27. Lynch, *The Northern IRA*, p. 50.
28. Dáil Éireann debate, 4 Jan. 1922, Vol. T (11).
29. Walsh biography, pp. 62–3.
30. Report of Dáil peace committee, EODP/NLI/MS 48,281/1/12.
31. Dáil Éireann debate, 6 Jan. 1922, Vol. T (12).
32. *Irish Examiner*, 6 Jan. 1922.
33. *Skibbereen Eagle*, 7 Jan. 1922.
34. "Irish Ratification of the Peace Treaty," *Current History* (California, 1922), 15 (5), p. 853.
35. Briscoe, *For the Life of Me*, p. 139.
36. Dáil Éireann debate, 10 Jan. 1922, Vol. T (17).
37. *Evening Herald*, 10 Jan. 1922.
38. John Borgonovo, "IRA Conventions" in (eds. John Crowley, Donal Ó Drisceoil, Mike Murphy), *Atlas of the Irish Revolution* (Cork, 2017), p. 670.
39. Macardle, *Republic*, p. 654.
40. Laurence White, "O'Connor, Roderick (Rory)," *Dictionary of Irish Biography* (DIB) (https://www.dib.ie/biography/oconnor-roderick-rory-a6614), (17 Aug. 2022).
41. Walsh biography, p. 69.
42. Thomas McNally interview, OMN/UCDA/P17b/99.
43. Tom Carragher, Marron Papers, MCM, p. 6.
44. Séamus Woods interview, OMN/UCDA/P17b/107.
45. McCluskey, *GAA in Monaghan*, pp. 39–40.
46. Tim Pat Coogan, *Michael Collins: A Biography* (London, 1990), p. 344.
47. McGonnell WS/574, p. 13.
48. Okan Ozseker, *Forging the Border: Donegal and Derry in Times of Revolution 1911–1940* (Newbridge, 2019), pp. 130–3.
49. Robert Lynch, "The Clones affray, 1922–massacre or invasion?," *History Ireland*, 12 (3), (Autumn 2003).
50. O'Duffy to Florence O'Donoghue, 27 Jul. 1944, EODP/NLI/MS, 48,281/3/5.
51. Hopkinson, *Green Against Green*, pp. 62–4.
52. O'Malley, *The Singing Flame*, p. 61.
53. Valiulis, *Mulcahy*, pp. 132–3.
54. *Irish Independent*, 23 Mar. 1922.
55. Roger McCorley WS/389/IMA/BMH, pp. 33–7.
56. Tom McNally interview, OMN/UCDA/P17b/99.
57. O'Duffy to Charlie Daly, 4 Mar. 1922, CÓFLA/LOK/iii.c.10, 0002.03.
58. Lynch, *Northern IRA*, pp. 100–1.
59. Patrick Diamond interview, CÓFLA/LOK/IV/B/01.
60. O'Hegarty, *Victory*, p. 119.
61. O'Malley, *Singing Flame*, p. 54.
62. MacEoin, *Survivors*, p. 133.
63. O'Malley, *Singing Flame*, p. 76.
64. Seán Dowling interview, quoted in MacEoin, *Survivors*, pp. 410–1.
65. Meda Ryan, *Liam Lynch: The Real Chief* (Cork, 1986), p. 103.
66. O'Donoghue, *No Other Law*, pp. 251–2.
67. Dáil Éireann debate, 11 May 1922, Vol S2 (10).
68. *Irish Independent*, 13 Apr. 1922.
69. Dáil Éireann debate, 17 May 1922, S2 (11).
70. Rory O'Connor to *The Republic*, 15 Sep. 1922, Aiken Papers, UCDA/P104/1253.
71. Matthew Lewis, "The Fourth Northern Division and the Joint-IRA Offensive, April–July 1922," *War in History*, 21 (3), Jul. 2014, pp. 315–8.
72. Donal Hall, *Louth: The Irish Revolution, 1912–23* (Dublin, 2019), p. 95.
73. Coogan, *Michael Collins*, p. 350.
74. John M. Regan, "Michael Collins: Military Dictator," *History Ireland: The Split* (Dublin, 2021), p. 56.
75. *Irish Independent*, 9 Jun. 1922.
76. Briscoe, *For the Life of Me*, p. 164.
77. Michael Gallagher, "The Pact General Election of 1922," *Irish Historical Studies*, 22 (84), (Sep. 1979), p. 412.
78. *Northern Standard*, 16 Jun. 1922.
79. *Belfast Newsletter*, 16 Jun. 1922.

## Chapter 5

1. *Longford Leader*, 24 Jun. 1922.
2. Calton Younger, *Ireland's Civil War* (New York, 1969), p. 248.
3. Aodh MacAodha to Seán MacEoin, 23 Jun. 1922, Seán MacEoin Papers, UCDA/P151/150.
4. T. Ryle Dwyer, *The Squad* (Cork, 2005), pp. 256–8.
5. Briscoe, *For the Life of Me*, p. 165.
6. David Lloyd George to Michael Collins, 22 Jun. 1922, Mulcahy Papers, UCDA/P7/B/244.
7. *Reminiscences* 5, p. 2.
8. Macready, *Annals*, pp. 655–6.
9. *Irish Examiner*, 16 Oct. 1933.
10. Macready, *Annals*, p. 655.
11. Liam Deasy, *Brother Against Brother* (Cork, 1982), p. 48.
12. O'Donoghue, *No Other Law*, p. 259.
13. Ryan, *Lynch*, p. 119.
14. Younger, *Civil War*, pp. 327–8.
15. Briscoe, *For the Life of Me*, p. 171.
16. Hopkinson, *Green Against Green*, pp. 124–5.
17. *Irish Independent*, 14 Jul. 1922.

18. *Republican War News*, 7 Jul. 1922.
19. *Republican War News*, 25 Jul. 1922.
20. Regan, "Military Dictator," p. 58.
21. Walsh biography, p. 69A.
22. Dominick Doherty pension application, IMA/MSPC/24SP6707.
23. Hopkinson, *Green Against Green*, p. 170.
24. Thomas Fitzpatrick pension application, IMA/MSPC/ 24SP13219.
25. Woods interview, OMN/UCDA/P17b/107.
26. Walsh biography, p. 82A–B.
27. Lynch to the Acting DI, 15 Jul. 1922, Maurice Twomey Papers, UCDA/P69/28/108.
28. Ryan, *Lynch*, p. 127.
29. Walsh biography, p. 82A.
30. *Freeman's Journal*, 24 Jul. 1922.
31. Younger, *Civil War*, pp. 364–5.
32. O'Duffy to Collins, 21 Jul. 1922, Mulcahy Papers, UCDA/P7/B/68.
33. Younger, *Civil War*, pp. 364–5.
34. John Borgonovo, *The Battle for Cork: July-August 1922*, (Cork, 2011), p. 71.
35. *Evening Herald*, 24 Jul. 1922.
36. Younger, *Civil War*, p. 362.
37. Hopkinson, *Green Against Green*, p. 146.
38. *Poblacht na hÉireann*, 14 Sep. 1922.
39. Younger, *Civil War*, p. 374.
40. Hopkinson, *Green Against Green*, p. 152.
41. *The Free State*, 12 Aug. 1922.
42. Colum Kenny, *The Enigma of Arthur Griffith* (Newbridge, 2020), p. 230.
43. O'Duffy, "Account of the History and Policies of Sinn Féin," p. 8.
44. Diary of Sir Horace Plunkett, 19 Aug. 1922, Sir Horace Plunkett Papers, NLI/MS, 42,222.
45. Townshend, *Republic*, p. 432.
46. Walsh biography, p. 85.
47. *Ibid*., p. 83.
48. On the death of Collins, EODP/NLI/MS, 48,281/6.
49. Batt O'Connor, *With Michael Collins in the Fight for Independence* (London, 1929), pp. 181–2.
50. *Anglo-Celt*, 25 Jul. 1936.
51. *Southern Star*, 17 Aug. 1935.
52. Walsh biography, p. 85.
53. *Iris an Gharda*, 10 Sep. 1923.
54. *Connaught Telegraph*, 8 Sep. 1934.
55. Hopkinson, *Green Against Green*, p. 201.
56. Walsh biography, p. 85.
57. Liam McNiffe, *A History of the Garda Síochána* (Dublin, 1997), p. 29.
58. Vicky Conway, *Policing Twentieth Century Ireland: A History of the Garda Síochána* (London, 2014), pp. 27–8.
59. Blythe WS/939, pp. 150–1.
60. Kevin O'Higgins to Mulcahy, 1 Sep. 1922, quoted in *The Nation*, Jun. 1936.
61. McNiffe, *Garda Síochána*, p. 23.
62. Younger, *Civil War*, p. 489.
63. Blythe WS/939, p. 174.
64. *Business Post*, 11 Aug. 2019.
65. Eunan O'Halpin, *Defending Ireland: The Irish State and Its Enemies Since 1922* (Oxford, 1999), pp. 7–9.
66. Blythe WS/939, p. 175.
67. McNiffe, *Garda Síochána*, p. 27.
68. *Westmeath Independent*, 25 Nov. 1922.
69. Conor Brady, *Guardians of the Peace* (Dublin, 2000), p. 73.
70. *Ibid*., p. 78.
71. Blythe WS/939, p. 175.
72. *Northern Standard*, 1 Dec. 1922.
73. *Westmeath Independent*, 25 Nov. 1922.
74. O'Duffy canvassed on behalf of Michael Staines in a 1929 Senate by-election. See O'Duffy to James Green Douglas, 1929, Senator James Green Douglas Papers, NLI/MS 49,581/49/8.
75. Dalton to O'Duffy, 2 Sep. 1922, Mulcahy Papers, UCDA/P17a/191.
76. Blythe WS/939, p. 176.
77. Seán Enright, *The Irish Civil War: Law, Execution and Atrocity* (Newbridge, 2019), pp. 21–2.
78. Mary MacSwiney to Frank Aiken, 22 Apr. 1924, EODP/NLI/MS 48,283/6/1.
79. Deasy, *Brother Against Brother*, p. 122.
80. Hopkinson, *Green Against Green*, pp. 232–3.
81. Frank Pakenham & Thomas P. O'Neill, *Eamon de Valera* (Dublin, 1970), p. 217.
82. Gregory Allen, *The Garda Síochána: Policing Independent Ireland 1922–1982* (Dublin, 1999), pp. 61–2.
83. Macardle, *Republic*, p. 858.
84. Peter Cottrell, *The Irish Civil War 1922–23* (London, 2008), p. 24.
85. Brady, *Guardians*, pp. 98–9.
86. McGarry, *O'Duffy*, p. 113.
87. *Anglo-Celt*, 23 Jul. 1923.

## *Chapter 6*

1. *Freeman's Journal*, 23 Apr. 1923.
2. *Irish Independent*, 11 Jun. 1925.
3. *Evening Herald*, 23 May 1923.
4. *United Irishman*, 28 Jul. 1923.
5. *Irish Independent*, 24 May 1923.
6. *New York Evening Post*, c. May 1925.
7. *New York Times*, 2 May 1923.
8. *Guth an Ghárda* 1 (6).
9. McNiffe, *Garda Síochána*, pp. 119–20.
10. *Irish Press*, 31 Jan. 1936.
11. Allen, *Garda Síochána*, p. 61.
12. Walsh biography, pp. 117–8.
13. Allen, *Garda Síochána*, p. 64.
14. *Guth an Ghárda* 1(11).
15. *Strabane Chronicle*, 6 Jun. 1925.
16. *Belfast Newsletter*, 3 Jun. 1925.
17. *Irish Independent*, 11 Jun. 1925.
18. *New York Evening Post*, c. May 1925.
19. *Meath Chronicle*, 1 Sep. 1923.
20. Memorandum on meeting with O'Duffy, 17 May 1923, EODP/NLI/MS 48,283/3.
21. *An tÓglach*, 5 May 1923.
22. Walsh biography, p. 96.
23. Pádraig Ó Caoimh, *Richard Mulcahy: From the Politics of War to the Politics of Peace, 1913–1924* (Newbridge, 2019), pp. 174–82.

24. *The Liberator* (Tralee), 20 Mar. 1924.
25. Regan, *Counter-Revolution*, p. 192.
26. Donal Corcoran, "Public Policy in an emerging state: The Irish Free State 1922–25," *Irish Journal of Public Policy*, 2009, (1) 1.
27. Regan, *Counter-Revolution*, p. 184.
28. *The Liberator* (Tralee), 20 Mar. 1924.
29. Mary MacSwiney to Aiken, 22 Apr. 1924, EODP/NLI/MS 48,283/6/1).
30. Minutes of Executive Council meeting, 24 May 1924, NAI, Department of the Taoiseach (TSCH)/3/S3442 B.
31. Army Organization, NAI/TSCH/3/S3442 B, p. 1.
32. O'Duffy to the Executive Council, 2 May 1924, NAI/TSCH/3/S3442 B.
33. *The Nationalist* (Tipperary), 23 Aug. 1924.
34. *Kerryman*, 18 Oct. 1924.
35. MacMahon, *A Fist to the Black-Blooded*, p. 42.
36. Patrick Long, "MacMahon, Peadar," *DIB*, (https://www.dib.ie/biography/macmahon-peadar-a5260), (accessed 14 Sep. 2022).
37. *Kerry News*, 18 Feb. 1925.
38. *Guth an Ghárda*, 1 (15).
39. *Kerryman*, 18 Oct. 1924.
40. Walsh biography, p. 97.
41. Allen, *Garda Síochána*, pp. 91–2.
42. Brady, *Guardians*, p. 111.
43. Conway, *Policing*, pp. 35–40.
44. *Westmeath Independent*, 25 Nov. 1922.
45. Fearghal McGarry, "Violence, citizenship and virility: The making of an Irish fascist," *History Ireland*, 6 (13), (Nov./Dec. 2005).
46. Memorandum by O'Duffy, 30 Oct. 1930, NAI/JUS/H247/41A.
47. *Guth an Ghárda*, 1 (36).
48. Brady, *Guardians*, p. 73.
49. *Reminiscences* 6, pp. 8–11.
50. *Irish Independent*, 21 Jul. 1931.
51. McNiffe, *Garda Síochána*, pp. 34–9.
52. *Iris An Gárda*, 1 (48).
53. Walsh biography, p. 98.
54. *Irish Independent*, 24 May 1923.
55. McGarry, *O'Duffy*, p. 121.
56. Walsh biography, pp. 101–2.
57. *Reminiscences* 5, p. 3.
58. *Daily Mail*, 20 Aug. 1928.
59. *Honesty*, 29 May 1926.
60. Walsh biography, p. 229.
61. Michael Gallagher & Michael Marsh, *Days of Blue Loyalty: The Politics and Membership of the Fine Gael party* (Dublin, 2002), p. 17.
62. Brian Hanley, *The IRA: 1926–1936* (Dublin, 2002), p. 173.
63. O'Duffy to Henry O'Friel, Aug. 1931, EODP/NLI/MS 48,285/4/5.
64. Memo on Communism and on Kindred Organizations, 24 Nov. 1932, NAI/TSCH/97/9/73.
65. O'Duffy to Henry O'Friel, Aug. 1931, EODP.
66. Emmet O'Connor, *Reds and the Green: Ireland, Russia and the Communist Internationals 1919–43* (Dublin, 2004), p. 175.
67. Eoin O'Duffy, "The Spread of Communism," 12 Dec. 1931, EODP/NLI/MS 48,285/6/2.
68. Briscoe, *For the Life of Me*, p. 224.
69. *The Nation*, 17 Dec. 1927.
70. Allen, *Garda Síochána*, pp. 90–1.
71. Brady, *Guardians*, pp. 145–6.
72. Blythe WS/939, p. 177.
73. Mel Farrell, *Party Politics in a New Democracy: The Irish Free State, 1922–37* (London, 2017), p. 168.
74. O'Hegarty, *Victory*, p. 125.
75. O'Duffy to O'Higgins, 6 Dec. 1926, NAI/TSCH/S5260.
76. Allen, *Garda Síochána*, p. 70.
77. *Iris an Ghárda*, Aug. 1927.
78. Walsh biography, p. 137.
79. Dáil Éireann debate, 7 Feb. 1934, 50 (7).
80. Walsh biography, p. 137.
81. *Irish Independent*, 4 Jul. 1928.
82. *Irish Independent*, 14 Jul. 1927.
83. Briscoe, *For the Life of Me*, p. 234.
84. Joseph Lee, *Ireland 1912–1985: Politics and Society* (Cambridge, 2006), p. 154.
85. Gallagher & Marsh, *Days of Blue Loyalty*, p. 18.
86. Fearghal McGarry, *Frank Ryan* (Dublin, 2010), p. 22.
87. Conway, *Policing*, pp. 43–4.
88. Walsh biography, p. 227.
89. McGarry, *O'Duffy*, p. 129.
90. Walsh biography, p. 236.
91. *The Blueshirt*, 22 Dec. 1934.
92. *Westmeath Independent*, 25 Nov. 1922.
93. *Limerick Leader*, 28 May 1930.
94. *Leitrim Observer*, 14 Jun. 1930.
95. Dáil Éireann debate, 1 Mar. 1934, 50 (16).
96. Diarmaid Ferriter, *Occasions of Sin: Sex and Society in Modern Ireland* (London, 2009), p. 138.
97. *Kerry Reporter*, 4 May 1929.
98. Walsh biography, pp. 126–7.
99. Allen, *Garda Síochána*, p. 101.
100. Newspaper cutting from *Hjemmet*, c. 1933, EODP/NLI/MS 48,286/11.
101. *Irish Press*, 4 Feb. 1933.
102. McGarry, *O'Duffy*, p. 211.
103. Jack Traynor, "The Italian arms importation scheme, 1920–1921," *TheIrishStory.com*, (https://www.theirishstory.com/2021/07/27/the-italian-arms-importation-scheme-1920-1921/), (accessed 19 Feb. 2023).
104. *United Irishman*, 10 Dec. 1932.
105. Maurice Manning, *The Blueshirts* (Dublin, 2006), p. 214.
106. Walsh biography, p. 156.
107. *Sunday Independent*, 3 May 1931.
108. Walsh biography, p. 156.
109. *Strabane Chronicle*, 30 May 1931.
110. *Irish Independent*, 20 Apr. 1931.
111. *Irish Independent*, 10 Apr. 1931.
112. Walsh biography, pp. 156–7.
113. *Northern Standard*, 24 Feb. 1933.
114. Eoin O'Duffy, "Ireland at an Olympiad," EODP/NLI/MS 48,299/1/3, pp. 16–7.
115. *Irish Press*, 3 May 1932.
116. Walsh biography, pp. 158–9.
117. O'Duffy, "Ireland at an Olympiad," p. 22.

118. *Strabane Chronicle*, 8 Oct. 1932.
119. Eoin O'Duffy, "The Struggle for Irish Athletics," EODP/NLI/MS 48,299/2/4.
120. Walsh biography, pp. 161–3.
121. *Irish Times*, 20 Sep. 2020.
122. Jason Knirck, "Afterimage of the Revolution: Kevin O'Higgins and the Irish Revolution," *Éire-Ireland*, 38 (3/4), (2003).
123. Manning, *Blueshirts*, p. 23.
124. McGarry, *O'Duffy*, pp. 187–8.
125. *Irish Times*, 2 Nov. 1970.
126. Allen, *Garda Síochána*, p. 105.
127. Regan, *Counter-Revolution*, pp. 287–8.
128. Ronan Fanning, *Éamon de Valera: A Will to Power* (London, 2015), p. 158.

## Chapter 7

1. *Irish Independent*, 23 Apr. 1932.
2. O'Duffy, "Ireland at an Olympiad," p. 7.
3. Diarmaid Ferriter, *What If? Alternative Views on Twentieth-Century Ireland* (Dublin, 2006), p. 111.
4. Regan, *Counter-Revolution*, pp. 290–5.
5. MacMahon, *A Fist to the Black-Blooded*, p. 65.
6. McGarry, *O'Duffy*, p. 191.
7. Letter of Introduction, 7 May 1930, EODP/NLI/MS 48,283 /4.
8. *Irish Press*, 26 Feb. 1932.
9. *Irish Times*, 2 Jun. 2018.
10. Regan, *Counter-Revolution*, p. 294.
11. *Kerry Reporter*, 2 Apr. 1932.
12. *Irish Times*, 23 Jun. 2007.
13. *Northern Standard*, 24 Feb. 1933.
14. Walsh biography, pp. 150–2.
15. *Northern Standard*, 24 Feb. 1933.
16. Tim Fanning, *The Salamanca Diaries: Father McCabe and the Spanish Civil War* (Newbridge, 2019), p. 178.
17. Walsh biography, p. 152.
18. Mike Cronin, *The Blueshirts and Irish Politics* (Dublin, 1997), p. 77.
19. Cronin Controversy, EODP/NLI/MS 48, 286/9).
20. Manning, *Blueshirts*, pp. 21–3.
21. Information Leaflet from the ACA, c. 1932, EODP/NLI/MS 48,265/5.
22. Briscoe, *For the Life of Me*, pp. 248–9.
23. Dale Montgomery, "'They were the men who licked the IRA until they squealed': Blueshirt masculine identity 1932–36," in (eds.) Caroline Magennis & Raymond Mullen, *Irish Masculinities: reflections on literature and culture* (Dublin, 2011).
24. Information Leaflet, EODP.
25. *Kerry News*, 16 Dec. 1932.
26. *Irish Press*, 17 Dec. 1932.
27. Fanning, *A Will to Power*, p. 168.
28. Maurice Manning, *James Dillon: A Biography* (Dublin, 2000), pp. 70–1.
29. *Fermanagh Herald*, 4 Mar. 1933.
30. Walsh biography, pp. 168–9.
31. *Ibid.*, p. 182.
32. *Irish Independent*, 23 Feb. 1933.
33. *Dundalk Democrat*, 25 Feb. 1933.
34. Margaret Pearse to O'Duffy, 25 Feb. 1933, EODP/NLI/MS 48,285/10.
35. Manning, *Dillon*, p. 71.
36. Manning, *Blueshirts*, p. 27.
37. *Irish Post*, 2 Mar. 2001.
38. Manning, *Blueshirts*, pp. 53–4.
39. Policy of New Movement, Dec. 1934, NAI/JUS/8/286.
40. Information Leaflet, EODP.
41. St Patrick's Day Message, 17 Mar. 1934, NAI, Department of Justice (JUS)/8/257.
42. Mike Cronin, "The Blueshirt movement, 1932–5: Ireland's Fascists?," *Journal of Contemporary History*, 3 (2), (1995), p. 315.
43. *United Irishman*, 29 Jul. 1933.
44. *Belfast Newsletter*, 16 Mar. 1933.
45. *Kerry Reporter*, 25 Mar. 1933.
46. Walsh biography, pp. 182–3.
47. *Irish Press*, 16 May 1933.
48. *The Liberator* (Tralee), 13 Mar. 1934.
49. *Irish Independent*, 19 May 1933.
50. Walsh biography, p. 183.
51. *Irish Press*, 18 Jul. 1933.
52. *Kerry Champion*, 24 Nov. 1934.
53. Seanad Éireann debate, 22 Aug. 1933, Vol. 17, No. 15.
54. Roy Foster, *W.B. Yeats: A Life, Vol. II: The Arch-Poet, 1915–1939* (Oxford, 2003), p. 472.
55. *An Phoblacht*, 12 Aug. 1933.
56. *Evening Echo*, 13 Aug. 1934.
57. Lee, *Ireland 1912–1985*, p. 183.
58. *Kerry News*, 21 Jul. 1933.
59. Dale Montgomery, "'No Suggestion of Suffragettism': the Blue Blouses in Ireland, 1933–1936," *Women's History Review*, 23 (5), pp. 776–92.
60. Dermot Keogh, *Jews in Twentieth-Century Ireland* (Cork, 1998), p. 96.
61. *Irish Press*, 1 Aug. 1933.
62. *Irish Examiner*, 3 Aug. 1933.
63. *The Blueshirt*, 5 Aug. 1933.
64. *Irish Press*, 12 Jul. 1934.
65. *Irish Independent*, 28 May 1934.
66. Eoin O'Duffy, *An Outline of the Political, Social and Economic Policy of Fine Gael* (Dublin, 1934), p. 4.
67. Antonio Costa Pinto, *Corporatism and Fascism: The Corporatist Wave in Europe* (Abingdon, 2017), p. 5.
68. Roger Griffin, *The Nature of Fascism* (London, 1993), pp. 120–4.
69. Eoin O'Duffy, *The Labour Policy of Fine Gael* (Dublin, 1934), p. 9.
70. *United Ireland*, 21 Oct. 1933.
71. Seanad Éireann debate, 21 Mar. 1934, 18 (12).
72. Walsh biography, p. 187.
73. *Southern Star*, 2 Sep. 1933.
74. *United Irishman*, 5 Aug. 1933.
75. *Irish Independent*, 26 Sep. 1933.
76. *An Phoblacht*, 19 Aug. 1933.
77. *Irish Press*, 9 Aug. 1933.
78. *Anglo-Celt*, 29 Jul. 1933.
79. *Irish Independent*, 29 Jul. 1933.

80. *Leitrim Observer*, 29 Jul. 1933.
81. *Anglo-Celt*, 29 Jul. 1933.
82. Anthony J. Jordan, *John A. Costello: Compromise Taoiseach* (Dublin, 2007), p. 37.
83. McGarry, *O'Duffy*, pp. 205–7.
84. John P. Swift, *John Swift: An Irish Dissident* (Dublin, 1991), p. 90.
85. Peter Martin, "The political career of Michael Tierney, 1920–44," *Irish Historical Studies*, May 2011, 37 (147), p. 422.
86. Seán Donnelly, "Michael Tierney and the Intellectual Origins of Blueshirtism, 1920–1938," *Fascism*, 10, 2021, pp. 94–103.
87. Foster, *Yeats*, pp. 473–4.
88. Mary Carden, "The Few and the Many: An Examination of W. B. Yeats's Politics," *Studies: An Irish Quarterly Review*, 58 (229), Spring 1969, pp. 56–61.
89. Foster, *Yeats*, p. 478.
90. Paul Scott Stanfield, *Yeats and Politics in the 1930s* (London, 1988), pp. 63–4.
91. Elisabeth Cullingford, *Yeats, Ireland and Fascism* (London, 1981), p. 205.
92. Stanfield, *Yeats and Politics in the 1930s*, p. 65.
93. Cronin, "The Blueshirt Movement," p. 318.
94. Manning, *Blueshirts*, p. 75.
95. Donnelly, "Tierney," p. 98.
96. Cronin, *Blueshirts and Irish Politics*, p. 94.
97. David Fitzpatrick, *Ernest Blythe in Ulster: The Making of a Double Agent?* (Cork, 2018), p. 172.
98. Eugene Broderick, *Intellectuals and the Ideological Hijacking of Fine Gael, 1932–1938* (Newcastle-upon-Tyne, 2010), pp. 107–8.
99. "The Diast," May 1933, Ernest Blythe Papers, UCDA/P24/690.
100. *The Blueshirt*, 5 Aug. 1933.
101. Oswald Mosley, *Fascism: 100 Questions Asked and Answered* (London, 1936), p. 8.
102. *Evening Herald*, 9 Aug. 1933.
103. *United Irishman*, 22 Apr. 1933.
104. *Irish Independent*, 14 Aug. 1933; *Irish Press*, 12 Aug. 1933.
105. *Irish Independent*, 21 Aug. 1933.
106. *Irish Independent*, 7 Sep. 1933.
107. *The Blueshirt*, 12 Aug. 1933.
108. Trevor White, *Alfie: The Life and Times of Alfie Byrne* (Dublin, 2017), p. 85.
109. Cronin, "The Blueshirt Movement," p. 316.
110. Manning, *Dillon*, p. 74.
111. Brady, *Guardians*, p. 270.
112. Donnacha Ó Beacháin, *Destiny of the Soldiers: Fianna Fáil, Irish Republicanism and the IRA, 1926–1973* (Dublin, 2011), pp. 147–8.
113. *An Phoblacht*, 12 Aug. 1933.
114. Terry de Valera, *A Memoir* (Dublin, 2004), pp. 58–9.
115. Walsh biography, p. 185.
116. Máire Mhac an tSaoi, *The Same Age as the State* (Dublin, 2003), p. 126.
117. J. Bowyer Bell, *The Secret Army: A History of the IRA 1915–1970* (London, 1972), p. 128.
118. Receipt for firearms surrendered, 29 Jul. 1933, EODP/NLI/MS 48,285/12/2.
119. *Strabane Chronicle*, 5 Aug. 1933.
120. Revocation of firearms certificate, 29 Jul. 1933, EODP/NLI/MS 48,285/12/1.
121. *Northern Standard*, 4 Aug. 1933.
122. *An Phoblacht*, 5 Aug. 1933.
123. Dáil Éireann debate, 1 Aug. 1933, Vol. 49 (9).
124. *The Blueshirt*, 5 Aug. 1933.
125. *Irish Press*, 10 Aug. 1933.
126. *The Blueshirt*, 5 Aug. 1933.
127. *Irish Press*, 12 Aug. 1933.
128. *Irish Workers' Voice*, 19 Aug. 1933.
129. *Evening Herald*, 12 Aug. 1933.
130. *Dublin Evening Mail*, 12 Aug. 1933.
131. Bell, *Secret Army*, p. 133.
132. *An Phoblacht*, 12 Aug. 1933.
133. Manning, *Blueshirts*, p. xi.
134. McGarry, *O'Duffy*, p. 217.
135. Ferriter, *What If?*, pp. 111–2.
136. *United Irishman*, 26 Aug. 1933.
137. J. Anthony Gaughan, *Thomas O'Donnell: A Political Odyssey* (Dublin, 1983), p. 225.
138. Mike Cronin, "The socio-economic background and membership of the Blueshirt movement, 1932–5," *Irish Historical Studies*, 23 (114), (Nov. 1994), p. 239.
139. *Dublin Evening Mail*, 12 Aug. 1933.
140. O'Duffy speech at Mansion House, 18 Aug. 1934, NAI/JUS/8/276).
141. *Kerry News*, 14 Aug. 1933.

## Chapter 8

1. *Anglo-Celt*, 19 Aug. 1933.
2. *Fermanagh Herald*, 26 Aug. 1933.
3. Hanley, *The IRA*, p. 85.
4. *Anglo-Celt*, 19 Aug. 1933.
5. *United Irishman*, 29 Jul. 1933.
6. *Irish Press*, 9 Aug. 1933.
7. *Anglo-Celt*, 19 Aug. 1933.
8. *The Blueshirt*, 19 Aug. 1933.
9. *An Phoblacht*, 26 Aug. 1933.
10. "Report by O'Duffy," 22 Sep. 1924, Blythe Papers, UCDA/P24/222.
11. *Irish Press*, 13 Jan. 1936.
12. *The Blueshirt*, 19 Aug. 1933.
13. *United Irishman*, 26 Aug. 1933.
14. Manning, *Dillon*, p. 78.
15. Stephen Collins & Ciara Meehan, *Saving the State: Fine Gael from Collins to Varadkar* (Dublin, 2020), p. 36.
16. Walsh biography, p. 186A.
17. *Irish Independent*, 2 Sep. 1933.
18. *Fermanagh Herald*, 2 Sep. 1933.
19. Notes on organization, Blythe Papers, UCDA/P24/652.
20. *Irish Independent*, 4 Sep. 1933.
21. *Irish Independent*, 18 Sep. 1933.
22. *Irish Press*, 23 Oct. 1933.
23. Lee, *Ireland 1912–1985*, p. 179.
24. Gallagher & Marsh, *Days of Blue Loyalty*, pp. 22–3.
25. *Irish Press*, 2 Sep. 1933.

26. *Irish Freedom*, 1 Sep. 1933.
27. O'Duffy, *An Outline*, p. 25.
28. *Irish Independent*, 9 Sep. 1933.
29. O'Duffy, *An Outline*, p. 6.
30. *Irish Press*, 2 Sep. 1933.
31. *Longford Leader*, 15 Sep. 1934.
32. John Henry Whyte, *Church and State in Modern Ireland, 1923–1979* (Dublin, 1980), p. 81.
33. *Kerryman*, 9 Sep. 1933.
34. Walsh biography, p. 187.
35. Regan, *Counter-Revolution*, p. 350.
36. James Hogan, *Could Ireland become Communist? The facts of the case* (Dublin, 1935).
37. O'Duffy, *An Outline*, p. 15.
38. *United Ireland*, 4 Nov. 1933. The *United Ireland* newspaper succeeded the CnaG journal *United Irishman* which ceased publication in 1933.
39. Cronin, *Blueshirts and Irish Politics*, p. 92.
40. Walsh biography, p. 186.
41. O'Duffy, *An Outline*, p. 5.
42. *Fermanagh Herald*, 2 Sep. 1933.
43. *Roscommon Herald*, 5 May 1933.
44. *Irish Press*, 24 Oct. 1933.
45. *Irish Independent*, 14 Jun. 1933.
46. *Irish Workers' Voice*, 21 Oct. 1933.
47. Garda dossier on Liam Walsh, NAI/JUS/2011/25/160.
48. Meeting of IFG, NAI/JUS/2011/25/160.
49. White, *Alfie*, p. 85.
50. Kevin Rafter, *Fine Gael: Party at the Crossroads* (Dublin, 2009), p. 28.
51. *Irish Press*, 19 Oct. 1933.
52. *Meath Chronicle*, 27 Jan. 1934.
53. *Sunday Independent*, 21 Jan. 1934.
54. Headquarters to Inspection Officers, 29 Nov. 1933, NAI/JUS/93/3/19).
55. *Anglo-Celt*, 28 Oct. 1933.
56. *Fermanagh Herald*, 28 Oct. 1933.
57. *Belfast Newsletter*, 4 Dec. 1933.
58. *Irish Examiner*, 31 Oct. 1933.
59. *Irish Independent*, 24 Oct. 1928.
60. Leo McCauley to Joseph Walshe, 20 Sep. 1933, NAI, Department of Foreign Affairs (DFA)/17/141.
61. *The Times* (London), 7 Oct. 1933.
62. *Evening Herald*, 26 Jan. 1934.
63. *An Phoblacht*, 9 Dec. 1933.
64. *Belfast Newsletter*, 4 Dec. 1933.
65. O'Duffy to James FitzGerald-Kenney, 7 Oct. 1931, NAI/JUS/8/306.
66. *Irish Independent*, 9 Dec. 1933.
67. Mike Cronin, "Cronin, Edmund ('Ned') John," *DIB*, (https://www.dib.ie/biography/cronin-edmund-ned-john-a2215), (6 Nov. 2022).
68. Regan, *Counter-Revolution*, p. 348.
69. Seanad Éireann debate, 13 Dec. 1933, 17 (28).
70. O'Duffy to Department of Justice, 8 Nov. 1928, NAI/JUS/8/684.
71. Manning, *Blueshirts*, p. 109.
72. Jordan, *Costello*, p. 37.
73. *Irish Press*, 29 Sep. 1933.
74. Regan, *Counter-Revolution*, p. 347.
75. *Donegal Democrat*, 16 Dec. 1933.
76. *Leitrim Observer*, 1 Jun. 1935.
77. *Irish Times*, 25 May 1933.
78. *Irish Independent*, 18 Dec. 1933.
79. *Evening Herald*, 24 May 1935.
80. *The Times* (London), 20 Dec. 1933.
81. Jordan, *Costello*, p. 37.
82. Quoted in McGarry, *O'Duffy*, p. 229.
83. *United Ireland*, 23 Dec. 1933.
84. Walsh biography, p. 188.
85. *Evening Herald*, 30 Dec. 1933.
86. *Irish Examiner*, 29 Dec. 2006.
87. *United Ireland*, 6 Jan. 1934.
88. *Southern Star*, 13 Jan. 1934.
89. *Irish Examiner*, 26 Feb. 1934.
90. *Irish Examiner*, 1 Jan. 1934.
91. *Donegal News*, 3 Feb. 1934.
92. *Belfast Newsletter*, 9 Jan. 1934.
93. *The Times* (London), 29 Aug. 1933.
94. *Offaly Independent*, 27 Jan. 1934.
95. *Irish Independent*, 2 Jan. 1993.
96. *Offaly Independent*, 27 Jan. 1934.
97. *Irish Times*, 19 Feb. 1934.
98. Walsh biography, p. 187.
99. *Irish Press*, 12 Jan. 1934.
100. *United Ireland*, 17 Feb. 1934.
101. Manning, *Blueshirts*, p. 117.
102. *Evening Echo*, 13 Jul. 1974.
103. Mike Cronin, "Catholicising Fascism, Fascistising Catholicism? The Blueshirts and the Jesuits in 1930s Ireland," *Totalitarian Movements and Political Religions*, Jun. 2007, 8 (2), p. 405.
104. O'Duffy, *Labour Policy*, p. 8.
105. A. James Gregor, *The Faces of Janus: Marxism and Fascism in the Twentieth Century* (New Haven, 2000), p. 40.
106. Dáil Éireann debate, 13 Mar. 1934, 51 (5).
107. *The Nation*, May 1936.
108. *United Ireland*, 17 Feb. 1934.
109. James Q. Whitman, "Of corporatism, fascism, and the First New Deal," *American Journal of Comparative Law*, Autumn 1991, 39 (4), pp. 747–78.
110. *United Ireland*, 13 Dec. 1933.
111. Cronin, *Blueshirts and Irish Politics*, pp. 95–7.
112. *Irish Times*, 9 Feb. 1934.
113. Broderick, *Ideological Hijacking*, p. 71.
114. *United Ireland*, 10 Feb. 1934.
115. Alana Lentin & Ronit Lentin, *Race and State* (Newcastle-upon-Tyne, 2006), p. 10.
116. *United Ireland*, 10 Feb. 1934.
117. Walsh biography, p. 188.
118. *United Ireland*, 14 Jul. 1934.
119. Jack Traynor, "Attempts to gain Leon Trotsky asylum in the Irish Free State," *The IrishStory.com*, (https://www.theirishstory.com/2021/09/14/attempts-to-gain-leon-trotsky-asylum-in-the-irish-free-state/), (accessed 9 Nov. 2022).
120. Broderick, *Ideological Hijacking*, p. 34.
121. *United Ireland*, 3 Mar. 1934.
122. *Roscommon Herald*, 5 May 1934.
123. Farrell, *Party Politics*, p. 265.
124. *United Ireland*, 24 Feb. 1934.
125. *Northern Standard*, 16 Feb. 1934.

126. Dáil Éireann debates, 28 Feb. 1934, 50 (15).
127. Interview with Maureen Haughey, 2013, Irish Life and Lore Series: The 1916 Rising Oral History Collection.
128. Jordan, *Costello*, p. 39.
129. *Belfast Newsletter*, 26 Mar. 1934.
130. *Irish Examiner*, 22 Mar. 1934.
131. Dáil Éireann debate, 22 Mar. 1934, 51 (11).
132. *Irish Press*, 7 Apr. 1934.
133. *Irish Press*, 23 Oct. 1933.
134. O'Duffy, *An Outline*, p. 5.
135. *Irish Independent*, 7 Apr. 1934.
136. *Irish Independent*, 16 Apr. 1934.
137. *Irish Press*, 21 Apr. 1934.
138. Seanad Éireann debate, 25 Apr. 1934, 18 (16).
139. *Nationalist and Leinster Times*, 16 Jun. 1934.
140. *Dundalk Democrat*, 28 Apr. 1934.
141. *Kerryman*, 1 Oct. 1966.
142. *Irish Independent*, 5 Apr. 1934.
143. *Belfast Newsletter*, 3 May 1934.
144. *Irish Press*, 29 May 1934.
145. *Irish Independent*, 4 May 1934.
146. Dale Montgomery, "'Helping the Guards': Illegal Displays and Blueshirt Criminality, 1932–36," *Éire-Ireland*, 49 (1 & 2), 2014, p. 41.
147. *Irish Independent*, 28 May 1934.
148. *Irish Press*, 12 Apr. 1934.
149. Manning, *Blueshirts*, pp. 155–6.
150. *Kerry Reporter*, 5 May 1934.
151. *The Nationalist* (Tipperary), 13 Jun. 1934.
152. *Irish Examiner*, 4 Jun. 1934.
153. *Dundalk Democrat*, 9 Jun. 1934.
154. *Irish Independent*, 26 Jun. 1934.
155. Manning, *Blueshirts*, p. 131.
156. *Irish Independent*, 28 Jun. 1934.
157. *Irish Independent*, 5 Jul. 1934.
158. Paul Bew, Ellen Hazelkorn, Henry Patterson (eds.), *The Dynamics of Irish Politics* (London, 1989), p. 57.
159. *Irish Workers' Voice*, 7 Jul. 1934.
160. General Purpose Committee meeting, 14 Jun. 1934, Fine Gael Papers, UCDA/P39/min/2.
161. *Fermanagh Herald*, 12 May 1934.
162. *Irish Times*, 11 Jun. 1934.
163. Hanley, *The IRA*, p. 89.
164. Barry McLoughlin, *Fighting for Republican Spain, 1936–38: Frank Ryan and the Volunteers from Limerick in the International Brigades* (Limerick, 2014), p. 39.
165. Regan, *Counter-Revolution*, p. 358.
166. Memo by Sir Edward Harding of a conversation with John Dulanty, 19 Feb. 1934, Public Records Office (PRO), TNA/DO/35/398/6.
167. *Kerry Champion*, 11 Aug. 1934.
168. Lyons, *Ireland since the Famine*, p. 525.
169. Manning, *Dillon*, pp. 95–6.
170. Uinseann MacEoin, *The IRA in the Twilight Years, 1923–1948* (Dublin, 1997), p. 264.
171. Robert Fisk, *In Time of War: Ireland, Ulster and the Price of Neutrality 1939–45* (Philadelphia, 1983), p. 369.
172. Manning, *Dillon*, p. 125.
173. *Irish Examiner*, 5 Jul. 1934.
174. *Connaught Telegraph*, 28 Jul. 1934.
175. *Belfast Newsletter*, 9 Jul. 1934.
176. *Irish News*, 24 Aug. 1934.
177. James Loughlin, *Fascism and Constitutional Conflict: The British Extreme Right and Ulster in the Twentieth Century* (Liverpool, 2019), p. 121.
178. *Irish Press*, 11 Jul. 1934.
179. *Longford Leader*, 18 Aug. 1934.
180. Salvatore Garau, "Anticipating Norwegian Fascism: The Radicalization of Urban Right-Wing Nationalism in Inter-war Norway," *European History Quarterly*, 2013, 43 (4).
181. Jonathan Trigg, *Hitler's Vikings: The History of the Scandinavian Waffen-SS: The Legions, The SS-Wiking and the SS-Nordland* (Stroud, 2012), p. 36.
182. *An Phoblacht*, 25 Aug. 1934.
183. Cronin, *Blueshirts and Irish Politics*, pp. 51 & 195.
184. Walsh biography, p. 188.
185. Eoin O'Duffy, *Why I Resigned from Fine Gael* (Dublin, 1934), p. 9.
186. *Strabane Chronicle*, 18 Aug. 1934.
187. Montgomery, "Illegal Displays and Blueshirt Criminality, 1932–36," pp. 25–6.
188. Proposal for the Organization of FG, 28 Aug. 1934, Blythe Papers, UCDA/P24/632.
189. *Northern Standard*, 24 Aug. 1934.
190. Manning, *Blueshirts*, p. 142.
191. *Northern Standard*, 24 Aug. 1934.
192. McGarry, *O'Duffy*, p. 263.
193. Martin, "Tierney," p. 423.
194. *Drogheda Independent*, 29 Sep. 1934.
195. *Irish Examiner*, 3 Sep. 1934.
196. Hogan to FitzGerald, 1935, Desmond FitzGerald Papers, UCDA/P80/1148.
197. O'Duffy, *Why I Resigned*, pp. 18–9.
198. *Nationalist and Leinster Times*, 8 Sep. 1934.
199. *Donegal News*, 1 Sep. 1934.
200. *Connaught Telegraph*, 8 Sep. 1934.
201. Manning, *Blueshirts*, pp. 155–6.
202. Fitzpatrick, *Blythe in Ulster*, p. 183.
203. *Irish Examiner*, 14 Sep. 1934.
204. *Longford Leader*, 15 Sep. 1934.
205. *Strabane Chronicle*, 15 Sep. 1934.
206. Manning, *Dillon*, p. 101.
207. O'Duffy, *Why I Resigned*, pp. 12–21.
208. *Irish Independent*, 2 Oct. 1934.
209. O'Duffy, *Why I Resigned*, p. 25.
210. McGarry, *O'Duffy*, p. 266.
211. Manning, *Dillon*, p. 102.
212. Cronin, *Blueshirts and Irish Politics*, p. 115.
213. P.J. Coughlan, *The Truth: The Story of the Blueshirts: Politics, Agriculture, Nationality* (Skibbereen, 1935), pp. 1–2.
214. Dillon to MacDermot, 26 Sep. 1934, NAI/JUS/1065/2/4.
215. Manning, *Dillon*, p. 102.
216. Coughlan, *The Truth*, pp. 6–7.
217. Manning, *Blueshirts*, p. 159.
218. *Irish Independent*, 2 Oct. 1934.
219. Donal O'Sullivan, *The Free State and Its*

*Senate: A Study in Contemporary Politics* (London, 1940), p. 408.

220. *The Nationalist* (Tipperary), 22 Sep. 1934.
221. O'Duffy, *Why I Resigned*, p. 6.
222. *Roscommon Herald*, 15 Sep. 1934.
223. Ó Beacháin, *Destiny of the Soldiers*, p. 87.

## *Chapter 9*

1. Manning, *Dillon*, p. 104.
2. *Irish Press*, 2 Oct. 1934.
3. *Roscommon Herald*, 29 Sep. 1934.
4. Walsh biography, p. 194.
5. Manning, *Blueshirts*, p. 164.
6. *Donegal Democrat*, 29 Sep. 1934.
7. *Donegal News*, 8 Dec. 1934.
8. *Irish Independent*, 3 Oct. 1934.
9. *Irish Press*, 5 Oct. 1934.
10. *The Liberator* (Tralee), 2 Oct. 1934.
11. Manning, *Blueshirts*, p. 163.
12. *Donegal Democrat*, 6 Oct. 1934.
13. *Irish Independent*, 13 Oct. 1934.
14. Pauric J. Dempsey, "Belton, Patrick," *DIB*, (https://www.dib.ie/biography/belton-patrick-a0572), (21 Dec. 2022).
15. Coughlan, *The Truth*, p. 9.
16. MacEoin, *Twilight Years*, p. 312.
17. O'Duffy to Quinn, 3 Oct. 1934, NAI/JUS/8/286.
18. *Irish Independent*, 31 Oct. 1934.
19. *Kerry Reporter*, 10 Nov. 1934.
20. *Donegal Democrat*, 17 Nov. 1934.
21. *The Blueshirt*, 13 Oct. 1934.
22. *Irish Press*, 17 Nov. 1934.
23. O'Duffy to Quinn, 3 Oct. 1934, NAI/JUS/8/286.
24. McGarry, *O'Duffy*, p. 274.
25. Circular letter from O'Duffy, c. 1935, EODP/NLI/MS 48,290/1.
26. O'Duffy to supporters, 4 Dec. 1934, NAI/JUS/8/286.
27. *Kilkenny People*, 8 Dec. 1934.
28. *Irish Independent*, 27 Nov. 1934.
29. *Kerry News*, 3 Dec. 1934.
30. *Longford Leader*, 8 Dec. 1934.
31. *Irish Press*, 24 Nov. 1934.
32. *Irish Examiner*, 17 Jan. 1936.
33. LoY appeal, Dec. 1934, NAI/JUS/8/286.
34. Michael A Ledeen, *Universal Fascism: The Theory and Practice of the Fascist International, 1928–36* (New York, 1972), p. 113.
35. Martin Kristoffer Hamre, "'Nationalists of All Countries, Unite!': Hans Keller and Nazi Internationalism in the 1930s," *Contemporary European History* (2022), p. 6.
36. *Donegal News*, 8 Dec. 1934.
37. Graham Macklin, *Failed Führers: A History of Britain's Extreme Right* (Abingdon, 2020), p. 93.
38. Hans Keller, *Volksgemeinschaft und Völkerfriede; Sitzungbericht der Berliner Tagung* (Berlin, 1935), p. 34. (My thanks to Martin Hamre for this reference).
39. *Drogheda Independent*, 14 Oct. 1961.
40. *Evening Echo*, 19 Mar. 1934.
41. *Irish Independent*, 28 May 1934.
42. Hans Keller, *Der kampf um die völkerordnung* (Berlin, 1939), pp. 124–5. (My thanks to Martin Hamre for this reference).
43. Nathaniël Kunkeler & Martin Kristoffer Hamre, "Conceptions and Practices of International Fascism in Norway, Sweden and the Netherlands, 1930–40," *Journal of Contemporary History*, 57 (1), Jan. 2022, p. 50.
44. Paolo Monelli, *Mussolini: An Intimate Life* (London, 1953), p. 133.
45. *Kerry News*, 17 Dec. 1934.
46. *Irish Press*, 18 Dec. 1934.
47. *Irish Press*, 29 Dec. 1934.
48. Raul Cârstocea, "Native Fascists, Transnational Anti-Semites: The International Activity of Legionary Leader Ion I. Moţa," in Arnd Bauerkämper and Grzegorz Rossoliński-Liebe (eds.), *Fascism Without Borders: Transnational Connections and Cooperation between Movements and Regimes in Europe from 1918 to 1945* (Oxford, 2017), pp. 228–9.
49. *The Nation*, 29 Jun. 1935.
50. *Irish Press*, 29 Dec. 1934.
51. *Irish Press*, 19 Dec. 1934.
52. Walsh biography, p. 194.
53. *Irish Press*, 29 Dec. 1934.
54. Cronin, *Blueshirts and Irish Politics*, p. 52.
55. Aristotle Kallis, "From CAUR to EUR: Italian Fascism, the "myth of Rome" and the pursuit of international primacy," *Patterns of Prejudice*, (2016), 50 (4–5), pp. 372–3.
56. *United Ireland*, 22 Dec. 1934.
57. *United Ireland*, 4 Jan. 1935.
58. *Irish Independent*, 1 Apr. 1935.
59. Alexander Raven Thomson to Liam Walsh, 7 May 1936, EODP/NLI/MS 48,288/2.
60. Walsh to Thomson, 15 May 1936, EODP/NLI/MS 48,288/3.
61. Thomson to Walsh, 21 May 1936, EODP/NLI/MS 48,288/4.
62. Walsh to Thomson, 3 Jun. 1936, EODP/NLI/MS 48,288/5.
63. Thomson to Walsh, 4 Jun. 1936, EODP/NLI/MS 48,288/6.
64. John Rodden & John Rossi, "Ireland's Quixotic Cruzada: The Irish and the Spanish Civil War," *Society*, 58, (2021), p. 98.
65. *The Fascist*, Jun. 1939.
66. *Irish Press*, 2 Jan. 1935.
67. *Connacht Tribune*, 12 Jan. 1935.
68. *Irish Press*, 20 Feb. 1935.
69. *Irish Independent*, 13 Feb. 1935.
70. Lee, *Ireland 1912–1985*, p. 201.
71. Cronin, *Blueshirts and Irish Politics*, p. 25.
72. Regan, *Counter-Revolution*, p. 370.
73. MacEoin, *Survivors*, p. 16.
74. Cronin, "Cronin, Edmund ('Ned') John," *DIB*.
75. *Belfast Newsletter*, 18 Mar. 1935.
76. *The Irish Workers' Voice*, 14 Sep. 1935.
77. *Anglo-Celt*, 10 Nov. 1934.
78. *Irish Press*, 2 Jan. 1935.
79. Hanley, *The IRA*, p. 89.

80. Martin White, *The Greenshirts: Fascism in the Irish Free State 1935–45* (London, 2004), PhD thesis, pp. 42–3.
81. RUC Inspector General to Dawson Bates, 21 Jun. 1935, PRONI/HA/32/1/615.
82. Ó Beacháin, *Destiny of the Soldiers*, p. 148.
83. Bell, *Secret Army*, p. 146.
84. Hanley, *The IRA*, p. 89.
85. *Tipperary Star*, 15 Jun. 1935.
86. "Job Stott," *WartimeNI.com*, (https://archives.wartimeni.com/person/job-stott/), (accessed 20 Dec. 2022).
87. *Derry Journal*, 7 Sep. 1934.
88. Loughlin, *Fascism and Constitutional Conflict*, p. 103.
89. *The Blueshirt*, 1 May 1935.
90. *Irish Independent*, 8 Aug. 1935.
91. Loughlin, *Fascism and Constitutional Conflict*, p. 128.
92. *Irish Independent*, 26 Apr. 1935.
93. Inspector General to Dawson Bates, 21 Jun. 1935, PRONI.
94. Thirty-Two Clubs, PRONI/HA/32/1/615.
95. McGarry, *O'Duffy*, p. 280.
96. *Irish Examiner*, 18 May 1935.
97. *Evening Herald*, 8 Jun. 1935.
98. White, *Greenshirts*, p. 52.
99. *Westmeath Independent*, 15 Jun. 1935.
100. White, *Greenshirts*, p. 65.
101. *The Blueshirt*, 1 Jun. 1935.
102. *Meath Chronicle*, 18 Jul. 1936.
103. *Irish Independent*, 10 Jun. 1935.
104. White, *Greenshirts*, pp. 88–90.
105. *Tipperary Star*, 15 Jun. 1935.
106. *Irish Press*, 24 Jul. 1935.
107. O'Halpin, *Defending Ireland*, p. 118.
108. *Irish Independent*, 12 Aug. 1935.
109. *Irish Examiner*, 10 Jun. 1935.
110. Ard Fheis League of Youth (O'Duffy Section), 6 Jul. 1935, NAI/JUS/8/307.
111. *Tipperary Star*, 15 Jun. 1935.
112. *Belfast Newsletter*, 21 Jun. 1935.
113. *Irish Press*, 23 Oct. 1934.
114. *Connaught Telegraph*, 26 Oct. 1935.
115. *Irish Independent*, 4 Jul. 1935.
116. *Irish Examiner*, 4 Jul. 1935.
117. *Dundalk Democrat*, 20 Jul. 1935.
118. White, *Greenshirts*, pp. 77–9.
119. *Drogheda Independent*, 28 Sep. 1935.
120. *The Nation*, Aug. 1936.
121. White, *Greenshirts*, pp. 81.
122. Monelli, *Mussolini*, p. 138.
123. Charles Bewley to Joseph P. Walshe, 12 Nov. 1935, NAI/DFA/19/50A.
124. Bewley to Walshe, 6 Nov. 1936, NAI/DFA/19/50A.
125. Cian McMahon, "Irish Free State newspapers and the Abyssinian crisis, 1935–6," *Irish Historical Studies*, 36 (143), 2009, pp. 371–2.
126. *Irish Independent*, 9 Dec. 1935.
127. *Irish Press*, 13 Sep. 1935.
128. Cian McMahon, "Eoin O'Duffy's Blueshirts and the Abyssinian crisis," *History Ireland*, 10 (2), 2002.
129. *Irish Press*, 14 Sep. 1935.
130. *Irish Press*, 19 Sep. 1935.
131. *Irish Press*, 24 Sep. 1935.
132. *Evening Echo*, 20 Sep. 1935.
133. *Irish Independent*, 24 Sep. 1935.
134. *Connaught Telegraph*, 26 Oct. 1935.
135. *Donegal Democrat*, 7 Nov. 1936.
136. McGarry, *O'Duffy*, p. 275.
137. *Dundalk Democrat*, 14 Sep. 1935.
138. *Irish Press*, 4 Mar. 1936.
139. White, *Greenshirts*, pp. 90–2.
140. *The Nation*, Apr. 1936.
141. *United Ireland*, 7 Mar. 1936.
142. *Irish Press*, 9 Dec. 1935.
143. *Irish Independent*, 10 Feb. 1936.
144. *Irish Independent*, 17 Jan. 1936.
145. *The Nationalist* (Tipperary), 4 Dec. 1935.
146. *The Nation*, Jul. 1936.
147. *Kerry News*, 2 Dec. 1935.
148. *Offaly Independent*, 16 Nov. 1935.
149. *The Nation*, Apr. 1936.
150. *Irish Press*, 7 May 1936.
151. Dáil Éireann debate, 24 Apr. 1936, 61 (11).
152. *The Nation*, Jul. 1936.
153. *Tipperary Star*, 14 Mar. 1936.
154. *Irish Independent*, 9 Mar. 1936.
155. *Sunday Independent*, 4 Oct. 1936.
156. *Anglo-Celt*, 25 Jul. 1936.
157. Special Branch report, 20 Jun. 1936, NAI/JUS/8/296.
158. *The Nation*, Aug. 1936.
159. *Anglo-Celt*, 25 Jul. 1936.
160. *The Nation*, Aug. 1936.
161. *Southern Star*, 20 Jun. 1936.

## Chapter 10

1. Enrique Moradiellos, *Franco: Anatomy of a Dictator* (London, 2018), p. 39.
2. Fearghal McGarry, "Irish Newspapers and the Spanish Civil War," *Irish Historical Studies*, 33 (129), 2002, pp. 69–70.
3. T. Ryle Dwyer, *Éamon de Valera* (Dublin, 1980), p. 224.
4. Fearghal McGarry, "Ireland and the Spanish civil war," in Declan M. Downey & Julio Crespo MacLennan (eds.), *Spanish-Irish Relations through the Ages* (Dublin, 2008), p. 218.
5. Paul Blanshard, *The Irish and Catholic Power* (London, 1954), p. 88.
6. J. Bowyer Bell, "Ireland and the Spanish Civil War, 1936–1939," *Studia Hibernica*, 9, 1969, p. 149.
7. Dáil Éireann debate, 27 Nov. 1936, 64 (8).
8. *Evening Herald*, 21 Sep. 1936.
9. *Irish Independent*, 22 Aug. 1936.
10. ICF pamphlet (Dublin, 1936), NLI/BB6301.
11. *Irish Press*, 31 Aug. 1936.
12. Bell, *Secret Army*, p. 163.
13. McGarry, "Ireland and the Spanish," p. 219.
14. Richard English, *Radicals and the Republic: Socialist Republicanism in the Irish Free State, 1925–1937* (Oxford, 2003), p. 37.
15. *Connaught Telegraph*, 15 Aug. 1936.

16. *Irish Independent*, 10 Aug. 1936.
17. Eoin O'Duffy, *Crusade in Spain* (Dublin, 1938), pp. 36–7.
18. O'Duffy, *Crusade*, p. 55.
19. Walsh biography, p. 205.
20. O'Duffy, *Crusade*, pp. 11–3.
21. *Irish Independent*, 13 Aug. 1936.
22. *Irish Examiner*, 20 Aug. 1936.
23. *Irish Press*, 31 Aug. 1936.
24. O'Duffy, *Crusade*, p. 14.
25. *Irish Independent*, 1 Sep. 1936.
26. *The Worker*, 29 Aug. 1936.
27. Bell, "Ireland and the Spanish," pp. 151–2.
28. *The Liberator* (Tralee), 25 Aug. 1936.
29. Memorandum by Attorney General, 9 Oct. 1936, NAI/JUS/AGO/1/488.
30. Dwyer, *De Valera*, p. 224.
31. O'Duffy, *Crusade*, p. 15.
32. Robert Stradling, *The Irish and the Spanish Civil War, 1936–39* (Manchester, 1999), pp. 28–30.
33. List of officers attached to Cuartel General, 31 Dec. 1936, EODP/NLI/MS 48,292/3/5.
34. *Belfast Newsletter*, 17 Sep. 1936.
35. Organization chart for the Irish Brigade, Sep. 1936, EODP/NLI/MS 48,292/1.
36. *Irish Press*, 29 Sep. 1936.
37. Judith Keene, *Fighting for Franco: International Volunteers in Nationalist Spain during the Spanish Civil War* (New York, 2007), pp. 117–21.
38. O'Duffy, *Crusade*, pp. 22–4.
39. McGarry, "Ireland and the Spanish," p. 223.
40. Christopher Othen, *Franco's International Brigades: Adventurers, Fascists, and Christian Crusaders in the Spanish Civil War* (London, 2008), p. 113.
41. *Sligo Champion*, 3 Oct. 1936.
42. McKeown report, 7 Oct. 1936, NAI/JUS/AGO/1/488.
43. Walsh to O'Duffy, 28 Dec. 1936, NAI/JUS/2011/25/77
44. O'Duffy, *Crusade*, p. 61.
45. *Ibid.*, pp. 56–7.
46. Manning, *Blueshirts*, p. 197.
47. McKeown report, 7 Oct. 1936, NAI/JUS/AGO/1/488.
48. *Limerick Chronicle*, 12 Oct. 1936.
49. Contract of Agreement, 28 Nov. 1936, EODP/NLI/MS 48,292/4.
50. O'Duffy, *Crusade*, pp. 195–200.
51. Niall Cullen, "'Oh Ireland! What a Disappointment You Have Been to the Basque People': Irish Non-Intervention in the Spanish Civil War," *Society*, 58, 2021, p. 104.
52. Matt J. Doolan, "Fascism never entered the picture," *New Hibernia*, 3 (7), 1986.
53. Fearghal McGarry, *Irish Politics and the Spanish Civil War* (Cork, 1999), p. 34.
54. *Irish Independent*, 21 Nov. 1936.
55. Niamh McGuinness, "A Bandera volunteer remembers," 2006, (http://irelandscw.com/band-DMcG.htm), (accessed 1 Jan. 2023).
56. Stradling, *Irish and Spanish*, p. 29.
57. Report on George Geraghty, 15 Jan. 1937, NAI/JUS/2011/25/77.
58. John Dorney, "'God's Battle': O'Duffy's Irish Brigade in the Spanish Civil War," *TheIrishStory.com*, (https://www.theirishstory.com/2018/10/24/gods-battle-oduffys-irish-brigade-in-the-spanish-civil-war/#_ednref4), (accessed 31 Dec. 2022).
59. Walshe to Kerney, 15 Feb. 1937, NAI/DFA/Letter Books Rome/Madrid 1936–37.
60. O'Duffy, *Crusade*, pp. 58–64.
61. *Evening Echo*, 30 Oct. 1936.
62. *Irish Press*, 29 Oct. 1936.
63. O'Duffy, *Crusade*, pp. 65–6.
64. Irish Brigade for Spain, 12 Jan. 1937, NAI/JUS/2011/25/77.
65. Garda dossier on Walsh, NAI.
66. Walsh to Coughlan, 3 Jan. 1936, EODP/NLI/MS 48,290/4/5.
67. O'Duffy, *Crusade*, pp. 88–90.
68. O'Duffy Brigade Diary, Nov. 1936–Jun. 1937, EODP/NLI/MS 48,292/2 [hereafter, Brigade Diary].
69. *Irish Press*, 23 Nov. 1936.
70. Matt Beckett, "The Irish Brigade," 1990, (http://irelandscw.com/band-Beckett.htm), (accessed 2 Jan. 2023).
71. *Evening Echo*, 4 Sep. 1967.
72. Dulanty to Walshe, 26 Feb. 1937, NAI/DFA/2006/39.
73. Fanning, *Salamanca Diaries*, p. 146.
74. O'Duffy, *Crusade*, pp. 87–92.
75. *Irish Independent*, 21 Nov. 1936.
76. *Irish Independent*, 4 Dec. 1936.
77. *Irish Press*, 24 Dec. 1936.
78. *Evening Echo*, 4 Sep. 1967.
79. *Irish Press*, 24 Dec. 1936.
80. Mariano Amoedo to Eoin O'Duffy, 4 Dec. 1936, EODP/NLI/MS 48,292/5.
81. Coughlan to Walsh, Dec. 1936, NLI/EODP/MS 48,290/4/6.
82. Francis McCullagh, *In Franco's Spain* (London, 1937), p. 150.
83. O'Duffy, *Crusade*, pp. 94–5.
84. McGarry, *O'Duffy*, p. 291.
85. *Offaly Independent*, 19 Dec. 1936.
86. *Northern Standard*, 25 Dec. 1936.
87. *Limerick Chronicle*, 25 Jul. 1995.
88. O'Duffy, *Crusade*, pp. 101–2.
89. Report to Minister, 31 Dec. 1936, NAI/JUS/2011/25/77.
90. Dulanty to Walshe, 26 Feb. 1937, NAI 2006/39.
91. *Belfast Newsletter*, 8 Jan. 1937.
92. Irish Brigade for Spain, 8 Jan. 1937, NAI/JUS/2011/25/77.
93. *Evening Herald*, 24 Feb. 1937.
94. *Round Table*, 27 (105), p. 163.
95. *Irish Independent*, 19 February 1937.
96. John Horgan, "'The great war correspondent': Francis McCullagh, 1874–1956," *Irish Historical Studies*, 36 (144), 2009, p. 561.
97. Mark O'Brien, "In war torn Spain," *Media, War & Conflict*, 10 (3), 2017, pp. 352–3.
98. Dulanty to Walshe, 26 Feb. 1937, NAI 2006/39.
99. Members of Irish Brigade, NAI/JUS/2011/26/77/8.

100. Members of Irish Brigade, NAI/JUS/2011/26/77/20.
101. Adrian Hoar, *In Green and Red: The Lives of Frank Ryan* (Dingle, 2004), p. 153.
102. "Will you help Frank Ryan?," TNA/KV2/1291.
103. Stradling, *Irish and Spanish*, p. 153.
104. McLoughlin, *Fighting for Republican Spain*, p. 168.
105. Richard Baxell, *Unlikely Warriors: The British in the Spanish Civil War and the Struggle Against Fascism* (London, 2012), p. 389.
106. John Newsinger, "Blackshirts, Blueshirts, and the Spanish Civil War," *The Historical Journal*, 44 (3), 2001, p. 841.
107. O'Duffy, *Crusade*, pp. 110–5.
108. Dulanty to Walshe, 26 Feb. 1937, NAI/DFA/2006/39.
109. *Irish Democrat*, 24 Apr. 1937.
110. O'Duffy, *Crusade*, p. 116.
111. Fanning, *Salamanca Diaries*, p. 149.
112. McCullagh, *In Franco's Spain*, p. 153.
113. Brigade Diary.
114. Fanning, *Salamanca Diaries*, p. 148.
115. *Irish Democrat*, 5 Jun. 1936.
116. *Irish Press*, 23 Nov. 1936.
117. O'Duffy, *Crusade*, p. 112–4.
118. Beckett, "The Irish Brigade."
119. *Wexford Echo*, Dec. 1988.
120. McGuinness, "A Bandera volunteer remembers."
121. *New York Times*, 4 Apr. 1937.
122. Dulanty to Walshe, 27 Feb. 1937, NAI 2006/39.
123. NAI/DFA/Madrid Embassy 19/4 87.
124. O'Duffy, *Crusade*, p. 133.
125. *Irish Independent*, 20 Feb. 1937.
126. Dulanty to Walshe, 27 Feb. 1937, NAI 2006/39.
127. McCullagh, *In Franco's Spain*, p. 160.
128. Keene, *Fighting for Franco*, p. 123.
129. Beckett, "The Irish Brigade."
130. McGuinness, "A Bandera volunteer remembers."
131. O'Duffy, *Crusade*, p. 109.
132. Manning, *Blueshirts*, p. 200.
133. O'Duffy, *Crusade*, p. 138.
134. Beckett, "The Irish Brigade."
135. Brigade Diary.
136. Othen, *Franco's International Brigades*, p. 107.
137. *Kerryman*, 27 Feb. 1937.
138. *Irish Press*, 24 Feb. 1937.
139. *Irish Press*, 1 Mar. 1937.
140. McCullagh, *In Franco's Spain*, pp. 262–3.
141. O'Duffy, *Crusade*, pp. 144–7.
142. *Irish Times*, 30 Apr. 1987.
143. *Irish Press*, 10 Mar. 1937.
144. *Irish Democrat*, 8 May 1937.
145. O'Duffy, *Crusade*, p. 148.
146. Walshe to Kerney, 6 Mar. 1937, NAI/DFA/Madrid/IP/3/6.
147. *Irish Democrat*, 3 Apr. 1937.
148. Report on Gunning, 22 Jul. 1940, NAI/DFA/4/244/22.
149. Report of Irish Legation (Berlin), 10 Aug. 1939, NAI/DFA/4/244/22.
150. Bernard S. Wall to Desmond FitzGerald, 1 Dec. 1937, FitzGerald Papers, UCDA/P80/1287.
151. Report on Gunning, 2 Jun. 1938, NAI/DFA/4/244/22.
152. McGarry, *Ryan*, p. 71.
153. Gunning to FitzGerald, 15 Jul. 1937, FitzGerald Papers, UCDA/P80/627.
154. Kerney interview with Gunning, 10 Jun. 1938, NAI/DFA/4/244/22.
155. Walshe to Kerney, 8 Mar. 1937, NAI/DFA/Madrid/IP3/6.
156. McCullagh, *In Franco's Spain*, p. 151.
157. Stradling, *Irish and Spanish*, p. 116.
158. Manning, *Blueshirts*, p. 201.
159. Othen, *Franco's International Brigades*, p. 118.
160. Newsinger, "Blackshirts, Blueshirts, and the Spanish Civil War," p. 841.
161. Keene, *Fighting for Franco*, pp. 125–6.
162. McGarry, *O'Duffy*, p. 307.
163. *Limerick Chronicle*, 25 Jul. 1937.
164. McCullagh, *In Franco's Spain*, p. 264.
165. Garda report, 4 Nov. 1936, NAI/JUS/2011/25/77
166. McCullagh, *In Franco's Spain*, p. 296.
167. Kerney to Walshe, 12 May 1937, NAI/DFA/Madrid/IP/3/6.
168. *Irish Times*, 26 Jun. 1937.
169. *Irish Times*, 17 Jul. 1986.
170. Fanning, *Salamanca Diaries*, p. 153.
171. Baxell, *Unlikely Warriors*, p. 286.
172. Special Branch report, 22 Jun. 1937, NAI/JUS/2011/25/77.
173. *Irish Times*, 17 Jul. 1986.
174. *Irish Democrat*, 24 Jul. 1937.
175. Kerney interview with Gunning, 10 Jun. 1938, NAI/DFA/4/244/22.
176. Stradling, *Irish and Spanish*, p. 94.
177. Keene, *Fighting for Franco*, p. 126.
178. Baxell, *Unlikely Warriors*, p. 378.
179. *Irish Democrat*, 24 Apr. 1937.
180. Kerney to Walshe, 8 Jun. 1937, NAI/DFA/Madrid/IP/3/6.
181. Keene, *Fighting for Franco*, p. 126.
182. *Irish Press*, 22 Jun. 1937.
183. Kerney Interview with Gunning, 10 Jun. 1938, NAI/DFA/4/244/22.
184. Stradling, *Irish and Spanish*, p. 100.
185. Fanning, *Salamanca Diaries*, pp. 168–72.
186. *Ibid.*, pp. 174–9.
187. O'Duffy, *Crusade*, p. 241.
188. *Irish Press*, 22 Jun. 1937.
189. *Irish Examiner*, 22 Jun. 1937.
190. *Irish Press*, 12 Jun. 1937.
191. *Irish Independent*, 30 Jun. 1937.
192. *Irish Press*, 19 Jun. 1937.
193. *The Evening Star* (Dunedin), 13 Aug. 1937.
194. Special Branch report, 22 Jun. 1937, NAI/JUS/2011/25/77.
195. O'Duffy, *Crusade*, p. 246.
196. *Donegal Democrat*, 26 Jun. 1937.
197. *Kerryman*, 30 Jan. 1998.

198. *Connaught Telegraph*, 26 Jun. 1937.
199. White, *Alfie*, p. 87.
200. Sylvère Lotringer, "The Thin Man: An Interview with Brendan Behan," *Field Day Review*, 2005, p. 9.
201. Baxell, *Unlikely Warriors*, p. 378 and 391.
202. *Irish Independent*, 24 Jun. 1937.
203. *Irish Press*, 14 Aug. 1937.
204. *Irish Democrat*, 21 Aug. 1937.
205. *Nationalist and Leinster Times*, 14 Aug. 1937.
206. McGarry, "Ireland and the Spanish," p. 228.
207. MacEoin, *Twilight Years*, p. 753.
208. Mark McNally, "Fianna Fáil and the Spanish civil war 1936–1939: The rhetoric of hegemony and equilibrium," *Journal of Political Ideologies*, 14 (1), 2009, p. 83.
209. O'Duffy, *Crusade*, p. 249.
210. Manning, *Blueshirts*, p. 202.
211. McGarry, "Ireland and the Spanish," p. 229.
212. Special Branch report, 22 Jun. 1937, NAI/JUS/2011/25/77.

## Chapter 11

1. Walsh biography, p. 212.
2. *The Nation*, 1 Jun. 1936.
3. *Irish Press*, 14 Jul. 1936; cf. Marriage Certificate of Robert Butler and Margaret Roche, Dublin, 29 Aug. 1938.
4. White, *Greenshirts*, p. 117.
5. John Pollard, "Corporatism and political Catholicism: The impact of Catholic corporatism in inter-war Europe," in Pinto (ed.), *Corporatism and Fascism*, pp. 50–1.
6. *The Nation*, 1 Jul. 1936.
7. *Irish Press*, 25 Apr. 1938.
8. Michael McDunphy to O'Duffy, 9 Jul. 1938, NAI/PRES/1/P474.
9. Walsh biography, p. 205.
10. *Irish Independent*, 21 Jun. 1938.
11. *Sunday Independent*, 3 Jul. 1938.
12. *Irish Press*, 2 Aug. 1938.
13. Kevin Kerrane, "Orwell's Ireland," *The Irish Review (Cork)*, 36/37, 2007, p. 25.
14. *Irish Press*, 17 Mar. 1938.
15. *Irish Examiner*, 30 Dec. 1938.
16. *Irish Independent*, 3 May 1939.
17. Walshe to de Valera, 4 Feb. 1939, NAI/DFA/227/4.
18. *Evening Herald*, 20 Feb. 1939.
19. Briscoe, *For the Life of Me*, p. 255.
20. Dwyer, *De Valera*, p. 231.
21. *Irish Independent*, 3 May 1939.
22. Wilhelm Abegg to O'Duffy, 17 Oct. 1938, EODP/NLI/MS 48,290/7.
23. Keogh, *Jews in Twentieth-Century Ireland*, p. 92.
24. *The Nation*, Aug. 1936.
25. Gerry Mullins, *Dublin Nazi No. 1: The Life of Adolf Mahr* (Dublin, 2007), pp. 56–7.
26. Memorandum for Lt. Col. S.N. Shoesmith, Dec. 1941, TNA/KV/3/120.
27. R.M. Douglas, "The Pro-Axis Underground in Ireland, 1939–1942," *The Historical Journal*, 49 (4), 2009, pp. 1158–9.
28. Interview with Attracta Maher and Sr Joanna Brennan-Whitmore, 2013, Irish Life and Lore Series: The 1916 Rising Oral History Collection.
29. McGarry, *O'Duffy*, p. 323.
30. Garda dossier on Walsh, NAI.
31. Towards Ireland's Attitude to International Affairs, c. 1939, EODP/NLI/MS 48,290/9.
32. Douglas, "Pro-Axis Underground," p. 1158.
33. Towards Ireland's Attitude to International Affairs, EODP.
34. Search of house of Captain Liam Walsh, 26 May 1940, NAI/JUS/2011/25/160.
35. Douglas, "Pro-Axis Underground," p. 1163.
36. Meeting of IFG, 14 Apr. 1940, NAI/JUS/2011/25/160.
37. Manning, *Blueshirts*, pp. 214–5.
38. *Reminiscences* 1, p. 1.
39. Adolf Hitler, *Mein Kampf* (Boston, 1943) (trans. Ralph Manheim), p. 3.
40. John A. Holden to Walsh, 2 May 1940, NAI/JUS/2011/25/160.
41. *Republican Review*, 23 Jun. 1938.
42. David O'Donoghue, *The Devil's Deal: The IRA, Nazi Germany and the Double Life of Jim O'Donovan* (Dublin, 2010), p. 297.
43. *Wolfe Tone Weekly*, 12 Apr. 1939.
44. *Wolfe Tone Weekly*, 18 Dec. 1937.
45. *Irish Freedom*, 1 Aug. 1937.
46. MacEoin, *Twilight Years*, p. 621.
47. Report from Garda Chief Superintendent (Tipperary Division), 29 Dec. 1938, NAI/JUS/2011/25/103.
48. Report from Garda Chief Superintendent (Tipperary Division), 1 Feb. 1939, NAI/JUS/2011/25/103.
49. MacEoin, *Twilight Years*, p. 835.
50. Brian Hanley, "'Oh Here's to Adolph Hitler': The IRA and the Nazis," *History Ireland*, 13 (3), 2005, p. 32.
51. Memorandum by Cecil Liddell, 11 Apr. 1943, TNA/KV 3/120.
52. MacBride, *That Day's Struggle*, pp. 122–3.
53. G2 memorandum on Séamus O'Donovan, Sep. 1945, IMA/G2/3738.
54. O'Donoghue, *Devil's Deal*, p. 288.
55. Joseph McKenna, *The IRA Bombing Campaign Against Britain, 1939–1940* (Jefferson, 2016), pp. 83–139.
56. Kurt Haller interview, TNA/KV2/769 [hereafter, Haller interview], p. ii.
57. Haller interview, p. vi.
58. Manning, *Blueshirts*, p. 202.
59. *Ibid.*, p. 260.
60. Carolle J. Carter, *The Shamrock and the Swastika: German Espionage in Ireland during World War II* (Palo Alto, 1977), pp. 102–3.
61. Stephen Hayes, "My Strange Story," *The Bell*, 17 (5), 1951, p. 14.

62. Intelligence report on possible German action in Ireland in the event of war, 20 Jul. 1939, TNA/KV 3/120.
63. NAI/JUS/8/732.
64. Hayes, "My Strange Story," p. 15.
65. P. Connell to Garda Commissioner, 16 Feb. 1939, NAI/JUS/2011/25/103.
66. *Irish Times*, 12 Jun. 1939.
67. Report on Anti-Partition Party, 24 Jun. 1939, NAI/JUS/2011/25/103.
68. T. Murphy report, 17 Jul. 1939, NAI/JUS/2011/25/103.
69. *Irish Times*, 21 Feb. 1940.
70. R.M. Douglas, *Architects of the Resurrection: Ailtirí na hAiséirghe and the Fascist "New Order" in Ireland* (Manchester, 2009), p. 78.
71. McGarry, *O'Duffy*, p. 332.
72. Summary of our Most Secret Information from Dublin, 22 Aug.–4 Sep. 1943, TNA/DO/121/87, p. 3.
73. *Irish Press*, 6 Oct. 1939.
74. Walsh biography, p. 221.
75. Garda Order to Search the house of Walsh, 23 May 1940, EODP/NLI/MS 48,301/1/1.
76. Emergency Powers (2) Order for the arrest of Walsh, 5 Jun. 1940, EODP/NLI/MS 48,301/1/2.
77. Arrest of Walsh, 4 Jun. 1940, NAI/JUS/2011/25/160.
78. MacEoin, *Twilight Years*, p. 645.
79. McGarry, *O'Duffy*, p. 338.
80. Hayes, "My Strange Story," p. 15.
81. *An Phoblacht*, Oct. 1951.
82. Haller interview.
83. MacEoin, *Twilight Years*, p. 930.
84. Keogh, *Jews in Twentieth-Century Ireland*, p. 167.
85. *Irish Independent*, 24 Jul. 1940.
86. Christopher Norton, "The Internment of Cahir Healy MP, Brixton Prison July 1941–December 1942," *Twentieth Century British History*, 18 (2), 2007.
87. McGarry, *O'Duffy*, p. 333.
88. Carter, *The Shamrock and the Swastika*, p. 96.
89. O'Halpin, *Defending Ireland*, p. 245.
90. Terence O'Reilly, *Hitler's Irishmen* (Dublin, 2008), p. 117.
91. Hayes, "My Strange Story," p. 16.
92. O'Halpin, *Defending Ireland*, p. 146.
93. Fitzpatrick, *Blythe in Ulster*, p. 187.
94. *Sunday Chronicle*, 2 Jul. 1940.
95. Walsh biography, p. 222.
96. Broadcast of "Today in Ireland," 7 Nov. 1940, RTÉ Archives, Acetate Disc Collection.
97. De Valera to O'Duffy, 12 Aug. 1940, (https://www.mullenslaurelpark.com/catalogue/lot/7db398414ece0007aa0c2ad77c213dd4/8d18a33c49d230f6f512e23c3c7b4265/collectors-cabinet-auction-lot-183/), (accessed 18 Feb. 2023).
98. Walsh biography, p. 222 (appendix 1).
99. Richard English, *Ernie O'Malley: IRA Intellectual* (Oxford, 1999), p. 169.
100. Garda dossier on Walsh, NAI.
101. Görtz's account of his mission, Richard J. Hayes Papers, NLI/MS 22,983, p. 37.
102. Summary of Our Most Secret Information from Dublin, 18 Apr.–1 May 1943, TNA/DO/121/87, p. 2.
103. Hayes, "My Strange Story," pp. 47–51.
104. Summary of Our Most Secret Information from Dublin, 8–21 Aug. 1943, TNA/DO/121/87, p. 2.
105. Hoar, *In Green and Red*, p. 279.
106. Görtz's account of his mission, NLI, p. 37.
107. Summary of Our Most Secret Information in Dublin, 30 May–12 Jun. 1943, TNA/DO/121/87, p. 3.
108. Carter, *The Shamrock and the Swastika*, p. 184.
109. Special Communiqué issued by the Army Council, 10 Sep. 1941, EODP/NLI/MS 48,290/14/1.
110. Short Summary of German Cables Nos. IR0001, 0002 and 0003, TNA/DO/121/87.
111. Enno Stephan, *Spies in Ireland* (London, 1963), (trans. Arthur Davidson), pp. 231–2.
112. Short Summary of German Cables Nos. IR0001, 0002 and 0003, TNA.
113. McGarry, *O'Duffy*, pp. 337–8.
114. Stephan, *Spies in Ireland*, p. 271.
115. Carter, *The Shamrock and the Swastika*, p. 187.
116. British intelligence file on Joseph Gerard Andrews, TNA/KV/2/3119.
117. McGarry, *O'Duffy*, p. 339.
118. Summary of Our Most Secret Information from Dublin, Jan./Feb. 1944, TNA/DO/121/87, p. 3.
119. T. Ryle Dwyer, *Behind the Green Curtain: Ireland's Phoney Neutrality during World War II* (Dublin, 2010).
120. *Fermanagh Herald*, 11 Apr. 1942.
121. *Irish Independent*, 6 Apr. 1942.
122. Pearse Reynolds, "'A First-Class Split': Political conflict in Irish athletics, 1924–40," *History Ireland*, 20 (4), 2012, p. 33.
123. *Irish Examiner*, 10 Oct. 1944.
124. *Irish Examiner*, 2 Nov. 1942.
125. Walsh biography, p. 213.
126. *Irish Times*, 13 May 1942.
127. *Irish Independent*, 30 Dec. 1942.
128. *The Nationalist* (Tipperary), 22 Mar. 1944.
129. Walsh biography, p. 214.
130. *Irish Independent*, 2 Aug. 1943.
131. *Irish Examiner*, 12 Jan. 1944.
132. Walsh biography, p. 219.
133. Death return of O'Duffy, 31 Dec. 1944, (https://www.irishgenealogy.ie/), (accessed 11 Jan. 2023).
134. Walsh biography, p. 229.
135. *The Irish Times*, 18 Jul. 1944.
136. *The Frontier Sentinel* (Newry), 5 Aug. 1944.
137. Walsh biography, p. 220.
138. *The Frontier Sentinel* (Newry), 5 Aug. 1944.
139. "General Eoin O'Duffy (Mount Merrion Resident)," 8 Jan. 2020, Mount Merrion Historical Society, (https://www.mountmerrionhistorical.com/General_Eoin_O_Duffy.html), (accessed 12 Jan. 2023).
140. Walsh biography, pp. 226–8.
141. McGarry, *O'Duffy*, p. 339.

142. Walsh biography, p. 226.
143. *Irish Times*, 28 Aug. 1942.
144. Walsh biography, pp. 226–8.
145. *The Frontier Sentinel* (Newry), 5 Aug. 1944.
146. Walsh biography, p. 229.

## Epilogue

1. *Irish Independent*, 4 Dec. 1944.
2. *Irish Times*, 4 Dec. 1944.
3. *Irish Press*, 10 Feb. 1945.
4. *Irish Press*, 27 Feb. 1945.
5. *Irish Times*, 1 Dec. 1944.
6. *Irish Independent*, 4 Dec. 1944.
7. *Monaghan Argus*, 15 Oct. 1949.
8. *Evening Echo*, 13 Jun. 1995.
9. *Irish Examiner*, 27 Aug. 1946.
10. Coogan, *GAA and the War of Independence*, p. 264.
11. *Northern Standard*, 3 Dec. 2009.
12. *The Times* (Ireland edition), 19 May 2021.
13. Guy Beiner, "When Monuments Fall: The Significance of Decommemorating," *Éire-Ireland*, 56 (1&2), 2021, pp. 31–61.
14. Noël Browne, *Against The Tide* (Dublin, 1986), p. 228.
15. "In Memory of Michael Patrick Lynch," 29 Sep. 2017, (https://youtu.be/Qo_vDGuSPmQ), (accessed 26 Feb. 2023).
16. https://web.archive.org/web/20230227234253/https://www.irishpatriotstore.com/collections/t-shirts/products/eion-oduffy-t-shirt, (accessed 27 Feb. 2023).
17. https://www.facebook.com/events/jobstown-community-centre/celebrating-the-death-of-eoin-oduffy/1233586340498274/, (accessed 15 Jan. 2023).
18. "Treaty Live," Jan. 2022, Internet Movie Database (IMDB), (https://www.imdb.com/title/tt18246540/), (accessed 16 Aug. 2022).
19. https://twitter.com/paddycullivan/status/1480239824196022273, (accessed 18 Feb. 2023).
20. *Irish Independent*, 21 May 2022.
21. Othen, *Franco's International Brigades*, p. 119.
22. MacMahon, *A Fist to the Black-Blooded*, p. 128.
23. Meehan & Collins, *Saving the State*, pp. 36 and 43.

## Postscript

1. *Irish Independent*, 21 Oct. 1999.
2. McGarry, *O'Duffy*, pp. 162–9.
3. Aidan Beatty, "The Life That God Desires: Masculinity and Power in Irish Nationalism, 1884–1938" (Chicago, 2015), PhD thesis, p. 13.
4. Mary Kenny, *The Way We Were: Catholic Ireland Since 1922* (Dublin, 2022), p. 76.
5. *Irish Independent*, 2 Feb. 1945.
6. Stradling, *Irish and Spanish*, pp. 208–9.
7. Summary of Our Most Secret Information from Dublin, 30 May–12 Jun. 1943, TNA/DO/121/87, p. 3.
8. *Daily Mail*, 23 Jul. 2013.
9. *Irish Independent*, 20 Feb. 1937.
10. *Donegal News*, 16 Jun. 1934.
11. Allen, *The Garda Síochána*, p. 97.
12. Walsh biography, p. 227 (handwritten note opposite). The reference to an ex-minister linking O'Duffy with a prominent lady in the Senate could be read to mean the comments were made in the Senate chamber by the unnamed former minister. There is, however, no parliamentary record of this.
13. Mary McAuliffe. *Senator Kathleen A. Browne: Patriot, Politician and Practical Farmer* (Roscrea, 2008), p. 104.
14. Seanad Éireann debate, 21 Mar. 1934, 18 (12).
15. McAuliffe, *Browne*, p. 42.
16. Bernard Browne, "Kathleen A. Browne," *The Past: The Organ of the Uí Cinsealaigh Historical Society*, 32, 2016, p. 112.

# Bibliography


Allen, Gregory. *The Garda Síochána: Policing Independent Ireland 1922–82*. Dublin: Gill & Macmillan, 1999.

Baxell, Richard. *Unlikely Warriors: The British in the Spanish Civil War and the Struggle Against Fascism*. London: Aurum, 2012.

Brady, Conor. *Guardians of the Peace*. Dublin: Prendeville Publishing Ltd, 2000.

Broderick, Eugene. *Intellectuals and the Ideological Hijacking of Fine Gael, 1932–1938*. Newcastle-upon-Tyne: Cambridge Scholars Publishing, 2010.

Carter, Carolle J. *The Shamrock and the Swastika: German Espionage in Ireland during World War II*. Palo Alto: Pacific Books, 1977.

Collins, Stephen, and Ciara Meehan. *Saving the State: Fine Gael from Collins to Varadkar*. Dublin: Gill, 2020.

Conway, Vicky. *Policing Twentieth Century Ireland: A History of the Garda Síochána*. London: Routledge, 2014.

Coogan, Tim Pat. *GAA and the War of Independence*. London: Head of Zeus, 2018.

Cronin, Mike. *The Blueshirts and Irish Politics*. Dublin: Four Courts Press, 1997.

Dooley, Terence. *The Irish Revolution, 1912–23: Monaghan*. Dublin: Four Courts Press, 2017.

Douglas, Raymond M. *Architects of the Resurrection: Ailtirí na hAiséirghe and the Fascist "New Order" in Ireland*. Manchester: Manchester University Press, 2009.

Dwyer, T. Ryle. *Behind the Green Curtain: Ireland's Phoney Neutrality during World War II*. Dublin: Gill, 2010.

_______.*Éamon de Valera*. Dublin: Gill & Macmillan, 1980.

_______. *"I Signed My Death Warrant": Michael Collins & the Treaty*. Cork: Mercier Press, 2007.

_______. *The Squad and the Intelligence Operations of Michael Collins*. Cork: Mercier Press, 2005.

English, Richard. *Ernie O'Malley: IRA Intellectual*. Oxford: Oxford University Press, 1999.

Enright, Seán. *The Irish Civil War: Law, Execution and Atrocity*. Newbridge: Irish Academic Press, 2019.

Fanning, Ronan. *Éamon de Valera: A Will to Power*. London: Faber & Faber, 2015.

Farrell, Mel. *Party Politics in a New Democracy: The Irish Free State, 1922–37*. London: Macmillan, 2017.

Ferriter, Diarmaid. *Occasions of Sin: Sex and Society in Modern Ireland*. London: Profile Books, 2009.

Fisk, Robert. *In Time of War: Ireland, Ulster and the Price of Neutrality 1939–45*. Philadelphia: University of Pennsylvania Press, 1983.

Fitzpatrick, David. *Ernest Blythe in Ulster: The Making of a Double Agent?* Cork: Cork University Press, 2018.

Foster, R.F. *W.B. Yeats: A Life, Vol. II: The Arch-Poet, 1915–1939*. Oxford: Oxford University Press, 2003.

Gallagher, Michael, and Michael Marsh. *Days of Blue Loyalty: The Politics and Membership of the Fine Gael party*. Dublin: PSAI Press, 2002.

Glennon, Kieran. *From Pogrom to Civil War: Tom Glennon and the Belfast IRA*. Cork: Mercier Press, 2013.

Hanley, Brian. *The IRA: 1926–1936*. Dublin: Four Courts Press, 2002.

Hopkinson, Michael. *Green Against Green: A History of the Irish Civil War*. New York: St Martin's Press, 1988.

Jordan, Anthony J. *John A. Costello: Compromise Taoiseach*. Dublin: Westport Books, 2007.

Keene, Judith. *Fighting for Franco: International Volunteers in Nationalist Spain during the Spanish Civil War*. New York: Hambledon Continuum, 2007.

Keogh, Dermot. *Jews in Twentieth-Century Ireland*. Cork: Cork University Press, 1998.

Lewis, Matthew. *Frank Aiken's War: The Irish Revolution 1916–23*. Dublin: University College Dublin Press, 2014.

Loughlin, James. *Fascism and Constitutional Conflict: The British Extreme Right and Ulster in the Twentieth Century*. Liverpool: Liverpool University Press, 2019.

Lynch, Robert. *The Northern IRA and the Early Years of Partition 1920–1922*. Newbridge: Irish Academic Press, 2006.

Manning, Maurice. *The Blueshirts*. Dublin: Gill & Macmillan, 2006.
______. *James Dillon: A Biography*. Dublin: Merlin Publishing, 2000.
McCullagh, David. *De Valera, Volume I: Rise 1882–1932*. Dublin: Gill, 2017.
McGarry, Fearghal. *Eoin O'Duffy: A Self-Made Hero*. Oxford: Oxford University Press, 2005.
______. *Frank Ryan*. Dublin: University College Dublin Press, 2010.
______. *Irish Politics and the Spanish Civil War*. Cork: Cork University Press, 1999.
McNiffe, Liam. *A History of the Garda Síochána*. Dublin: Merlin Publishing, 1997.
Mullins, Gerry. *Dublin Nazi No. 1: The Life of Adolf Mahr*. Dublin: Liberties Press, 2007.
Murray, Patrick. *Oracles of God: The Roman Catholic Church and Irish Politics, 1922–37*. Dublin: University College Dublin Press, 2000.
Ó Beacháin, Donnacha. *Destiny of the Soldiers: Fianna Fáil, Irish Republicanism and the IRA, 1926–1973*. Dublin: Gill, 2011.
Ó Caoimh, Pádraig. *Richard Mulcahy: From the Politics of War to the Politics of Peace, 1913–1924*. Newbridge: Irish Academic Press, 2019.
O'Connor, Emmet. *Reds and the Green: Ireland, Russia and the Communist Internationals 1919–43*. Dublin: University College Dublin Press, 2004.
O'Donoghue, David. *The Devil's Deal: The IRA, Nazi Germany and the Double Life of Jim O'Donovan*. Dublin: New Island Books, 2010.
O'Halpin, Eunan. *Defending Ireland: The Irish State and Its Enemies Since 1922*. Oxford: Oxford University Press, 1999.
Regan, John M. *The Irish Counter-Revolution 1921–1936: Treatyite Politics and Settlement in Independent Ireland*. Dublin: Gill, 2001.
Stanfield, Paul Scott. *Yeats and Politics in the 1930s*. London: Macmillan, 1988.
Stradling, Robert. *The Irish and the Spanish Civil War, 1936–39*. Manchester: Manchester University Press, 1999.
Valiulis, Maryann Gialanella. *Portrait of a Revolutionary: General Richard Mulcahy and the Founding of the Irish Free State*. Dublin: Irish Academic Press, 1992.
Younger, Calton. *Ireland's Civil War*. New York: Taplinger Publishing Company, 1969.

# Index

Milton Keynes UK
Ingram Content Group UK Ltd.
UKHW050319180124
436198UK00005B/43

General Eoin O'Duffy